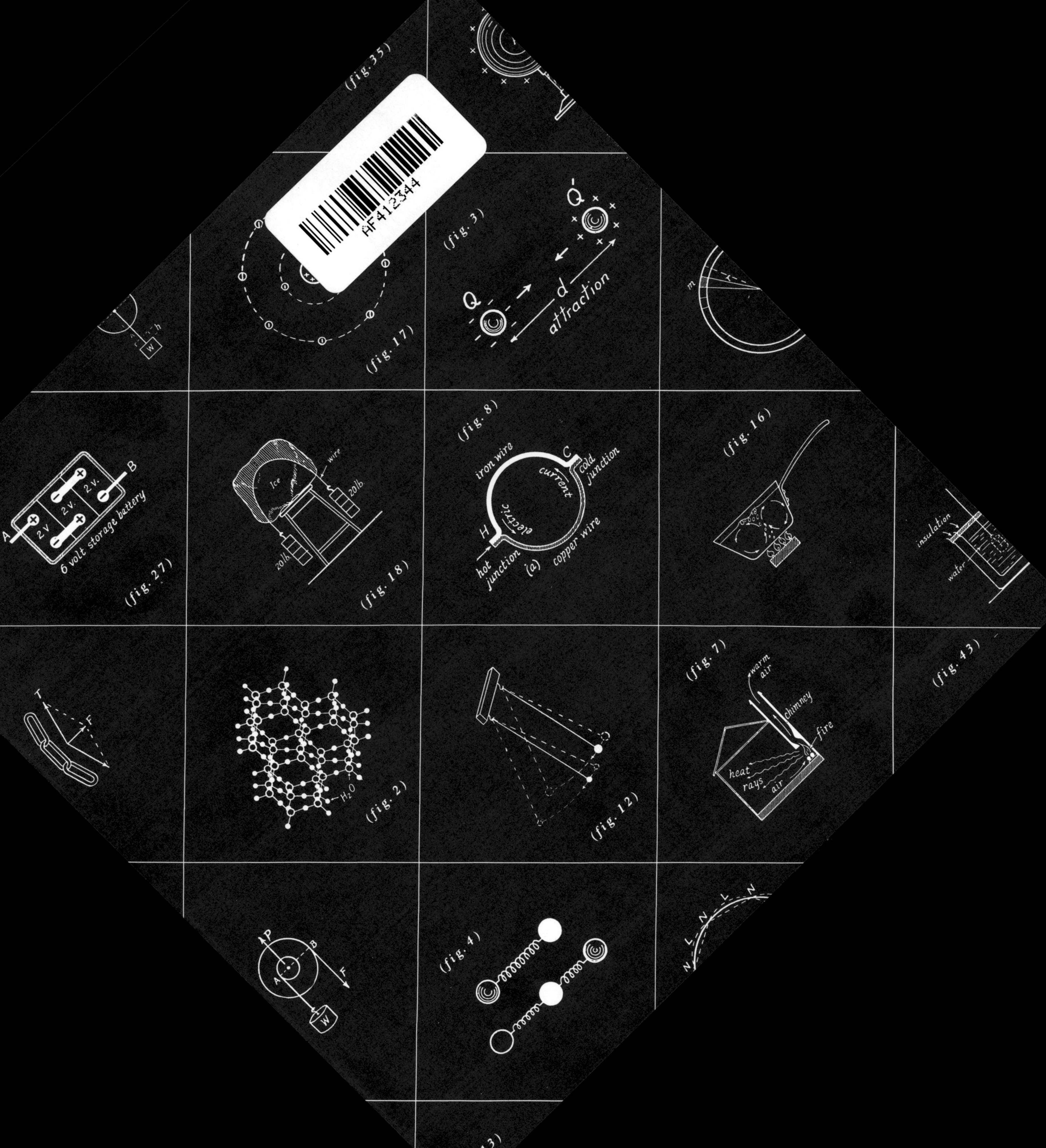

(fig. 35)
(fig. 17)
(fig. 3)
Q
Q
d
attraction
(fig. 27)
A
B
2 v.
2 v.
2 v.
2 v.
6 volt storage battery
(fig. 18)
Ice
wire
20 lb
20 lb
(fig. 8)
iron wire
C
current
cold junction
electric
H
hot junction
(a) copper wire
(fig. 16)
(fig. 7)
warm air
chimney
fire
heat rays
air
(fig. 43)
insulation
water
T
F
H₂O
(fig. 2)
(fig. 12)
P
B
F
A
W
(fig. 4)
N
N
N

TO OUR
family, friends, and clients

$$F = (a \times p)^4$$

(1.B)

(1.B) In this equation, we assume that *a* symbolically represents *film(video)* + *design* + *illustration* + *photography* + *support services* while *p* in this equation symbolically represents *sourcebook*.

T H E

ALTERNATIVE

PICK

1 9 9 5

fourth annual edition

PUBLISHERS: Maria Ragusa/Juliette Wolf PRODUCTION TEAM: Christina Holbrook/Carol Schultheiss ART DIRECTION: Victor Mazzeo
BOOK DESIGN: BlackBird Creative COPY: nomad Short Subjects LIMITED EDITION METAL BOXES: Brett Waller ILLUSTRATION ACCOUNTS REP-
RESENTATIVE: Liane Nikitovich LISTINGS AND DISTRIBUTION COORDINATOR: Fanny (flee) Lee LISTINGS: Patty Gang ACCOUNTS RECEIVABLE:
Sandy Mansfield TYPESETTING: Type & Tone DATA SYSTEMS COORDINATOR: Ian Clarke LEGAL ADVISOR: Burt A. Lewis FINANCIAL ADVISORS:
Dave Dobbins/Ira Reiter PRINTER: Palace Press, Hong Kong. ISBN# 0-9632606-3-4

$$\frac{energy\ \textit{times}\ \text{lust}\ \textit{applied}\ \text{to mass}}{} \ .$$

$$(1.C)$$

cheap hotels,
lovely bedrooms

music video directors + production companies + animation (special effects)

+ stock film + location (sound stages) .

(1 . D)

7 West 18th Street
New York City 10011
N.Y. Telephone: 212.627.3600
Contact: Amy Lauren

President: Stavros Merjos

1611 Electric Ave.
Venice CA. 90291
L.A. Telephone: 310.452.9999
Contact: Rebecca Skinner

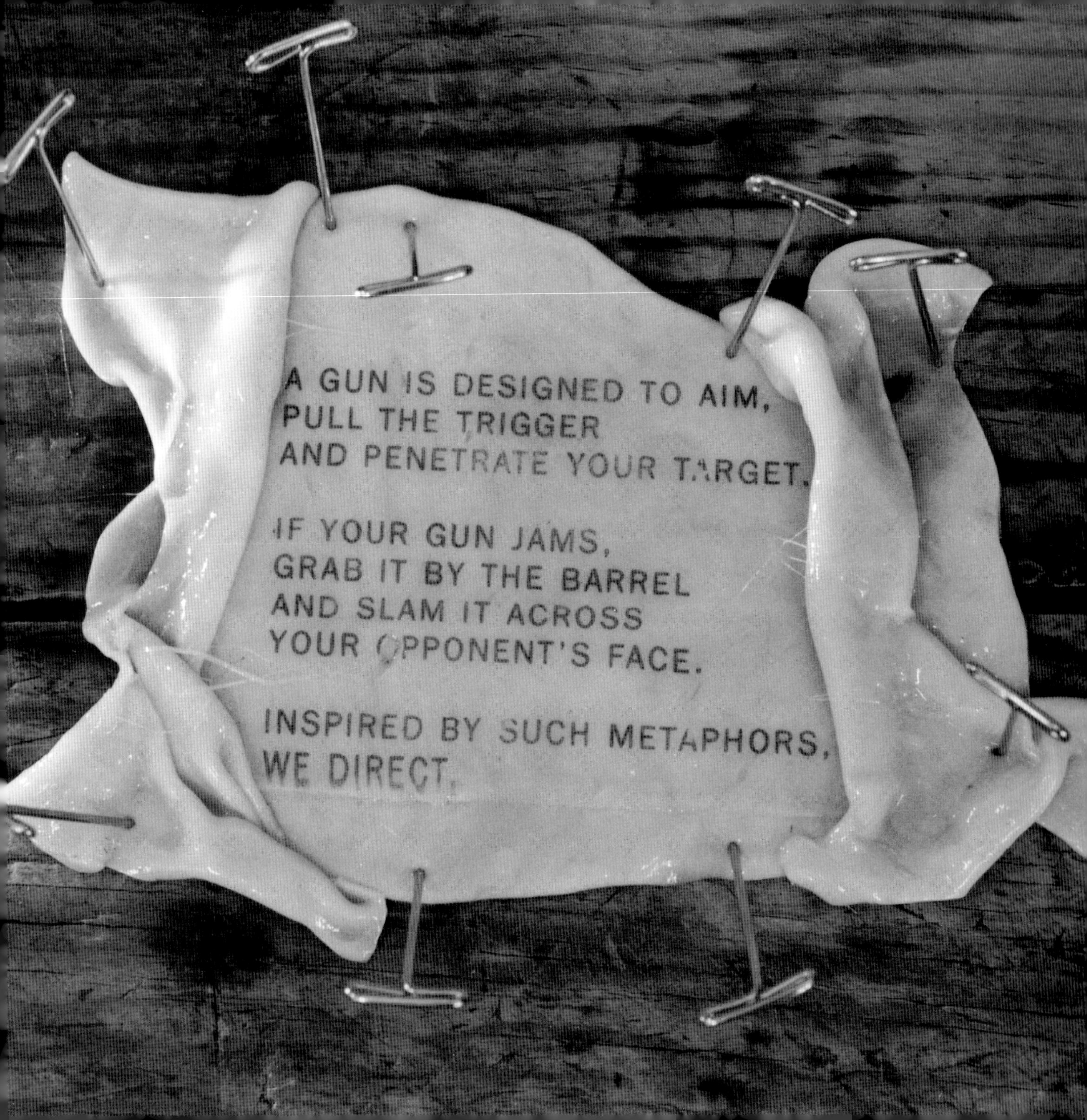

A GUN IS DESIGNED TO AIM,
PULL THE TRIGGER
AND PENETRATE YOUR TARGET.

IF YOUR GUN JAMS,
GRAB IT BY THE BARREL
AND SLAM IT ACROSS
YOUR OPPONENT'S FACE.

INSPIRED BY SUCH METAPHORS,
WE DIRECT.

SINCERE AS
POTASSIUM NITRATE
+ SULFUR
+ CARBON,

nomad

FOR MUSIC SHORTS, CALL INDUSTRIAL ARTISTS   310.393.3400

FOR COMMERCIALS, CALL BEDFORD FALLS   310.395.3553   312.751.0557   212.627.3888

FOR A CONVERSATION, CALL nomad   919.832.0250

Gallen Mei
5 4 3
New York 212.929.0540

Gallen Mei

[Director & Photographer]

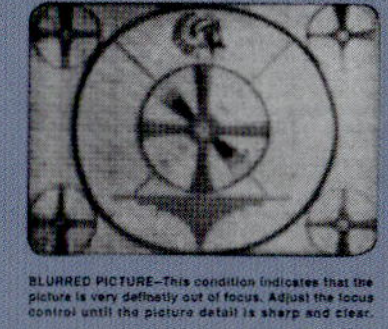

Miami 305.453.9660   San Francisco 415.928.5070

music video directors + production companies + animation (special effects)

+ stock film + location (sound stages)
——————————————————— .

(1 . 1)

$$F = (a \times p)^4$$

TABLE (1.2). FILM & VIDEO

Directors	Directors
Abbott, Abdul Malik Public Pictures / 212-431-0998	Bate, Brad Major League Productions, Inc. / 312-440-1430
Abramson, Neil Palomar Pictures / 213-525-2900	Bay, Michael Propaganda Films / 213-462-6400
Aitken, Satellite Satellite Films / 213-465-9300	Bayer, Sam HSI / 310-452-9999
Aldridge, Miles Oil Factory, Inc. / 213-466-7306	Becker, Goode E. O Pictures / 213-466-0324
Alquist, Sean The End / 213-782-9000	Bell, Adam Bell Boy Productions / 800-827-2355
Amos, Matthew Propaganda Films / 213-462-6400	Benaur, Tom Commotion Pictures / 415-777-2034
Anderson, David Chelsea Pictures / 212-431-3434	Berkman, Stephen The End / 213-962-2424
Andresen, Paul Oil Factory, Inc. / 213-466-7306	Bernstein, Adam Epoch Films / 310-440-2656
Applebaum, Chris Satellite Films / 213-465-9300	Beyer, John Leisure Jazz Video / 504-943-4343
Atkins, Martyn Oil Factory, Inc. / 213-466-7306	Beyer, Nico Propaganda Films / 213-462-6400
Avis, Meiert Windmill Lane Productions / 310-305-8116	Bieber, Tim Mr. Big Productions, Inc. / 312-463-3590
Badger, Matthew Woo Art International / 212-989-7870	Big TV! Palomar Pictures / 213-525-2900
Baine, Brian Buckholtz Prod., Inc. / 504-891-0912	Billard, George Flatiron Films / 212-620-0781
Baker, Graham Original Video / 310-393-0200	Blake, Stephan Underdog Films / 213-936-3111
Ball, Marc Scene Three / 615-385-2820	Blunder, Marcus Propaganda Films / 213-954-1100
Ballone, Karen Public Pictures / 212-431-0998	Boatner, Derrick W. GPA / 212-532-6000
Barclay, Gerald Liberty Studios / 212-532-1865	Bogen, Neil Original Video / 310-393-0200
Barclay, Paris Black & White Television / 213-878-2585	Boklund, Fredrik Oil Factory, Inc. / 213-466-7306
Barish, Geoffrey HSI / 310-452-9999	Bonet, Lisa Oil Factory, Inc. / 213-466-7306

Table (1.3). Film & Video

Directors	Directors
Bowden, Gavin Original Video / 310-393-0200	Carrillo, Hugo Daisy Force Pictures / 213-462-8881
Boyd, Paul Propaganda Films / 213-462-6400	Carter, Alan Flattery Yukich, Inc. (F.Y.I.) / 213-850-6106
Boyd, William Smash! Films / 213-957-7657	Carter, Alan Flattery Yukich, Inc. (F.Y.I) / 213-850-6106
Brambilla, Marco O Pictures, Inc. / 213-466-0324	Caruso, Robert Commotion Pictures / 415-777-2034
Brandt, Nicholas Propaganda Films / 213-462-6400	Ceorner, Louis Buckholtz Prod., Inc. / 504-891-0912
Bray, Kevin DNA / 213-463-2826	Cheek, Norwood Moxie Pictures / 213-957-5420
Brian, Jeb Above & Beyond Pictures / 615-385-3203	Cheng, Rod The Underground / 213-954-1100
Brooks, Craig S. Power Films / 213-653-7665	Christian, Brad / 310-393-0200 Original Video
Buckholtz, Tom Buckholtz Prod., Inc. / 504-891-0912	Christopher, Steven Riviera Films / 212-496-7929
Buckley, Dick Squeak Pictures / 818-980-0800	Christopherson, Peter Squeak Pictures / 818-980-0800
Burdin, Gary Innovative Media Productions / 818-755-0155	Clark, Larry Riviera Films / 212-496-7929
Burlingame, Michael Sonic Vision / 213-663-4082	Clarke, Matt Primalux Video / 212-206-1402
Burns, Chris 1171 Production Group / 213-655-1171	Clemene, Chuck Angel City Productions / 213-465-6802
Byrd, Jeffrey W. F.M. Rocks / 310-587-1501	Clemens, Clint HSI / 310-452-9999
Califano, Gary Firehouse Films / 212-491-6500	Cohen, Adam Bennu Productions, Inc. / 212-213-8511
Callner, Marty Cream Cheese / 213-465-8495	Cole, Matt Rainmaker Productions / 615-320-7267
Cameron, David The A&R Group / 213-650-4722	Coles, Dwyane Public Pictures / 212-431-0998
Care, Peter Satellite Films / 213-465-9300	Cooper, Peter Firehouse Films / 212-491-6500
Carolan, Drew The End / 213-782-9000	Coppola, Roman Original Video / 310-393-0200

$$F = (a \times p)^4$$

TABLE (1.4). FILM & VIDEO

Directors	Directors
Core, Ericson Dreamtime Pictures / 213-933-5515	Dixon, Phillip DNA / 213-463-2826
Cousins, Scott Public Pictures / 212-431-0998	Doane, Darren Dreamtime Pictures / 213-933-5515
Crutcher, Greg Picture Vision / 212-995-9797	Dobkin, David A+R Group / 213-650-4722
Cummings, Jr., Richard Underdog Films Inc. / 213-936-3111	Dobson, Craig Bennu Productions, Inc. / 212-213-8511
Cundieff, Rusty Oil Factory, Inc. / 213-466-7306	Domner, John The Underground / 213-954-1100
Curreri, robert Notorious Pictures / 718-768-6074	Donovan, Kevin Industrial Artists / 310-393-3400
Cury, Brian UN Productions, Inc. / 201-488-1111	Dorfman, Jay Unherd of Productions / 212-251-8671
Dark and Meade Squeak Pictures / 818-980-0800	Doucette, Andrew Silvey & Company / 213-936-2137
Darken, Brett North Star Productions / 615-297-1457	Dougherty, George Industrial Artists / 310-393-3400
Davis, Tamara O Pictures / 213-466-0324	Dubin, Adam Shine / 213-852-1006
de Paola, Mark de Paola Productions / 310-550-5910	Dwek, Nevil Open City Films / 212-343-1850
De Thame, Gerard HSI / 310-452-9999	Dylan, Jesse Shine / 213-852-1006
DeCerchio, Tom HSI / 310-452-9999	Egan, Nick Satellite Films / 213-465-9300
Deaton, Robert Deaton Flanigen / 615-329-2095	Elledge, Paul Mr. Big Productions, Inc. / 312-733-8021 Rep: Ann Bieber / 312-463-1921
Demchuck, Bob Scene East Productions / 212-749-2399	Falcon, Errol Falcon Productions / 305-442-1318
Dempster, Kim O Pictures, Inc. / 213-466-0324	Fincher, David Propaganda Films / 213-462-6400
Dey, Thomas Portfolio/Blackdog / 212-633-6030	Finger, Lea Owen Electric / 212-941-5944
DiSalvio, James Epoch Films / 310-440-2656	Flanigen, George Deaton Flanigen / 615-329-2095
Dick, Nigel Squeak Pictures / 818-980-0800	

Table (1.5). Film & Video

Directors	Directors
Flansbergh, John Moxie Pictures / 213-957-5420	Glover, Lefty Liberty Studios / 212-532-1865
Flatiron Film Flatiron Films / 212-924-6668	Godley, Kevin Chelsea Pictures / 212-431-0199
Fletcher, Ian Dreamtime Pictures / 213-933-5515	Gold, Greg Propaganda Films / 213-462-6400
Forti, Brian Forti/Layne Entertainment / 305-599-2818	Gondry, Michel Palomar Pictures / 213-525-2900
Fox, Ken F.M. Rocks / 310-587-1501	Goodman, Katie Sonic Vision / 213-663-4082
Franchot, Pascal Power Films / 213-653-7665	Grant, Brian Flattery Yukich, Inc. (F.Y.I) / 213-850-6106
Fred Stuhr The Underground / 213-954-1100	Grasso, Carlos Squeak Pictures / 818-980-0800
Friedman, Bradley Vide U Productions / 310-657-4385	Gray, F. Gary F.M. Rocks / 212-251-8686
Friedman, Carol Dominick Films / 212-925-4951	Greenberg, Bryan Red Hots / 818-954-0092
Froehle, Paula M. Sonic Vision / 213-663-4082	Grieg, Gary Raimondi Films / 202-342-9559
Fuqua, Antoine Propaganda Films / 213-462-6400	Groot, John Modern Image / 312-943-5722
Gable, Jim Graying & Balding Inc. / 213-962-7551	Guillet, Guy Notorious Pictures / 718-768-6074
Gabrielson, Robert Scene Three / 615-385-2820	Gwynn, Cat O Pictures / 213-466-0324
Garrett, Okuwah Power Films / 213-936-3111	Haft, Steven Propaganda Films / 213-462-6400
Gaudet, Joe F.M. Rocks / 310-587-1501	Halsband, Michael Planet Pictures / 213-461-2695
Geoghegan, Michael The Underground / 213-954-1100	Hamad, Ron Kucharo Group / 602-253-4888
George, Tryan Smash! Films / 213-957-7657	Hamilton, J.R. Del-Rey Communication / 708-655-0020
Gibson, Wayne HSI / 310-452-9999	Handa, Yasushu PMC Pictures / 310-202-4929
Giraud, Paul HSI / 310-452-9999	Hanesh, Brian Paradox Studios & Prods. / 213-962-6688

$$F = (a \times p)^4$$

TABLE (1.6). FILM & VIDEO

Directors	Directors
Harding, C.B. Picture Vision / 212-995-9797	Humphery, Mark A+R Group / 213-650-4722
Harmon, Jason Oil Factory, Inc. / 213-466-7306	Hunter, Paul Oil Factory, Inc. / 213-466-7306
Harrick, Keith Studio Productions / 615-298-5818	Huss, Michael Above & Beyond Pictures / 615-385-3203
Harrison, Phil Epoch Films / 310-440-2656	Ice Cube The End / 213-782-9000
Hartley, Hal Pellington/Gorai/Crossroads / 212-647-1300	Ice T DNA / 213-483-2826
Haussman, Michael The A&R Group / 213-650-4722	Ifergan, Erich O Pictures / 213-466-0324
Hawke, Ethan The End / 213-782-9000	Israelson, Peter Picture Vision / 212-995-9797
Hayward, Julia Industrial Artists / 310-393-3400	Jacobs, Dani Squeak Pictures / 818-980-0800
Hedgecock, Brent Planet Pictures / 213-461-2695	Jakobsson, Agust F.M. Rocks / 310-587-1501
Hennesey, Martin Stone GPA / 212-532-6000	Janiak, Seb Propaganda Films / 213-462-6400
Henry, Craig Power Films / 213-653-7665	Jim Gabour Jim Gabour Moving Pictures / 504-529-5956
Hermelin, Julie Oil Factory, Inc. / 213-466-7306	Joanou, Phil O Pictures / 213-466-0324
Hershleder, Jim DNA / 213-463-2826	Johnson, Michael Blue Desert Pictures / 602-941-4109
Heslop, Richard Oil Factory, Inc. / 213-466-7306	Jonze, Spike Satellite Film / 213-465-9300
Hewitt, Peter Quick on the Draw / 213-655-5791	Joyce, Graeme A+R Group / 213-650-4722
Hillcoat, Jill Oil Factory, Inc. / 213-466-7306	Jurgensen, Jens Riviera Films / 212-496-7929
Hogan, David Original Video / 310-393-0200	Karr, Dean 1171 Production Group / 213-655-1171
Hughes, Albert & Allen Oil Factory, Inc. / 213-466-7306	Keely, Wayne Bennu Productions, Inc. / 212-213-8511
Hughes, Bronwen O Pictures / 213-466-0324	Keller, Brian Kucharo Group / 602-253-4888

$$F = (a \times p)^4$$

TABLE (1.7). FILM & VIDEO

Directors	Directors
Kellison, Kurt Sonic Vision / 213-663-4082	Lamardo, Felix R. Pulsar Entertainment / 212-686-2717
Kelly, David Propaganda Films / 213-462-6400	Lambert, Mary Industrial Pictures / 310-393-3400
Kennedy, Scott Industrial Artists / 310-393-3400	Lateef, Ahmed Silvereye Production, Inc. / 818-501-4232
Kerner, Water L@it2'd / 213-856-0700	Lauer, Peter Maddhatter Films / 213-957-7777
Kerslake, Kevin Silvey & Company / 213-936-2137	Lauper, Cyndi Daisy Force Pictures / 213-462-8881
Keshishian, Alek Propaganda Films / 213-462-6400	Lavett, Darren J. Maddhatter Films / 213-957-7777
Kessler, Stephen HSI / 310-452-9999	Layne, Kevin Forti/Layne Entertainment / 305-599-2818
Killen, Michael Above & Beyond Pictures / 615-385-3203	Leitman, Ruth Moxie Pictures / 213-957-5420
Kirklys, Steven Propaganda Films / 213-462-6400	Leshem, Matti Planet Pictures / 213-461-2695
Klasfeld, Marc / 212-532-1626 MKSR Films	Levine, Richard Daisy Force Pictures / 213-462-8881
Klein, John Epoch Films / 310-440-2656	Lim, Abe Riviera Films / 212-496-7929
Kliot, Jason Open City Films / 212-343-1850	Lindquist, Mark The End / 213-782-9000
Kohr, Mark Satellite Films / 213-465-9300	Lipschultz, Mindi L@it2'd / 213-856-0700
Kolarek, Frank Kolarek Film & Video / 212-947-7515	Lockwood, Brian Smash! Films / 213-957-7657
Koszell, Kathy Above & Beyond Pictures / 615-385-3203	Lokken, Maria Unherd of Productions / 212-251-8671
Kovacs, Peter Dreamtime Pictures / 213-933-5515	Lowe, Jeff Public Pictures / 212-431-0998
Kurt & Bart Planet Pictures / 213-461-2695	Maag, Gary Maag Productions, Inc. / 612-339-2345
L.J. Krevsling GPA / 212-532-6000	Maclean, Allison Pellington/Gorai/Crossroads / 212-647-1300
LaFrance, Don Smash! Films / 213-957-7657	Maguire, Barry Oil Factory, Inc. / 213-466-7306

TABLE (1.8). FILM & VIDEO

Directors	Directors
Mahurin, Matt O Pictures / 213-466-0324	Melie, Ora Maximum Respect Prod. / 201-435-5309
Malkin, Max Shine / 213-852-1006	Mercilion, Tom Propaganda Films / 213-462-6400
Mallet, David Flattery Yukich, Inc. / 213-850-6106	Meseke, Dale Kolarek Film & Video / 212-947-7515
Markey, Dave Hero / 818-505-8833	Meza, Eric Original Video / 310-393-0200
Marro, Stephen Marro & Associates / 212-463-0397	Miller, Chip Red Hots / 818-954-0092
Marshall, Denny Freestyle Media Group / 310-530-9195	Miller, John Llyod Scene Three Inc. / 615-385-2820
Martin, Bruce 1171 Production Group / 213-655-1171	Miller, Sue Travis Red Hots / 818-954-0092
Martin, Douglas Design & Direction, Inc. / 310-395-6730	Minutello, Frank On Track Video / 212-645-2040
Masuak, Greg Oil Factory, Inc. / 213-466-7306	Miron, Francois Sonic Vision / 213-663-4082
Matthews, Matt Wright-Banks Films / 310-470-0491	Modi Modivation Films / 213-850-6607
Matthies, Eric H-Gun Productions / 312-808-0134	Mondino, Jean-Baptiste Palomar Pictures / 213-525-2900
Maxwell, Simon The Underground / 213-954-1100	Money, Jim Angel City Productions / 213-465-6802
May, James Studio Productions / 615-298-5818	Moore, Jeff O Pictures / 213-466-0324
McClelland, Kirk Kirk McClelland Productions / 813-355-2456	Moore, Jeff Stan Stan Moore Productions / 615-791-6237
McDaniel, Melodie Palomar Pictures / 213-525-2900	Morahan, Andy HSI / 310-452-9999
McDaniels, Ralph F.W.A. Productions / 212-268-3849	Morton, Rocky & Annabel Jankel Daisy Force Pictures / 213-462-8881
McDermott, Dylan Black & White Television / 213-467-8822	Mulcahy, Russell Propaganda Films / 213-462-6400
McFarlane, Keir Palomar Pictures / 213-525-2900	Muller, Sophie Oil Factory, Inc. / 213-466-7306
→ Mei, Gallen Gallen Mei Productions / 415-928-5070 pages 4 - 5	Musick, Gary Gary Musick Productions, Inc. / 615-259-2400

TABLE (1.9). FILM & VIDEO

Directors	Directors
Nelson, Larry Edge Productions / 615-824-2430	Pellington, Mark Pellington/Gorai/Crossroads / 212-647-1300
Newman, Tim Wright-Banks Films / 310-319-9900	Penczner, Marcus Rainmaker Productions / 615-320-7267
Nichol, Doug Palomar Pictures / 213-525-2900	Peredoehl, Eric I.A.M. / 408-749-9757
Nispel, Marcus Portfolio/Blackdog / 212-633-6030	Perillo, Mary Mary Perillo Inc. / 212-608-3943
Nydrle, Peter	Philips, Toby F.M. Rocks / 310-587-1501
Ockenfels 3, Frank W. HSI / 310-452-9999	Phillips, Jeffrey Studio Productions / 615-298-5818
Ohrling, Michael Kucharo Group / 602-253-4888	Pinkett, Jada F.M. Rocks / 310-587-1501
Orlando, Dominic DNA / 213-463-2826	Pirozek, Sarah Dame Work / 212-675-3263
Owen, Michael Owen Electric / 212-941-5944	Pistole, Roger Studio Productions / 615-298-5818
Painter, Chris Picture Vision / 212-995-9797	Pitts, Martin One Heart Productions / 213-466-7306
Parker, Alex Daisy Force Pictures / 213-462-8881	Plansker, Jeffrey Propagand Films / 213-848-3777
Parker, Bill Renge Films, Inc. / 213-656-5941	Plowden, Piers DNA / 213-463-2826
Parks, Jon Mirage Productions / 804-788-1450	Pollock, Neil The End / 213-782-9000
Patillo, Dwight E. F.M. Rocks / 310-587-1501	Pomeroy, Dan Red Hots / 818-954-0092
Paul, Reid Major League Productions, Inc. / 312-440-1430	Poussaint, Neil Moxie Pictures / 213-957-5420
Paul, Rod Rod Paul Productions / 404-321-7900	Preiss, Jeff Epoch Films / 310-440-2656
Payson, John Original Video / 310-393-0200	Proyas, Alex Propaganda Films / 213-462-6400
Peck, Tony Industrial Artists / 310-393-3400	Quay Brothers, The The End / 213-782-9000
Peckham, Russell Peckham Productions / 914-631-5050	Raboy, Marcus The End / 213-782-9000

$$F = (a \times p)^4$$

TABLE (1.10). FILM & VIDEO

Directors	Directors
Rachman, Paul Hero / 818-505-8833	Rozen, Andre Commotion Pictures / 415-777-2034
Raimondi, Paul Raimondi Films / 202-342-9559	Sacramento, Frank Oil Factory, Inc. / 213-466-7306
Ranch, Floyd Riviera Films / 212-496-7929	Sanji Propaganda Films / 213-462-6400
Reed, Peyton Moxie Pictures / 213-957-5420	Schenck, Rocky DNA / 213-463-2826
Reichek, Robin Orbit Productions, Inc. / 213-993-0199	Schewe, Jeff Major League Productions, Inc. / 312-440-1430
Reiss, John Original Video / 310-393-0200	Schwartzberg, Louie Schwartzberg & Company / 818-508-1444
Riviera, Peter Underdog Films / 213-936-3111	Scopels, Stephen Imagemaker Productions / 615-244-1700
Roberts, Amanda PMC Pictures / 310-202-4929	Scott, Jake Portfolio/Blackdog / 212-633-6030
Robertson, Dave Southwest Productions / 505-247-3300	Sednaoui, Stephane Propaganda Films / 213-462-6400
Robertson, Dustin O Pictures / 213-466-0324	Seminara, George Public Pictures / 212-431-0998
Robertson, Woody September Moon Production Network / 810-355-3700	Sena, Dominic Propaganda Films / 213-462-6400
Robinson, Pam Smash! Films / 213-957-7657	Shainberg, Steven Industrial Artists / 310-393-3400
Rodriguez, Robert Oil Factory, Inc. / 213-466-7306	Shankman, Adam Power Films / 213-653-7665
Roland, Glenn Glenn Roland Films / 310-475-0937	Shea, Jim Planet Pictures, Inc. / 213-461-2695
Romanek, Mark Satellite Films / 213-465-9300	Shelton, Millicent The End / 213-782-9000
Romhanyi, Pedro Oil Factory, Inc. / 213-466-7306	Siegel, Niles On Track Video / 212-645-2040
Rosenberg, Merlyn Propaganda Films / 212-462-6400	Sigsmondi, Gloria Propaganda Films / 213-954-1100
Ross, Ken Picture Vision / 212-995-9797	Simpson, Jane Silvey & Company / 213-936-2137
Royes, Tim A+R Group / 213-650-4722	Smith, Jeff Above & Beyond Pictures / 615-385-3203

$$F = (a \times p)^4$$

TABLE (1.11). FILM & VIDEO

Directors	Directors
Smyth, Richie PMC Pictures / 310-202-4929	Thorgerson, Storm The End / 213-782-9000
Snyder, Zack The End / 213-782-9000	Thorton, Spencer Innovative Media Productions / 818-755-0155
Soultanakis, Nico Palomar Pictures / 213-525-2900	Tolot, Alberto Smash! Films / 213-957-7657
Speaks, John Original Video / 310-393-0200	Trail, Thomas F.M. Rocks / 310-587-1501
Spring, Jim Riviera Films / 212-496-7929	Tuckett, Phil NFL Films / 609-778-1600
Springsteen, Pamela Picture Vision / 212-995-9797	Tyler, Jan Tyler Productions / 615-385-2244
Stacey, Terry Notorious Pictures / 718-768-6074	Van Sant, Gus Riviera Films / 212-496-7929
Sterner, John Firehouse Films / 212-491-6500	Vaughan, Jesse F.M. Rocks / 310-587-1501
Stobaugh, William Planet Pictures / 213-461-2695	Vaughn, Steve GPA / 212-532-6000
Stokes, Ben H-Gun Productions / 312-808-0134	Verbinski, Gore Palomar Pictures / 213-525-2900
Stone, III, Charles S. Woo Art International, Inc. / 212-989-7870	Walker, Paula Strato Films / 213-344-0988
Stratton, Eric Edge Productions / 615-822-8206	Ward, Bill DNA / 213-463-2826
Strictland, Stan Rainmaker Productions / 615-320-7267	Warner, Leta Squeak Pictures / 818-980-0800
Taft, Josh Shine / 213-852-1006	Waters, Jon Sonic Vision / 213-663-4082
Tardio Jr., Neil Original Video / 310-393-0200	Watson, Albert F.M. Rocks / 310-587-1501
Tarsem A&R Group / 213-650-4722	Watson, Charlie The End / 213-782-9000
Temple, Julien Nitrate Films / 213-782-3400	Watson, Kim Squeak Pictures / 818-980-0800
Thomas, Pam Satellite Films / 213-466-0324	Wayne, Tony Tony Wayne, Inc. / 212-683-0733
Thomson, Brian Wright-Banks Film / 310-470-0491	Webster, D.J. F.M. Rocks / 310-587-1501

$$F = (a \times p)^4$$

Table (1.12). Film & Video

Directors	Directors
Weinrich, Jeth DNA / 213-463-2826	Zimmerman, Eric Industrial Artists / 310-393-3400
Weiss, Mark Weissguy Productions / 908-291-2989	Zodiac F.W.A. Productions / 212-268-3849
Weiss, Mike Open City Films / 212-343-1850	

Directors	Production Companies
Wells, Tammara One Heart Productions / 213-466-3288	
Wenner, Gerry Planet Pictures, Inc. / 213-461-2695	1171 Production Group / 213-655-1171 303 S. Sweetzer St., LA, CA 90048
White, Shell The Underground / 213-954-1100	16 Carrots Production Services / 212-645-9071 16 Abingdon Sq., NYC, NY 10014
Wille, Jodi DNA / 213-463-2826	900 Frames / 212-661-6569 140 E. 46th St., Ste 3C, NYC, NY 10017
Williams, Mark Open City Films / 212-343-1850	A&R Group, The / 212-679-7199 38 W. 21st St., NYC, NY 10010
Williams, Russell Raimondi Films / 202-342-9559	A&R Group, The / 213-650-4722 1015 N. Fairfax Ave., LA, CA 90046
Williams, Ruth Liberty Studios / 212-532-1865	**Directors:**
Winter, Alex Satellite Films / 213-465-9300	David Cameron Eric Clapton, Stereo MC'S, PM Dawn
Wittenmeier, Charles The End / 213-782-9000	David Dobkin Dada, Blues Traveler, Sonic Youth
Wiz Oil Factory, Inc. / 213-466-7306	Michael Haussman Madonna, Joe Cocker, Chris Isaak
Woo, John Woo Art International / 212-989-7870	Mark Humphrey Born Jamericans, Genius
Wooton, Albert Maverick Video / 210-655-1111	Graeme Joyce Stone Temple Pilots, Dig Greta
Yeaworth, Jonathan Gary Musick Productions, Inc. / 615-259-2400	Tim Royes Eternal, Melisa Etheridge, Terrorvision
Yukich, Jim Flattery Yukich, Inc. (F.Y.I.) / 213-850-6106	Tarsem R.E.M., Deep Forest, Suzanne Vega
Zanes, Paula Greif Epoch Films / 310-440-2656	Above & Beyond Pictures / 615-385-3203 P.O. Box 121426, Nashville, TN 37212
Zanuck, Lili Fini DNA / 213-463-2826	Akiva Films / 718-802-0531 31 Washington St., Brooklyn, NY 11201
	Alternative Visions / 615-726-2005 114 17th Ave. South, Nashville, TN 37203

TABLE (1.13). FILM & VIDEO

Production Companies	Production Companies
Angel City Productions / 213-465-6802 7000 Romaine St., LA, CA 90038	DNA, Inc. / 213-463-2826 6535 Santa Monica Blvd., Ste.B, LA, CA 90038
BFCS / 212-838-4417 84 Wooster, NYC, NY 10012	Daisy Force Pictures / 213-462-8881 441 W. Magnolia Blvd., LA, CA 91505
BFCS / 213-960-2400 1040 N. Las Palmas, Hollywood, CA 90038	Dame Work / 212-675-3263 360 W. 20th St., #107, NY, NY 10011
Badman / 213-461-8659 905 N. Cole Ave., Hollywood, CA 90038	de Paola Productions / 310-550-5910 1560 Benedict Canyon, Beverly Hills, CA 90210
Bennu Productions, Inc. / 212-213-8511 171 Madison Ave., NYC, NY 10016	Deaton Flanigen Productions / 615-329-2095 1014 17th Ave. So., Nashville, TN 37212
Black & White TV / 213-467-8822 6683 Sunset Blvd., #1, LA, CA 90028	Del-Rey Communications / 708-655-0020 P.O. Box 5274, Oak Brook, IL 60522
Black Ball Films / 312-235-9341 916 N. Daman Ave., Chicago, IL 60622	Desert Music Pictures / 213-937-0951 3780 Wilshire Blvd, 202, LA, CA 90010
Black Dog Films / 310-659-1017 634 N. La Peer Dr., LA, CA 90069	Design & Direction, Inc. / 310-395-6730 437 San Vincente Blvd, Ste. C, Santa Monica, CA 90402
Blue Desert Pictures / 602-941-4109 5900 E. Thomas, #H 130, Scottsdale, AZ 85251	Detour Pictures / 212-353-8106 352 Bowery, 2nd Floor, NYC, NY 10012
Brinkerhoff Associates, Martin / 714-660-9396 17767 Mitchell, Irvine, CA 92714	Directions, Inc. / 212-691-2202 89 Fifth Ave., NYC, NY 10003
Buckholtz Prod., Inc. / 504-891-0912 737 Eleonore St., New Orleans, LA 70115-3216	Dominick Films / 212-925-4951 60 Grand St., NYC, NY 10013
Chelsea Pictures / 301-450-0999 1750 14th St., Ste. E, Santa Monica, CA 90404	Doom / 213-850-6560 3309 Carse Dr., LA, CA 90068
Chelsea Pictures / 212-431-3434 122 Hudson St., 6th Fl., NYC, NY 10013	Drawing Board / 212-929-4572 63 E. Ninth St., 14N, NYC, NY 10003
Classic Concepts / 212-268-3849 444 W. 35th St., 1D, NYC, NY 10001	Dreamtime Pictures / 213-933-5515 7218-1/2 Beverly Blvd., LA, CA 90038
Commotion Pictures / 415-777-2034 118 King St., Ste.200, SF, CA 94107	Dublin Productions / 612-332-8864 414 Third Ave. N., Minneapolis, MN 55401
Company, The / 818-766-5680 11330 Ventura Blvd., Studio City, CA 91604	Edge Productions / 615-824-2430 109 Jackstaff, Hendersonville, TN 37075
Cream Cheese / 213-465-8495 959 N. Cole, Ste. 460, LA, CA 90038	Emotion Pictures / 312-235-3410 1057 N. Leavitt, Ste 1, Chicago, IL 60622
Creative Edge Studio / 615-320-1403 1416 Church St., Nashville, TN 37203	End, The / 213-782-9000 8060 Melrose, Hollywood, CA 90046
Cummings Productions, Inc., Bob / 615-385-4400 1204 Elmwood Ave., Nashville, TN 37212	End, The / 212-387-8800 119 Fifth Ave., NYC, CNY 10003

TABLE (1.14). FILM & VIDEO

Production Companies	Production Companies
Epoch Films / 310-440-2656 1450 N. Spaulding Ave., LA, CA 90046	→ HSI Productions / 310-452-9999 1611 Electric Ave., Venice, CA 90291 page 1
Epoch Films / 212-226-0661 122 Hudson St., NYC, NY 10013	**Directors:** Geoffrey Barish
F.M. Rocks / 310-587-1501 1351 Third St. Pomenade, Santa Monica, CA 90401	Samuel Bayer Clint Clemens
F.W.A. Productions / 212-268-3849 444 W. 35th St., Ste. 1D, NYC, NY 10001	Tom DeCerchio Gerard De Thame
Falcon Productions / 305-442-1318 133 Aragon Ave., Coral Gables, FL 33134	Wayne Gibson Paul Giraud
Firehouse Films / 212-491-6500 / 213-957-6820	Stephen Kessler Andy Morahan
Flatiron Films / 212-924-6668 1 Union Sq. West, Ste.307, NYC, NY 10003	Frank W. Ockenfels 3
Flattery Yukich, Inc. (F.Y.I.) / 213-850-6106 3605 Cahuenga Blvd. W., LA, CA 90068	Happy Feet Productions / 310-273-1086 425 N. Oakhurst Dr., #207, Beverly Hills, CA 90210
Force of Habit Productions / 415-585-2200 196 Newton St., SF, CA 94112	Hedquist Productions / 515-472-6798 P.O. Box 1475, Fairfield, IA 52556
Forti/Layne Entertainment / 305-599-2818 7355 NW 41st St., Miami, FL 33166	Hero Films / 818-505-8833 11101 Hortense St., N. Hollywood, CA 91602
Freestyle Media Group / 310-530-9195	High Five Productions / 213-969-9555 3723 W. Olive Ave., Burbank, CA 91505
GPA/Grodin Production Assoc. / 212-532-6000 157 E. 35th St., NYC, NY	High Five Productions / 615-321-2540 903 18th ave South, Nashville, TN 37212
Gabour Moving Pictures, Jim / 504-529-5956 921 Canal St., Ste. 740, New Orleans, LA 70112	I.A.M. / 408-749-9757 P.O. Box 2430, Santa Clara, CA 95055
Glassman TV & Film Prod. / 212-369-3010 417 E. 87th St., NYC, NY 10128	Imagemaker Productions / 615-244-1700 220 Great Circle Rd., #118, Nashville, TN 37228
Graying & Balding Inc. / 213-962-7551 6311 Romaine St., #7306, Hollywood, CA 90038	Industrial Artists / 310-393-3400 409 Santa Monica Blvd., Santa Monica, CA 90401
H-Gun Productions / 312-808-0134 2024 S. Wabash, 7th Fl, Chicago, IL 60616	Kolarek Film & Video, Frank / 212-947-7515 286 Fifth Ave., NYC, NY 10001
→ HSI Productions / 212-627-3600 7 West 18th St., NYC, NY 10011 page 1	Kucharo Group, The / 602-253-4888 624 N. Fifth St., Phoenix, AZ 85004
	L@it2'd / 213-856-0700 6815 W. Willoughby Ave., Ste. 102, Hollywood, CA 90038
	Directors: Water Kerner & Mindi Lipschultz Janet Jackson "Because of Love"

$F = (a \times p)^4$

TABLE (1.15). FILM & VIDEO

Production Companies	Production Companies
Leisure Jazz Video / 504-943-4343 P.O. Box 56757, New Orleans, LA 70156-6757	NFL Films / 609-778-1600 330 Fellowship Rd., Mount Laurel, NJ 08054
Liberty Studios / 212-532-1865 238 E. 26th St., NYC, NY 10010	New Generation Pictures / 212-675-1809 7 W. 20th St., #2F, NYC, NY 10011
Longo, Robert / 212-431-8627 224 Centre St., NYC, NY 10013	Nitrate Films, Inc. / 213-782-3400 8455 Beverly Blvd., #410, LA, CA 90048
Lorcott Productions, Inc. / 212-633-8868 255 W. 26th St., NYC, NY 10001	Noir Music Videos / 310-449-1141 2121 Cloverfield, Ste.201, Santa Monica, CA 90404
MKSR Films / 212-532-1626 311 E. 25th St., Ste.1C, NYC, NY 10010	→ nomad SHORT SUBJECTS / 919-832-0259 501 Washington St., Raliegh, NC 27605 pages 2 - 3
Maag Productions, Inc. / 612-339-2345 126 N. Third St., Ste. 508, Minneapolis, MN 55401	North Star Productions / 615-297-1457 3608 Sperry Ave, Nashville, TN 37215
Major League Productions, Inc. / 312-440-1430 111 E. Chestnut St., Ste. 42C, Chicago, IL 60611	Notorious Pictures, Inc. / 718-768-6074 409 Ninth St., Brooklyn, NY 11215
Marro-Matson / 212-463-0397 121 W. 19th St., 10th Fl., NYC, NY 10011	Nydrle, Peter / 213-935-5228 170 N. Gardner, LA, CA 90036
Maverick Video Prod., Inc / 210-655-1111 4235 Centergate, San Antonio, TX 78217	O Pictures, Inc. / 213-466-0324 5636 Melrose Ave., Hollywood, CA 90029
Maximum Respect Prod. / 212-780-3466 / 201-435-5309	O Wow / 212-691-3500 153 Waverly Place, NYC, NY 10014
McClelland Productions, Kirk / 813-355-2456 831 D Mecca Dr., Sarasota, FL 34234	Oil Factory / 213-466-7306 1655 Cherokee, 3rd fl., Hollywood, CA 90028
→ Mei, Gallen Productions / 415-928-5070 1405 Gough St., #3, SF, CA 94109 pages 4 - 5	**Directors:** Miles Aldridge
Mirage Productions / 804-788-1450 333 N. 17th St., Richmond, VA 23219	Paul Andersen (formerly TV Eye)
Modern Image Productions, Inc. / 312-943-5722 1522 N. Hudson, Chicago, IL 60610	Martyn Atkins
Modivation Films & Parallax / 213-850-6607 2126 Ewing St., LA, CA 90039	Fredrik Boklund
Moore Productions, Stan / 615-791-6237 321 Kentons Way, Franklin, TN 37064	Lisa Bonet Rusty Cundieff
Moxie Pictures / 213-957-5420 1040 N. Sycamore, LA, CA 90038	Jason Harmon Julie Hermelin
Mr. Big Productions, Inc. / 312-463-1921 3312 W. Belle Plaine, Chicago, IL 60618	Richard Heslop John Hillcoat
Musick Productions, Inc., Gary / 615-259-2400 912 Twin Elms Ct., Nashville, TN 37210	Albert & Allen Hughes Paul Hunter Barry Maguire

$$F = (a \times p)^4$$

Table (1.16). Film & Video

Production Companies	Production Companies
Greg Masuak	Planet Pictures, Inc. / 213-461-2695 6311 Romaine St., #7235, Hollywood, CA 90038
Sophie Muller	
Robert Rodriguez	Power Films / 213-653-7665 653 N. Fairfax, LA, CA 90036
Pedro Romhanyi	
Frank Sacramento	Primalux Video / 212-206-1402 30 W. 26th St., NYC, NY 10010
Wiz	
On Track Video / 212-645-2040 124 W. 24th St., NYC, NY 10011	PrimeLight Productions / 718-543-3991 750 Kappock St., Ste. 805, Riverdale, NY 10463
One Heart Productions / 213-466-3288 6255 Afton Place, Hollywood, CA 90028	Propaganda Films / 213-462-6400 940 N. Mansfield Ave., Hollywood, CA 90038
One Wolrd Productions / 213-960-2480 1040 N. Las Palmas Ave., Hollywood, CA 90038	Public Pictures / 212-431-0998 476 Broome St., Ste. 6B, NYC, NY 10013
Open City Films / 212-343-1850 198 Sixth Ave., NYC, NY 10013	Pulsar Entertainment / 212-686-2717 121 Madison Ave., Ste 8F, NYC, NY 10016
Original Video / 310-393-0200 2045 Barrington Ave., LA, CA 90025	RSA USA, Inc. / 212-725-1900 192 Lexington Ave., 16th Fl, NYC, NY 10016
Original Video / 212-686-0200 60 Madison Avenue, NYC, NY 10010	Raimondi Films / 202-342-9559 2121 Wisconsin Ave. NW, Washington, DC 20007
Owen Electric / 212-941-5944 84 Wooster St., #5C, NYC, NY 10012	Rainmaker Productions / 615-320-7267 / 615-320-7267 815 18 Ave. S., Nashville, TN 37203
PMC Pictures / 310-202-4929 9336 W. Washington Blvd, Culver City, CA 90232	Raven Knite Productions / 213-462-8841 663 Lillian Way, LA, CA 90004
Palomar Pictures / 213-525-2900 5657 Wilshire Blvd., 5th fl., LA, CA 90036	Rebo Group / 212-989-9466 530 W. 25th St., 2nd Fl, NYC, NY 10001
Paradox Studios & Prods. / 213-962-6688 6200 De Longpre Ave., Ste. C, Hollywood, CA 90028	Red Hots / 818-954-0092 813 N. Cordova St., Burbank, CA 91505-2924
Paul Productions, Rod / 404-321-7900 1820 Briarwood Industrial Ct., Atlanta, GA 30329	Riviera Films / 212-496-7929 13 W. 89th St., #1, NYC, NY 10012
Peckham Productions / 914-631-5050 65 S. Broadway, Tarrytown, NY 10591	Roland Films, Glenn / 310-475-0937 P.O. Box 341408, LA, CA 90034
Pellington/Gorai/Crossroads / 212-647-1300 136 W.21St., 5th fl., NYC, NY 10011	Samurai Productions / 212-391-1020 45 W. 45th St., 12th Fl., NYC, NY 10036
Perrilo, Inc., Mary / 212-608-3943 125 Cedar St., Ste. 8S, NYC, NY 10006	Satellite Films / 213-465-9300 940 N. Mansfield Ave., Hollywood, CA 90038
Pershing Productions, Verne / 213-463-1511 1800 N. Argyle Ave., #100A, Hollywood, CA 90028	Scene East Productions / 212-749-2399 229 W. 97th St., NYC, NY 10025
Picture Vision / 212-995-9797 900 Broadway, Ste. 604, NYC, NY 10003	Scene Three / 615-385-2820 1813 Eighth Ave. So., Nashville, TN 37203

TABLE (1.17). FILM & VIDEO

Production Companies	Production Companies

Schwartzberg & Company / 818-508-1444
12700 Ventura Blvd, 4th Fl, Studio City, CA 91604

Scorched Earth Productions / 212-777-2300
640 Broadway, NYC, NY 10012

September Moon Prod. Network / 810-355-3700
25925 Telegraph, Ste. 190, Southfield, MI 48034

Shine / 213-852-1006
7551 Melrose Ave, #4, LA, CA 90046

Shooting Stars Productions, Inc. / 212-888-8999
38 E. 57th St., 12th Fl, NYC, NY 10022

Silvereye Production, Inc. / 818-501-4232
4163 Murietta Ave, Sherman Oaks, CA 91423

Silvey/Company / 213-936-2137
8306 Wilshire Blvd, #2300, Beverly Hills, CA 90211

Slingshot Productions / 818-999-2539

Smash! Films / 213-957-7657
1020 N. Cole Ave., Hollywood, CA 90038

Sonic Vision Management / 213-663-4082
2525 Panorama Terrace, LA, CA 90039

Representing Riviera Films Directors:

Katie Goodman

Jon Waters

Michael Burlingame
  Yoko Ono "Love"
  Roger Miller "Wounded World"
  Mariah Carey "Anytime You Need a Friend"
   (dance mix")

Gus Van Sant
  Red Hot Chili Peppers "Under the Bridge"
  Chris Isaak "San Francisco Days"
  David Bowie "Fame '90"

Larry Clark
  Chris Isaak "Solitary Man"

Jim Spring & Jens Jergensen
  Mercury Rev "Chasing a Bee"
  Jon Spencer Blues Explosion "Rachel"
  Dinosaur Jr. "Whatever's Cool With Me"

Also Representing The Following Directors:

Kurt Kellison and Paula M. Froehle
  Helmet "Give It" (co-directors)
  4 Non-Blondes "Dear Mr. President" (co-directors)
  Eleventh Dream Day "Makin' Like a Rug"

Francois Miron
  Monster Magnet "Tab 25"
  Moby "Drop a Beat"
  Aphex Twin "Ambient Work Part 2"

Southwest Productions / 505-247-3300
812 Gold SW, Alburquerque, NM 87102

Spotlight Prod. Srvcs. / 214-484-6173
2435 W. Northwest Hwy., Dallas, TX 75220

Spy Films / 212-979-9400 / 213-271-2424
141 Fifth Ave., Ste.8N, NYC, NY 10010

Squeak Pictures / 818-980-0800
3753 Cahuenga Blvd. West, Studio City, CA 91604

Directors:

Dick Buckley
  Robert Plant "If I was a Carpenter"
  James Ingram "Get Ready"

Peter Christopherson
  Nine Inch Nails "Wish" & "March of the Pigs"
  Rage Against the Machine "Freedom"
  Robert Plant "I Believe"

Dark and Meade
  John Mellencamp "Human Wheels"
  "Wild Night"

Nigel Dick
  Living Color "Sunshine of Your Love"
   (from the movie "True Lies")
  Alice in Chains "Down in a Hole"
  Guns 'n Roses "Sweet Child O' Mine"

Carlos Grasso
  Cracker "Low"
  Grant Lee Buffalo "Fuzzy" & "Mighty Joe Moon"
  Sam Phillips "Baby I Can't Please You"

Dani Jacobs
  Tears for Fears "Break It Down Again"
  The Cranes "Shinning Road"
  Jeffery Gaines "I Like You"

$$F = (a \times p)^4$$

TABLE (1.18). FILM & VIDEO

Production Companies	Production Companies

Leta Warner
   Brian McKnight "One Last Cry"
   Lauren Christy "Steep"
   Jonathan Butler "Down On My Knees"
Kim Watson
   R Kelly "Bump and Grind"
   Keith Washington "Believe That"
   Will Downing "There's No Living Without You"

Starving Artist / 310-859-8930
329 N. Wetherly Dr., Beverly Hills, CA 90211

Stone Films / 212-595-6991 / 310-578-7565
225 W. 70th St., NYC, NY 10023

Strato Films / 213-344-0988
4859 College View Ave., LA, CA 90041

Sunrise Films / 800-545-3869

Tennessee Prod. Center Inc. / 615-577-5597
10840 Chapman Hwy, Seymour, TN 37865

Third Ave. Productions / 206-728-8290
2720 Third Ave., Seattle, WA 98121

Thunder & Lightning Productions / 212-675-4358
P.O. Box 392, NYC, NY 10276

Two Headed Monster / 213-957-5370
6161 Santa Monica Blvd., Ste.#200, LA, CA 90038

Tyler Productions / 615-385-2244
3010 West End Ave., Ste 9c, Nashville, TN 37203

UN Productions, Inc. / 201-488-1111
84 Kennedy St., Hackensack, NJ 07601

Ultra Image, Inc. / 703-579-2699
3421 M St. NW, Ste. 1646, Washington, DC 20007

Underdog Films Inc. / 213-936-3111
5657 Wilshire, Ste.280, LA, CA 90036

Underground, The / 213-954-1100
633 N. La Brea Ave., LA, CA 90036

Unherd of Productions / 212-251-8671
475 Park Ave South, 10th Fl., NYC, NY 10016

Vendetta Pictures / 213-874-2094
7211 Santa Monica Blvd., Ste. 800, LA, CA 90046

Viagraph Production / 213-939-7720
922-1/2 S. Curson Ave., LA, CA 90036

Vide U Productions / 310-657-4385
1034 Shenandoah St., Ste. 6, LA, CA 90035

Wayne, Inc., Tony / 212-683-0733
300 E. 33rd St., #5M, NYC, NY 10016

Weissguy Productions / 908-291-2989
P.O. Box 398, Rumson, NJ 07760

Westcom Creative Group / 503-484-4314
2295 Coburg Rd, Ste.105, Eugene, OR 97401

Windmill Lane Productions / 310-305-8116
2017 Pacific Ave, Venice, CA 90291

Wright-Banks Film / 310-470-0491
1334 Westwood Blvd, #9, LA, CA 90024

Xopix / 512-478-3593
501 North IH 35, Austin, TX 78702

Zink Group / 212-929-2949
245 W. 19th St., NYC, NY 10011

Animation

4 Front Video Design / 212-944-7055
1500 Broadway, Ste. 509, NY, NY 10036

Abracadabra Animations / 203-869-3646
64 Loughlin Ave., Cos Cob, CT 06807

Advanced Imaging / 203-284-1224
350 Center St., Ste. 207, Wallingford, CT 06492

Animation & Effects / 415-355-7635
221 Naomi Ave., Pacifica, CA 94044

AutoGraphics / 213-464-2244
6335 Homewood Ave., Hllywd, CA 90028

B.D. Fox & Friends / 310-394-7150
1111 Broadway, Santa Monica, CA 90401

Bandelier Films / 505-345-8021
3815 Osuna Rd N.E., Alberquerque, NM 87109

Bechtold Studio / 818-562-1751
430 S. Niagara St., Burbank, CA 91505

$F = (a \times p)^4$

TABLE (1.19). FILM & VIDEO

Animation	Animation
Becker Studios,Inc. / 212-925-3974 500 Broadway, NYC, NY 10012	Composite Image Systems / 213-463-8811 1144 N. Las Palmas Ave., Hllywd, CA 90038
Betelgeuse Productions / 212-251-8600 44 E. 32nd St., Penthouse, NY, NY 10016	Corey Design Studio, The / 212-532-0599 / 914-365-3077 433 Park Ave. S, NYC, NY 10016
Blue Sky Productions / 914-941-5260 100 Executive Blvd., Ossining, NY 10562 Rep: Whitney Rauh / 212-972-0670	Cornell/Abood / 818-508-1215 4400 Water Canyon Ave. Ste. 100, Studio City, CA 91604
Blumenthal, Warshaw / 212-867-4225 104 E. 40th St., NYC, NY 10016	Crosspoint Post & Transfer / 303-232-9572 940 Wadsworth Blvd., Lakewood, CO 80215
Boss Film Studios / 310-823-0433 13335 Maxella Ave., Marina Del Rey, CA 90292	Curious Pictures / 212-674-1400 440 Lafayette St., NY, NY 10003
Broadway Video Design / 212-265-7600 1619 Broadway, NY, NY 10019	DC Post / 202-466-7678 1155 21st. St. N.W., Washington D.C. 20036
Brooklyn Model Works / 718-834-1944 60 Washington Ave., Brooklyn, NY 11205	DI Group, The / 617-267-6400 651 Beacon St., Boston, MA 02215
Buzzco Associates, Inc. / 212-473-8800 33 Bleecker St. #5A, NYC, NY 10012	daSilva Animation / 212-535-5760 311 E. 85th St., NYC, NY 10028
Calico Creations / 818-407-5200 9340 Eton Ave., Chatsworth, CA 91311	Digital Artworks / 503-344-6541 2295 Coburg Rd., Ste. 104, Eugene, OR 97401
California Communications Inc. / 213-466-8511 6900 Santa Monica Blvd., LA, CA 90038	Digital Post & Graphics / 206-623-3444 1921 Minor Ave., Seattle, WA 98101
Cascom Int., Inc. / 615-329-4112 806 4th Ave. S., Nashville, TN 37210	Dovas Animation / 718-230-4570 202 St. James Pl., Brooklyn, NY 11238
Celluloid Studios / 303-595-3152 1422 Delgany St., Denver, CO 80202	Dream Quest Images / 805-581-2671 2635 Park Ctr. Dr., Simi Valley, CA 93065
Charlex / 212-719-4600 2 W. 45th St., NYC, NY 10036	Duck Soup Productions / 310-478-0771 2205 Stoner Ave., LA, CA 90064 Rep: Whitney Rauh / 212-972-0670
Cinema Research Corp. / 213-460-4111 6860 Lexington Ave., Hllywd, CA 90038	Edefx Group / 212-983-2686 219 E. 44th St., 9th Fl., NY, NY 10017
Class Entertainment / 213-465-0300 6777 Hollywood Blvd., LA, CA 90028	Edefx Group / 305-593-6911 7355 N.W. 41st St., Miami, FL 33166
Colossal Pictures / 415-550-8772 2800 Third St., SF, CA 94107	Editel/Chicago / 312-440-2360 301 E. Erie, Chicago, IL 60611
Commotion / 213-882-6637 3131 Cahuenga Blvd. W., LA, CA 90068	Editel/Los Angeles / 213-931-1821 729 N. Highland Ave., Hollywood, CA 90038

$$F = (a \times p)^4$$

TABLE (1.20). FILM & VIDEO

Animation	Animation
Editel/N.Y. / 212-867-4600 222 E. 44th St., NYC, NY 10017	Hot Source Media / 703-527-5992 1916 Wilson Blvd., Ste. 304, Arlington, VA 22201
Exit Productions / 212-925-8750 180 Franklin St., NYC, NY 10013	Ice Tea Productions / 212-557-8185 160 E. 38th St., #15G, NYC, NY 10016
Fantasy II Film Effects / 818-843-1413 504 S. Varney St., Burbank, CA 91502	In-Sight Pix / 310-399-0858 321 Hampton Dr., Ste. 210, Venice, CA 90291
Flying Colours / 415-363-8767 499 Seaport Ct., Ste. 205, Redwood City, CA 94063	Industrial Light & Magic / 415-258-2000 P.O. Box 2459, San Rafael, CA 94912
Frame-Runner / 212-874-1730 1995 Broadway, NY, NY 10023	Ink Tank, The / 212-869-1630 2 W. 47th St., 14th Fl., NYC, NY 10036
Fred Wolf Films / 818-846-0611 4222 W. Burbank Blvd., Burbank, CA 91505	Interface Video / 202-861-0500 1233 20th St. N.W., Washington D.C. 20036
Friedman Consortium, Ltd., Harold / 310-821-0100 1350 Abbot Kinney Blvd, Venice, CA 90291	J.J. Sedelmaier Productions / 212-627-8700 199 Main St., Penthouse, White plains, NY 10601
Friedman Consortium, Ltd., Harold / 212-688-6434 404 55th St., Ste. 14A, NYC, NY 10022	Jim Keeshen Productions / 310-478-7230 1950 Sawtelle Blvd., Ste. 220, LA, CA 90025
GRFX Productions / 213-461-3688 6314 Santa Monica Blvd., Hollywood, CA 90038	Kinetics / 312-644-2767 215 W. Ohio St., 3rd Fl., Chicago, IL 60610
GT Group / 212-246-0154 630 Ninth Ave., Ste 1000, NYC, NY 10036	Klasky Csupo / 213-463-0145 1258 N. Highland Ave., Hollywood, CA 90038
Geppetto Soft Sculpture, Inc. / 718-398-9792 107 Lexington Ave., Brooklyn, NY 11238	Kroyer Films / 818-841-8188 2312 W. Olive Ave., Burbanks, CA 91506
Graphics for Industry / 212-889-6202 8 W. 30th St., NYC, NY 10001	Kurtz & Friends / 818-841-8188 2312 W. Olive Ave., Burbank, CA 91506
HBO Studio Productions / 212-512-7800 120A E. 23rd St., NYC, NY 10010	Laszewski, Barbara / 615-269-0025 1905 Wildwood Ave., Nashville, TN 37212
Hanna-Barbera Prods., Inc. / 213-851-5000 3400 Cahuenga Blvd., Hollywood, CA 90068-1376	Liberty Studios / 212-532-1865 238 E. 26th St., NYC, NY 10010
Hash, Inc. / 206-750-0042 2800 E. Evergreen Blvd., Vancouver, WA 98661	Lieberman Productions, Jerry / 212-431-3452 76 Laight St., NYC, NY 10013
Hearst Animation Productions / 310-478-1700 1640 S. Sepulveda Blvd., 4th Fl., LA, CA 90025	Lumeni Productions / 818-956-2200 1632 Flower St., Glendale, CA 91201
Henson Productions, Jim / 212-794-2400 117 E. 69th St., NYC, NY 10021	Marvel Productions, Ltd. / 310-444-8644 1440 S. Sepulveda Blvd., LA, CA 90025
Homer & Associates / 213-462-4710 1420 N. Beachwood Dr., Hllywd, CA 90028	MetroLight Studios / 213-932-0400 5724 W. Third St., Ste.400, LA, CA 90036

TABLE (1.21). FILM & VIDEO

Animation	Animation
Metroplex Multimedia / 310-202-9988 3614 Overland Ave., LA, CA 90034	Pixar / 510-236-4000 1001 W. Cutting Blvd., Richmond, CA 94804
Motion City Films / 310-264-4870 1847 Centinela Ave., Santa Monica, CA 90404	Pixelworks / 510-277-0447 3120 Crow Canyon Rd., Ste. A, San Ramon, CA 94583
Motion Works / 818-995-3982 13412 Ventura Blvd., Ste. 200, Sherman Oaks, CA 91423	Planet Blue / 213-871-8280 1040 N. Las Palmas, LA, CA 90038
Napoleon Videographics / 212-967-6655 460 W. 42nd St., NYC, NY 10036	Post Group, The / 407-560-5600 Roy Disney Production Center, Lake Buena Vista, FL 32830
Novocom Productions / 213-461-3688 6314 Santa Monica Blvd., Hllywd, CA 90038	Post House, The / 213-464-0116 1311 N. Highland Ave., Hllywd, CA 90028
OCS/Freeze Frame/Pixel Magic / 818-760-0862 10635 Riverside Dr., Toluca Lake, CA 91602	Post Masters / 615-256-7678 50 Vantage Way, Ste. 100, Nashville, TN 37228
Olive Jar Studios, Inc. / 617-783-9500 35 Soldiers Field Pl., Boston, MA 02135	Post Perfect / 212-972-3400 220 E. 42nd St., NY, NY 10017
On Tape Productions / 415-421-5551 724 Battery St., SF, CA 94111	R&B Films / 818-956-8406 1810A S. Victory Blvd., Glendale, CA 91201
One Eighty One Productions / 212-229-1811 92 Vandam St., 3rd Fl., NYC, NY 10013	R/Greenberg Associates / 213-957-6868 6526 Sunset Blvd., Hollywood, CA 90028
Ovation Animation / 212-529-4111 81 Irving Pl., NYC, NY 10003	R/Greenberg Associates / 212-239-6767 350 W. 39th, NYC, NY 10018
Pacific Data Images / 408-745-6755 1111 Karlstad Dr., Sunnyvale, CA 94089	R/Greenberg Associates / 212-239-6767 350 W. 39th, NYC, NY 10018
Pacific Data Images / 213-960-4042 650N. Bronson Ave., Ste. 400W, LA, CA 90004	RGA/LA / 213-957-6868 6526 Sunset Blvd., Hollywd, CA 90028
Pacific Data Images / 213-960-4042 650 N. Bronson Ave., Ste. 400 W, LA, CA 90004	ReZ.n8 Productions / 213-957-2161 6430 Sunset Blvd., Ste. 1000, Hllywd, CA 90028
Pacific Focus / 808-593-8848 1013 Kawaiahao St., Honolulu, HI 96814	Realtime Video / 415-705-0188 60 Broadway, SF, CA 94111
Pacific Ocean Post / 310-458-3300 730 Arizona Ave., Santa Monica, CA 90401	Renegade Animation / 818-556-3395 1314 Scott Rd., Burbank, CA 91504
Perpetual Motion Pictures / 805-294-0788 P.O. Box 55182, Valencia, CA 91385	Rhythm & Hues, Inc. / 213-851-6500 910 N. Sycamore Ave., Hollywood, CA 90038
Pinnacle Effects / 206-441-9878 2334 Elliott Ave., Seattle, WA 98121	Roland House / 703-525-7000 2020 N. 14th St., Ste. 600, Arlington, VA 22201
Pittard Sullivan Fitzgerald / 213-462-1190 6430 Sunset Blvd., Ste. 200, LA, CA 90028	

$$F = (a \times p)^4$$

TABLE (1.22). FILM & VIDEO

Animation	Animation
Schwartzberg & Company / 818-508-1444 12700 Ventura Blvd, 4th Fl, Studio City, CA 91604	Video Works / 212-782-1700 24 W. 40th St., NY, NY 10018
Serious Robots Computer / 800-827-0914 1101 Capital Blvd., Raleigh, NC 27603	Vinton's Claymation, Will / 503-225-1130 1400 NW 22nd Ave., Portland, OR 97210
Sight Effects / 310-392-0999 321 Hampton Dr., Ste. 104, Venice, CA 90291	Visual Concept Engineering / 818-367-9187 13300 Ralston Ave., Sylmar, CA 91342
Silverstraw Productions / 818-752-9040 10635 Riverside Dr., Toluca Lake, CA 91602	Warner Bros. Animation / 818-379-9401 15303 Ventura Blvd., Sherman Oaks, CA 91403
Six Foot Two Productions / 415-925-9909 49 Murray Ave., Larkspur, CA 94939	Woo Art / 212-989-7870 133 W. 19th St., 3rd Fl., NYC, NY 10011
Sony Pictures Imageworks / 310-280-7600 10202 W. Washington Blvd., Culver City, CA 90232	Xaos / 415-558-9267 600 Townsend St., 271E, SF, CA 94103
Soundwave / 202-861-0560 1100 N. Glebe Rd., Ste. 100, Arlington, VA 20201	Yale Video / 714-693-5300 1360 N. Hancock St., Anaheim, CA 92807
Spaff Animation / 818-761-6744 10843 Magnolia Blvd., Ste. 1, N. Hllywd, CA 91601	Zander's Animation Parlour / 212-477-3900 118 E. 25th St., NYC, NY 10010
Steve Michelson Productions / 415-626-3080 280 Utah St., SF, CA 94103	Zander's Animation Parlour / 212-477-3900 118 E. 25th St., NY, NY 10010
Studio Productions, Inc. / 213-856-8048 650 N. Bronson Ave., Ste. 223, Hollywood, CA 90004	
TV Art / 213-650-7747 8430 Santa Monica Blvd., Ste. 200, W. Hllywd, CA 90069	**Stock Film**
Tape House Computer Ink & Paint / 212-557-9611 222 E. 44th St., NYC, NY 10017	Archive Films / 212-620-3955 / 800-876-5115 530 W. 25th St., NYC, NY 10001
Tape House Editorial Co., The / 212-557-4949 216 E. 45th St., 2nd Fl., NYC, NY 10017	Cinenet Cinema Network / 805-527-0093 2235 First St., Ste.111, Simi Valley, CA 93065
Terry X 2 / 818-304-9080 21 W. Dayton St., Pasadena, CA 91105	Clip Joint for Film, The / 818-842-2525 833-B N. Hollywood Way, Burbank, CA 91505
ThreeSpace / 310-837-4450 10544 W. Pico Blvd., LA, CA 90064	Energy Productions / 818-508-1444 12700 Ventura Blvd. 4th Fl., Studio City, CA 91604
Unitle Video-Hollywood / 213-878-5800 3330 Cahuenga Blvd. W., LA, CA 90068	Energy Productions / 212-686-4900 / 800-462-4379 163 E. 36th St. Ste. 1B, NYC, NY 10016
Video Image/VIFX / 310-822-8872 5333 McConnell Ave., LA, CA 90066	

Table (1.23). Film & Video

Stock Film	Sound Stages

Stock Film

FIB Intellectual Property / 213-614-4195
707 Wilshire Blvd.
7-23, LA, CA 90017

Image Bank Film / 212-529-6700
111 Fifth Ave., NYC, NY 10003

Image Bank Film, West / 310-264-4850
2400 Broadway, Ste. 220, Santa Monica, CA 90404

National Geographic Film Library / 202-857-7659
1600 M St., N.W., Washington, DC 20036

Paradise Stock Footage / 808-955-1000
1833 Kalakaua Ave., Ste.404, Honolulu, HI 96815

Paramount Film Library / 213-956-5510
5555 Melrose Ave., LA, CA 90038

Petrified films / 212-242-5461
430 W. 14th St., Rm.204, NYC, NY 10014

Republic Pictures / 310-302-1710
12636 Beatrice St., LA, CA 90066

Spectral Communications / 818-840-0111
178 S. Victory Blvd., Ste.106, Burbank, CA 91502

Stock Shots / 818-760-2098
10422 Burbank Blvd., N. Hllywd, CA 91601

Sound Stages

Apricot Entertainment / 213-469-4000
940 N. Orange Dr., Hollywood, CA 90038

Buena Vista Studios / 818-560-7100
500 S. Buena Vista St., Burbank, CA 91521

Empire Stages of NY / 718-392-4747
50-20 25th St., Long Island City, NY 11101

Garson Studios, The College of Santa Fe
505-438-1150 / 800-926-1150
1600 St. Michaels Dr., Santa Fe, NM 87505

Sound Stages

Imagemaker, Inc. / 615-244-1700
220 Great Circle Rd.,Ste 118, Nashville, TN 37228

J. Horvath Productions/ Stage, Inc. / 212-463-0061
335 W. 12th St., NYC, NY 10014

Kaufman Astoria Studios / 718-392-5600
34-12 36th St., Astoria, NY 11106

Lifetime Television Studios / 718-706-3513
34-12 36th St., Astoria, NY 11106

Nashville Cartage and Sound
615-386-3700 / 615-386-9797
3630 Redmon St., Nashville, TN 37209

Oakridge Studios / 818-502-5500
1239 S. Glendale Ave., Glendale, CA 91205

Paisley Park Studios / 612-474-8555
7801 Audubon Rd., Chanhassen, MN 55317

Paramount Pictures / 213-956-5000
5555 Melrose Ave., LA, CA 90038

Paramount Pictures / 212-373-7000
15 Columbus Circle, NYC, NY 10023

Paramount Pictures / 213-956-5000
5555 Melrose Ave., LA, CA 90038

Rhythm and Hues / 213-851-6500
910 N. Sycamore, Hollywood, CA 90038

SIR Film Stages & Lighting / 310-287-3600
3322 LaCienega Pl., LA, CA 90016

Silvercup Studios / 718-784-3390 / 212-349-9600
42-22 22nd St., LIC, NY 11101

Tennessee Performing Arts Ctr. / 615-741-7975
505 Deaderick St., Nashville, TN 37219

Universal City Studios / 818-777-3000
100 Universal City Plaza, Universal City, CA 91608

Walt Disney Studios, The / 818-560-5151
500 S. Buena Vista St., Burbank, CA 91521

Warner Bros. Studios / 818-954-6000
4000 Warner Blvd., Burbank, CA 91522

$$F = (a \times p)^4$$

TABLE (1.24). FILM & VIDEO

Notes	Notes

a star *is* dead
__________ .

(2.A)

infinite mass baby.

i wanna be your

black hole

(designers + art directors)

$$\frac{\times \text{ (lettering + computer graphics + new technology + retouching + separators)}}{}\ .$$

(2.B)

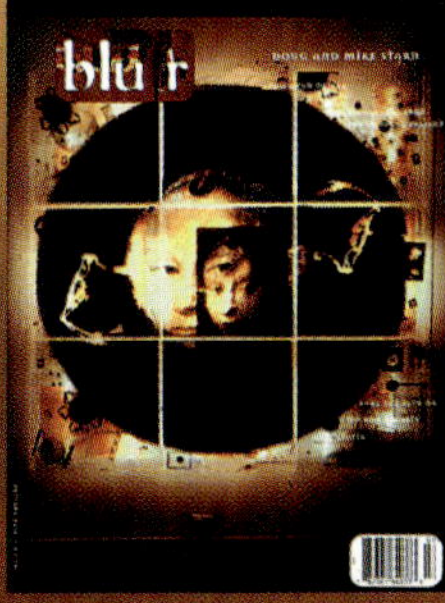

BLU R

BIKINI

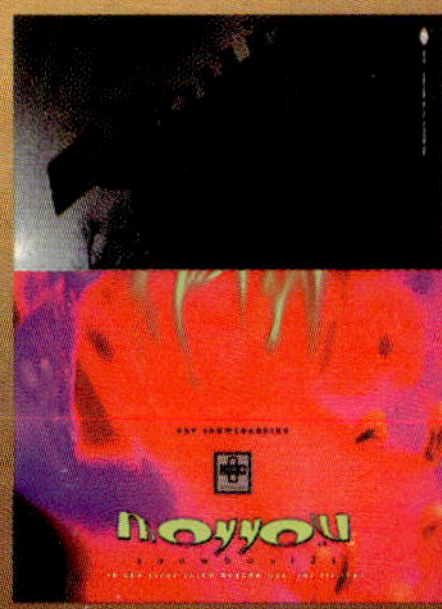

MORROW SNOWBOARDS

the Crow

ELVIS
THE TRIBUTE

frankenstein

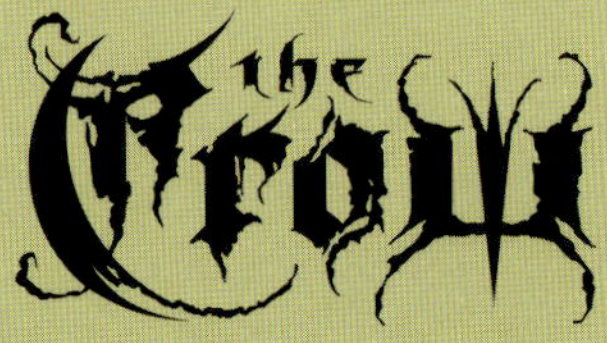

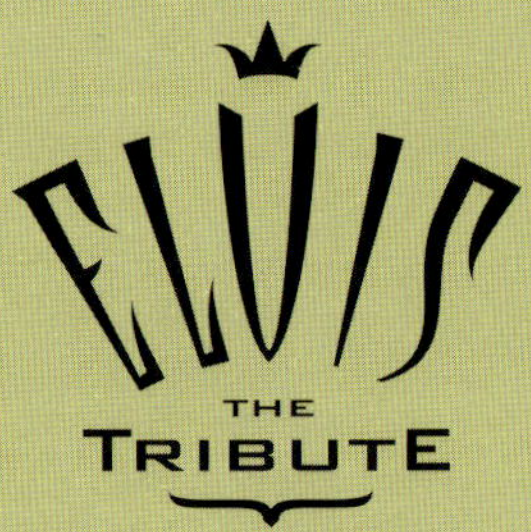

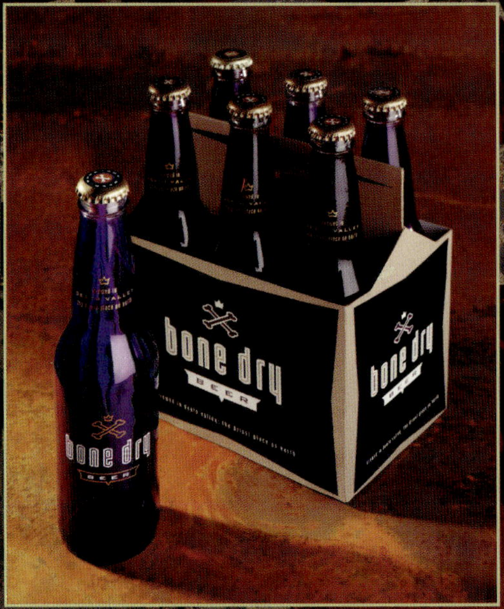

margo chase design

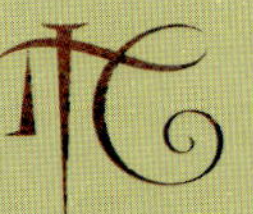

2255 bancroft ave • la ca • ph 213.668.1055 • fax 213.668.2470

M W
makin' waves

RED
HERRING
DESIGN

ACME
Road Tested
LOONEY TUNES

LEADERSHIP
THE
LEADERSHIP
DIFFERENCE

JAZZ

TOUR '94
[Steely Dan]

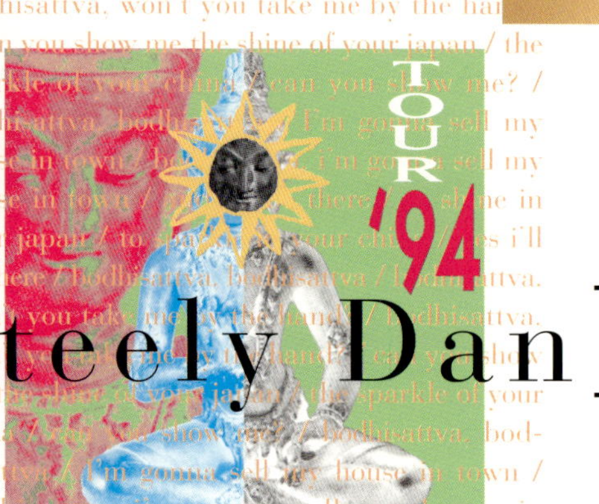

{212} 219-0557

95 Horatio St. #6-W, New York NY 10014 voice 212.645.7379 fax 212.645.3582

design | illustration | good deeds

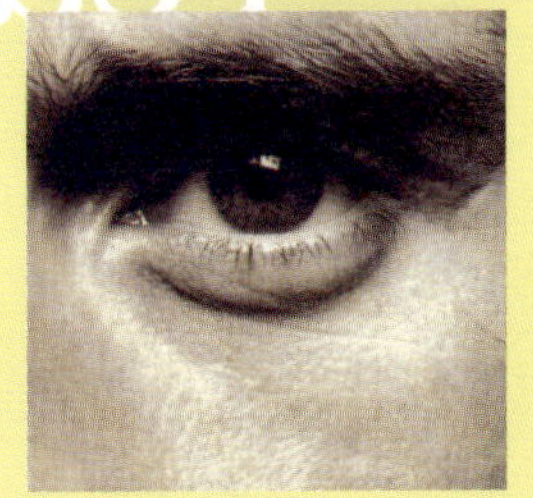

MUSIC
THERE IS STUFF ON THIS PAGE FOR: GUESS? • McDONALD'S//DAVIS BALL COLOMBATTO, • MAD LOVE/DISNEY • JOURNEY •
JUNGLE BOOK/DISNEY • MERCURY RECORDS/ZIPATONI
Out of Control
JUNGLE BOOK
Gospelfest '94
MOR SO FAR
anything is possible
mark alien
310.396.6471

PARIS
MAD LOVE
THERE IS STUFF ON THIS PAGE DONE FOR; GUESS? •MERCURY RECORDS/ZIPITONI • ATLANTIC RECORDS • OUTER LIMITS/MGM • JOURNEY • CASPER > MCA/UNIVERSAL,
•CAP'N CRUNCH/ B.B.V... THE INTEGER GROUP / COORS , •PRIMORTALS/> B.D, FOX • MAD LOVE DISNEY • I LIKE IT LIKE THAT / COLUMBIA PICTURES • RCA
LEONARD NIMOY'S PRIMORTALS
LOS ANGELES
THE OUTER LIMITS
Do not adjust your set. we are in control.
Why am I afraid to tell you who I Am?
BRANDY
Mad Love
mark alen
310.396.6471

like It Or nOt,
We cop to the Design of the
'95 Altaernative Pick

BlackBird Creative
919.8 59.7418
"Call for Our Portfolio
Of Work"

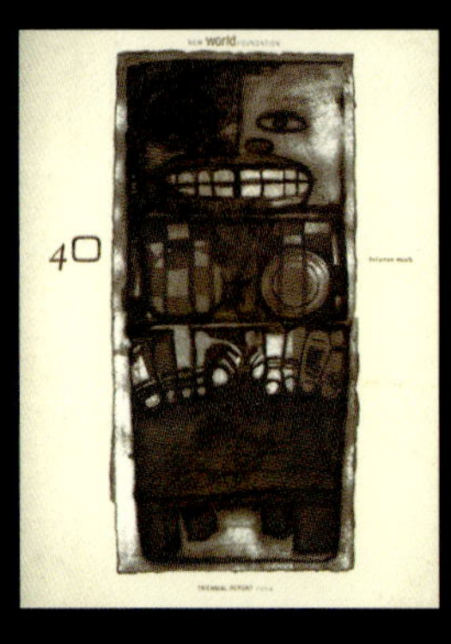

catgraphics

Princess® is a regis-tered trademark of AT&T. Pepsi® is a registered trademark of PepsiCo. Props to Paul Aresu, Color-wheel, Macbeth, & Peter Zeray. All other rights reserved.

straight

kinky

2 1 2
2 2 6
8 9 6 9

darect

2 1 2
8 3 8
2350

dorothy

da rep

338 2550

werner
design
werks

Aug 27. I laughed out loud today, just to show people how glad I am to be here.
F I S H
614 [STUDIO]
4 64 092 8
FAX
614 464 0944
REPRESENTED BY ID+A
[ny] 212 633 2388

firehou
se lol ar
+ de
si n
t
art direction
print
animation
illustration
PRODUCE OF U.S.A.
BLUE
DIVIDER

CHANGE
FORTUNE
FORTUNE
FORTUNE

KNICKElbine
pAUL
GRAPHIC DIRECTION and
ILLUSTRATION
P: 612 724 1618
F: 612 724 0405

The Masseur
From K-tel
MAKES
AN
IDEAL
GIFT
K-TEL RECORDS
MUSIC + PRODUCT

STAY
TUNED
STAY
TUNED
HOWARD'S SISTER

MORE
WORK
DANCE
X PRESS

compact disc packages

annual reports

logos

packaging

brochures

murrell
(murrell)
design group

(404) 892-5494

+ James Murrell
40 INWOOD CIRCLE.
ATLANTA. GEORGIA.
30309. FAX:404.874.6894

illustration:john weber

Paramount
Electronic
NEXT
20 km
Highway

VOO
DOO
The Rolling Stones

US3

VOTE
LOUD

SIMCHA time
Mickey Katz
Plays Music For
weddings, Bar Mitzvahs
& Brisses
{The Klezmer Sessions}

are
you

MeGABoOM
Thinking

T
SOL
a YUL um
R

BUTTHOLE
independent
worm
saloon
SURFERS

hEATHER
VAN
HAAFTEN
213 660 5970

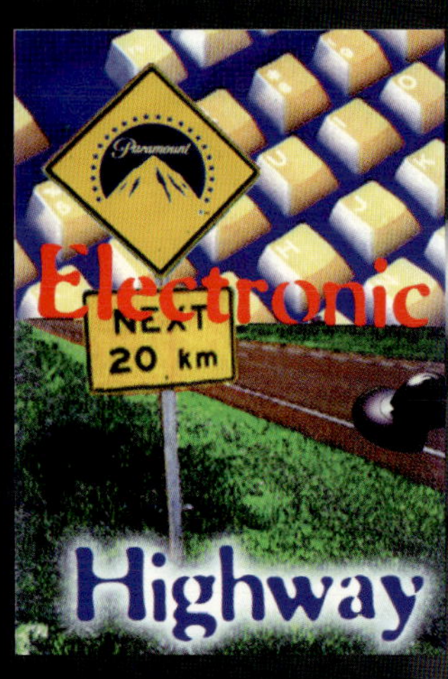

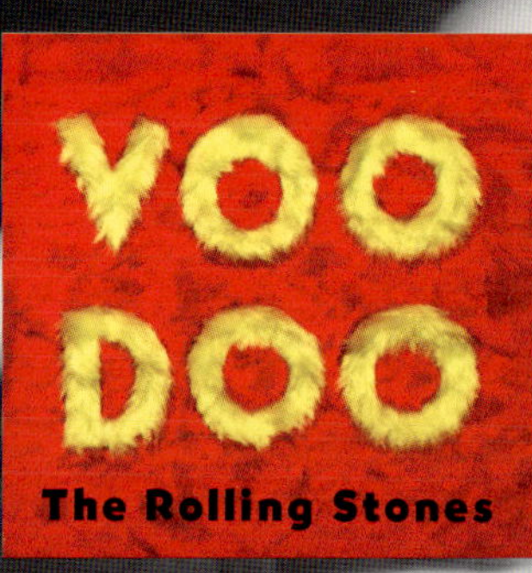

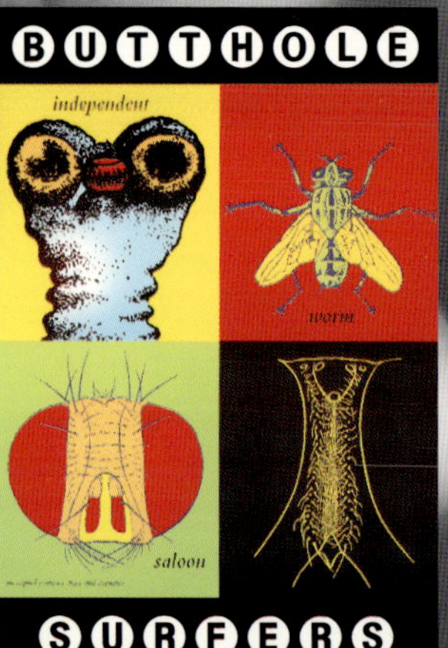

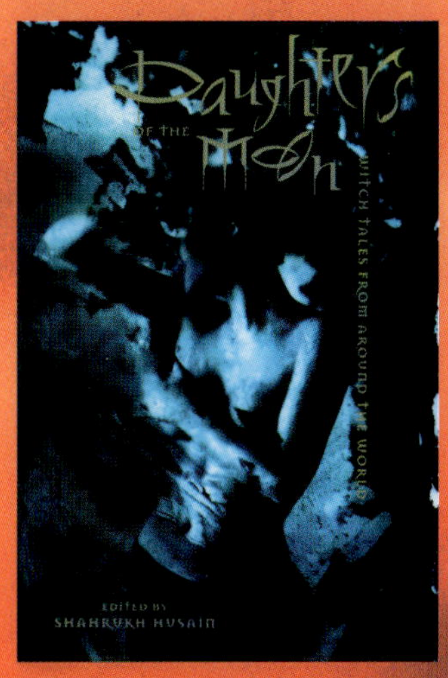

LORNA STOVALL

ART DIRECTION · DESIGN · LETTERING · 213.931.5984

REY international
4120 Michael Avenue   Los Angeles, California 90066
Art Direction • Design • Consulting
310 305 9393
Album Packaging • Logotypes • Advertising • Posters • Publications
MCA SOUNDTRACKS

CALL FOR BOOK AND YOUR VERY OWN COPY OF THE CABAZON DICTIONARY

upper california
dave parmley
408.395.6615

lower california
eric ruffing
310.546.7135

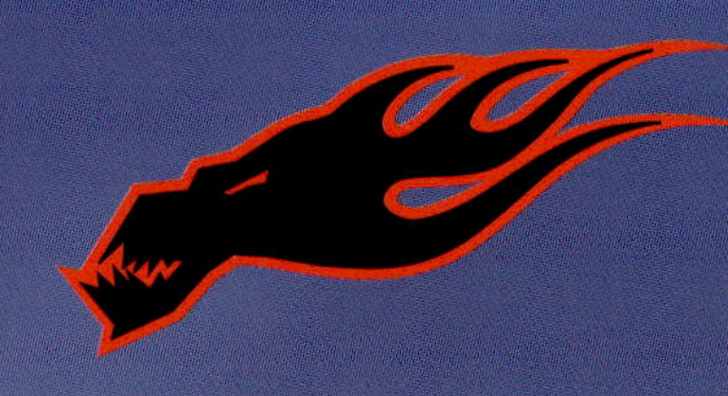

ART DIRECTION

MARKS

PACKAGING

IMAGE TWEAKS

ADVERTISING

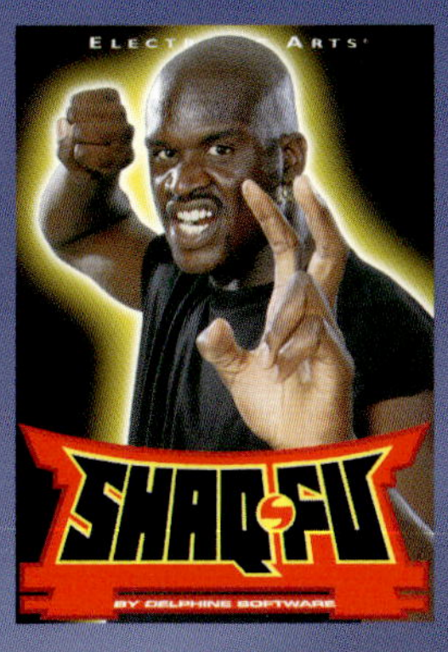

upper california
dave parmley
408.395.6615

lower california
eric ruffing
310.546.7135

13TH FLOOR
ourmindswanderwhereothersfeartogo

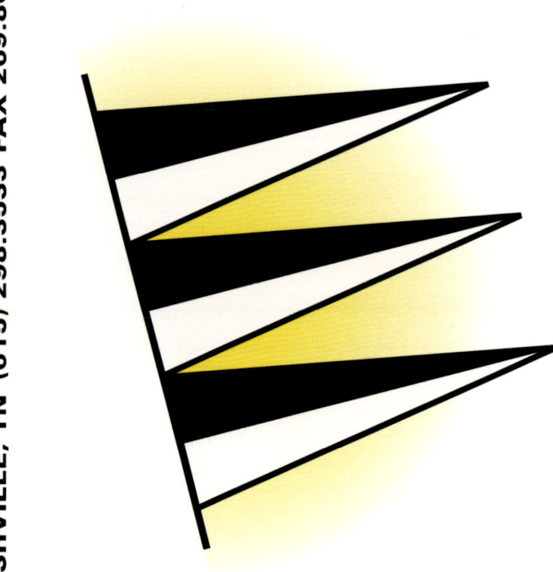

TEAM DESIGN, INC. 1414 17TH AVENUE SOUTH

NASHVILLE, TN (615) 298.3533 FAX 269.8686

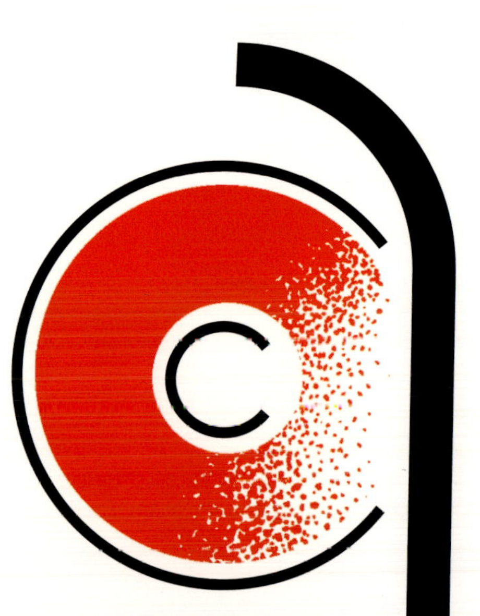

Whitney
MICK JAGGER
BERNARD MAISNER
HAND—LETTERING
Hi.
PLYMOUTH
neon
KROKUS
STAND ON IT AND
IT SCREAMS.
I'M AT THE
PLYMOUTH
DEALER!
MOODY BLUES
REVLON
Revolutionary
Spiegel
WORLD CLASS
Barry
Manilow
BOLERO
Virtue lies
in moderation.
Stanley Jordan
BOLERO
HOUSE ROCKER
RECORD
OPEN-
ABSOLUT PROVERB
REPRESENTED BY GERALD & CULLEN RAPP
108 EAST 36 ST. NY, NY 10016
FAX: 212.889.3341   PHONE: 212.889.3337
C.C. Adcock
ADRENALINE
Chicken Classics
EXTREME
Allow the bearer, W. H.
Lamon & friend, with
any baggage to pass from
Washington to Richmond
and return—
April 11, 1865   A. Lincoln
Clapton
PSYCHO TRAINING
by
CONVERSE
HOUSE
11
IT'S
Mr. Phipps
TATER
CRISPS
QUEST
BODY LANGUAGE
Concept & Calligraphy
Bernard Maisner
Photography & Design
Helane Blumfield
The body is a sacred garment. -Martha Graham ...in this body the soul passes...from one
body to another. -Bhagavad-Gita. Energy is eternal delight! -William Blake. A rose is a rose
is a rose. -Gertrude Stein. I unsealed the mystical... -Elizabeth Barrett Browning. Nobody has
ever measured, even poets, how much a heart can hold. -Zelda Fitzgerald. One is not born, but rather
becomes, a woman. -Simone de Beauvoir. Sweet joy befall thee! -William Blake.

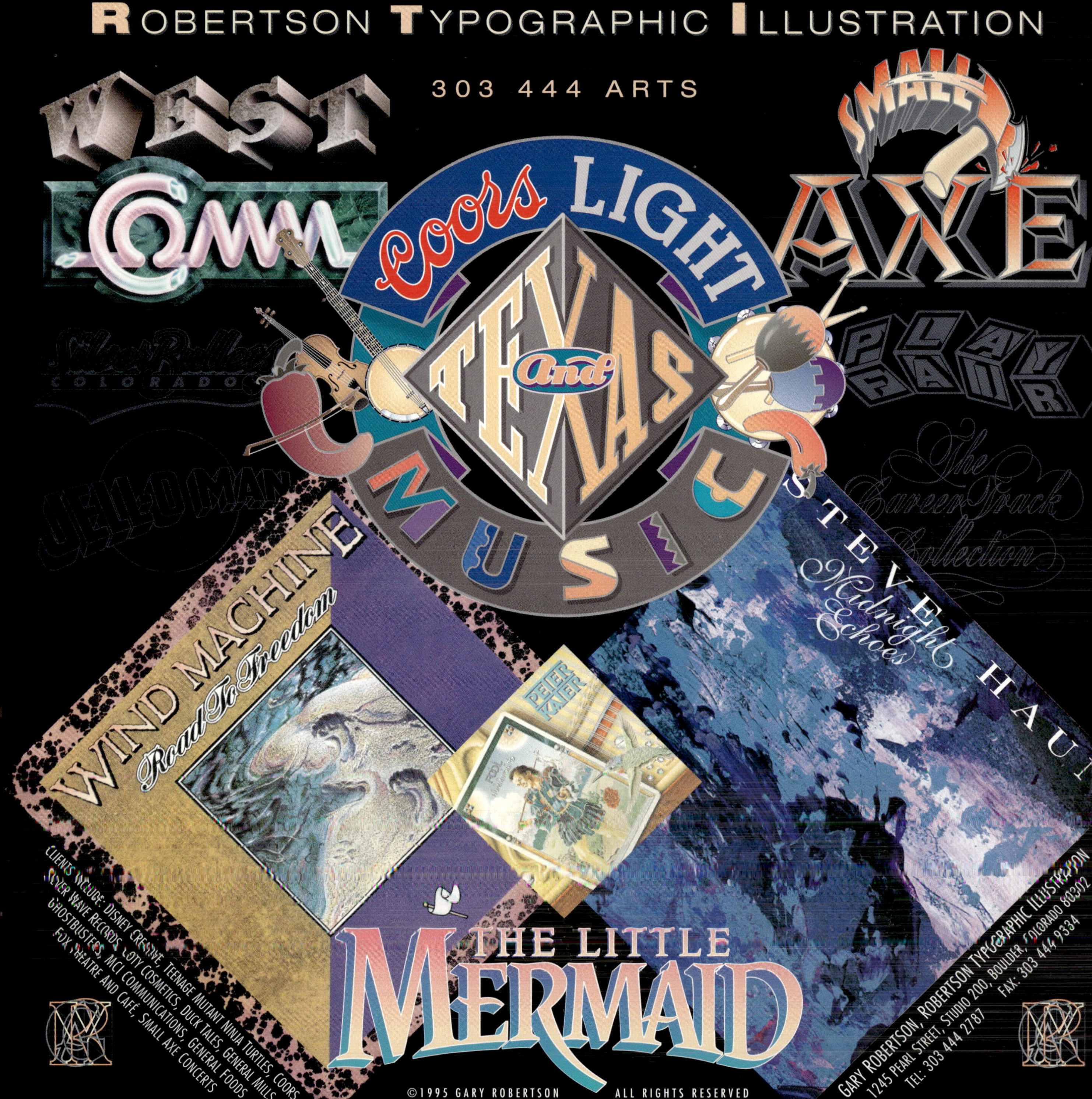

ROBERTSON TYPOGRAPHIC ILLUSTRATION
303 444 ARTS
WEST COMM
SMALL AXE
Coors LIGHT
TEXAS and MUSIC
Silver Bullet COLORADO
PLAYR FAIR
JELLO MAN
The Career Track Collection
WIND MACHINE
Road To Freedom
STEVE HAUL
Midnight Echoes
PETER KATER
THE LITTLE MERMAID
CLIENTS INCLUDE: DISNEY CREATIVE, TEENAGE MUTANT NINJA TURTLES, COORS
SILVER WAVE RECORDS, CITY COSMETICS, DUCK TALES, GENERAL MILLS
GHOSTBUSTERS, MCI COMMUNICATIONS, GENERAL FOODS
FOX, THEATRE AND CAFE, SMALL AXE CONCERTS
GARY ROBERTSON, ROBERTSON TYPOGRAPHIC ILLUSTRATION
1245 PEARL STREET, STUDIO 200, BOULDER, COLORADO 80302
TEL: 303 444 2787   FAX: 303 444 9334
©1995 GARY ROBERTSON   ALL RIGHTS RESERVED

pawn shop press

let us bounce some ideas off you

213•653•9331   or   213•935•7356

5000 BC•SUMER

Pictograms of traded goods were carved on heavy stone tablets. As the world's first catalogue, it's weight alone would postpone mail order for several thousand years.

2400 BC•EGYPT

Heiroglyphics first appear as written language. Originally only used by priests, symbols like these are used by everyone today, to find out **where** to go when they **have to go...**

800 BC•GREECE

Once a revered symbol used for Apollo, god of healing and prophecy; today modern mice are related to cartoons and computer pads... Where did this rodent go wrong?

149 AD•CHINA

A eunuch named T'sai Lun, invents paper and becomes known as the "god of papermaking" thus permanently proving that the most useful part of the human body is indeed the brain.

390 AD•INDIA

The fig tree becomes a Buddhist symbol of harmony with the earth, and human enlightenment, eventually making paper recycling a very Zen thing to do.

470 AD•MEXICO

The image of the Mayan winged sun begins to appear simultaneously all over the western world. Since there were no fax machines, those wings must have been pretty powerful!

1995 AD•USA

At the end of the 20th century, a group of humans come together in the West known as Ultimo Incorporated, to create design that would communicate the important messages of the known universe.

Descended from the great historic attempts at communication, armed with some useless musical and poetic abilities and a computer, they set out to create new cultural symbols even though they were not priests.

Proceeding with respect and knowledge of the earth's resources, as well as a particular bias toward social issues they have managed to remain sane and productive even to this day.

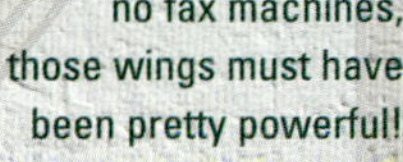

Book concept and design
Client: Ultimo Inc.
1993

Ultimo Inc.

a brief historic account

Book design
Client: Sensaii Ltd.
1994

• founded 1986 •

past and present contributions include:

concept • copywriting • design • product development

& marketing consultation for a wide variety of clients

documented activities to date:

advertisements • posters • packaging,

capabilities materials • sales tools • catalogs • books •

corporate identification • on-air graphic design

& odd but necessary equipment

for commerce & communication in the world

point of origin:

41 Union Square West,

Suite 209 • New York NY • 10003,

Phone: 212-645-7858 • Fax: 212-989-2836

contact:

Clare Ultimo or Elena Olivares

New program promotion
Client: A&E Network
1994

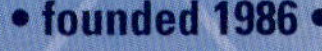

Promotional Poster
Client: Nuyorican Poet's Cafe
1994

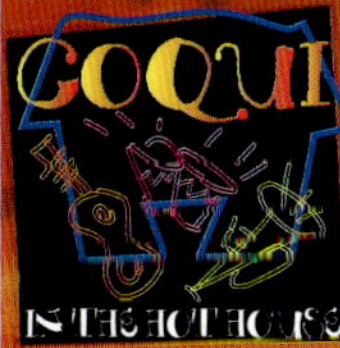
CD Design
Client: Coqui International
1993

INSIGHT
COMMUNICATIONS
Corporate Identity
Client: Insight Communications, Inc.
1994

Sales Promotion Kit
Client: Warner Music International
1993

USDA
CHOICE

ART
CHANTRY
206·
441·
3369
188
·
Lb.

Bonus
Buy!

(designers $+$ art directors)

$$\times \, \frac{\text{(lettering} + \text{computer graphics} + \text{new technology} + \text{retouching} + \text{separators})}{}$$.

$$(2.1)$$

$$F = (a \times p)^4$$

TABLE (2.2). DESIGN

Designers	Designers
→ 13th Floor / 408-395-6615 16175 Rose Ave., Monte Sereno, CA 95030 pages 20 - 21	Arnold Goodwin Communications, Inc. / 312-944-6276 4 E. Ohio St., Chicago, IL 60611
→ 13th Floor / 310-546-7135 3309 Pine Ave., Manhattan Beach, CA 90266 pages 20 - 21	Arnold Saks Assoc., Inc. / 212-861-4300 350 E. 81st St., 4th Fl., NYC, NY 10028
30Sixty Design Inc. / 213-850-5311 2801 Cahuenga Blvd. West, LA, CA 90068	Arrias, Julia / 310-459-7895 1294 Calle de Sevilla, Pacific Palisades, CA 90272
A Vision Entertainment / 212-275-2000 1290 Ave. of Americas, 4th Fl, NYC, NY 10019	Art Connection / 617-599-3292 109 Green St., Lynn, MA 01902
AG Communications Systems / 602-582-7000 2500 W. Utopia Rd., Phoenix, AZ 85027	Art Direction / 303-443-7603 2120 13th St., Boulder, CO 80302
AGA Design / 212-642-9500 1515 Broadway, 42nd Fl., NY, NY 10036-5703	Art Hotel / 310-854-6154 607 Huntley Dr., W. Hollywood, CA 90069
Abrams Design, Kym / 312-654-1005 213 W. Institute Pl., Ste. 608, Chicago, IL 60610	Art Paul Design / 312-266-0621 175 East Delaware Place, Chicago, IL 60611
Adler & Assocs., Stan / 212-366-4860 305 Seventh Ave., 19th Fl., NYC, NY 10001	Arthur Design / 818-884-8748 4751 Del Moreno Pl., Woodland Hills, CA 91364
Agramonte Hynes Design / 718-349-7449 97 Greenpoint Ave., #3R, Brooklyn, NY 11222	Ascienzo Design / 212-366-9173 109 W. 27th St., NYC, NY 10001
Akagi Remmington Design / 415-397-4668 632 Commercial St., 4th Fl., SF, CA 94111	Ashby, Neal / 202-775-0101 1020 19th St. N.W., Ste. 200, Washington D.C. 20036
Alfstad Blank Group / 212-463-8600 22 W. 19th St., 4th Fl, NYC, NY 10011	Aspect Ratio / 213-467-2121 1347 N. Cahuenga Blvd., LA, CA 90028
→ Allen, Mark / 310-396-6471 129 20th St., Manhattan Beach, CA 90266 pages 6 - 7	Attention Design! / 310-207-6068 11938 Dorothy St., Ste. 4, Brentwood, CA 90049
Anderson & Lembke / 212-886-2100 79 Fifth Ave., NYC, NY 10003	Avchen & Assocs., Inc. / 612-339-1206 401 N. Third St., Ste. 410, Minneapolis, MN 55401
Anderson Design Co., Charles S. / 612-339-5181 30 N. First St., Minneapolis, MN 55401	Avery Design Consultants, Eileen / 213-221-1639 1918 N. Main St., Ste. 204, LA, CA 90031
Anderson Thomas Design / 615-327-9894 110 29th Ave. N., Ste. 301, Nashville, TN 37203	BLT & Assocs. / 213-465-9687 844 N. Seward St., LA, CA 90038
Ark Interface / 206-654-4182 1201 Third Ave., Ste. 2380, Seattle, WA 98101	Baczewska, Christine / 212-260-1159 45 1st Ave., #3Q, NYC, NY 10003
	Baer Design, Kimberly / 310-399-3295 620 Hampton Dr., Venice, CA 90291
	Bagby Design, Inc. / 312-755-3100 455 N. City Front Plaza, Ste. 1600, Chicago, IL 60611

Table (2.3). Design

Designers	Designers
Baggetta & Associates / 310-644-0361 4920 W. 123rd Pl., Hawthorne, CA 90250	Bentz, Charles / 212-302-9088 110 W. 40th St., Ste. 1108, NYC, NY 10018
Baggetta & Assocs. / 503-699-0252 1321 Haven Stone Dr., West Linn, OR 97068	Bergman Firesign Design, Marlene / 818-509-1121 11498 Laurelcrest Dr., Studio City, CA 91604
Baker Design Assoc. / 310-453-6613 1450 20th St., Santa Monica, CA 90404	Bernhardt Fudyma Design Group / 212-889-9337 133 E. 36th St., NYC, NY 10016
Baker Design, Eric / 212-598-9111 11 E. 22nd St., 5th Fl., NYC, NY 10010	Berry Design / 404-664-9531 755 Mid-Broadwell Rd., Alpharetta, GA 30201
Bali Design, Alain / 213-962-7933 7060 Hollywood Blvd., #503, LA, CA 90028	Beynon Company, The / 213-936-8175 5750 Wilshire Blvd., Ste. 190, LA, CA 90036
Banever, Carol / 213-874-2438 944 N. Martel Ave., LA, CA 90046	Big Bang Graphics / 213-664-6287 1300 Micheltorena St., LA, CA 90026
Banks & Assocs. / 310-476-5289 507 Veteran Ave., LA, CA 90024	Big Bolt / 212-244-2658 338 E. 5th St., #5, NYC, NY 10003
Banowetz & Co. / 214-741-7300 2115 Jackson St., Dallas, TX 75201	Big Fat TV / 212-420-0808 873 Broadway, Ste. 500, NY, NY 10003
Barany Communications, Leslie / 212-627-8488 121 W. 27th St., #202, NYC, NY 10001	Big Hand Productions / 214-526-2888 4514 Travis, Ste. 220, Dallas, TX 75205
Barnard Design / 718-858-9466 155 Hicks St., Brooklyn Heights, NY 11201	Binder, Andrew Paul / 818-508-8621 12812 Landale St., Studio City, CA 91604
Barnes Design Office / 312-527-0157 455 East Illinois, Ste. 363, Chicago, IL 60611	→ Binkley, Gina / 615-256-1110 Illustration / page 35
Barnes, Bill / 615-385-9955 1922 Woodmont Blvd, Nashville, TN 37215	Black, Stephen / 415-459-3316 P.O. Box 550, San Anselmo, CA 94979
Barnett Design Group / 212-431-7130 270 Lafayette St., Ste. 801, NYC, NY 10012	→ BlackBird Creative / 919-859-7418 7312-4 Hihenge Ct., Raleigh, NC 27615 pages 8 - 9
Bartel Design Group / 213-662-6869 4459 Avocado St., LA, CA 90027	BlackDog / 415-258-9663 239 Marin St., San Rafael, CA 94901
Bartels & Company / 314-781-4350 3284 Ivanhoe Ave., St. Louis, MO 63139	Blair Communications / 213-871-0889 2104 Holly Drive, LA, CA 90068
Bell Design & Lettering, Jill / 310-372-4204 2501 Clark Lane, Unit C, Redondo Beach, CA 90278	Blue Brick / 212-982-3880 611 Broadway, Ste. 828, NYC, NY 10012
Bellini Design / 312-649-1710 325 W. Huron, #706, Chicago, IL 60610	Blue Sky Design / 404-237-0667 2970 Peachtree Rd., Atlanta, GA 30305
Bender & Assocs., Lawrence / 415-327-3821 512 Hamilton Ave., Palo Alto, CA 94301	

$$F = (a \times p)^4$$

Table (2.4). Design

Designers	Designers
Bonauro, Tom / 415-648-5233 601 Minnesota St., #216, SF, CA 94107	Bureau / 212-242-3108 142 W. 14th St., Rm. 603, NYC, NY 10011
Bonnell Design / 212-757-4420 409 W. 44th St., NYC, NY 10036	Burke Design / 310-280-3488 1341 Ocean Ave., Ste. 131, Santa Monica, CA 90401
Boom! Graphics / 213-876-3896 1402 N. Sierra Bonita Ave., LA, CA 90046	Burnett Group, The / 212-254-3344 39 E. 20th Street, 7th Fl., NYC, NY 10003
Bottiglieri, Dessolena / 212-473-4592 126 East 12th St. #6C, NYC, NY 10003	Burning Bush Studio / 206-622-4475 500 Aurora Ave. N., Seattle, WA 98109
Boyd Communications / 213-933-8383 6624 Melrose Ave., LA, CA 90038	Byram, Steve / 201-869-7493 52 68th St., Apt. #1, Guttenberg, NJ 07093
Boynton Design Co. / 407-254-5595 1716 W. Shores Rd., Melbourne, FL 32935	Coy, Los Angeles / 310-837-0173 9520 Jefferson Blvd., Culver City, CA 90232
Bradley, Lyn / 714-589-8365 43 Inverary, Dove Canyon, CA 92679	→ Cabazon Design / 503-220-8236 322 NW 5th, Ste. 312, Portland, OR 97209 page 19
Braithwaite, Mickey / 615-329-4573 1710 Hayes, Ste. 207, Nashville, TN 37203	Cahan & Assocs. 818 Brannan St., #300, SF, CA 94103
Branstetter Studio, Jim / 214-891-0813 6616 Ascott Lane, Dallas, TX 75214	Calliope Vision / 818-567-4626 128 Longfellow St., Thousand Oaks, CA 91360
Brawner, Becky / 615-356-1244 Unlikely Suburban Design 732 Richfield Dr., Nashville, TN 37205	Campbell, Fisher, Ditko / 602-955-2707 3333 E. Camelback Rd., Ste. 200, Phoenix, AZ 85018
Brebner Company, The / 212-242-1223 45 W. 18th St., 7th Fl., NYC, NY 10011	Carbone Smolan Assocs. / 212-807-0011 22 W. 19th St., 10th Fl., NYC, NY 10011
Bright & Assocs. / 310-450-2488 901 Abbot Kinney Blvd., Venice, CA 90291	Carl Waltzer Digital Service / 212-475-8748 873 Broadway, #412, NYC, NY 10003
Brochure Masters / 818-884-9722 6931 Topanga Canyon Blvd., Canoga Park, CA 91303	Carpenter Design & Marketing, Inc. / 310-837-0732 10020 National Blvd., LA, CA 90034
Brock Design / 213-932-0283 8075 W. 3rd St., #300, LA, CA 90048	Carson Design, David / 619-338-8080 432 F St., Ste. 503, San Diego, CA 92101
Brunt Designs, Bill / 615-297-9442 631 Second Ave. S., Nashville, TN 37212	Carter, Julie / 213-962-2521 2890 Westshire Dr., LA, CA 90068-1932
Bulter Shine & Stern / 415-331-6049 10 Liberty Ship Way, #4118, Sausalito, CA 94965	→ Cat Graphics / 212-226-8969 259 Elizabeth St., #3B, NY, NY 10012 page 10
Buntin Group / 615-244-5720 1001 Hawkins St., Nashville, TN 37203	Catalano, Donalyn Brooks / 213-353-9473 1940 Delta St., LA, CA 90026

$F = (a \times p)^4$

Table (2.5). Design

Designers	Designers
Catalog Design & Prod., Inc. / 415-468-5500 1485 Bayshore Blvd., #25, SF, CA 94124 3002	Copeland Hirphler Design & Comm. / 404-892-3472 40 Inwood Circle, Atlanta, GA 30309
Cato, Bob / 212-517-2073 157 E. 72nd St., NYC, NY 10021	Cordova Design / 213-733-7388 5037 W. Jefferson Blvd., LA, CA 90016
→ Chantry, Art Design / 206-441-3369 2315 Western Ave., Ste. 201, Seattle, WA 98121 page 28	Corey Design Studio, The 212-529-7238 / 914-365-3077 27 Chestnut Oval, Orangeburg, NY 10962
→ Chase Design, Margo / 213-668-1055 2255 Bancroft Ave., LA, CA 90039 pages 2 - 3	Cormier Illustration & Design / 818-303-6066 2251 Oakshade Rd., Bradbury, CA 91010
Cheng, Fu-Ding / 310-396-1466 209 Seventh Ave., Venice, CA 90291	Corsentino Design / 212-239-0849
Christensen & Assoc., Glen / 818-771-0246 6530 Independent Ave., Canoga Park, CA 91305	Corsillo Manzone / 203-656-3394 1006 Post Rd, Darien, CT 06820
Chwast, Seymour / 212-674-8080 215 Park Ave. So., #1300, NYC, NY 10003	Cossette / 416-922-2727 931 Young St., Toronto, Ontario, M4W 2H2 CANADA
Cimarron/Bacon/O'Brien / 213-936-6162 6824 Melrose Ave., Hollywood, CA 90038	Coulson Design / 408-458-1166 108 Locust St., Ste. A, Santa Cruz, CA 95060
Cimarron/Bacon/O'Brien / 213-461-5850 758 N. Highland Ave., Hollywood, CA 90038	Coulter, John / 213-655-8474 8127 Melrose Ave., #4, LA, CA 90046
Cincotta, Janice / 212-799-2305 113 W. 74th St., #4F, NY, NY 10023	Craig Communications / 415-292-7599 175 Alhambra St., #101, SF, CA 94123
Clark Communications Group / 800-886-2522 2024 West St., Annapolis, MD 21401	Creative Juices / 310-791-3237 3817 W. 226th St., Torrance, CA 90505
→ Clum, Scott / 503-873-6402 417 N. Second St., #5E, Silverton, OR 97381 page 1	DZ Communications / 818-761-6495 11288 Ventura Blvd., #727, Studio City, CA 91604
Cochran, Bobbye & Assocs. / 312-404-0375 433 W. Webster, Chicago, IL 60614	DZN The Design Group / 213-365-6401 672 S. La Fayette Park Pl., #26, LA, CA 90057
Collins & Chu / 714-731-7200 430 W. Main St., Tustin, CA 92680	Daggar, Elizabeth / 718-596-1858 216 Washington Ave., Brooklyn, NY 11205
Concept Arts Studios / 213-461-3696 6422 Selma Ave., Hollywood, CA 90028	Damore Johann Design / 415-957-9737 300 Brannan St., Ste. 610, S.F., CA 94107
Concepts + / 818-994-3339 / 213-873-1121 15450 Cabrito Rd., Van Nuys, CA 91406	David Anderson Design / 708-848-1020 539 North Linden, Oak Park, IL 60302
	DeCordova, Herb / 718-969-3125 152-18 Union Tpke., Flushing, NY 11367
	DeVault, Katherine / 615 260 0202 2400 Sunset Pl., Nashville, TN 37212

$$F = (a \times p)^4$$

Table (2.6). Design

Designers	Designers
Deep Design / 404-396-6666 5901 Peachtree-Dunwoody Rd., Atlanta, GA 30328	Designframe / 212-924-2426 116 E. 16th St., 10th Fl., NYC, NY 10003
Defrin Design, Inc., Bob / 212-799-4793 140 Riverside Dr., NYC, NY 10024	Designthing / 212-989-9325 1 Union Sq. W., NYC, NY 10003
Desanges, Saint-Jivago / 213-931-1984 P.O. Box 24 AA 2, LA, CA 90024	Deutsch Design / 212-966-7710 25 Mercer St., NYC, NY 10013
Deserted Design / 212-421-5624 865 First Ave., 16C, NYC, NY 10017	Diehl, Michael / 818-552-4110 1415 Norton Ave., Glendale, CA 91202
Design & Direction, Inc. / 310-395-6730 437 San Vincente Blvd., Ste. C, Santa Monica, CA 90402	Dietz Design / 206-781-7818 8349 20th Ave. NW, Seattle, WA 98117
Designory, The / 310-432-5707 211 E. Ocean Blve., #600, Long Beach, CA 90802	Dig-etel Design / 415-626-8337 328 Hayes St., SF, CA 94102-4421
Design Art, Inc. / 213-467-2984 6311 Romaine St., Ste. 7311, LA, CA 90038	Directions / 818-340-2443 23679 Calabasas Rd., #365, Calabasas, CA 91302
Design Element, The / 213-656-3293 8624 Wonderland Ave., LA, CA 90046	Diskin, Cecelia / 718-783-3647 759 President St., 4I, Brooklyn, NY 11215
Design Guys / 612-338-4462 119 N. 4th St., #410, Minneapolis, MN 55401	Ditko, Steve / 602-955-2707 3333 E. Camelback Rd., Phoenix, AZ 85018
Design Line, The / 404-451-5158 4360 Chamblee-Dunwoody Rd., Atlanta, GA 30341	Doret, Michael / 213-467-1900 / 310-376-2275 6545 Cahuenga Terrace, Hollywood, CA 90068
Design Matters / 212-867-8791 330 E. 38th St., NYC, NY 10016	DoubleSpace / 212-366-1919 170 Fifth Ave., NYC, NY 10010
Design Metro / 503-452-8195 643 SW Westwood Dr., Portland, OR 97201	Downing, Allan / 617-449-4784 50 Francis St., Needham, MA 02192
Design North / 414-639-2080 8007 Douglas Ave., Racine, WI 53402	Doyle Advertising & Graphic Design / 617-424-1844 419 Boylston St., Boston, MA 02116
Design One / 415-954-0710 1500 San Some St., Ste. 203, SF, CA 94111	Doyle Design Group, Clay / 213-848-8492 7836 Santa Monica Blvd., W. Hollywood, CA 90046
Design Team One, Inc. / 513-381-4774 22 W. 7th St., 7th Fl., Cincinnati, OH 45202	Drawing Board Design / 212-229-5211 160 Varick St., 12th Fl., NYC, NY 10013
Design Works, The / 310-553-9374 2307 Fox Hill Dr., LA, CA 90064	Drenttel Doyle Partners / 212-463-8787 1123 Broadway, Ste. 600, NYC, NY 10010
Design! / 706-272-3770 109 King St., Ste. C, Dalton, GA 30720	Drissi Advertising / 213-383-4080 638 S. Van Ness St., LA, CA 90005
Design: Diane Painter / 615-383-2005 1700 Shackleford Rd., Nashville, TN 37215	Duffy Design / 612-339-3247 901 Marquette Ave. S., Ste. 3000, Mpls, MN 55402

TABLE (2.7). DESIGN

Designers	Designers
Duke Design Co. / 818-980-0900 11264 Sunshine Terr., Studio City, CA 91604	Evans, Richard / 818-954-9918 412 S. Kenneth Rd., Burbank, CA 91501
Dyer/Mutchnick Group, Inc. / 213-655-1800 8360 Melrose Ave., 3rd Fl., LA, CA 90069	Exaline / 615-399-1991
EM2 Design / 404-221-1741 503 Means St., Ste. 402, Atlanta, GA 30318	Eye Noise / 407-894-3550 1215 E. Robinson St., Orlando, FL 32801
Eames, Tim / 310-455-3266 1104 Canyon Trail, Topanga, CA 90290	Fahrenheit / 617-536-4482 169 W. Newton St., Boston, MA 02118
East West Design / 310-275-6900 1110 S. Robertson Blvd., Ste. #6, LA, CA 90035	Fame / 612-342-9801 60 S. Sixth St., Ste. 2600, Mpls., MN 55402
Eaton & Assocs. Design Co. / 612-338-2266 708 S. Third St., Minneapolis, MN 55415	Fattal & Collins / 310-822-2777 4640 Admiral T Way, Marina Del Rey, CA 90292
Ed Walter Design / 212-966-7800 584 Broadway, Ste. 1108, NYC, NY 10012	Fili, Louise / 212-989-9153 71 Fifth Ave., NYC, NY 10003
Edwards, Ron / 818-786-3162 / 808-325-6744 13107 Strathern St., N. Hollywood, CA 91605	Fina Design / 212-677-2755 23 West 9th St., Ste. 2F, NYC, NY 10011
Ehlers, Lesley / 212-683-2773 244 Fifth Ave., NYC, NY 10011	Fine Art Studio / 714-832-6595
Eiber Design, Rick / 206-632-8326 31014 S.E. 58th St., Preston, WA 98050	Fiorentino Assocs. Inc. / 212-243-2236 134 W. 26th St., Ste. 902, NY, NY 10001
Eisenberg & Assocs. / 214-528-5990 3311 Oak Lawn, Ste. 300, Dallas, TX 75219	→ Firehouse 101 Art + Design / 614-464-0928 492 Armstrong St., Columbus, OH 43215 pages 12 - 13
Electric Paint / 213-462-4332 6335 Homewood Ave., Hollywood, CA 90028	Focus 2 / 214-741-4007 2105 Commerce St., Ste. 102, Dallas, TX 75201
Ellis Design / 615-254-0483 25 Lindsley Ave., Nashville, TN 37210	Fontographics / 310-659-0122 998 S. Robertson Blvd., #202, LA, CA 90035
Emprye Design / 212-677-1138 156 Sullivan St., #6, NYC, NY 10012	Fortune Design Studio / 206-483-5953 16932 NE 141st Pl., Woodinville, WA 98072
Engel Design, Inc., Andy / 818-760-1551 4370 Tujunga Ave., #220, Studio City, CA 91604	Foster Design / 617-262-5899 222 Newbury Street, Boston, MA 02116
English, Valerie / 212-475-8748 Carl Waltzer Digital Services, Inc. 873 Broadway, #412, NYC, NY 10003	Four Corners Design / 818-899-8987 P.O. Box 10426, Burbank, CA 91510
	Fox & Friends, Inc., B.D. / 310-394-7150 1111 Broadway, Santa Monica, CA 90401
Erbe Design, Maureen / 310-839-1954 1948 S. LaCienega Blvd., LA, CA 90034	Frandsen, Marilyn / 213-466-7398 1041 North McCadden Pl., LA, CA 90038

$$F = (a \times p)^4$$

TABLE (2.8). DESIGN

Designers	Designers
Franek Design Assocs., Inc. / 202-363-4441 5101 Wisconsin Ave., N.W., Washington, DC 20016	Gold Advertising, Bill / 212-941-0990 584 Broadway, Ste. 702, NYC, NY 10012
Frankfurt Balkind Partners / 212-421-5888 244 E. 58th St., NYC, NY 10022	Good Graphic Design, Peter / 203-526-9597 3 N. Main St., Chester, CT 06412
Frankfurt Balkind Partners / 213-965-4800 6135 Wilshire Blvd., 3rd Fl., LA, CA 90048	Goodspeed Creative / 212-475-4580 165 Lexington Ave., NYC, NY 10016
Frazier Design / 415-863-9613 600 Townsend St., #412 W., SF, CA 94103	Gorman Design, Pat / 212-620-0506 5 E. 17th St., NYC, NY 10003
Frog Design, Inc. / 408-734-5800 1327 Chesapeake Terrace, Sunnyville, CA 94089	Graca Design Group, James / 805-339-9304 1891 Goodyear Ave., Ste. 607, Ventura, CA 93003
Fulcrum Design / 415-641-5542 2121 Bryant St., #301, SF, CA 94110	Graffito, Inc. / 410-837-0070 601 N. Eutaw St., #704, Baltimore, MD 21201
Fulton Design Group, Jacobs / 415-328-4669 745 Emerson St., Palo Alto, CA 94301	Graphic Factor / 818-398-1212 1487 E. Washington Blvd., Pasadena, CA 91104
Funk & Assoc. Marketing Comm. / 503-485-1932 1255 Pearl St., Eugene, OR 97401	Graphic Orb, Inc. / 818-980-2266 12155 Riverside Dr., N. Hollywood, CA 91607
Gary Group, The / 310-842-8400 9046 Lindblade St., Culver City, CA 90232	Graphic Productions / 714-898-7992 11642 Knott St., #13, Garden Grove, CA 92641
Gee Design, Earl / 415-543-1192 501 Second St., Ste. 700, SF, CA 94107	Graphics Studio, The / 213-466-2666 811 N. Highland Ave., LA, CA 90038
Georgopoulos Design Assocs. / 213-972-0171 837 Traction Ave., Ste. #203, LA, CA 90013	Graphique Design Group / 808-325-6678 73-1270 Awakea St., Kailua Kona, HI 96740
Giles, David C. / 212-349-2569	Grasso Assocs., Lou / 212-371-1820 425 Madison Ave., NY, NY 10017
Gilmore, Steven / 213-939-8560 6017 Colgate Ave., LA, CA 90036	Gravy / 310-319-3718 522 Wilshire Blvd., Ste. D, Santa Monica, CA 90401
Girvin Design, Tim / 206-623-7808 1601 Second Ave., 5th Fl., Seattle, WA 98101	Green Design Studio, Peter / 818-953-2210 4219 Burbank, Burbank, CA 91505
Glaser, Milton / 212-889-3161 207 E. 32nd St., NYC, NY 10016	→ Greenberg Kingsley / 212-645-7379 95 Horatio St., #6W, NYC, NY 10014 page 5
Global Dog House / 310-315-4808 3000 W. Olympic Blvd., Santa Monica, CA 90004	Greeson, Robert / 214-826-5697 6118 Ellsworth, Dallas, TX 75214
Go Graphics/Printing / 310-578-0490 P.O. Box 66305, LA, CA 90066	Greiman Inc., April / 213-227-1222 620 Moulton Ave., Ste. 211, LA, CA 90031
Godat/Jonczyk Design / 602-620-6337 807 S. Fourth Ave., Tucson, AZ 85701	

Table (2.9). Design

Designers	Designers
Group/Chicago Inc. / 312-787-4504 400 West Erie, #302, Chicago, IL 60610	Hixo, Inc. / 512-477-0050 2905 San Gabriel, Ste. #300, Austin, TX 78705
Hafeman Design Group / 312-829-6829 935 W. Chestnut, Chicago, IL 60622	Hoar, John / 804-798-3352
Handman Design / 212-599-0161 265 Madison Ave., NYC, NY 10016	Hopkins/Baumann / 212-727-2929 236 W. 26th St., NYC, NY 10001
Hansen Design Assocs., Ted / 619-233-0422 1955 4th Ave., San Diego, CA 92101	Hornall Anderson Design Works / 206-467-5800 1008 Western Ave., #600, Seattle, WA 98104
Hard Werken Design / 213-934-2186 5514 Wilshire Blvd., LA, CA 90036	Hound Dog Studio / 615-327-9577 1710 Hayes St., Nashville, TN 37203
Hardy, Paul / 212-947-5209 448 W. 37th St., NYC, NY 10018	Hurrell Design Group Inc. / 404-892-5494 40 Inwood Circle, Atlanta, Georgia 30309
Harrison Design Group / 415-928-6100 665 Chestnut St., 3rd Fl., SF, CA 94133	I Design / 310-393-8521 923 5th St., #6, Santa Monica, CA 90403
Hawthorne/Wolfe / 314-231-1844 1818 Chouteau Ave., St. Louis, MO 63103	Icon Design / 212-229-2344 421 Hudson St., Ste. #625, NYC, NY 10014
Heiden Design, John / 213-668-9073 2353 Moreno Dr., LA, CA 90039	Ignition Design / 212-254-4324
Heller New York / 212-307-0007 1841 Broadway, NYC, NY 10023	Ikon / 615-292-7798 PO Box 121741, Nashville, TN 37212
Hello Studio / 212-941-8373 285 W. Broadway, #280, NYC, NY 10013	Ikon Creative Services, Inc. / 310-204-5711 3760 S. Robertson Blvd., Ste. 202, Culver City, CA 90232
Henry Dreyfuss Design / 212-957-8600 423 W. 55th St., NY, NY 10019	Illusion Factory, The / 818-223-8400 23875 Ventura Blvd., #104, Calabasas, CA 91302
Herr, Randy / 213-664-8046 1608 N. Cahuenga Blvd., #387, Hllywd, CA 90028	Image Design, Inc. / 615-242-4646 2280 Metrocenter Blvd., Nashville, TN 37228
Hershey Assocs. / 213-669-1001 2959 Glendale Blvd., LA, CA 90039	ImageWorks / 818-773-8773 19725 Sherman Way, #385, Winnetka, CA 91306
→ Hess, Lydia / 503-234-4757 1246 SE 49th St., Portland, OR 97215 Illustration / page 33	Impact Promotions & Design / 312-751-3500 101 E Erie St., Chicago, IL 60611-2897
Hewson Design Associates / 212-925-2776 270 Lafayette St., Rm. 1110, NYC, NY 10012	Industrial Strength Design / 310-578-6486 516 Boccaccio Ave., #C, Venice, CA 90291
	Infinite Ltd. / 818-303-1386 859 N. Hollywood Way, #214, Burbank, CA 91505
Higashi Glaser Design / 703-372-6440 822 Caroline St., #2, Fredericksburg, VA 22401	Insight Communications / 818-507-1909 1721 Victory Blvd., Glendale, CA 91201

$$F = (a \times p)^4$$

TABLE (2.10). DESIGN

Designers	Designers
Intralink Film Graphic Design / 310-859-7001 155 N. La Peer Dr., LA, CA 90048	Keswick Hamilton/Sygma / 213-380-3933 3519 W. Sixth St., LA, CA 90020
Isley Design, Alexander / 212-941-7945 361 Broadway, Ste. 111, NYC, NY 10013	Kinetik Communication Graphics / 202-797-0605 1615 17th St. NW, 2nd Fl., Washington D.C. 20009
Ivener Design Group / 310-452-0770 1501 Main St., Ste. 204, Venice, CA 90291	→ Knickelbine, Paul / 612-724-1618 4706 31st Ave. So., Minneapolis, MN 55406 page 14
Iwerks Entertainment / 818-841-7766 4540 W. Valerio St., Burbank, CA 91505	Koepke Design / 508-525-2229 10 Oakes Ave., Ste. 3, Magnolia, MA 01930
J.S. Graphics / 818-551-9293 318 E. Glen Oaks Blvd., Glendale, CA 91207	Kosh Design Studio / 213-465-9919 6671 Sunset Blvd., Ste. 1574A, Hllywd, CA 90028
Jager Dipaola Kemp / 802-864-5884 308 Pine Street, Burlington, VT 05401	Kotas, Karl / 212-675-0052 445 W. 19th St., 1E, NY, NY 10011
Jane Doe Design / 601-949-6942 1117 Kenwood Pl., Jackson, MS 39202	Kovach Design Co. / 312-587-0074 4 E. Ohio St., Chicago, IL 60611
Jermann, Paul / 213-934-4557 165 N. Sycamore Ave., LA, CA 90036	Kovin Design / 215-968-7820 236 Leigh High Dr., Richboro, PA 18954
JesseJames Creative / 212-675-7424 19 W. 21st St., Rm 1105, NYC, NY 10010	Krahn Design / 805-495-3874 31 Marimar St., Thousand Oaks, CA 91360
Johnson & Wolverton / 503-241-6145 1314 NW Irving, #702, Portland, OR 97209	Krause Mora, Pamela / 213-650-1940 1400 N. Havenhurst Dr., LA, CA 90046
Johnson Olson / 612-722-8050 3107 E. 42nd St., Mpls., MN 55406	L.A. Design Firm / 310-478-7011 11500 W. Olympic Blvd., LA, CA 90064
Johnson Wolverton / 503-241-6145 1314 NW Irving #702, Portland, OR 97209	Lam Design / 914-948-4777 661 N. Broadway, White Plains, NY 10603
Johnson, Christopher & Assoc. / 212-246-4455 154 W. 57th St., #114, Carnegie Hall, NY, NY 10019	Larsen Design Office, Inc. / 612-835-2271 7101 York Ave. S., Ste. 120, Minneapolis, MN 55435
Justdesign / 212-620-4672 160 Fifth Ave., #905, NYC, NY 10010	Larson, Mark / 914-679-1010 9A Millstream Rd., Woodstock, NY 12498
Kampa Design / 512-441-6831 2414A S. Lamar, Austin, TX 78704	Larson, Ron / 213-465-8451 940 N. Highland, #E, LA, CA 90038
Kaulfuss Designers, Inc. / 312-943-2161 1000 N. Halsted St., Chicago, IL 60622	Lauren, Deborah / 212-677-1138 156 Sullivan St., NYC, NY 10012
Kegler, Alan / 716-881-5723 306 Lexington Ave., Buffalo, NY 14222	LeBoy, Lori Design Studio / 213-913-2790 913 Sanborn Ave., LA, CA 90029
Kellum Design, Ron / 212-979-2661 151 First Ave., Ph 1, NYC, NY 10003	

TABLE (2.11). DESIGN

Designers	Designers
LePrevost Corp, The / 310-457-3742 29350 Pacific Coast Hwy, #6, Malibu, CA 90265	Lumel Design, Inc. / 818-769-5332 12517 Chandler Blvd., #101, N. Hollywood, CA 91607
Lead Pencil Design Studio, The / 213-463-0154 6671 Sunset Blvd., #1523-B, Hollywood, CA 90028	M & Company / 212-343-2408 225 Lafayette St., Ste. #904, NYC, NY 10012
Leah Lettering & Design, Bonnie / 714-841-4046 19351 Sun Ray Lane, Huntington Beach, CA 92648	M Group / 615-251-0162 209 Tenth Ave. S., #208, Nashville, TN 37203
Lee, Johnny / 213-464-4567 424 N. Larchmont Blvd., Ste. #3, LA, CA 90004	M.A.D. / 415-331-4430 1237 San Carlos, Sausalito, CA 94965
Lee, Walter W. / 818-792-8770 85 N. Chester Ave., Pasadena, CA 91106	M2Art / 212-599-1616 225 E. 43rd St., 4th Fl., NYC, NY 10017
Leonhardt Group, The / 206-624-0551 1218 Third Ave., #620, Seattle, WA 98101	MS Design / 212-242-6525 / 908-223-5937 20 W. 20th St., Ste. #401, NYC, NY 10010
Levinson & Assocs. / 415-397-5717 1005 Sansome, Ste. 242, SF, CA 94111	Mackin & Dowd / 410-426-8010 3110 Juno Pl., Baltimore, MD 21214
Lim, Howard / 310-394-3005 1002 14th St., #8, Santa Monica, CA 90403	Maddock Douglas, Inc. / 708-279-3939 257 N. West Ave., Elmhurst, IL 60126
Liska & Assocs., Steve / 312-943-4600 676 N. St. Clair St., Ste. 1550, Chicago, IL 60611	Maddogs & Englishman / 212-505-1427 56 E. 11th St., 5th Fl., NY, NY 10003
Little & Company / 612-375-0077 1010 S. Seventh St., Minneapolis, MN 55415	Madsen, Eric / 612-339-6868 430 First Ave. N., Ste. 690, Mpls., MN 55401
Lloyd, Doug / 212-941-5524 165 Hudson St., 5B, NYC, NY 10013	Maginnis Inc. / 312-915-0592 1440 N. Dayton, Ste. 203, Chicago, IL 60622
Looking / 213-226-1086 660 S. Ave 21, Unit 5, LA, CA 90031	⟶ Maisner Hand Lettering, Bernard Rep: Gerald & Cullen Rapp / 212-889-3337 page 23
Lorelei Graphic Design Studio / 310-470-0975 1044 Manning Ave., LA, CA 90024	Makela, Scott / 612-922-2271 3711 Glendale Terrace, Minneapolis, MN 55410
Loudmouth Graphics / 310-578-9683 624-B Venice Blvd., Venice, CA 90291	Manhattan Design / 212-620-0506 5 E. 17th St., NYC, NY 10003
Louey/Rubino Design Group, Inc. / 310-396-7724 2525 Main St., #204, Santa Monica, CA 90405	Marketing And / 310-841-6600 8522 National Blvd., Ste. 109, Culver City, CA 90232
Louie, Lorraine / 212-941-7329 80 Varick St., Ste. 3B, NYC, NY 10013	Marks Communications, Inc. / 213-957-9904 2690 Beachwood Dr., LA, CA 90068
Lowry & Assocs. / 310-558-3691 8800 Venice Blvd., LA, CA 90034	Martin, Doug / 310-395-6730 437 San Vincente Blvd., Santa Monica, CA 90402
Lukasiewicz Design / 212-581-3344 119 W. 57th St., 11th Fl., NYC, NY 10019	

$$F = (a \times p)^4$$

TABLE (2.12). DESIGN

Designers	Designers
Mason Design Group, The Karen / 206-340-0644 540 1st Ave S., Studio # 206, Seattle, WA 98104	Michelle Weibman / 212-410-6796 160 E. 88th St., 11J, NYC, NY 10028
Massey, Inc., John / 312-871-5029 2131 N. Cleveland St., Chicago, IL 60614	Middleberg & Assocs. / 212-888-6610 130 E. 59th St., 12th Fl., NYC, NY 10022
Matare Design / 310-392-6069 237 Pacific St., #A, Santa Monica, CA 90405	Miho, James N. / 818-577-9015 1200 Chateau Rd., Pasadena, CA 91105
Matsuno Design Group / 818-247-4200 719 W. Broadway, Glendale, CA 91204	Millerburg, Inc., John / 213-663-4143 3084 St. George St., LA, CA 90027
Mauck & Assocs. / 515-243-6010 303 Locust St., Ste. 200, Des Moines, IA 50309	Minds Eye Design / 310-444-7387 11666 Goshen Ave., Ste. 308, Brentwood, CA 90049
Mazzeo, Victor / 212-645-1898 340 W. 17th St., #4C, NYC, NY 10011	Minobe Design / 818-244-7520 1721 Victory Blvd., Glendale, CA 91201
McCayco / 310-842-9004 8761 W. Washington Blvd., Culver City, CA 90232	Modern Dog Design Co. / 206-282-8857 601 Valley St., Ste. 309, Seattle, WA 98109
McConnell & Associates / 615-329-1044 321 29th Ave. N., Nashville, TN 37203	Monahan, Leo / 818-843-6115 1912 Hilton Dr., Burbank, CA 91504
McDaniel Design, Inc. / 201-762-3601 29 Schaefer Rd., Maplewood, NJ 07040	Moo-V-Adz / 213-655-4693 6721 Drexel Ave., LA, CA 90048
McMacken, David / 707-996-5239 19481 Franquelin Pl., Sonoma, CA 95476	Moran Studios / 714-722-0992 711 W. 17th St., Costa Mesa, CA 92627
McRoberts Mitchell Visual Comm. / 212-431-5166 54 Greene St., NYC, NY 10013	Morava & Oliver / 310-453-3523 2054 Broadway, Santa Monica, CA 90404
Mednick Group, The / 310-842-8444 8522 National Blvd., Culver City, CA 90232	Morla Design / 415-543-6548 463 Bryant St., SF, CA 94107
Melia Design Group / 404-659-5584 905 Bernina Ave., Atlanta, GA 30307	Morris, Rick Design / 213-255-6615 5013 Hartwick St., LA, CA 90041
Melton Design, Margery / 213-872-1824 12952 Dickens St., Studio City, CA 91604	Muccino Design Group / 408-993-1870 448 S. Market St., SF, CA 95113
Mendl, Trella / 212-645-5606 59 W. 19th St. #2C, NYC, NY 10011	Murrell Design Group / 404-892-5494 40 Inwood Circle, Atlanta, GA 30309 page 15
Menihan Designs / 617-524-0399 53 Boynton St., Boston, MA 02130	Murrie Lienhart Rysner / 312-943-5995 58 W. Huron St., Chicago, IL 60610
Merrill McWillie Design / 818-769-8414 4556 Simpson Ave., Studio City, CA 91607	Nancekivell Group, The / 612-341-8003 400 N. First St., Ste. 100, Minneapolis, MN 55401
Merville Design / 805-579-8825 2140 Woodwind Ct., Simi Valley, CA 93063	

TABLE (2.13). DESIGN

Designers	Designers
Naughton & Assocs., Carol / 312-951-5353 213 West Institute Place, Chicago, IL 00010	Parsons Design, Glenn / 310-559-6571 0522 National Blvd., Culver City, CA 00232
Nesnadny & Schwartz, Inc. / 216-791-3637 10803 Magnolia Dr., Cleveland, OH 44106	Pattee Design / 515-255-6801 3200 Ingersoll Ave., #D, Des Moines, IA 50312
Network Art Service / 818-843-5078 630 S. Mariposa St., Burbank, CA 91506	→ Pawn Shop Press / 213-653-9331 / 213-935-7356 858 N. Curson Ave., LA, CA 90046 page 25
Nichols Graphic Design, Mary Ann / 212-727-9818 80 Eighth Ave., Ste. 900, NYC, NY 10011-5126	Paykos Design, Melanie / 310-287-3420 3633 Hayden Ave., Culver City, CA 90232
→ Nomad Short Subject / 919-832-0250 501 Washington St., Raleigh, NC 27605 Film / pages 2 - 3	Pearl Design / 310-473-4935 1318 1/2 Amhearst Ave., LA, CA 90025
Nomura Graphic Design, Lynn / 818-568-3596 284 S. Madison Ave., #105, Pasadena, CA 91101	Pedersen Design, Inc. / 212-683-5450 141 Lexington Ave., NYC, NY 10016
North Light, Ltd. / 213-386-9140 3055 Wilshire Blvd., #490, LA, CA 90010	Pentagram Design Inc. / 415-981-6612 620 Davis St., SF, CA 94111
Nucleus / 312-243-2055 853 N. Wood St., Chicago, IL 60622	Pentagram Design Inc. / 212-683-7000 212 Fifth Ave., NYC, NY 10010
Olinsky, Frank / 718-875-6584	Perr, Janet / 201-993-8494 33 Wyndmoor Dr., Morristown, NJ 07960
Onaitis Design / 213-878-6255 12514 Sarah St., #188, Studio City, CA 91604	Persechini & Company / 310-314-8622 1501 Main St., Ste. 202, Venice, CA 90291
Orton Communication / 818-716-9072 6800 The Sunset Ridge, #200, West Hills, CA 91307	Pettis, Valerie / 212-683-7382 88 Lexington Ave., Ste. 17G, NYC, NY 10016
Osborne Design, Mackie / 213-463-4602 5140 1/2 Clinton St., LA, CA 90004	Ph.D / 310-829-0900 / 310-396-7627 1524a Cloverfield Blvd, Santa Monica, CA 90404
Owen, Tania / 615-298-1444 2804 Brightwood Ave., Nashville, TN 37212	Philpott, Kathleen / 213-930-0116 516 S. Orange Grove, LA, CA 90036
Ozubko, Chris / 206-284-8122 3044 38th Ave. W., Seattle, WA 98199	Phinney Bischoff Design / 206-322-3484 614 Boylston Ave. E., Seattle, WA 98102
Pacific Art & Light / 818-895-7662 15831 Romar St., North Hills, CA 91343	Photo Sphere Art Studio / 310-392-5457 2211 4th St., #210, Santa Monica, CA 90405
Paperny & Assocs., Vladimir / 818-506-4596 10625 Magnolia Blvd., N. Hollywood, CA 91601	Pink Coyote / 212-475-0430 611 Broadway, Ste. 908, NYC, NY 10012
Parham Santana Inc. / 212-645-7501 7 W. 18th St., NYC, NY 10011	Pinkhaus Design Corp. / 305-854-1000 2424 S. Dixie Hwy., Ste. 200, Miami, FL 33133
Parks, Greg / 213-665-1730 2126 Cove Ave., LA, CA 90039	

$$F = (a \times p)^4$$

TABLE (2.14). DESIGN

Designers	Designers
Pittard Sullivan Fitzgerald / 213-462-1190 6430 Sunset Blvd., Ste. 200, LA, CA 90028	Rambo, Michael / 212-387-0870 140 E. 17th St., NYC, NY 10003
Planet Design Company / 608-256-0000 229 State St., Madison, WI 53703	Ramey, Lee Ann / 615-385-0375 3001 Brightwood Ave., Nashville, TN 37212
Platinum Design, Inc. / 212-366-4000 14 W. 23rd St., 2nd Fl., NYC, NY 10010	Raumberger Design, Gabrielle / 310-582-2211 1634 19th St., Santa Monica, CA 90404
→ Plunkert, David / 410-235-7803 3647 Falls Rd., Baltimore, MD 21211 Illustration / page 14	ReVerb / 213-936-7305 5514 Wilshire Blvd., #900, LA, CA 90036-3800
Poindexter Design / 818-508-1284 3792 Berry Dr., Studio City, CA 91604	→ Red Herring Design, Inc. / 212-219-0557 449 Washington St., NYC, NY 10013 page 4
Point Blank Design / 818-841-8706 2205 W. Olive Ave., #C, Burbank, CA 91506	Red Square Design / 212-620-0363 1133 Broadway, Ste. 1401, NY, NY 10010
Polese & Clancy / 617-367-6730 10 Commercial Wharf W., Boston, MA 02110	Reece Graphics / 505-345-2004 2129 Osuna N.E., Ste. 111, Albuquerque, NM 87113
Powers, Mary / 415-431-2831 1371 Page St., SF, CA 94117	Reiner Design / 212-673-1302 26 E. 22nd St., NYC, NY 10010
Pressley Jacobs Design / 312-263-7485 101 N. Wacker Drive, Chicago, IL 60606	Reneric and Company / 213-465-3166 1041 N. McCadden Pl., LA, CA 90038
Pushpin Group, The / 212-674-8080 215 Park Ave. So., #1300, NYC, NY 10003	→ Rey International / 310-305-9393 4120 Michael Ave., LA, CA 90066 page 18
Quan, Carolyn / 212-343-1108 / 416-599-3590 285 W. Broadway, NYC, NY 10013	Rickabaugh Graphics / 614-337-2229 384 W. Johnstown Rd, Gahanna, OH 43230
Quick on the Draw / 213-848-3777 8225 1/2 Santa Monica Blvd, LA, CA 90046	→ Ride Design/Scott Clum / 503-873-6402 417 N. Second St., #5E, Silverton, OR 97381 page 1
Quill Creative / 214-689-3614 1111 W. Mockingbird, Ste. 830, Dallas, TX 75247	Rigsby Design, Inc. / 713-660-6057 5650 Kirby Drive, Ste. #260, Houston, TX 77005
Quon, Mike / 212-226-6024 568 Broadway, Ste. 703, NYC, NY 10012	Riordon Design Group Inc., The / 905-271-0399 1001 Queen St. West, Mississauga, ON, L5H 4E1
RBMM / 214-987-4800 7007 Twin Hills, Ste. 200, Dallas, TX 75231-5164	→ Robertson Typographic Illustration / 303-444-2787 1245 Pearl St., #200, Boulder, CO 80302 page 24
Radoyce Assocs. Design / 310-822-2150 513 Wilshire Blvd., #304, Santa Monica, CA 90401	Roinstad, Eric / 213-933-4743 645 1/2 S. Ridgeley, LA, 90036
Raess Design / 310-446-9524 1842 Holmby Ave., LA, CA 90025	

$F = (a \times p)^4$

TABLE (2.15). DESIGN

Designers	Designers
Roman, Carmelo / 615-256-6463 96 Taylor St., Nashville, TN 37208	Scott Design / 214-744-1777 3200 Main, Unit 37, Dallas, TX 75226
Romeo Empire Design / 212-274-0214 154 Spring St., #3, NYC, NY 10012	Segura Inc. / 312-649-5688 361 W. Chestnut St., 1st Fl., Chicago, IL 60610
Romero Design Group, Javier / 212-420-0656 24 E. 23rd St., 3rd Fl., NYC, NY 10010	Seiniger Advertising / 310-777-6800 9320 Wilshire Blvd., Beverly Hills, CA 90212
Ross, Culbert & Lavery / 212-206-0044 15 W. 20th St., 9th Fl., NYC, NY 10011	Senophle, Debra / 213-466-8100 2285 N. Beachwood Dr., #1, Hllywd, CA 90068
Roxas & Wikle Creative Services / 714-744-3511 58 Plaza Sq., Ste. E, Orange, CA 92666	Serino/Coyne, Inc. / 212-626-2700 1515 Broadway, 36th Fl., NYC, NY 10036
Russell & Assoc., Inc., Anthony / 212-431-8770 584 Broadway, Ste. 701, NYC, NY 10012	Shahid & Company / 212-343-0493 76 Greene St., 3rd Fl., NYC, NY 10012
Ryder, Sheridan / 310-823-9520 2314 Grand Canal, Venice, CA 90291	Shannon Design / 612-362-2583 1700 Broadway N.E., Mpls, MN 55413
Sabaj Williams & Assocs. / 914-345-3555 45 Knollwood Rd., 5th Fl., Elmsford, NY 10523	Sherman, Wendy / 818-763-3858 11910 Louise Ave., #10, LA, CA 90066
Sackett Design / 415-543-1590 864 Fulsom St., SF, CA 94107	Sibley/Peteet Design / 214-761-9400 965 Slocum, Dallas, TX 75207
Sagon-Phior Group / 818-752-7370 5308 Vineland Ave., N. Hollywood, CA 91601	Siegel & Gale / 213-389-1010 3465 W. Sixth St., Ste. 300, LA, CA 90020
Salisbury Communications, Mike / 310-320-7660 2200 Amapola Ct., Ste. 202, Torrance, CA 90501	Sierbert Design Assocs. / 513-241-4550 1600 Sycamore St., Cincinnati, OH 45210
Samata Assocs. / 708-428-8600 101 S. First St., Dundee, IL 60118	Sign Language / 212-732-2449 86 Thomas St., 4th Fl., NYC, NY 10013
Sandstrom Design / 503-248-9466 808 S.W. Third, Portland, OR 97204	Silton, Susan / 213-660-4588 3359 Garden Ave., #1, LA, CA 90039
Sasaki, Yori / 206-860-8656 747 Bellevue Ave. E., Seattle, WA 98102	Silvio, Sam Design / 312-427-1735 633 S. Plymouth Ct., #204, Chicago, IL 60605
Sawyer Studios / 212-645-4455 115 W. 27th St., 8th Fl., NYC, NY 10001	Sine Language Graphics / 212-732-2449 86 Thomas St., 4th Fl., NY, NY 10013
Schiffer Design, David / 212-255-3464 381 Park Ave. S., NY, NY 10016	Sine Language Graphics / 212-732-2449 86 Thomas St., 4th Fl., NY, NY 10013
Schiffman Young Design Group / 213-930-1873 7421 Beverly Blvd., #4, LA, CA 90036	Singer Design / 212-481-3452 401 E. 34th St., Ste. S11C, NYC, NY 10016
Schuth, Rosa / 510-215-7043 404 W. Richmond Ave., Pt. Richmond, CA 94801	Skolos/Wedell / 617-242-5179 529 Main St., Charlestown, MA 02129

$$F = (a \times p)^4$$

Table (2.16). Design

Designers	Designers
Slatoff & Cohen / 212-243-8019 17 W. 20th St., 3rd Fl., NYC, NY 10011	→ Stovall, Lorna / 213-931-5984 1088 Queen Ann Pl., LA, CA 90019 page 17
Slover Design, Susan / 212-431-0093 584 Broadway, Ste. 903, NY, NY 10012	Strandell Design / 312-943-7553 218 East Ontario, Chicago, IL 60611
Smart Design / 212-807-8150 7 W. 18th St., NYC, NY 10011	Strata Design / 212-228-8870 28 W. 25th St., 10th Fl., NYC, NY 10010
Smith Smith & Smith / 310-540-3080 539 Ave. B, Redondo Beach, CA 90277	Stringham, Jodee / 212-966-1948 285 W. Broadway, #280, NYC, NY 10013
Smith, Tyler / 401-751-1220 127 Dorrance St., Providence, RI 02903	Stroster Graphics Co., M. / 312-525-2081 2057 N. Sheffield Ave., Chicago, IL 60614
Smoke Bomb Studio NYC / 718-389-3873 106 Norman Ave., Brooklyn, NY 11222	Structural Graphics / 203-767-2661 80 Plains Rd., Essex, CT 06426
Sola, Luis / 213-876-6481 3320 Floyd Terrace, LA, CA 90068	Stuart/Moss Design Inc. / 213-655-6555 470 S. San Vincente Blvd., LA, CA 90048
Soohoo Designers, Patrick / 310-836-8800 8800 Venice Blvd., LA, CA 90034	Studio Izbickas / 617-695-0606 99 Chauncy St., #409, Boston, MA 02111
Sposato, John / 212-477-3909 43 E. 22nd St., NYC, NY 10010	Studio North / 708-729-9221 1616 Greenbay Rd., N. Chicago, IL 60064
Spot Design / 212-645-8684 775 Ave of Americas, NYC, NY 10001	Studio Productions / 213-856-8048 650 N. Bronson Ave., Ste. 223, Hollywood, CA 90004
→ Stanislaw Fernandes / 212-533-2648 Equilibrium Design 874 Broadway, #305, NY, NY 10003 Illustration / pages 28 - 29	Studio Q / 212-343-1108 / 416-599-3590 285 W. Broadway, NYC, NY 10013
Stearney, Mark / 312-360-9033 621 S. Plymouth St., Ste. 202, Chicago, IL 60605	Studio Seireeni / 213-937-0355 708 S. Orange Grove Ave., LA, CA 90036
Stenning & Assocs., Barbara / 510-236-5973 534 Grandview Court, Point Richmond, CA 94801	Stylewrite Design Group / 212-255-1686 161 Sixth Ave., NYC, NY 10013
Stermole, Rick / 212-674-6714 226 E. 12th St., NYC, NY 10003	Sullivan Perkins / 214-922-9080 2811 McKinney Ave. Ste. 320, Dallas, TX 75204
Stevens Design, Joanne / 818-441-6432 1003 Diamond Ave., Ste. 206, S. Pasadena, CA 91030	Sunshine Studios / 213-464-5131 6305 Yucca St., #202, Hollywood, CA 90028
Stevens, John / 516-579-5352 53 Clear Meadow, E. Meadow, NY 11554	Supon Design Group / 202-822-6540 1700 K St. NW, Ste. 400, Washington, DC 20006
	Surface Film / 818-766-9039 5350 Strohm Ave., #22, N. Hollywood, CA 91601

TABLE (2.17). DESIGN

Designers	Designers
Sutton, Lisa / 310-398-5770 12136 Allin St., Culver City, CA 90290	Tri-Arts, Inc. / 213-461-4891 10401 W. Vine Dr., Ste. 920, LA, CA 90028
Swaine Studio, Inc. / 310-374-3533 2002 DuFour Ave., Redondo Beach, CA 90278	Triad / 415-925-3300 14 E. Sir Francis Drake, Larkspur, CA 94939
Swieter Design / 214-720-6020 3227 McKinney Ave., #201, Dallas, TX 75204	Ultimo, Inc. / 212-645-7858 41 Union Square W., Ste. 209, NYC, NY 10003 pages 26 - 27
Syme, Hugh / 317-529-0978 / 818-508-7137 3868 South Spiceland Road, Newcastle, IN 47362 Rep: Randy Pate / 805-529-8111	Underdog Design / 206-935-7456 4147 49th Ave. S.W., Seattle, WA 98116
T.L.R. & Assocs. / 213-381-7770 638 S. Van Ness Ave., LA, CA 90005	Unicorn / 213-381-3742 672 S. Lafayette Park Pl., #5, LA, CA 90057
TL Graphics / 814-453-3412 858 East 37th St., Erie, PA 16504	VNO Design / 615-269-8924 1807 Eighth Ave. So., Ste. 103, Nashville, TN 37203
TW Design / 404-237-3958 3490 Piedmont Rd., #1200, Atlanta, GA 30305	VSA Partners, Inc. / 312-427-6413 542 S. Dearborn, Ste. 202, Chicago, IL 60605
Takeda Designs, Marsha / 310-286-7475 1220 S. Smithwood Dr., #2, LA, CA 90035	Valencia, Anna / 212-387-0372 114 MacDougal St., Ste. 17, NYC, NY 10012
Tanagram, Inc. / 312-787-6831 855 W. Blackhawk Ave., Chicago, IL 60622	Valentine, Robert / 212-925-3103 17 Vestry St., NYC, NY 10013 Rep: Deborah Ayerst / 415-567-3570
Team Design / 615-298-3533 1414 17th Ave. So., Nashville, TN 37212 page 22	Van Haaften, Heather / 213-660-5970 1544 Westerly Terrace, LA, CA 90026 page 16
Teamwork Design / 213-224-8855 630 Moulton Ave., LA, CA 90031	Vance Wright Adams & Assocs. / 412-322-1800 930 N. Lincoln Ave., Pittsburgh, PA 15233
Thatcher Advertising & Design / 714-846-6474 4862 Tiara Dr., #204, Huntington Beach, CA 92649	Vaughn Wedeen Creative / 505-243-4000 407 Rio Grande N.W., Alberquerque, NM 87104
Thirst / 312-951-5251 855 W. Blackhawk, Chicago, IL 60622	Veal, Tracy / 213-469-9601 249 N. Larchmont Blvd., #1, LA, CA 90004
Three / 212-463-7025 236 W. 26th St., Ste.805, NYC, NY 10001	Via Media / 310-435-6998 203 Pine Ave., Long Beach, CA 90802
Tolleson Design / 415-626-7796 444 Spear St., Ste. #204, SF, CA 94105	Vigon, Larry / 213-882-6607 2635 La Cuesta Dr., LA, CA 90046
Toma, Roy & Assocs. / 303-293-8353 1201 18th St., Ste. 210, Denver, CO 80202	Vinas, Jaime / 212-473-3616 7 E. 20th St., NYC, NY 10003
Top Design Studio / 818-988-8028 7011 Hayvenhurst Ave., W. Van Nuys, CA 91406	

$$F = (a \times p)^4$$

Table (2.18). Design

Designers	Designers
Virtu / 213-465-3232 650 N. Bronson, Ste 142, LA, CA 90004	West-Towne Studios / 310-453-5000 1447 11th St., Bldg 300, Santa Monica, CA 90401
Visual Asylum / 619-233-9633 343 Fourth Ave., San Diego, CA 92101	Wexler, Glen / 213-465-0268 736 N. Highland Ave., LA, CA 90038
Vivid Images / 203-799-0180 233 Boston Post Rd., Orange, CT 06477	Whitfield Art Agency, Inc. / 615-244-6810 615 Seventh Ave. So., Nashville, TN 37203
Volan Design Assocs. / 303-449-3838 1800 38th St., Boulder, CO 80301	Williams Design Office, Steve / 215-579-4941 301 South State St., Newtown, PA 18940
WRC Entertainment / 216-566-7019 1100 Superior Ave., Ste. 1350, Cleveland, OH 44114	Williams Design, Angela / 415-567-5746 900 Chestnut St., #102, SF, CA 94109
WRK Design / 816-561-4189 602 Westport Rd., Kansas City, MO 64111	Wilson Design Group / 818-980-4400 11426 Ventura Blvd., 3rd Fl., Studio City, CA 91604
WYD Design / 203-227-2627 61 Wilton Rd., Westport, CT 06880	Wilson Design, Peter / 818-795-0126 23 E. Colorado Blvd., Ph#203, Pasadena, CA 91105
Wages Design / 404-876-0874 1201 W. Peachtree St., Ste. 3630, Atlanta, GA 30309	Wilson, Gavin / 718-965-0908 70 Sherman St., Brooklyn, NY 11215
Warkulwiz Design Assocs. / 215-988-1777 2218 Race St., 3rd Fl., Philadelphia, PA 19103	Wilson, Gayle Christensen / 510-798-8859 1748 Limewood Court, Concord, CA 94521
Watson Design / 310-376-9665 704 Flagler Lane, Redondo Beach, CA 90278	Winner/Clippinger & Assocs. / 213-931-1891 761 N. Highland Ave., LA, CA 90038
Wazoo / 213-658-5287 838 N. Sweetzer Ave., #5, LA, CA 90069	Wintner Design / 818-766-5650 11712 Moore Park St., Ste. 109, Studio City, CA 91604
Weingard, Ilene / 310-393-8521 923 5th St., #6, Santa Monica, CA 90403	Wise Design / 404-897-5200 75 Thirteenth St., Atlanta, GA 30309
Weiss Assocs., Jack / 708-866-7480 1103 Mulford St., Evanston, IL 60202	Wittman Design / 203-740-8745 11 Cawdor Burn Rd., Brookfield, CT 06804
Weissman/Photo/Graphics/Studio / 212-989-9694 463 West St., Suite B332, NYC, NY 10014	Woloch, Dennis / 212-427-1746 1700 York Ave., NYC, NY 10128
Wendi Horowitz / 212-645-9120 201 W. 21st St., 7C, NY, NY 10011	Wong, Ark & Hoi-Ping Law / 213-876-5981 7360 Woodrow Wilson Dr., LA, CA 90046
Werndorf & Assocs. / 213-467-7990 6315 Yucca St., Hollywood, CA 90028	Woo Art / 212-989-7870 133 W. 19th St., 3rd Fl., NYC, NY 10011
Werner Design Werks / 612-338-2550 126 N. Third St., Rm. 400, Minneapolis, MN 55401 page 11	Wood, Lynn / 603-882-3152 39 Sullivan Rd., Hudson, NH 03051
	World Graphics / 213-874-1571 3421 W. Cahuenga Blvd., Hollywood, CA 90068

TABLE (2.19). DESIGN

Computer Graphics

Worrell Design / 612-946-1966
8509 City W. Pky., Eden Prairie, MN 55344

X Height / 818-789-5232
4434 Matilija Ave., Sherman Oaks, CA 91423

Yager & Assocs., Bass / 213-466-9701
7039 Sunset Blvd., LA, CA 90028

Yee Graphics, Ray / 213-465-2514
424 N. Larchmont Blvd, LA, CA 90004

Young & Company / 213-878-0910
7325 Santa Monica, W. Hollywood, CA 90046

Youngblood Padraic & Assocs., Inc. / 818-773-1792
8956 Etiwanda Ave., Northridge, CA 91325

Zachow Design / 214-954-0774
2500 State St., Dallas, TX 75201

Zaken, Ossie Adv. & Design / 818-845-7711
3119 W. Burbank Blvd, Burbank, CA 91505

Ziga Design / 203-852-1640
24 Harstrom Place, Rowayton, CT 06853

Zimmerman Crowe Design / 415-777-5560
90 Tehma St., SF, CA 94105

Zimmerman Rose Columbus, Inc. / 416-534-3444
77 Mowat Ave., Ste. 506, Toronto, Canada M6K 3E3

Zunda Design, Charles / 203-622-5918
80 Mason St., Greenwich, CT 06830

x2 Design / 212-388-1889
108 E. 16th St., No. 402, NYC, NY 10003

Computer Graphics

Advanced Intergrated Tech / 904-882-3652
P.O. Box 942, Gulf Breeze, FL 32562

Artistic Group Imaging Services, The / 212-736-6663
151 W. 30th St., Ste. 1003, NY, NY 10001-4007

Blackman, Barry / 212-627-9777
40 W. 25th St., 6th Fl., NYC, NY 10010

Computer Graphics

Christensen & Assoc., Glen / 818-716-1926

Colorspace Inc. / 212-679-9064
38 E. 32nd St., NYC, NY 10016

Computer Aided Photo, Inc. / 404-993-7197
P.O. Box 28656, Atlanta, GA 30328

Digital Magic / 310-315-4720
3000 W. Olympic Blvd., Santa Monica, CA 90404

Duggal Computer Imaging
800-382-9000 / 212-242-7000
9 W. 20th St., NYC, NY 10011

Effects House, The / 212-924-9150
111 Eighth Ave., Ste. 914, NYC, NY 10011

Fischer, Ken & Carl / 212-794-0400
121 E. 83rd St., NYC, NY 10028-0821

Herbert, Jonathan / 212-571-4444
Computer Illustration
324 Pearl St., NYC, NY 10038

Horowitz, Ryszard / 212-243-6440
137 W. 25th St., NYC, NY 10001

Industrial Light & Magic / 212-255-0500
1 Union Sq. W., Ste. 205, NY, NY 10003

Industrial Light & Magic / 415-258-2000
P.O. Box 2459, San Raefal, CA 94912

J&R Incorporated / 714-476-2788
4040 McArthur Blvd., #220, Newport Beach, CA 92660

Jasin, Mark
Rep: Martha Prods., Inc. / 310-204-1771

K Squared, Inc. / 312-421-7345
1242 W. Washington, Chicago, IL 60607

MacPherson, Ron / 310-372-7777

Metafor Imaging / 818-584-4034
39 E. Walnut St., Pasadena, CA 91103

O'Dell Prods., Dale / 602-772-7208
1225-B Tapadero Dr., Dewey, AZ 86327

Pacific Data Images / 408-745-6755
1111 Karlstad Dr., Sunnyvale, CA 94089

$$F = (a \times p)^4$$

Table (2.20). Design

Separators	Separators
Pacific Data Images / 213-960-4042 650 N. Bronson, Ste. 400W, LA, CA 90004	Color Wheel Inc., The / 212-697-2434 227 E. 45th St., NYC, NY 10017
Presentation Source, The / 212-614-4111 230 Park Ave. So., NYC, NY 10003	Colorfast / 212-929-2440 121 Varick St., NYC, NY 10013
R/GA Print / 212-239-6767 350 W. 39th, NYC, NY 10018	ColourWorks / 615-876-7268 7535 Hickory Hills Ct., White Creek, TN 37189
Raphaele, Inc. / 713-524-2211 616 Hawthorne St., Houston, TX 77006	Dynagraf, Inc. / 617-268-1900 147 W. Fourth St., Boston, MA 02127
Struther, Doug Rep: Renard Represents / 212-490-2450 Rep: Artco / 212-889-8777	Earth Color / 212-564-2500 424 W. 33rd St., 12th Fl., NYC, NY 10001
Studio Q / 212-343-1108 285 W. Broadway, NYC, NY 10013	Final Film / 213-655-4501 470 S. San Vincente Blvd., LA, CA 90048
T-Square Etc. / 310-826-7033 1990 S. Bundy Dr., #190, LA, CA 90025	Four Color Imports / 502-896-9644 2843 Brownsboro Rd., Ste. 102, Louisville, KY 40206
Tcherevkoff, Michael / 212-229-1733 15 W. 24th St., NYC, NY 10010	G2 Graphices / 213-467-7828 7014 Sunset Blvd, LA, CA 90028
Varis Photo Media / 213-874-0129 922 N. Formosa Ave., LA, CA 90046	Goodsight Images, Inc. / 212-645-6100 216 W. 18th St., NYC, NY 10011
Waltzer Digital Services Inc., Carl / 212-475-8748 873 Broadway, #412, NY, NY 10003	Harris Graphics / 615-885-3616 219 Shady Grove Rd., Nashville, TN 37214
World Graphics / 213-874-1571 3421 W. Cahuenga Blvd., Hollywood, CA 90068	L.A. Filmco, Inc. / 818-848-3509 2070 Floyd St., Burbank, CA 91504

Separators	
Absolute Color Corp. / 212-868-0404 130 W. 30th St., NYC, NY 10001	M&B Graphics & Co. / 818-980-9494 6934 Tuganga Ave., N. Hollywood, CA 91605
Amko Color U.S.A. / 212-687-0400 301 Madison Ave, 5th Fl., NYC, NY 10017	Manhattan Color Graphics / 212-697-2434 227 E. 45th St., NYC, NY 10017
Bergeron, Friedricks / 818-563-4721 3140 Damon Way, Burbank, CA 91505	Pacific Rim Int'l Printing / 800-952-6567 / 310-207-6336 11726 San Vincente Blvd, Ste.280, LA, CA 90049
Business Link / 212-268-0777 / 800-969-8973 312 Fifth Ave., NYC, NY 10001	Pixel Tone / 212-691-8585 216 W. 18th St., 9th Fl., NYC, NY 10011
Color Separation, Inc. / 713-868-1100 1100 W. 23rd St., Houston, TX 77008	Separations Unlimited / 804-794-4864 11501 Allecingie Pkwy, Richmond, VA 23235
	Unlimited Color / 314-849-1181 11037 Gravois Industrial Court, St. Louis, MO 63128
	Waltzer Digital Services Inc., Carl / 212-475-8748 873 Broadway, #412, NY, NY 10003

gravity *causes* all masses to *move* toward each other ________________________ .

(3 . A)

jump

and the earth

will rise

to meet you

$$\text{illustrators} \times \frac{\text{(representatives + stock agencies)}}{} \; .$$

(3 . B)

PATRICK CUNNINGHAM 718.625.6902

WaxTrax! Records: The first 13 years.
BlackBox
913 642 6607 (voice)   913 642 5006 (fax)   djnvr@aol.com (e-mail)

ERIC DINYER

PLEASE DO NOT BEND COW
REGISTERED MAIL
CUT CUT CUT CUT
HOWDY
SECURITY REGISTERED
L.A. TIMES MAGAZINE
TV TIMES
WOMEN'S SPORT & FITNESS
THE WASHINGTON POST
AMERICAN MEDICAL NEWS
CALL RICK SEALOCK
ELECTRONIC ENTERTAINMENT
CALL: 403·276·5428
STUDIO FAX
BANZAI
EATS LTD.
PSYCHOLOGY TODAY
GUITAR PLAYER
SOME CLIENTS: US
FORUM MAGAZINE
ALSO IN:
AMERICAN ILLUSTRATION 12, 13
Society of NEWSPAPER DESIGN
Communication Arts 34, 35
AMERICAN SHOWCASE 18
THE STUDIO MAGAZINE AWARDS
'92 '93 '94

Anita Kunz

tel 416-364-3846   fax 416-368-3947

HENDERSON TYNER ART CO.
PH.910.748.1364

SERIES #

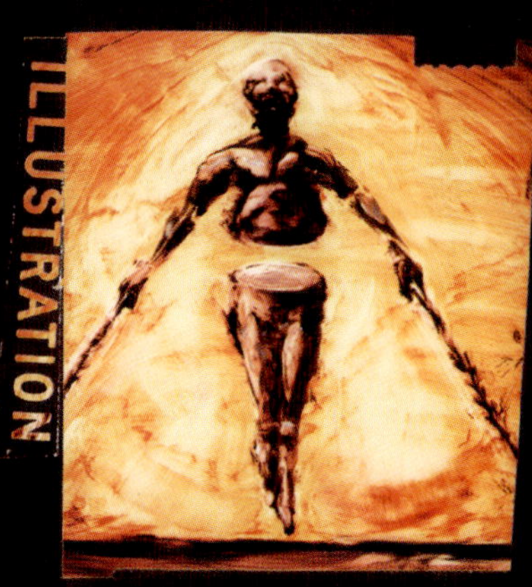
ILLUSTRATION

DAVID MISCONISH

404-231-9711

Jordin Isip 718-624-6538

Clients Include: The Atlantic Monthly, Atlantic Records, Entertainment Weekly, GQ, Ray Gun,
Rolling Stone, Sony Music, Spin, Time and The New York Times

Melinda Beck 718-624-6538

Clients Include: MTV, Nike, Island Records, Polygram Records, Rolling Stone, Spin, Ray Gun,
Entertainment Weekly, Ms. Magazine and The New York Times

Voo-Doo Lounge Entry
"Eve"

Voo-Doo Lounge Entry
"Metallic Bird Mask"

Cheshire Map Cat
Globe & Mail, CANADA

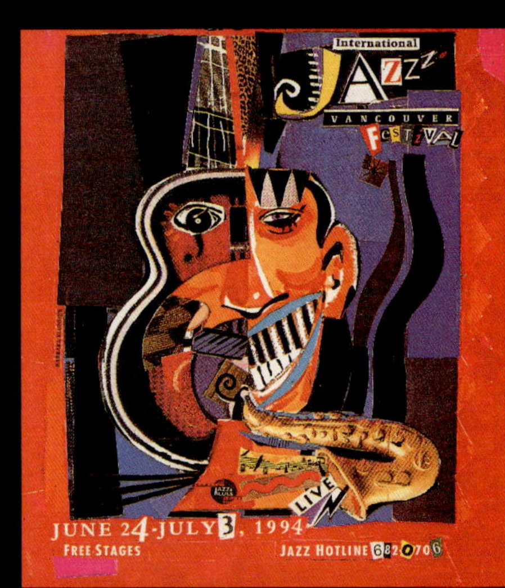

Jazz Poster
Vancouver, CANADA

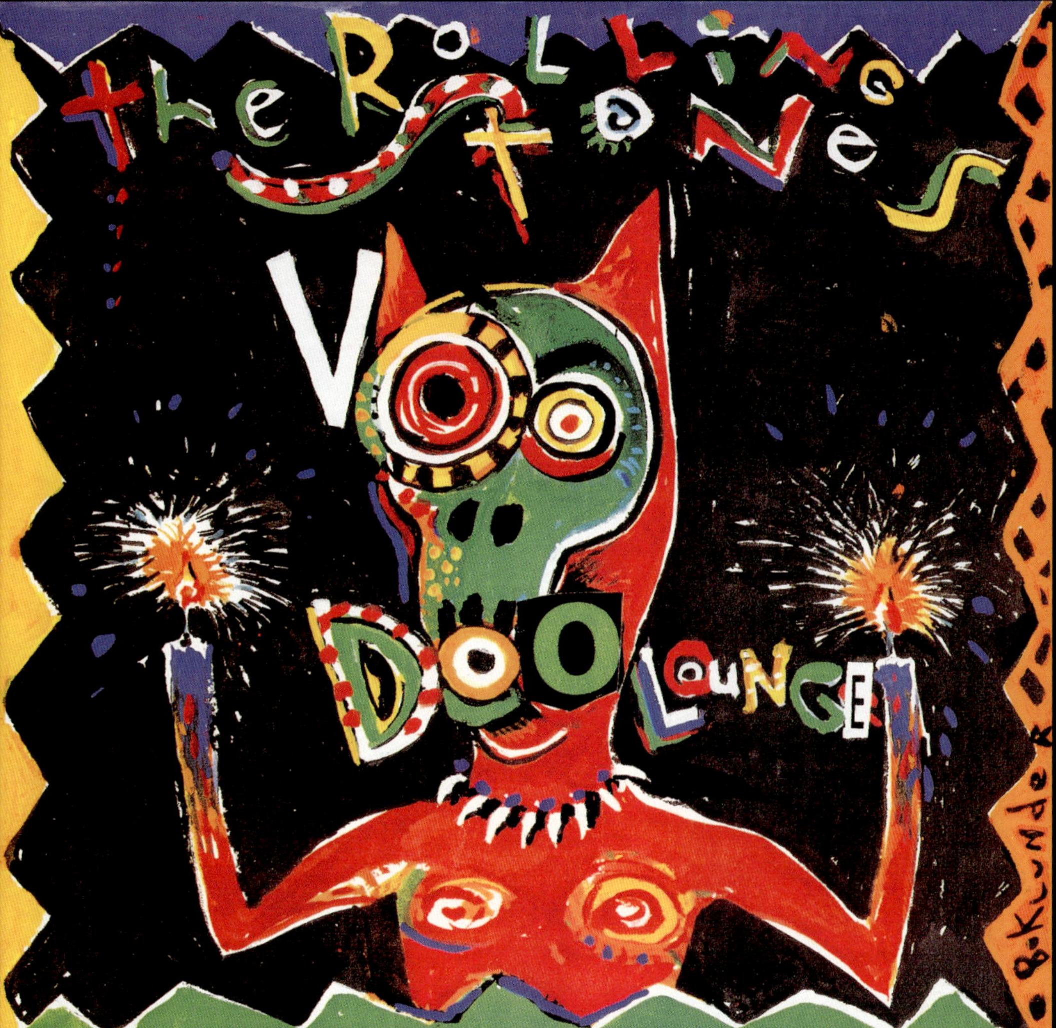

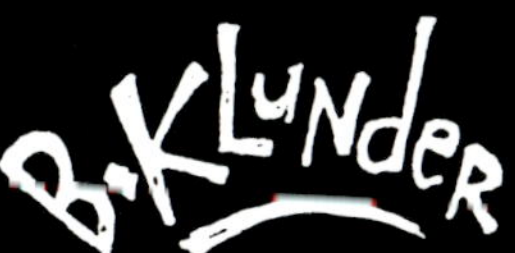

Rolling Stone's Voo-Doo Lounge
'94 Tour T-shirt

B.Klunder

Barbara Klunder, through Rep Art in Seattle (206) 281-0960, in Vancouver (604) 684-6826.

steven
LYONS
illustratio
415.459.7560
fax.453.8657
e-mail: slyons@aol.com

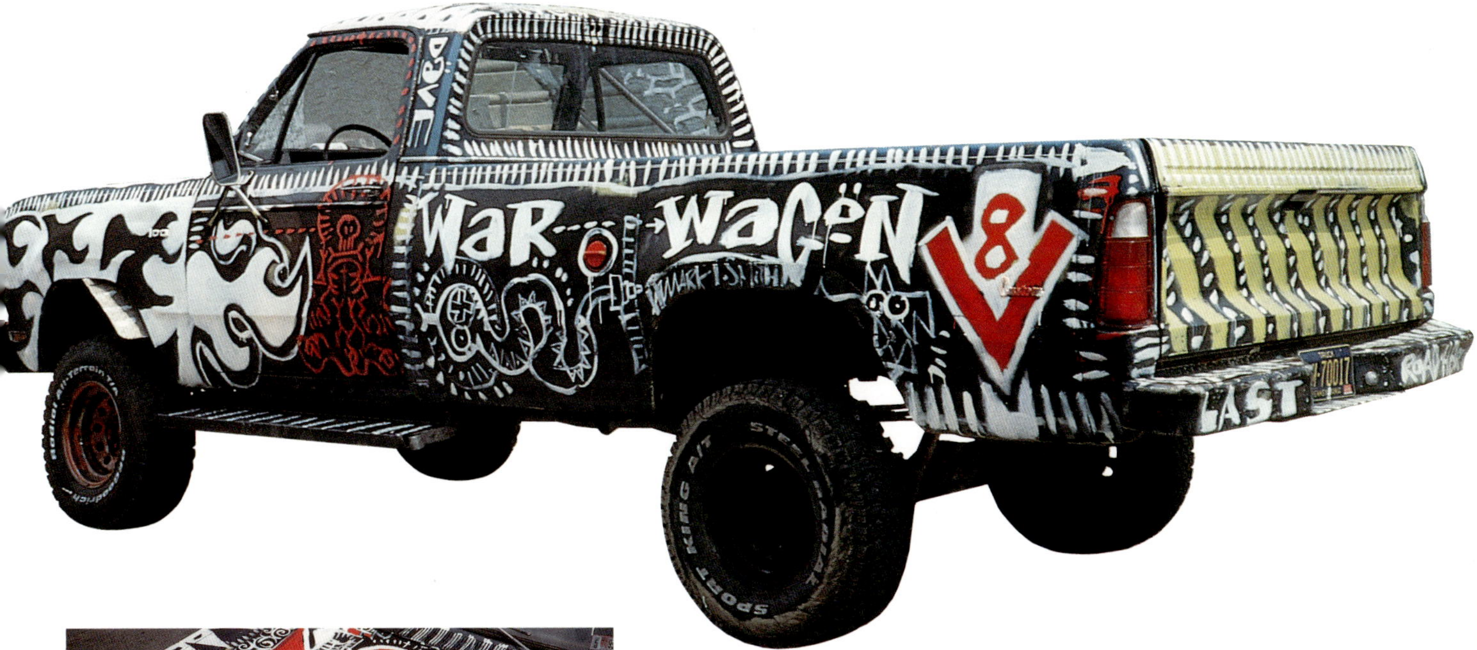

IN THE CITY OF ANGELS: (310)·281·5504

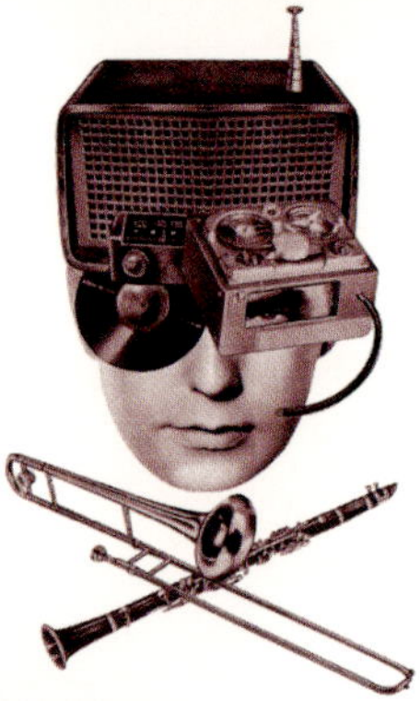

not
always
digital
unconventional
always

Proven good enough
for Time-Warner,
Recording Industry
Assoc. of America,
Rolling Stone and
many more.

created digitally for the 1993 Recording Industry Association Annual Report. Copyright 1994 David Plunkert. Musical cyborgs

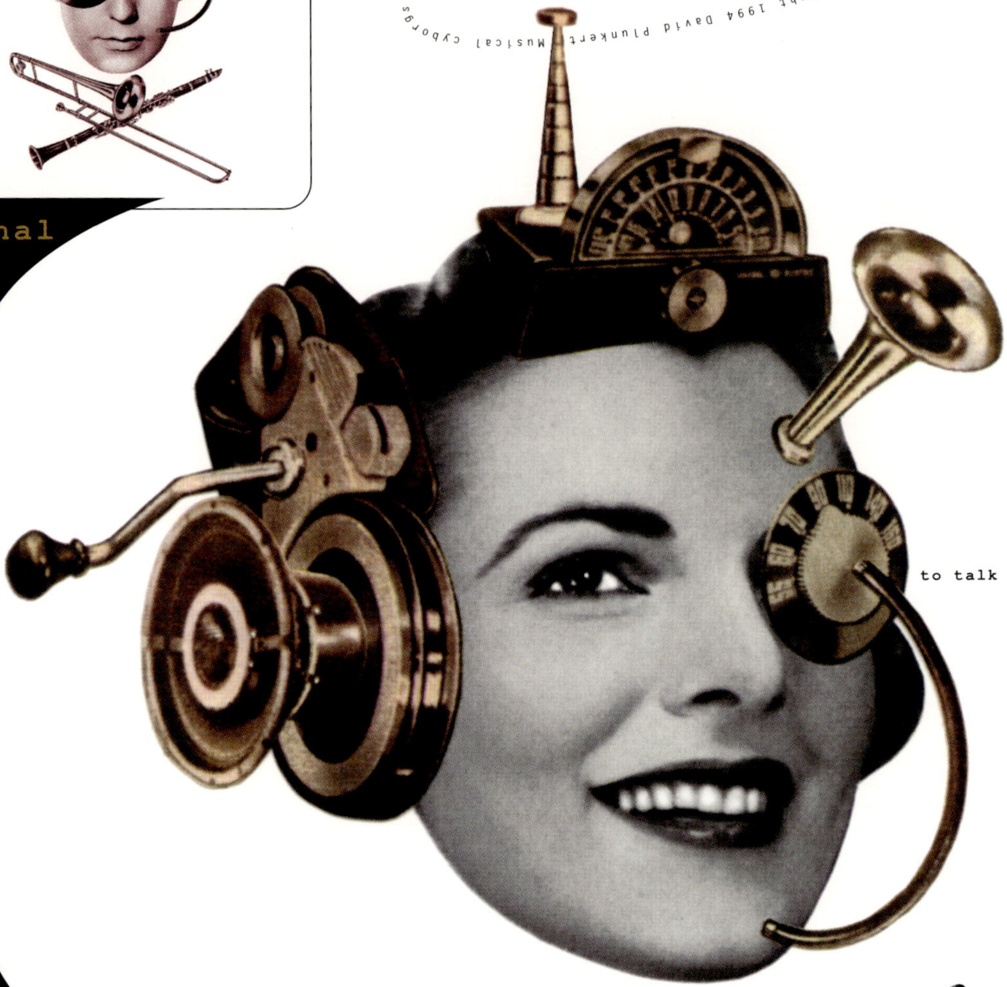

410 235.7803

to talk or send

David

PLUNKERT

Design + Illustration by David Plunkert

ask for "Dave"

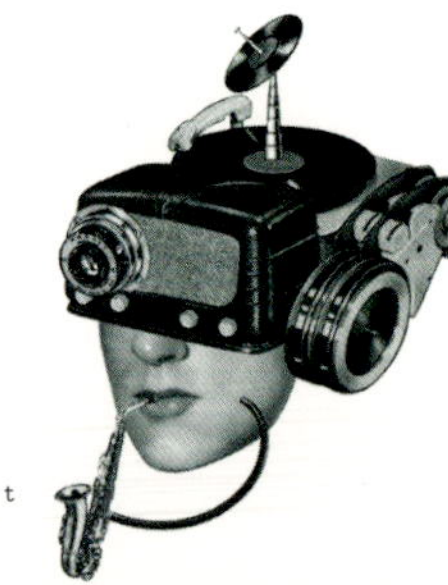

CAUTION: HIGH POWERED ILLUSTRATION
(908) - 382 - 5641. 908 - 382 - 5641. 908 - 382 -
5641. 382 -
5641 - 382
5641. 382 -
5641 382 -
564 382 -
5641. 382 -
564 - 382
KAI ART

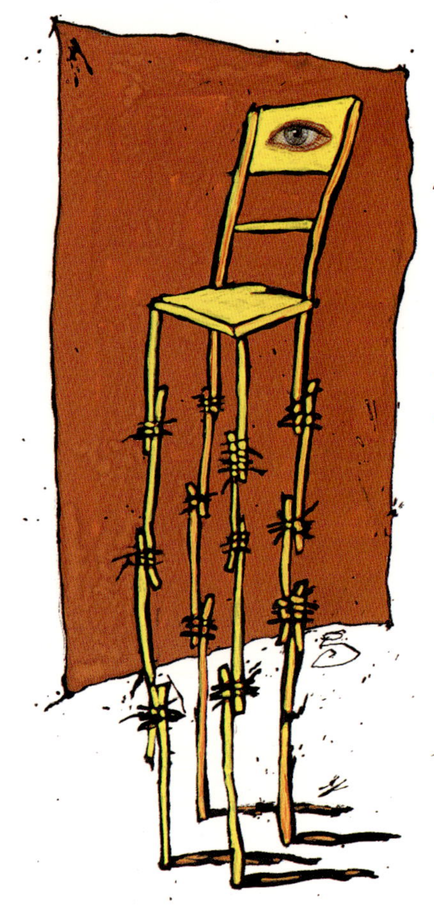

C O U R T N E Y
G R A N N E R

328 N. FIFTH STREET
PATTERSON, CA 95363
209.892.2973
FAX 209.892.3479

EDMUND GUY 309 RACE TRACK ROAD HOHOKUS NEW JERSEY 07423 201 251 7660

ROBOTA
BOB CONGE 716-473-0291

LESLIE BARANY
COMMUNICATIONS
121 WEST 27 STREET
SUITE 202 NEW YORK
NEW YORK 10001
TEL 212/627-8488
FAX 212/463-7983

DIMITRIOS PATELIS

B I L L**BOYKO**

TEL 4 1 6 . 6 5 6 . 6 6 1 6 FAX 4 1 6 . 6 5 6 . 6 6 6 4

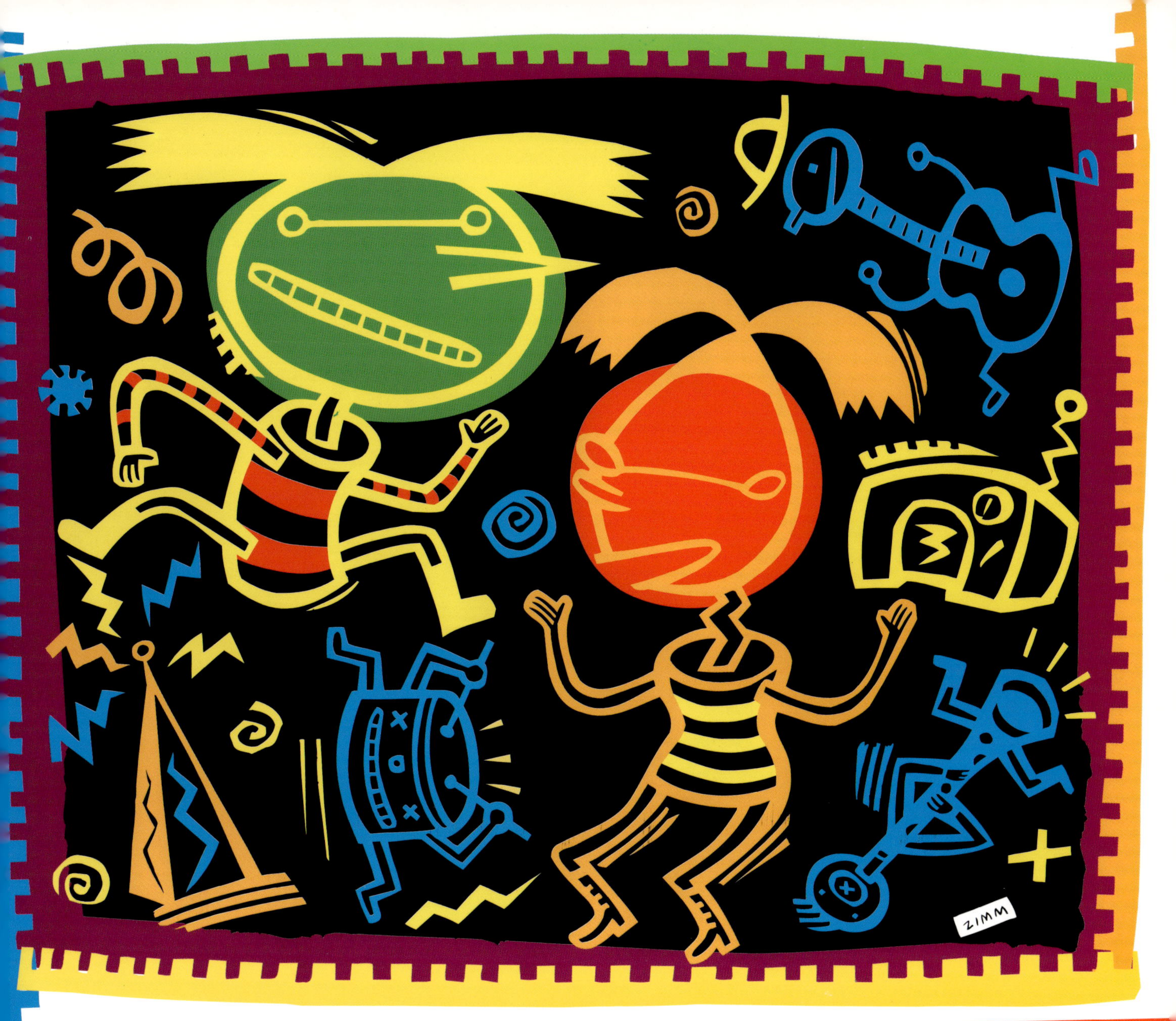

Did this drawing for my favorite AAA radio station, WNCW. They paid me with ten really cool CD's. one coffee thermos, enough tee-shirts for me and my family, two bumper stickers, ten songs in a row by request, two coffee mugs, a long chat with my favorite DJ, two buttons,and a years dues to public radio. They offered me two third row tickets to see Eric Clapton but I couldn't go. Thanks to WNCW.

Robert Zimmerman (704) 252 9689

R Zimm@AOL.com

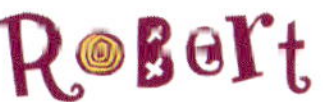

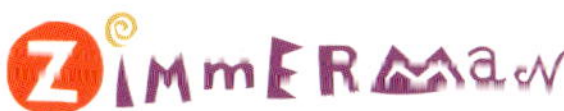

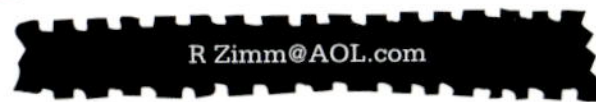

SANDRA
DAVE
619·298·0414
ME
ASMUSSEN

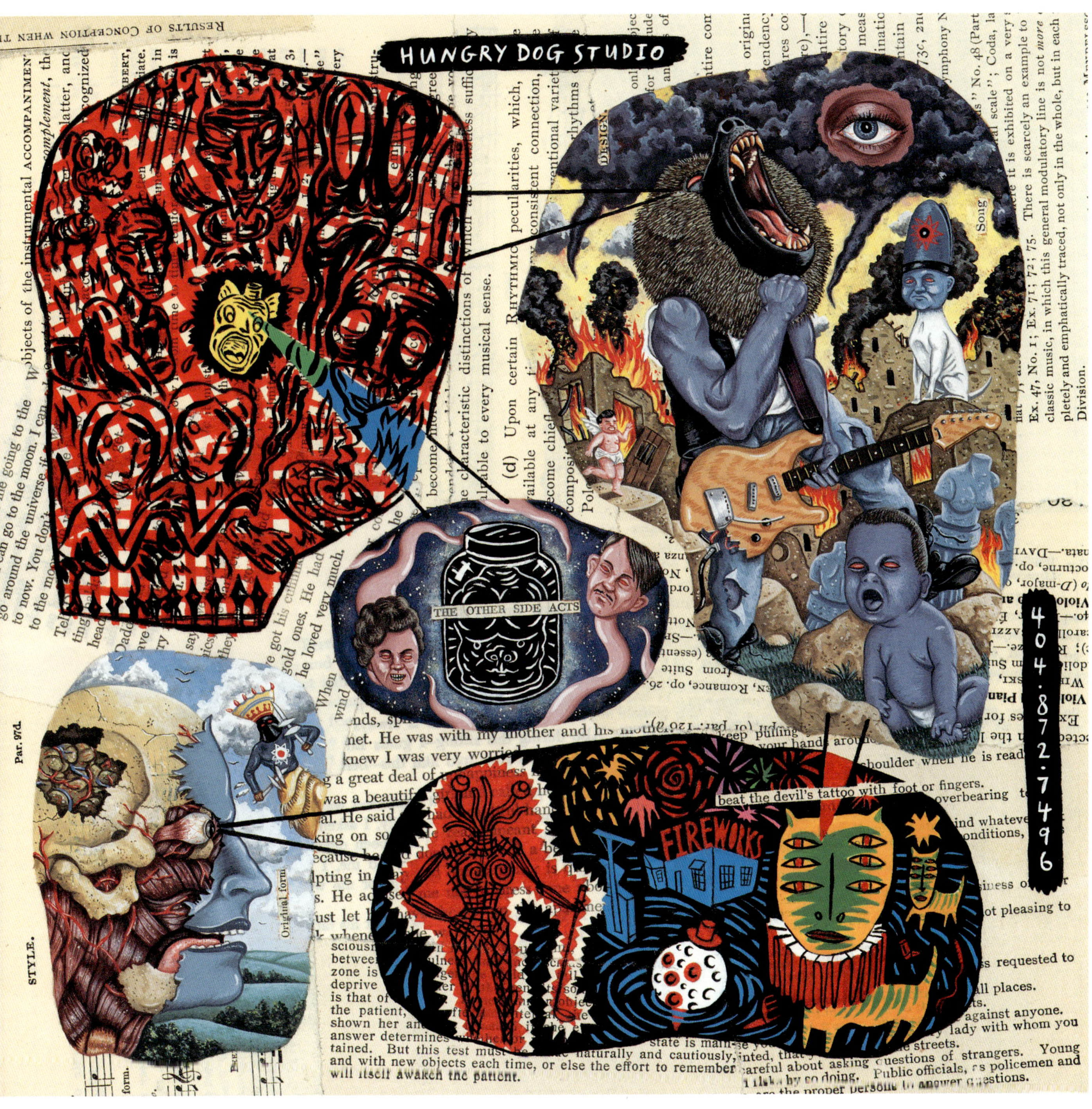

HUNGRY DOG STUDIO
THE OTHER SIDE ACTS
FIREWORKS
404.872.7496

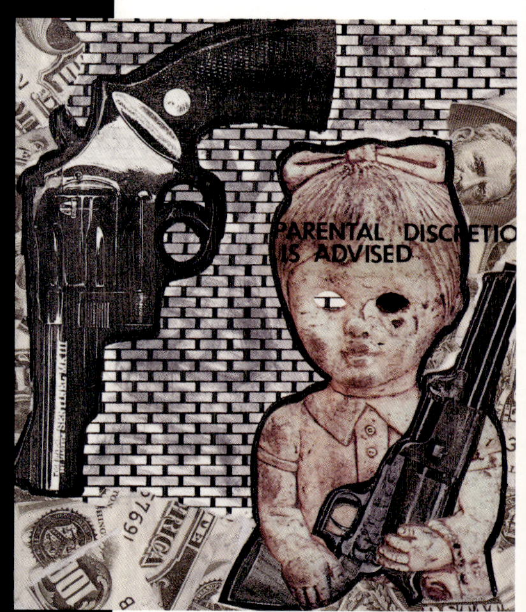

DONNA MC CORMACK

718. 229.7939

REF. NO. 11
NAME OF ARTIST . . . . . . JOELLE NELSON
DESCRIPTION . . . . DATE PREPARATION (ADJUSTING)
JANE JENNI
REPRESENTATIVE
472 PORTLAND AVE.
ST. PAUL, MN 55102
TEL. 612 224 6763
114

SCOTT ROBERTS ILLUSTRATOR

PHIL BOATWRIGHT
214·222·7571

WALTER
HUSTON
STREET SCENE
A MUSICAL PLAY OF MAGNIFICENCE AND GLORY!
BROADWAY THEATRE

THOSE 3 REPS
214·871·1316

StanislawFernandes

TELEPHONE (212) 533 2648
FAX (212) 353 0131

StanislawFernandes

TELEPHONE (212) 533 2648
FAX (212) 353 O131

DEBRA OSTROKOLOWICZ • 508.943.8451

Joe Ciardiello   2182 Clove Rd. Staten Island, NY 10305 (718)727-4757

Johnson
julie johnson
represented by Anita Grien
(2 1 2)   6 9 7 - 6 1 7 0
fax: (212) 697-6177 • 155 East 38th St • NYC 10016
Clients include:
Showtime Network Inc.,
Arts & Entertainment Network,
Levi Strauss & Co.,
L'Oreal, Revlon,
Bloomingdales, Macy's,
Saatchi & Saatchi, Publicis,
Lintas, Nynex, IBM,
Playboy, Cosmopolitan,
San Francisco Magazine,
Simon & Schuster, Doubleday,
Macmillan, HBJ
Johnson

Lydia J. Hess
Illustration
Phone 503-234-4757
Fax 503-233-1330

Pete Spino
619.225.9476
Portfolios
upon request

...LET IT RING...
...LET IT RING...
THE MACHINE WILL ANSWER IT...
THE MACHINE WILL ANSWER IT...
...LET IT RING...
...LET IT RING...
HELLO, I AM NOT HOME
NOT HOME

GINA R. BINKLEY

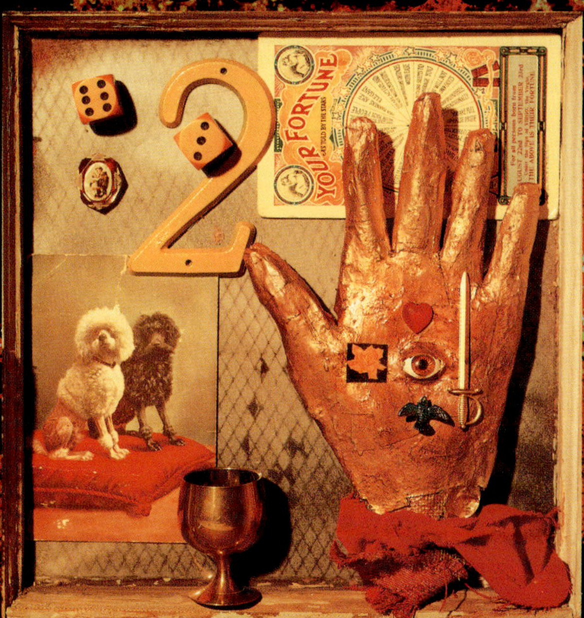

(3-D illustration)
nashville, tennessee
615.256.1110

"RARE MEAT"
[DAVID McMACKEN]
1983
RHINO RECORDS
PHONE & FAX 707 996-5239
THE CUCAMONGA TAPES

JOHN RITTER *illustration*

415.922.8577

san francisco, california

The Meices - Tastes Like Chicken   London/Polygram Records

eric white illustration
1142 Castro St
San Francisco CA 94114

Spotlight - Kurt Cobain   Time Magazine

P 415.821.3839
F 415.821.2034

Bantam Books
Bill Graham Presents
Business Week
Entertainment Weekly
Harper Collins
Los Angeles Times
Mondo 2000
Movieline
Virgin Interactive

Reflections on Sexual Harassment   Gentlemen's Quarterly

CYBeR KuTz
JOHN MURRAY ILLUSTRATION
617·424·0024

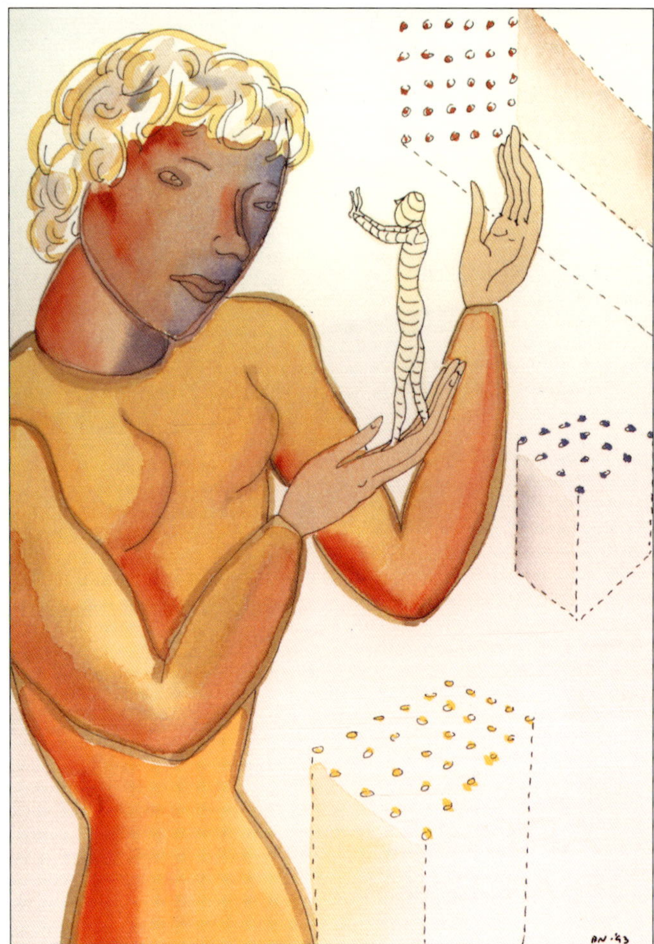

ATT•American Express

CBS•Fortune•Glamour

IBM•Levi Strauss

Foote, Cone, & Belding

New York Magazine

Lincoln Center•Mademoiselle

Newsweek•Time

Rolling Stone•Traveler

Barbara Nessim

63 Greene Street

NYC, NY 10012

Tel 212•219•1111

Fax 212•219•0989

BALOGH
ILLUSTRATION
DENNIS BALOGH
8183 JOYCE RD.
BROADVIEW HTS.
OHIO 44147
(216) 996-3556
(216) 546-9223

Kevin Peake

Mark Falls

Elvis Brook

...stration agents   tel: 305 576 0142   fax: 305 576 0138   toll free: 800 484 8592 [2787]

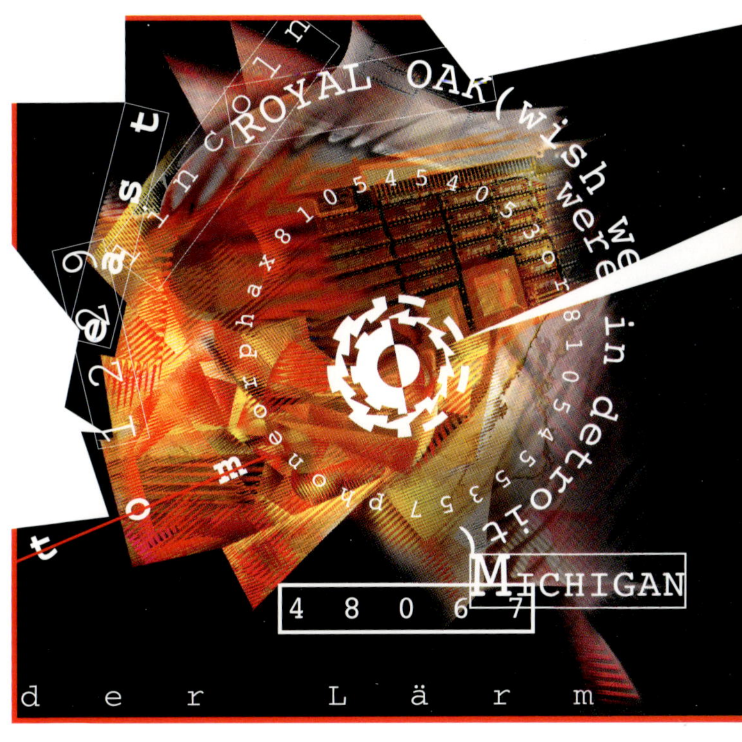

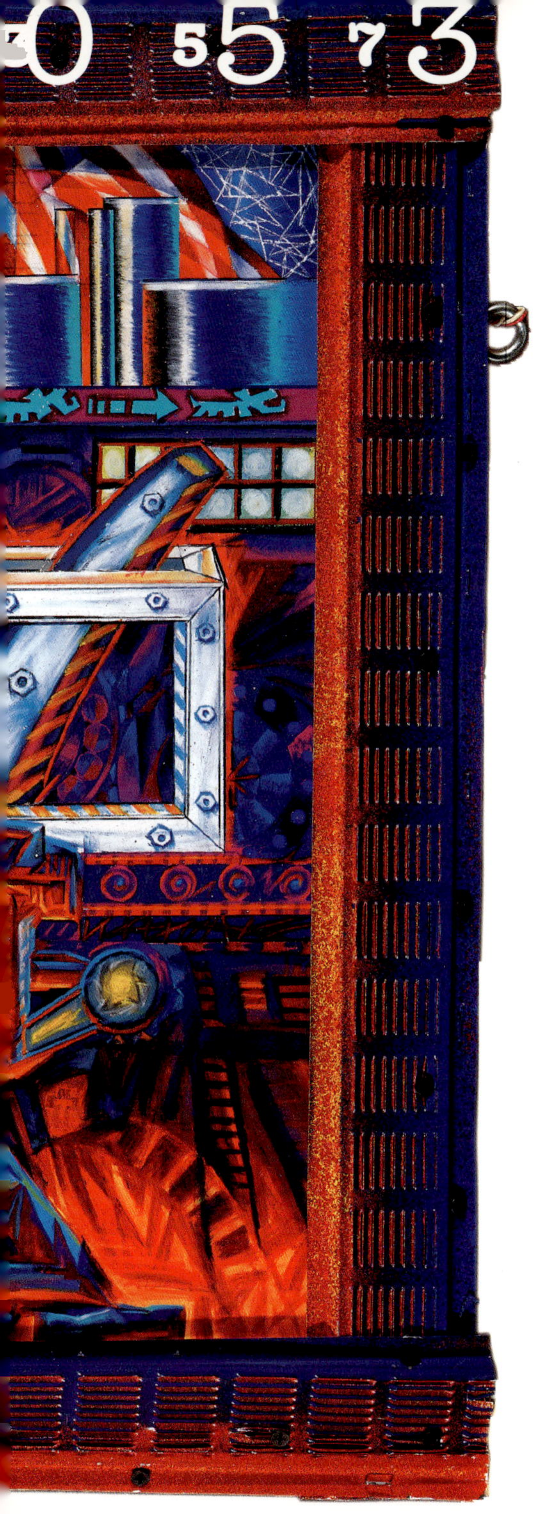
0 55 73

t o m
12 east lincoln
ROYAL OAK (wish we were in detroit)
MICHIGAN
4 8 0 6 7
d e r L ä r m

0 6   7 4 2   4 9 7 4

VOLVO
piven (212) 691-5133

LISA ADAMS ILLUSTRATION

TEL. 212.385.8189   FAX 212.385.9630

MARIA RENDON

TELS: (909)889-8979
(213)687-3664
FAX: (909)888-9932

6997 PERRIS HILL ROAD, SAN BERNARDINO CALIFORNIA 92404

CHANG PARK ILLUSTRATION
52-05 39th Rd. #2A, Woodside, NY 11377
(718) 651-3764

SERGIO BARADAT · 212 · 721 · 2588

Cherie
Bender

farfalla

305 • 891 • 1629

12105 N.E.
6th Ave Suite 404
Miami, Fla.
33161

53

dOugLas aNdeLin
415.927.1945
[party line]

dOUgLaS aNdELiN
415.927.1945
[work line]

LYNN GREEN ROOT

voice 601 366 5780   fax 601 939 1977

$$\overline{\text{illustrators} \times (\text{representatives} + \text{stock agencies})} \ .$$

(3.1)

$$F = (a \times p)^4$$

TABLE (3.2). ILLUSTRATION

Illustration Representatives	Illustration Representatives
Aline Inc., France / 213 933-2500 1076 S. Ogden Dr., LA, CA 90019	Braun, Kathy / 415-775-3366 75 Water St., SF, CA 94133
American Artists / 212-682-2462 353 W. 53rd St., NYC, NY 10019	Brooke & Company / 214-352-9192 4323 Bluffview Blvd., Dallas, TX 75209
Anders, Phil / 919-929-0011 307 Saint Thomas Dr., Chapel Hill, NC 27514	Cary & Company / 404-296-9666 / 404-296-9666 666 Bantry Lane, Stone Mt., GA 30083
Anderson, Paula / 312-321-0848 405 N. Wabash, Ste. 1212, Chicago, IL 60611	Collier, Jan / 415-383-9026 1205 W. California Ave., Mill Valley, CA 94941
Anton, Jerry / 212-633-9880 119 W. 23rd St., #203, NYC, NY 10011	Collignon, Daniele / 212-243-4209 200 W. 15th St., NYC, NY 10011
Art Source, The / 914-747-2220 P.O. Box 257, Pleasantville, NY 10570	Conrad, James / 415-921-7140 2149 Lyon St., #5, SF, CA 94115
Artco / 212-889-8777 / 203-222-8777 232 Madison Ave., Ste. 402, NYC, NY 10016	Cormany, Tom / 310-578-2191
Artists Associates / 212-755-1365 3788 Mill St., Shrub Oak, NY 10588	Cornell Agents / 310-301-8059 737 Milwood Ave., Venice, CA 90291
Artworks / 212-260-4153 89 Fifth Ave., Ste. 901, NYC, NY 10003	Creative Advantage / 518-370-0312 620 Union St., Schnectady, NY 12035
Asciutto Art Representatives, Inc. / 602-899-0600 1712 E. Butler Circle, Chandler, AZ 85225	Creative Freelancers / 212-398-9540 25 W. 45th St., NYC, NY 10036
Ayerst, Deborah / 415-567-3570 2546 Sutter St., SF, CA 94115	Creative Resource/Sylvia Franks, The / 310-276-5282 12056 Summit Circle, Beverly Hills, CA 90210
Baker, Kolea / 206-784-1136 2814 N.W. 72nd St., Seattle, WA 98117	Dedell, Jacqueline / 212-741-2539 58 W. 15th St., NYC, NY 10011
Barany Communications, Leslie / 212-627-8488 121 W. 27th St., Ste. 202, NYC, NY 10001 page 19	de Moreta, Linda / 510-769-1421 1839 Ninth St., P.O. Box 587, Alameda, CA 94501
Barracca & Assoc., Sal / 212-889-2400 381 Park Ave. So., NYC, NY 10016	Dodge, Sharon & Associates / 206-622-7035 1201 First Ave. So., Ste. 202, Seattle, WA 98134
Bartels Associates, Ceci 314-781-7377 / 212-912-1877 / 312-786-1560 3286 Ivanhoe, St. Louis, MO 63139	Ella, Inc. / 617-266-3858 / 212-972-8800 229 Berkeley St., Boston, MA 02116
Bernstein & Andriulli, Inc. / 212-682-1490 60 E. 42nd St., NYC, NY 10165	Famous Frames / 310-558-3325 5183 Overland Ave., Ste. A, Culver City, CA 90230
Berstein, Joanie / 612-374-3169 817 S. Westwood Dr., Minneapolis, MN 55416-3354	Fiat & Associates, Randi / 312-663-5300 1727 S. Indiana Ave., Chicago, IL 60616
	Foster, Pat / 212-685-4580 22 E. 36th St., Ste. 7, NYC, NY 10016

$F = (a \times p)^4$

Illustration Representatives	Illustration Representatives
Fox Art / 213-653-6484 8350 Melrose Ave., Ste. 201, LA, CA 90069	Head Productions / 718-624-1906 42 Delavan St., Brooklyn, NY 11231
Freeman, Lisa / 317-920-0068 740 E. 52nd St., Indianapolis, IN 46205	Hedge, Joanne / 213-874-1661 1838 El Cerrito Pl., #3, Hollywood, CA 90068
Friend & Johnson / 312-943-7885 676 St. Clair, #1550, Chicago, IL 60611	Holland, Mary & Company / 602-263-8990 6638 N. 13th St., Phoenix, AZ 85014
Friend & Johnson / 310-829-4326 1240 Harvard, #2, Santa Monica, CA 90404	Holmberg, Irmeli / 212-545-9155 280 Madison Ave., Ste. 1010, NYC, NY 10016
Friend & Johnson / 214-559-0055 3624 Oak Lawn Ave., Ste. 300, Dallas, TX 75219	Hull Associates, Scott / 513-433-8383 68 E. Franklin St., Dayton, OH 45459
Friend & Johnson / 212-808-0022 325 E. 41st St., Ste. 604, NYC, NY 10017	Incandescent Ink, Inc. / 305-454-6566 1849 S. Ocean Dr., Ste. 514, Hallandale, FL 33009
George, Nancy / 213-655-0998 7811 Waring Ave., LA, CA 90046	Jaz & Jaz / 206-282-8558 223 Prospect St., Seattle, WA 98109
Goldman Agency, David / 212-807-6627 41 Union Square, W., NYC, NY 10003	→ Jenni, Jane / 612-224-6763 472 Portland Ave., St. Paul, MN 55102 page 25
Goodman, Munro / 312-321-1336 405 N. Wabash Ave., #3112, Chicago, IL 60611	Jett & Associates / 502-635-1401 1408 S. Sixth St., Louisville, KY 40208
Gordon, Barbara / 212-686-3514 165 E. 32nd St., NYC, NY 10016	Johnson Associates, Evelyne / 212-532-0928 201 E. 28th St., NYC, NY 10016
Gouch, Kathy / 415-285-9911 148 Park St., SF, CA 94110	Kahn, Harvey / 201-467-0223 155 Millburn Ave., Millburn, NJ 07041
Graham, Corey / 415-956-4750 Pier 33 North, SF, CA 94111	Kamin & Assoc., Vincent / 312-787-8834 111 E. Chestnut, Ste. 256, Chicago, IL 60611
→ Grien, Anita / 212-697-6170 155 E. 38th St., NYC, NY 10016 page 32	Kastaris, Harriet / 314-773-2600 3301A S. Jefferson St., St. Louis, MO 63118
Hackett, Pat / 206-447-1600 101 Yesler Way, #502, Seattle, WA 98104-2552	Kimche, Tania / 212-242-6367 425 W. 23rd St., #10F, NYC, NY 10011
Hahn, Holly / 312-338-7110 707 N. Halsted St., P102, Chicago, IL 60622	Klimt, Bill & Maurine / 212-799-2231 15 W. 72nd St., #7U, NYC, NY 10023
Hankins & Tegenborg Ltd / 212-867-8092 60 E. 42nd St., #1940, NYC, NY 10165	Knable & Associates, Inc., Ellen / 310-855-8855 1233 S. La Cienega Blvd, LA, CA 90035
Hanson & Talent, Jim / 312-337-7770 777 N. Michigan Ave., Chicago, IL 60611	Knecht, Cliff / 412-761-5666 309 Walnut Rd., Pittsburgh, PA 15202
Harlib Associates, Inc., Joel / 312-329-1370 405 N. Wabash Ave., Ste. 3203, Chicago, IL 60611	Korn & Associates, Pamela / 717-595-9298 P.O. Box 521, Canadensis, PA 18325

$$F = (a \times p)^4$$

TABLE (3.4). ILLUSTRATION

Illustration Representatives	Illustration Representatives
Lavaty & Associates, Jeff / 212-355-0910 217 E. 86th St., NY, NY 10028	Pate & Assoc., Inc., Randy / 805-529-8111 P.O. Box 2160, Moorpark, CA 93021
Leff Associates, Jerry / 212-697-8525 420 Lexington Ave., NYC, NY 10170	Penny & Stermer Group, The / 212-505-9342 19 Stuy Oval, Ste. 2D, NYC, NY 10009
Lehmen Dabney, Inc. / 206-325-8595 1431 35th Ave. So., Seattle, WA 98144	Pepper, Missy / 415-543-6881 35 Stillman, #206, SF, CA 94107
Lilie, Jim / 415-441-4384 110 Sutter St., #706, SF, CA 94104	Photocom Inc. / 214-720-2272 3005 Maple Ave., Ste. 104, Dallas, TX 75201
Lindgren & Smith / 212-929-5590 250 W. 57th St., Ste. 916, NYC, NY 10107	Prapas, Christine / 503-246-9511 8402 SW Woods Creek Ct., Portland, OR 97219
Lott, George & Peter / 212-953-7088 60 E. 42nd St., #1146, NYC, NY 10165	→ Rapp, Gerald & Cullen / 212-889-3337 108 E. 35th St., NYC, NY 10016 Design / page 23
Lynch, Alan / 908-813-8718 11 Kings Ridge Rd., Long Valley, NJ 07853	Reactor / 212-967-7699
Manasse, Michele / 215-862-2091 200 Aquetong Rd., New Hope, PA 18938	Renard Represents, Inc. / 212-490-2450 501 Fifth Ave., NYC, NY 10017
Marlena / 212-289-5514 211 E. 89th St., Ste. A1, NYC, NY 10128	→ Rep Art / 206-281-0960 / 604-684-6826 pages 10 - 11
Martha Productions, Inc. / 310-390-8663 11936 W. Jefferson Blvd., Culver City, CA 90230	Repetoire / 214-369-6990 5521 Greenville #104-338, Dallas, Texas 75206
Mattelson, Judy / 212-684-2974 37 Cary Rd., Great Neck, NY 11021	Riley Illustration / 212-989-8770 155 W. 15th St., Ste. 4C, NYC, NY 10011
Mendola Ltd. / 212-986-5680 420 Lexington Ave., #PH, NYC, NY 10170	Rosenthal Represents / 310-390-9595 3443 Wade St., LA, CA 90066
Morgan Associates, Vicki / 212-475-0440 194 Third Ave., NYC, NY 10003	S.I. International / 212-254-4996 43 E. 19th St., 2nd Fl., NYC, NY 10003
Morgan, Michelle / 714-731-2611 129 Avenida Victoria, San Clemente, CA 92672	Salzman, Richard / 415-285-8267 716 Sanchez St, SF, CA 94114
Motion Artists, Inc. / 213-851-7737 1400 N. Hayworth Ave., W. Hollywood, CA 90046	Schuna Group, The / 612-343-0432 30 No. 1st St., #303, Mpls, MN 55401
Neis Group, The / 616-672-5756 11440 Oak Dr., Shelbyville, MI 49344	Scott, Freda, Inc. / 415-621-2992 244 Ninth St., SF, CA 94103
Newborn Group, The / 212-260-6700 270 Park Ave. S., Ste. 8E, NYC, NY 10010	Seigel, Fran / 212-486-9644 515 Madison Ave., #2200, NYC, NY 10022
Palulian, Joanne / 212-581-8338 / 203-866-3734 18 McKinley St., Rowayton, CT 06853	Sharpe + Assocs. / 310-641-8556 7536 Ogelsby Ave., LA, CA 90045

TABLE (3.5). ILLUSTRATION

Illustrators	Illustrators
Siegel, Tema / 212-696-4680 Craven Design 234 Fifth Ave., 4th Fl, NYC, NY 10001	Aizawa, Kaz / 213-254-3362 6140 Monterey Rd., #425, LA, CA 90042 Rep: Irmeli Holmberg / 212-545-9155
Solomon, Richard / 212-683-1362 121 Madison Ave., #5F, NYC, NY 10016	Ajhar, Brian / 717-595-3782 Rep: Pamela Korn / 717-595-9298
Storyboards / 310-305-1998 4052 Del Rey Ave., Ste. 108, Venice, CA 90292	Allen, Julian Rep: Lindgren & Smith / 212-929-5590
Straightline / 310-396-1213 279 S. Beverly Dr., Ste. 677, Beverly Hills, CA 90212	Allen, Terry / 718-727-0723 164 Daniel Low Terrace, Staten Island, NY 10301
Sweet Represents / 415-433-1222 716 Montgomery St., SF, CA 94111	Alonso, Erika / 212-727-1255
→ Those 3 Reps / 214-871-1316 2909 Cole, Ste. 118, Dallas, TX 75204 page 27	Altamore, Vincent / 718-263-2264 152-48 Melbourne Ave., Flushing, NY 11367
→ Tonal Values / 305-576-0142 111 N.E. 42nd St., Miami, FL 33137 page 43	Ameijide, Ray Rep: Gerald & Cullen Rapp / 212-889-3337
Wagoner, Jae / 310-392-4877 654 Pier Ave., Unit C, Santa Monica, CA 90405	Amit, Emmanuel Rep: Gerald & Cullen Rapp / 212-889-3337
Washington, Dick / 210-822-1336 4901 Broadway, Ste. 152, San Antonio, TX 78209	→ Andelin, Douglas / 415-927-1945 19 Bayview Ave., Larkspur, CA 94939 pages 54 - 55
Weber Group, The / 212-799-6532 125 W. 77th St., NYC, NY 10024	Appleton, Douglas / 818-304-1054 360 S. Los Robles Ave., #2, Pasadena, CA 91101
Wiley, David / 415-989-2023 870 Market St., #1053, SF, CA 94102	Archer, Doug Rep: Penny & Stermer Group / 212-505-9342

Illustrators	Illustrators
Abe, George Rep: Kolea Baker / 206 784-1136	Arculus, Callis / 705-432-2789 119 St. John's St., Cannington, Ontario L0E1E0
Abraham, Daniel / 800-372-9748 / 718-499-4006 372 Fifth Ave., Brooklyn, NY 11215	Arion, Katherine / 213-654-6252 / 818-912-3249 1162 N. Orange Grove Ave., W. Hollywood, CA 90046
Acuna, Ed / 203-255-7770 17 Ermine St., Fairfield, CT 06430 Rep: Artco / 212-889-8777	Armes, Steve / 214-721-0164 1509 Glenbrook Dr., Irving, Texas 75061
→ Adams, Lisa / 212-385-8189 40 Harrison St., #29F, NYC, NY 10013 page 49	Asbaghi, Zita / 718-275-1995 104-40 Queens Blvd., Forest Hills, NY 11375
	→ Asmussen, Don / 619-298-0414 3975 Hortensia St., Apt. E6, San Diego, CA 92110 page 22
	Atkins, Bill Rep: Sylvia Franks/ The Cre / 310-276-5282

TABLE (3.6). ILLUSTRATION

Illustrators	Illustrators
Ayers, Alan Rep: Sal Barracca & Assoc. / 212-889-2400	Bates, George / 212-475-3229 160 Third St., #6F, NYC, NY 10009
Bachem, Paul Rep: Artworks / 212-627-1554	Bates, Harry / 914-679-4695 P.O. Box 461, Bearsville, NY 12409
Baker, Don Rep: Kolea Baker / 206-784-1136	Battles, Brian / 619-267-3182 6316 Dissinger Ave., San Diego, CA 92139 Rep: Christine Prapas / 503-246-9511
Baldwin, Christopher Rep: Jaz & Jaz / 206-282-8558	Beach, Pearl Rep: Martha Productions / 310-390-8663
Baldwin, Scott Rep: Jacqueline Dedell / 212-741-2539	→ Beck, Melinda / 718-624-6538 44 Fourth Pl., #2, Brooklyn, NY 11231 page 9
→ Balogh, Dennis / 216-996-3556 / 216-546-9223 8183 Joyce Rd., Broadview Hghts, OH 44147 page 42	Beckdorf, John / 216-932-2489 3296 Ormond, Cleveland Heights, OH 44118
Banthien, Barbara Rep: Lindgren & Smith / 212-929-5590 Rep: Jan Collier / 415-383-9026	Beckerman, Richard / 212-228-3465 326 E. 13th St., #18, NYC, NY 10003
→ Baradat, Sergio / 212-721-2588 210 W. 70th St., PH 1606, NYC, NY 10023 page 52	Ben-Ami, Doron / 203-797-8847
Barnes, Michelle Rep: David Goldman / 212-807-6627	Bendell, Norm Rep: David Goldman / 212-807-6627
Barr, Ken Rep: Jerry Leff / 212-697-8525	→ Bender, Cherie / 305-891-1629 12105 N.E. Sixth Ave., Miami, FL 33161 page 53
Barrett, Andrea / 617-585-5791 164 Elm St., Kingston, MA 02364	Bendis, Keith Rep: David Goldman / 212-807-6627
Barrington, Brian / 714-731-8538 415 W. Main St., Tustin, CA 92680	Bennett, Gary Rep: Jett & Assocs. / 502-635-1401
Bartholomew, Caty / 718-965-0790 198 7th Ave., #4-R, Brooklyn, NY 11215	Benny, Mike / 916-677-9142 2773 Knollwood Dr., Cameron Pk., CA 95682
Bartolos, Michael / 415-863-4569	Benson, Linda Rep: Artworks / 212-627-1554
Baseman, Gary / 718-499-9358 443 12th St., #2D, Brooklyn, NY 11215 Rep: Jan Collier / 415-383-9026	Berendt, Eric / 510-462-6809 1989-A Sauto Rita Rd. #307, Pleasanton, CA 94566
Batchell, Tim / 312-939-6603 202 S. State St., Chicago, IL 60604 Rep: Chris Glenn / 312-670-7737	Bergendorff, Roger Rep: Ceci Bartels Assocs. / 314-781-7377
	Bergin, Robert Rep: Les Mintz / 305-454-6566

TABLE (3.7). ILLUSTRATION

Illustrators	Illustrators
Berkey, John Rep: Jeff Lavaty & Assoc. / 212-355-0910	Bobnick, Dick / 612-881-1008 9801 Dupont Ave. S., Bloomington, MN 55431
Bernstein, Audrey / 212-330-8778 290 Riverside Dr., #2A, NYC, NY 10025	Boehm, Roger / 714-499-6230 31726 Fourth Ave., S. Laguna, CA 92677 Rep: Corey Graham / 415-956-4750
Berrett, Randy Rep: Sweet Represents / 415-433-1222	Boies, Alex Rep: Jerry Leff / 212-697-8525
Biers, Nanette Rep: Vicki Morgan Associate / 212-475-0440	Boll, Maxine Rep: Michele Manasse / 215-862-2091
Billout, Guy / 212-431-6350 225 Lafayette St., Ste 1008, NYC, NY 10012-4015 Rep: France Aline Inc. / 213-933-2500 Rep: Conrad Represents / 415-921-7140	Bonhomme, Bernard Rep: Les Mintz / 305-454-6566
→ Binkley, Gina R. / 615-256-1110 209 10th Ave. So., Ste. 240, Nashville, TN 37203 page 35	Borda, Juliette / 718-624-6004 416 Clinton St., Brooklyn, NY 11231
Birchman, Fred Rep: Lehmen Dabney / 206-325-8595	Bowles, Doug / 816-523-6324 Rep: Richard Salzman / 415-285-8267
Birdseye Hunter / 415-492-9827 650 Bambo Terrace, San Rafael, CA 94903	Boyer-Nelles, Lyn / 616-267-9267 7482 Cook Road, Williamsburg, MI 49690 Rep: The Neis Group / 616-672-5756
Bjorkman, Steve / 714-261-1411 2402 Michelson, #275, Irvine, CA 92715 Rep: Renard Represents / 212-490-2450 Rep: Vincent Kamin / 312-787-8834	→ Boyko, Bill / 416-656-6616 16 Conrad Ave., Toronto, Ontario, Canada M6G3G5 page 20
Blackshear, Thomas / 719-636-5009 220 Elm Circle, Colorado Springs, CO 80906 Rep: France Aline Inc. / 213-933-2500	Bozzini, James Rep: Renard Represents / 212-490-2450
Bleck, Cathie Rep: Jacqueline Dedell / 212-741-2539	Brady, Elizabeth Rep: Jean Conlon / 212-966-9897
Blessen, Karen Rep: Brooke & Company / 214-352-9192 Rep: Vicki Morgan Assoc. / 212-475-0440	Bralds, Braldt / 203-868-7577 Rte. 3 Box 15A, Espanola, NM 87532 Rep: The Newborn Group / 212-260-6700
Bloch, Alex Rep: Asciutto Art Reps / 602-899-0600	Brandt, Kim Wilson / 718-237-8546 219 Crescent Ave., SF, NY 94110
Blubaugh, Susan M. / 212-570-6731 511 E. 81st St., #17, NYC, NY 10028	Braught, Mark Rep: Scott Hull Associates / 513-433-8383
→ Boatwright, Phil / 214-222-7571 2342 Stillwater Dr., Mesquite, TX 75181 Rep: Those 3 Reps / 214-871-1316 page 27	Brawner, Dan / 615-356-1244 732 Richfield Dr., Nashville, TN 37205 Rep: Jett & Assocs. / 502-635-1401
	Brennan, Neil Rep: Jeff Leff Assocs. / 212-697-8525

$$F = (a \times p)^4$$

TABLE (3.8). ILLUSTRATION

Illustrators	Illustrators
Brennan, Steve Rep: Artworks / 212-627-1554	Busch, Lon Rep: Gerald & Cullen Rapp / 212-889-3337
Brice, Jeff Rep: Kolea Baker / 206-784-1136	Bush, George Rep: Sal Barracca & Assoc. / 212-889-2400
Britt, Tracy Rep: Scott Hull Associates / 513-433-8383	Bush, Robert / 310-434-1697 P.O. Box 4830, Long Beach, CA 90804
Broda, Ron Rep: Jerry Leff / 212-697-8525	Bustamente, Gerald / 619-234-8803 2400 Kettner Blvd., Ste. 226, San Diego, CA 92101
Brodner, Steve / 212-740-8174 120 Cabrini Blvd., #116, NYC, NY 10033	Byram, Steve / 201-869-7493 52 68th St. #1, Guttenberg, NJ 07093
Brook, Elvis Rep: Tonal Values / 305-576-0142 page 43	Callanan, Brian Rep: Jerry Leff / 212-697-8525
Brooks, Lou / 212-245-3632 / 609-398-1955	Calver, Dave / 716-383-8996 70 Stoneham Dr., Rochester, NY 14625
Brown, Calef / 512-478-5389 1400 Concordia Ave., Austin, TX 78722 Rep: Lisa Freeman / 317-920-0068	Camejo, John / 410-332-6528 1606 Bramble Court, Bel Air, MD 21015
Brown, Michael David Rep: Gerald & Cullen Rapp / 212-889-3337	Capstone Studios / 213-936-1156 Rep: Randy Pate & Assoc. / 805-529-8111
Brown, Peter / 212-684-7080 235 East 22nd St., #16R, NYC, NY 10010 Rep: Alan Lynch / 908-813-8718	Carruthers, Roy Rep: The Newborn Group / 212-260-6700
Bruce, Sandra / 916-477-1909 13997 Emerald Ct., Grass Valley, CA 95945 Rep: Kathy Braun / 415-775-3366 Rep: Karen Dolby / 312-855-9336	Castellanos, Carlos / 407-791-7993 13174 80th Lane N., W. Palm Beach, FL 33412
Brunnick, Jeanne / 310-798-2771 1233 Hermosa Ave., Hermosa Beach, CA 90254	Castellitto, Mark / 201-939-8049 38 Sixth St., Woodridge, NJ 07075
Bryan, Mike Rep: Jerry Leff / 212-697-8525	Castelluccio, Federico / 201-625-9252 71 Parks Rd., Denville, NJ 07834
Burgard, Tim Rep: Motion Artists / 213-851-7737	Cayard, Bruce / 213-656-7194 2323 Merrywood Dr., LA, CA 90046
Burke, Philip / 716-297-0345 1945 Juron Dr., Niagara Falls, NY 14304	Ceballos, John Rep: Scott Hull Associates / 513-433-8383
Burnett, Lindy Rep: Ceci Bartels Assocs. / 314-781-7377	Cellini, Joseph / 201-944-6519 415 Hillside Ave., Leonia, NJ 07605 Rep: Renard Represents / 212-490-2450
Burns, Charles / 215-925-7618	Chan, Ron Rep: Jim Lilie / 415-441-4384
	Chandler, Karen / 516-671-0388 80 Lattingtown Rd., Locust Valley, NY 11560

TABLE (3.9). ILLUSTRATION

Illustrators	Illustrators
Cheng, Fu-Ding / 310-396-1466 209 Seventh Ave., Venice, CA 90291	→ Ciardiello, Joe / 718-727-4757 page 31
Chermayeff, Ivan Rep: Jacqueline Dedell / 212-741-2539	Cigliano, Bill / 312-973-0062 1525 W. Glenlake Ave., Chicago, IL 60660 Rep: Renard Represents / 212-490-2450
Chernishov, Anatoly / 201-327-2377 4 Willowbank Ct., Mahwah, NJ 07430	Clark, Bradley Rep: Penny and Stermer / 212-505-9342 Rep: Martha Productions / 310-390-8663
Cheung, Phil / 510-839-3975 750 MacArthur Blvd., #103, Oakland, CA 94610 Rep: Conrad Represents... / 415-921-7140	Clarke, Bob Rep: Barbara Gordon Assoc. / 212-686-3514
Chichoni, Oscar Rep: S.I. International / 212-254-4996	Clarke, Greg Rep: Jan Collier / 415-383-9026
Chodos-Irvine, Margaret / 206-624-2480 311 First Ave. S., Rm. 314, Seattle, WA 98104 Rep: Kolea Baker / 206-784-1136	Cleghorne, Stedroy / 718-855-7702 1175 Oxford St., #3, Brooklyn, NY 11217
Choi, Jaeeun / 718-237-0216 70 Clark St., #6C, Brooklyn, NY 11201	Cober, Alan E. / 914-941-8696 95 Croton Dam Rd, Ossining, NY 10562
Chorney, Steven / 805-376-2291 743 Morelia Ct., Thousand Oaks, CA 91360 Rep: Mendola / 212-986-5680 Rep: Joni Tuke / 312-787-6826	Cober-Gentry, Leslie / 203-452-0188 285 Mayfield Dr., Trumble, CT 06611
Chouinard, Roger / 310-451-0771 1026 Montana Ave., Santa Monica, CA 90403 Rep: Ellen Knable / 213-855-8855	Cochran, Bobbye & Assocs. / 312-404-0375 433 W. Webster, Chicago, IL 60614
Christensen, David M. / 714-761-3488 4338 Manchester Pl., Cypress, CA 90630 Rep: S.I. International / 212-254-4996 Rep: Maclaine & Friend / 404-881-6627	Colby, Gary / 412-761-5666 Rep: Mendola / 212-986-5680
Christensen, Kent / 212-744-3050 518 E. 80th St., #7R, NYC, NY 10021	Collicott, Chris / 213-876-5112 1151 1/2 N. La Brea Ave., LA, CA 90038
Christiansen, Lee Rep: Joanie Bernstein / 612-374-3169	Collier, John Rep: Richard Solomon / 212-683-1362
Chui, John Rep: Sylvia Franks / 310-276-5282	Collier, Michele Rep: Vincent Kamin / 312-787-8834 Rep: Linda de Moreta / 510-769-1421
Chwast, Eve Rep: Pushpin Associates / 212-674-8080	Collins, Christopher / 215-248-4641 27 E. Gowan Ave., Philadelphia, PA 19119
Chwast, Seymour 215 Park Ave. So., Ste. 603, NYC, NY 10003 Rep: Pushpin Associates / 212-674-8080	Colon, Raul Rep: The Weber Group / 212-799-6532
	Commander, Bob / 801-649-4356 / 801-649-4356 1565 Village Round Dr., Park City, Utah 84060
	Comp Art Plus / 212-921-1199 49 W. 45th St., NYC, NY 10036

$$F = (a \times p)^4$$

TABLE (3.10). ILLUSTRATION

Illustrators	Illustrators
Comport, Sally Wern / 813-579-4499 750 94th Ave., Ste. 203, St. Petersburg, FL 33702 Rep: Allan Comport / 813-579-4499	Cromwell, Janelle / 213-882-6011 1151 N. Fuller Ave., #3, LA, CA 90046
Conge, Bob / 716-473-0291 28 Harper St., Rochester, NY 14607 page 18	Csicsko, David Rep: Randi Fiat & Assoc. / 312-663-5300
Connelly, Gwen Rep: Jerry Leff / 212-697-8525	Cunningham, Patrick / 718-625-6902 131 Fourth Pl., Brooklyn, NY 11231 page 1
Connor, Todd Rep: Jaz & Jaz / 206-282-8558	Curry, Tom / 915-837-2311 901 W. Sulross, Alpine, TX 79830 Rep: Conrad Represents... / 415-921-7140
Consani, Chris / 310-546-6622 728 33rd St., Manhattan Beach, CA 90266 Rep: Rita Marie & Friends / 312-222-0337	Cusano, Steven R. / 610-565-8829 80 Talbot Ct., Media, PA 19063
Consing, Robert Rep: Motion Artists / 213-851-7737	Custodio, Bernard / 818-998-4242 / 818-705-4065 20103 Baltar St., Canoga Park, CA 91306
Continuity Studios / 212-869-4170 / 818-980-8852 62 W. 45th St., NYC, NY 10036	Czeczot, Andrzej Rep: Marlena / 212-289-5514
Cormier, Wil / 818-303-6066 2251 Oakshade Rd., Bradbury, CA 91010 Rep: Bill & Maurine Klimt / 212-799-2231 Rep: Famous Frames / 310-558-3325	D'Andrea, Bernard Rep: Jeff Lavaty & Assoc. / 212-355-0910
Cornelius, Ray-Mel / 214-946-9405 1526 Elmwood Blvd., Dallas, TX 75224 Rep: Friend and Johnson / 214-559-0055	Daggar, Elizabeth / 718-596-1858 216 Washington Ave., Brooklyn, NY 11205
Cosgrove, Dan Rep: Daniele Collignon / 212-243-4209	Daily, Don Rep: Jeff Lavaty & Assoc. / 212-355-0910
Couch, Greg Rep: Betsy Hillman / 415-391-1181 Rep: Joanne Paululian / 203-866-3734	Daley, Joann Rep: Mendola / 212-986-5680
Cox, Paul Rep: Richard Solomon / 212-683-1362	Daniels, Sid / 212-673-6520 12 E. 22nd St., NYC, NY 10010
Cozzolino, Paul / 516-795-2432 211 Glengarisff Rd., Massapequa Park, NY 11762 Rep: Marlena / 212-289-5514	Davis, Gary / 617-245-2628 1 Cedar Pl., Wakefield, MA 01880
Craft, Kinuko Y. Rep: Fran Seigel / 212-486-9644	Davis, Jack Rep: Gerald & Cullen Rapp / 212-889-3337 Rep: Richard Solomon / 212-683-1362
Creative Capers Rep: Bernstein & Andriulli / 212-682-1490	Davis, Paul / 212-420-8789 14 E. Fourth St., #504, NYC, NY 10012
	Dawson, John Rep: Fran Seigel / 212-486-9644
	Day, Rob / 317-253-9469 6095 Ralston Ave., Indianapolis, IN 46220

Illustrators	Illustrators
De Barros, A. Martins Rep: S.I. International / 212-254-4996	Detwiler, Darius / 210-662-0603 5018 Fawn Lake, San Antonio, TX 78244 Rep: Dick Washington / 210-822-1336 Rep: Mendola / 212-986-5680
De Michiell, Robert / 212-769-9192 250 West 85th St. #3D, NYC, NY 10024 Rep: Gerald & Cullen Rapp / 212-889-3337	Devlin, Bill Rep: Gerald & Cullen Rapp / 212-889-3337
De Seve, Peter / 718-398-8099 25 Park Pl., Brooklyn, NY 11217	Diaz, David / 619-438-0070 6708 Corinta St., Rancho La Costa, CA 92009
DeAnda, Ruben / 619-421-2845 890 Entrada Pl., Chula Vista, CA 91910	Dierksen, Jane Brunkan / 909-593-7227 5384 Shemiran St., La Verne, CA 91750 Rep: Holly Hahn / 312-338-7110
Deal, Jim / 206-285-2986 3451 24th Ave. W., Seattle, WA 98199 Rep: S.I. International / 212-254-4996	Dietz, Jim Rep: Barbara Gordon Assoc. / 212-686-3514
Dean, Bruce Rep: Nancy George / 213-655-0998	Dillon, Leo & Diane / 718-624-0023 221 Kane St., Brooklyn, NY 11231
Dearth, Greg Rep: Scott Hull Associates / 513-433-8383	Dinges, Michael Rep: Jim Hanson / 312-337-7770
Deas, Michael Rep: Newborn Group / 212-421-0050	Dininno, Steve / 516-431-1495 553 E. Fulton St., Long Beach, NY 11561 Rep: David Goldman / 212-807-6627 Rep: Corey Graham / 415-956-4750
Deas, Michael J. 708 Toulouse St., New Orleans, LA 70130 Rep: The Newborn Group / 212-260-6700	Dinyer, Eric / 913-642-6607 8974 Cedar Dr., Shawnee Mission, KS 66207 dinyr@aol.com pages 2 - 3
Deeter, Catherine Rep: Fran Seigel / 212-486-9644	Dismukes, John / 213-936-1156 Rep: Mendola / 212-986-5680
Delessert, Etienne / 203-435-0061 P.O. Box 1689, Lakeville, CT 06029	Dogue, Maurice / 718-875-2288
Dellorco, Chris Rep: Mendola Artists / 212-986-5680	Doktor, Patricia / 818-769-7321 4118 Beck Ave., Studio City, CA 91604
Delmonico, C. Crist / 201-285-0909 P.O. Box 9040, Morristown, NJ 07960	Dolobosky, Mena Rep: Helen Roman Assocs. / 203-222-1608
der Lärm / 810-545-4053 1229 E. Lincoln, Royal Oak, MI 48067 pages 44 - 45	Doty, Curt Rep: Les Mintz / 305-454-6566
Deschamps, Bob Rep: Gerald & Cullen Rapp / 212-889-3337	Doty, Eldon Rep: Kathy Braun / 415-775-3366
Descombes, Roland Rep: Jeff Lavaty & Assoc. / 212-355-0910	Dougan, Michael / 206-789-5969 5308 Ballard Ave. N.W., Seattle, WA 98107

$$F = (a \times p)^4$$

Table (3.12). Illustration

Illustrators	Illustrators
Downs, Richard / 909-677-3452 24294 Saradella Ct., Murrieta, CA 92562 Rep: Richard Salzman / 415-285-8267	Emerson, Carmela / 718-224-4251 217-11 54th Ave., Bayside, NY 11364 Rep: Creative Freelancers / 212-398-9540
Drawson, Blair / 416-693-7774 14 Leuty Ave., Toronto, Canada M4E2R3 Rep: Reactor / 212-967-7699	Emmett, Bruce Rep: Jeff Lavaty & Assoc. / 212-355-0910
Drescher, Henrik / 510-883-9616 2434 California St., Berkeley, CA 94703	Ericken, Marc / 415-362-1214 1045 Sansome St., #306, SF, CA 94111 Rep: Hankins & Tegenborg / 212-867-8092
Drew, Kim Rep: Jaz & Jaz / 206-282-8558	Erickson, Mary Anne / 914-246-3804 1203 Glasco Tpke, Saugerties, NY 12477
Drucker, Mort Rep: Artco / 212-889-8777	Ernster, Scott / 818-753-1504 12832 Bloomfield St., Studio City, CA 91604 Rep: Carol Chislovsky / 212-677-9100 Rep: Tom Maloney / 312-704-0500
Dudash, C. Michael / 802-496-6400 RR #1, Box 2803, Moretown, VT 05660	
Dudzinski, Andrzej Rep: Conrad Represents... / 415-921-7140 Rep: Vincent Kamin / 312-787-8834	Evans, Robert / 415-397-5322 1045 Sansome, #306, SF, CA 94111 Rep: Sweet Represents / 415-433-1222
Duggan, Lee Rep: Gerald & Cullen Rapp / 212-889-3337	Everitt, Betsy / 510-233-3241 582 Santa Rosa Ave., Berkeley, CA 94707
Duke, Chris Rep: Jeff Lavaty & Assoc. / 212-355-0910	Faia, Don / 408-662-8857 130 Camino Pacifico, Aptos, CA 95003
Dunnick, Regan Rep: Lindgren & Smith / 212-929-5590	Fairman, Dolores Rep: Jacqueline Dedell / 212-741-2539
Dvorak, Philip / 619-223-2776	→ Falls, Mark Rep: Tonal Values / 305-576-0142 page 43
Dykes, John S. / 203-222-8150 17 Morningside Dr. South, Westport, CT 06880	
Dynamic Duo, Inc., The / 203-454-4518 95 Kings Hwy So., Westport, CT 06880 Rep: Gerald & Cullen Rapp / 212-889-3337	Farber, Joan / 805-933-3016 12544 Sisar Rd., Ojai, CA 93023 Rep: Vicki Prentice Assoc. / 310-826-1332
Eberbach, Andrea Rep: Scott Hull Associates / 513-433-8383	Farnsworth, Bill / 203-355-1649 30 Elm St., New Milford, CT 06776
Edwards, Ron / 808-325-6744 / 808-325-6744 Rep: Richard Kapland / 818-223-7004	Fasolino, Teresa Rep: The Newborn Group / 212-260-6700
Eidrigevicius, Stasys Rep: Marlena / 212-289-5514	Febland, David / 212-580-9299 670 West End Ave., #11B, NYC, NY 10025
Eloqui / 301-334-4086 100 G Street, Mt. Lake Park, MD 21550	Feldman, Steve / 805-945-5966 / 818-442-8037 1402 W. Jackman St., Lancaster, CA 93534

TABLE (3.13). ILLUSTRATION

Illustrators	Illustrators
Fernandes, Stanislaw / 212-533-2648 874 Broadway, NYC, NY 10003 pages 28 - 29	Frampton, David Rep: Jacqueline Dedell / 212-741-2539
Fiedler, Joseph Daniel Rep: Lindgren & Smith / 212-929-5590	Fraser, Douglas Rep: Lindgren & Smith / 212-929-5590 Rep: Jan Collier / 415-383-9026
Field, Ann / 310-450-6413 2910 16th St., Santa Monica, CA 90405 Rep: Deborah Ayerst / 415-567-3570	Frazier Design / 415-863-9613
Fine Art Studio / 714-832-6595	Fredrickson, Mark A. / 602-252-5072 853 S. Pantano Pkwy., Tucson, AZ 85710 Rep: Marla Matson / 602-252-5072
Fisher, Carolyn / 406-585-2767 425 S. Black Ave., Bozeman, MT 59715 Rep: Marla Matson / 602-252-5072	Freeman, Helane / 818-891-5558 16717 Bahama St., Northridge, CA 91343
Fisher, Mark Rep: Les Mintz / 305-454-6566	Frisari, Frank / 718-848-5007 78-11 161 Ave., Howard Beach, NY 11414
Flaherty, David / 212-675-2038 1 Union Sq. W., Ste. 914, NYC, NY 10003	Fuchs, Bernie Rep: Harvey Kahn / 201-467-0223
Flatland / 310-394-0322 1128 Ocean Park Blvd., Santa Monica, CA 90405 Rep: Ceci Bartels / 314-781-7377 Rep: Daniele Collignon / 212-243-4209	Funkhouser, Kristen Rep: Richard Salzman / 415-285-8267
Fleming, Stanley / 415-397-4849 559 Pacific Ave., Rm. 35, SF, CA 94133	Gaadt, David Rep: Will Sumpter & Assocs. / 404-874-2014 Rep: Hankins & Tegenborg / 212-967-9092
Flemming, Ron Rep: Conrad Represents... / 415-921-7140 Rep: Bernstein & Andriulli / 212-682-1490	Gabor, Tim / 206-860-0089
Flesher, Vivienne / 415-921-2440	Gadino, Victor Rep: Bernstein & Andruilli / 212-682-1490
Florczak, Robert Rep: Randy Pate & Assoc. / 805-529-8111	Gaetano, Nick Rep: Harvey Kahn / 201-467-0223 Rep: Conrad Represents... / 415-921-7140
Forbes, H. / 212-677-7792 P.O. Box 2383, NYC, NY 10009	Gallagher, James / 718-857-5958 462 Bergen St., #3, Brooklyn, NY 11217
Fox, Brian / 508-674-0511 29 Massasort St., Somerset, MA 02725-1616	Gallardo, Gervasio Rep: Jeff Lavaty & Assoc. / 212-355-0910
Fox, Rosemary Rep: David Goldman / 212-807-6627	Gallipoli, Wayne / 203-937-8384 14 Gilbert St., West Haven, CT 06516
Frampton, Bill Rep: Daniele Collignon / 212-243-4209	Gannon, Lanie / 615-297-0040 4211 Idaho Ave., Nashville, TN 37209
	Garcia Illustration, Stephanie / 201-963-8089 85 Jefferson St., #13, Hoboken, NJ 07030

$$F = (a \times p)^4$$

TABLE (3.14). ILLUSTRATION

Illustrators	Illustrators
Garcia, Manuel Rep: Richard Salzman / 415-285-8267	Goodrich, Carter / 401-272-6094 100 Angell St., Providence, RI 02906
Garner, David / 212-663-5625 301 W. 110th St., NYC, NY 10026	Gosfield, Josh / 212-645-8826 200 Varick St., Ste. 508, NYC, NY 10014
Garns, Allen Rep: Martha Productions Inc / 310-390-8663 Rep: Susan Gomberg / 212-206-0066	Gottlieb, Penelope Rep: Nancy George / 213-655-0998
Gast, Josef Rep: Scott Hull Associates / 513-433-8383	Graber, Jack Rep: Creative Advantage / 518-370-0312
Gelb, Jacki Rep: Gerald & Cullen Rapp / 212-889-3337	Grace, Alexa / 212-254-4424 70 University Pl., NYC, NY 10003
Gergely, Peter / 914-446-2367 24 Roe Park, Highland Falls, NY 10928 Rep: Panni Gergely / 914-446-2367	Grace, Robert / 913-894-2460 12415 W. 101 Paris, Lenexa, KS 66215-1809
Giger, H.R. Rep: Leslie Barany / 212-627-8488	Graef, Wm. / 212-673-7509 333 E. 14th St., NY, NY 10003
Gin, Byron Rep: Martha Productions / 310-390-8663	Grandpre, Mary / 612-645-3463 475 Cleveland Ave. N, #222, St. Paul, MN 55104 Rep: Scott Hull / 513-433-8383
Giusti, Robert Rep: The Newborn Group / 212-260-6700	→ Granner, Courtney / 209-892-2973 328 N. Fifth St., Patterson, CA 95363 page 16
Glaser, Milton / 212-889-3161 207 E. 32nd St., NYC, NY 10016	Granryd, Linnea Rep: Lehmen Dabney / 206-325-8595
Glass, Randy / 213-851-6555 1950 Wattles Dr., LA, CA 90046 Rep: Gerald & Cullen Rapp / 212-889-3337 Rep: Sweet Represents / 415-433-1222	Graves, Keith / 512-259-8586 1403 Pinewood Cove, Leander, TX 78641 Rep: Bernstein & Andriulli / 212-682-1490
Glazer, Ted / 914-354-1524 28 Westview Rd., Spring Valley, NY 10977	Grebu, Devis / 914-674-0246 338 Sprain Rd., Scarsdale, NY 10583
Goetzinger, Rolf Rep: Lehmen Dabney / 206-325-8595	→ Green Root, Lynn / 601-366-5780 page 56
Goldin, David Rep: Joanne Palulian / 212-581-8338 / 203-866-3734	Greenberg, Sheldon Rep: Michele Manasse / 215-862-2091
Goldstrom, Robert Rep: The Newborn Group / 212-260-6700	Greg Michaelson / 213-660-5711 2365 N. Teviot, LA, CA 90039
Gonzalez, Danilo / 818-300-0132 324 N. Marengo Ave., Alhambra, CA 91801	Gregoretti, Rob / 718-779-7913 41-07 56th St., Woodside, NY 11377
	Griesbach/Martucci Rep: Jacqueline Dedell / 212-741-2539

TABLE (3.15). ILLUSTRATION

Illustrators	Illustrators
Grimes, Don / 214-821-9590 5635 Ridgedale, Dallas, TX 75206	Hamagami, John Rep: Ceci Bartels Assocs. / 314-781-7377
Gross, Alex Rep: Joanne Hedge / 213-874-1661	Hamlin, Janet / 718-638-1735 47 St. Mark's Ave., #3, Brooklyn, NY 11217
Grossman, Myron / 818-797-8422 2027 N. Lake Ave., Altadena, CA 91001	Hammond, Franklin Rep: Scott Hull / 513-433-8383
Guarnaccia, Steven / 201-746-9785 31 Fairfield St., Montclair, NJ 07042	Harrington, Glenn Rep: Barbara Gordon Assoc. / 212-686-3514 Rep: Harriet Kastaris / 314-773-2600
Guip, Amy / 212-674-8166 352 Bowery, #2, NYC, NY 10012	Hart, Thomas Rep: Gerald & Cullen Rapp / 212-889-3337
Guitteau, Jud / 503-282-0445 2506 NE 49th, Portland, OR 97213 Rep: Renard Represents / 212-490-2450 Rep: Betsy Hillman / 415-563-2243	Hart, Tom / 212-925-2220 225 Lafayette, #509, NYC, NY 10012
Gunsaullus, Marty Rep: Richard Salzman / 415-285-8267	Hayashida, Emma / 818-792-6069 3290 Primavera St., Pasadena, CA 91107
Gurvin, Abe / 714-499-2001 31341 Holly Dr., Laguna Beach, CA 92677 Rep: Fox Art / 213-653-6484 Rep: The Weber Group / 212-799-6532	Haynes, Bryan Rep: Randy Pate & Assoc. / 805-529-8111 Rep: Bernstein & Andriulli / 212-682-1490
Gusholk, Mike Rep: Les Mintz / 305-454-6566	Haynes, Michael Rep: Brooke & Co. / 214-352-9192
Gustafson, Mats Rep: Art & Commerce / 212-206-0737	Head, Gary Rep: Brooke & Company / 214-352-9192
→ Guy, Edmund / 201-251-7660 309 Race Track Rd., Ho Ho Kus, NJ 07423 page 17	Heavner, Becky / 703-683-0872 202 E. Raymond Ave., Alexandria, VA 22301
Hagio, Kunio Rep: Randy Pate & Assoc. / 805-529-8111	Heavner, Obadinah Rep: Lehmen Dabney / 206-325-8595
Halbert, Michael / 314-645-6480 2419 Big Bend, St. Louis, MO 63143 Rep: Mendola / 212-986-5680	Heiner Studio Rep: Martha Productions / 310-390-8663
Hall, Joan / 212-243-6059 155 Bank St., #H954, NYC, NY 10014	Heinze, Mitchell Rep: Sal Barracca & Assoc. / 212-889-2400
Hall, Kate Brennan Rep: Repertoire / 214-369-6990	→ Henderson, Hayes / 910-748-1364 815 Burke St., Winston-Salem, NC 27101 page 6
Halstead, Virginia / 818-705-4353 4336 Gayle Drive, Tarzana, CA 91356	Hendricks, Steve Rep: Nancy George / 213-655-0998

$$F = (a \times p)^4$$

Illustrators	Illustrators
Hennessy, Thomas / 415-388-7959 210 Chapman Rd., Mill Valley, CA 94941 Rep: France Aline Inc. / 213-933-2500	Holland, Brad / 212-226-3675 96 Greene St., NYC, NY 10012
Henry, Paul Rep: Bill & Maurine Klimt / 212-799-2231	Homad, Jewell Rep: Creative Freelancers / 212-398-9540
Hersey, John / 415-454-0771	Hong, Min Jae / 914-986-8040 54 Points of View, Warwick, NY 10990
→ Hess, Lydia / 503-234-4757 1246 SE 49th St., Portland, OR 97215 page 33	Hopkins, Chris / 206-347-5613 Rep: Joni Tuke / 312-787-6826 Rep: Randy Pate & Assoc. / 805-529-8111
Hess, Mark / 914-232-5870 88 Quicks Lane, Katonah, NY 10536 Rep: The Newborn Group / 212-260-6700	Hosner, William / 313-781-3466 3861 Pickford, Washington, MI 48094
Hewitt/Low Studios / 516-427-1404 144 Soundview Rd., Huntington, NY 11743	Howard, John H. Rep: The Newborn Group / 212-260-6700
High, Richard Rep: Jerry Leff / 212-697-8525	Huerta, Catherine / 212-627-0031 337 W. 20th St., #4M, NYC, NY 10011
Hill, Amy Rep: Les Mintz / 305-454-6566	Hull, John / 206-365-5522 / 213-254-4647 12726 12th NE, Seattle, WA 98125 Rep: Laurie Pribble / 818-574-0288
Hilliard, Fred Rep: Jerry Leff / 212-697-8525	→ Hungry Dog Studio / 404-872-7496 1361 Markan Ct., #3, Atlanta, GA 30306 page 23
Hilton-Putnam, Denise Rep: Richard Salzman / 415-285-8267	Hunt, Robert / 415-459-6882 107 Crescent Rd., San Anselmo, CA 94960 Rep: Randy Pate & Assoc. / 805-529-8111
Hitz, Christoph / 212-227-6670 77 Hudson St., NYC, NY 10013	Hunt, Scott / 212-924-1105 6 Charles St., #4C, NYC, NY 10014
Hodges, Mike Rep: Brooke & Company / 214-352-9192 Rep: Cary & Co. / 404-296-9666	Hunter, Stan Rep: Lavaty & Assoc. / 212-355-0910
Hoff, Terry / 415-359-4081 1525 Grand Ave., Pacifica, CA 94044 Rep: Jerry Leff / 212-697-8525	Hussar, Michael / 818-449-0183 Rep: Fance Aline Inc. / 213-933-2500
Hoffman, Martin Rep: Jeff Lavaty & Assoc. / 212-355-0910	Huyssen, Roger / 203-256-9192 54 Old Post Rd., Southport, CT 06490
Hokanson, Lars Rep: Fran Seigel / 212-486-9644	Ibusuki, James / 818-362-9899 13053 Beaver St., LA, CA 91342 Rep: Mendola Ltd. / 212-986-5680
Holladay, Reggie / 305-749-9031 7395 NW 51st St., Lauderhill, FL 33319	→ Isip, Jordan / 718-624-6538 44 Fourth Pl., #2, Brooklyn, NY 11231 page 8

Table (3.17). Illustration

Illustrators	Illustrators
Iskowitz, Joel / 914-679-6742 297 Ohayo Mountain Rd., Woodstock, NY 12498	Joly, Dave / 203-928-1042 15 King St., Putnam, CT 06260
Jackson, Barry / 818-769-7321 4118 Beck Ave., Studio City, CA 91604	Jones, Dan Rep: Richard Salzman / 415-285-8267
Jacobsen, Ken / 612-823-4662 1458 W. 33rd St., Minneapolis, MI 55408 Rep: Gretchen Harris / 612-822-0650 Rep: Liz Sanders / 714-495-3664	Jost, Larry Rep: Susan & Co. / 206-728-1300
Jaksevic, Nenad Rep: Barbara Gordon Assoc. / 212-686-3514	Juhasz, Victor Rep: The Newborn Group / 212-260-6700
James, Bill Rep: Mendola / 212-986-5680	Justinen, Lars Rep: Jerry Leff / 212-697-8525
Jarecka, Danuta / 212-353-3298 114 E. Seventh St., #15, NYC, NY 10009	Kadiev, Petko Rep: Motion Artists / 213-851-7737
Jarvis, David Rep: Pat Foster / 212-685-4580	Kai Art / 908-382-5641 92 Maple St., Colonia, NJ 07067 page 15
Jasin, Mark Rep: Martha Productions Inc / 310-390-8663	Kalish, Lionel Rep: Gerald & Cullen Rapp / 212-889-3337
Jasper, Jackie Rep: Barbara Gordon Assoc. / 212-686-3514	Kann, Victoria Rep: Jett & Associates / 502-635-1401
Jeffries, Shannon / 202-234-8958 1905 Kalorama Rd., N.W. #3, Washington D.C. 20009	Kastaris, Rip / 314-773-2600 3301-A S. Jefferson Ave., St. Louis, MO 63118 Rep: Harriet Kastaris / 314-773-2600
Jessell, Tim Rep: James Conrad / 415-921-7140 Rep: Bernstein & Andriulli / 212-682-1490	Katz, Les / 718-284-4779 451 Westminster Rd., Brooklyn, NY 11218 Rep: Sharon Drexler / 212-768-8072
Jinks, John Rep: Conrad Represents / 415-921-7140	Keleny, Earl Rep: Fran Seigel / 212-486-9644
Johnson, Bob Rep: Kathy Braun / 415-775-3366	Kelley, Barbara / 516-754-7374 533 Main St., Northport, NY 11768 Rep: Irmeli Holmberg / 212-545-9155 Rep: Janice Stefanski / 415-928-0457
Johnson, Doug / 212-260-1880 45 East 19th St., NYC, NY 10003	Kelley, Gary Rep: Richard Solomon / 212-683-1362
Johnson, Julie Rep: Anita Grien / 212-697-6170 page 32	King, J.D. / 518-822-0225 P.O. Box 91, Stuyvesant Falls, NY 12174
Johnson, Steve / 612-377-8728	King, Martha / 212-614-9059 P.O. Box 104, Stuyvesant Station, NY, NY 10009
Johnson, Val Rep: Les Mintz / 305-454-6566	

$$F = (a \times p)^4$$

TABLE (3.18). ILLUSTRATION

Illustrators	Illustrators
Kirk, Daniel Rep: Bernstein & Andriulli / 212-682-1490	Kunstler, Mort Rep: Jeff Lavaty & Assoc. / 212-355-0910
Klanderman, Leland Rep: Ceci Bartels Assocs. / 314-781-7377 Rep: Conrad Represents... / 415-921-7140	→ Kunz, Anita / 416-364-3846 230 Ontario St., Toronto, ON M5A 2V5 Rep: Edge Reps / 415-457-9336 / 212-343-2260 page 5
Kleber, John / 602-253-4129 2301 N. Tenth St., Phoenix, AZ 85006 Rep: Randi Fiat & Assoc. / 312-464-0964 Rep: Martha Productions / 310-390-8663	LaCava, Vincent / 212-725-8949 1186 Broadway, #939, NYC, NY 10001
Klein, David G. / 718-788-1818 408 Seventh St., Brooklyn, NY 11215	LaFever, Greg Rep: Scott Hull Associates / 513-433-8383
→ Klunder, Barbara Rep: Rep Art / 206-281-0960 / 604-684-6826 pages 10 - 11	LaFleur, Dave Rep: Scott Hull Associates / 513-433-8383
Knoff, Jean-Christian Rep: Maud Geng / 617-236-1920	Labbe, John / 212-529-2831 97 Third Ave., #2E, NYC, NY 10003
Kotas, Karl / 212-675-0052 445 W. 19th St., 1E, NYC, NY 10011	Lackow, Andy / 203-431-7980 135 Mamanasco Rd., Ridgefield, CT 06877
Kovalcik, Terry / 212-620-7772 80 Eighth Ave., #1308, NYC, NY 10011	Lagalia, Linda Rep: Asciutto Art Reps / 602-899-0600
Kowal, Thomas / 212-675-1694 535 Hudson St., PH E, NYC, NY 10014	Lamut, Sonja Rep: Barbara Gordon Assoc. / 212-686-3514
Kowalski, Mike Rep: Melissa Brock / 510-521-2012 Rep: Sharon Dodge / 206-622-7035	Laugeneckert, Mark / 314-451-5568 3664 Bassett Woods, Pacific, MO 63069
Krejca, Gary Rep: Mary Holland & Co. / 602-263-8990	Leary, Catherine Rep: Martha Productions / 310-390-8663
Kriegler, Richard Rep: Nancy George / 213-655-0998	Lee, Eric J.W. / 415-399-9575
Kriegshauser, Shannon Rep: Ceci Bartels Assocs. / 314-781-7377	Lee, Walter W. / 818-792-8770 85 N. Chester Ave., Pasadena, CA 91106
Krizmanic, Tatjana Rep: Bobbi Wendt / 415-252-1910	Lensch, Chris / 303-279-8304 Strangeboat Prod. 209 Ford St., Golden, CO 80401
Kubinyi, Laszlo Rep: Gerald & Cullen Rapp / 212-889-3337	Lesh, David Rep: Joanne Palulian / 212-581-8338 / 203-866-3734
Kung, Lingta Rep: Jerry Leff / 212-697-8525	Lesser, Ron Rep: Jerry Leff / 212-697-8525
	Lester, Mike / 706-234-7733 17 E. Third Ave., Rome, GA 30161

TABLE (3.19). ILLUSTRATION

Illustrators	Illustrators

Levine, Laura / 212-431-4787
444 Broome St., NYC, NY 10013

Leyonmark, Roger
Rep: Irmeli Holmberg / 212-545-9155

Liao, Sharmen / 818-458-7699
Rep: Gerald & Cullen Rapp / 212-889-3337

Lieberman Studio, Ron / 212-947-0653
109 W. 28th St., NYC, NY 10001

Liepke, Skip
Rep: Richard Solomon / 212-683-1362

Little, Ed / 203-350-6523
112 Wewaka Brook Rd, Bridgewater, CT 06752
Rep: Artco / 212-889-8777

Live Wire Studios / 216-694-2020
2020 Euclid Ave., 4th Fl, Cleveland, OH 44115

Livingston, Francis
Rep: Jerry Leff / 212-697-8525
Rep: Freda Scott, Inc. / 415-621-2992

Loch, Lindsey / 208-386-9074
833 Richmond St., Boise, ID 83706

Loew, David
Rep: Artco / 212-889-8777

Logrippo, Robert
Rep: Jeff Lavaty & Assoc. / 212-355-0910

Lohstoeter, Lori
Rep: Lindgren & Smith / 212-929-5590

Long, Loren
Rep: Lisa Freeman / 317-920-0068

Lopez, Rafael
Rep: Conrad Represents... / 415-921-7140

Lorenz, Lee
Rep: Gerald & Cullen Rapp / 212-889-3337

Louie, Lorraine / 212-941-7329
80 Varick St., Ste. 3B, NYC, NY 10013

Love, Sara
Rep: Lisa Freeman / 317-920-0068

Loveless, Roger
Rep: Sal Barracca & Assoc. / 212-889-2400

Lu, Kong
Rep: Lehmen Dabney / 206-325-8595

Ludlow, Roberta
Rep: Les Mintz / 305-454-6566

Lui, David
Rep: Les Mintz / 305-454-6566

Lukens, Jan / 919-945-2581
9455 Shallowford Rd., Lewisville, NC 27023

→ Lyons, Steven / 415-459-7560
136 Scenic Rd., Fairfax, CA 94930
slyons@aol.com
page 12

Lytle, John / 209-928-4849
17130 Yosemite Rd. P.O. Box 5155, Sonora, CA 95370

Macanga, Steve / 201-403-8967
20 Morgantine Rd., Roseland, NJ 07068

Macdonald, Ross / 212-966-2446
189 Franklin, #492, NYC, NY 10013
Rep: Reactor / 800-730-8945

Macleod, Lee
Rep: Bernstein & Andriulli / 212-682-1490

Macrae, Doug / 416-365-7079
507 King St., E., Ste. 302, Toronto, Ontario, Canada
M5A 1M3

Maddox, Kelly
Rep: Jerry Leff / 212-697-8525

Maffia, Daniel / 201-871-0435
236 S. Dwight Pl., Englewood, NJ 07631

Maggard, John
Rep: Scott Hull Associates / 513-433-8383

Magovern, Peg / 510-648-1444
Rep: Corey Graham / 415-956-4750

Mahoney, Pat / 415-647-7969
Rep: Corey Graham / 415-956-4750

Mahurin, Matt / 212-691-5115

$$F = (a \times p)^4$$

TABLE (3.20). ILLUSTRATION

Illustrators	Illustrators
Maisner, Bernard Rep: Gerald & Cullen Rapp / 212-889-3337 Design / page 23	Mattos, John / 415-397-2138 1546 Grant Ave., SF, CA 94133 Rep: Jett & Assocs. / 502-635-1401
Manchess, Gregory Rep: Richard Solomom / 212-683-1362	Mayer, Bill / 404-378-0686 240 Forkner Dr., Decatur, GA 30030
Mangiat, Jeff Rep: Mendola / 212-986-5680	Mayforth, Hal Rep: Gerald & Cullen Rapp / 212-889-3337
Manning, Michele Rep: Jerry Leff / 212-697-8525 Rep: Jan Collier / 415-383-9026	Mayse, Steve / 913-962-2285 7515 Allman, Lenexa, KS 66217 Rep: Bill Rabin & Assoc. / 312-944-6655 Rep: Sweet Represents / 415-433-1222
Mantel, Richard / 212-889-2254 114 E. 32nd St., Ste. 1505, NY, NY 10016 Rep: Lindgen & Smith / 212-929-5590	Mazemaster Rep: David Goldman / 212-807-6627
Marciulliano, Frank Rep: Jerry Leff / 212-697-8525	Mazzetti, Alan / 415-647-7677 834 Moultrie St., SF, CA 94110 Rep: Freda Scott, Inc. / 415-621-2992
Mardon, Allan Rep: Gerald & Cullen Rapp / 212-889-3337	McCollum, Rick Rep: Joanne Hedge / 213-874-1661
Marek, Mark / 201-384-1791 199 Owatonna St., Haworth, NJ 07641	Mc Cormack, Donna / 718-229-7939 page 24
Marshall, Craig Rep: Jim Lilie / 415-441-4384	McDonald, Mercedes / 408-268-0662 1459 Athenour Ct., San Jose, CA 95120 Rep: Nadine Represents / 415-456-7711 Rep: Friend & Johnson / 310-268-4107
Marten, Ruth / 212-645-0233 8 W. 13th St., #7RW, NYC, NY 10011	McElroy, Darlene Rep: Sylvia Franks / 310-276-5282 Rep: Christine Prapas / 503-246-9511
Martin, Larry Rep: Scott Hull Associates / 513-433-8383	McEntire, Larry Rep: Fran Seigel / 212-486-9644
Masuda, Coco / 212-753-9331 300 E. 51st. St., #6E, NY, NY 10022	McGinty, Mick Rep: Randy Pate & Assoc. / 805-529-8111 Rep: Christine Prapas / 503-246-9511
Mateu, Franc Rep: S.I. International / 212-254-4996	McGowan, Dan Rep: Susan Gomberg / 212-206-0066 Rep: Pat Hackett / 206-447-1600
Mathews, Adam / 215-884-9247 142 Bickley Rd., Glenside, PA 19038	McGrail, Rollin Rep: Ceci Bartels Assocs. / 314-781-7377
Mattelson, Marvin Rep: Judy Mattelson / 212-684-2974	
Mattingly, David B. / 201-659-7404 1112 Bloomfield St., Hoboken, NJ 07030	

TABLE (3.21). ILLUSTRATION

Illustrators	Illustrators
McGurl, Michael / 505-466-6889 14 Garbosa Rd, Santa Fe, NM 87505 Rep: Renard Represents / 212-490-2450	Mitchell, Briar Lee / 818-752-6809 11552 Hartsook Ave., Valley Village, CA 91601
McIntosh, Mark / 714-642-7445 391 Broadway, Costa Mesa, CA 92627 Rep: Jae Wagoner / 310-392-4877	Moline, Robin Rep: Conrad Represents... / 415-921-7140
McKowen, Scott Rep: Marlena / 212-289-5514	Moline-Kramer Rep: Les Mintz / 305-454-6566
McLain, Julia Rep: Les Mintz / 305-454-6566	Mongeau, Marc Rep: Marlena / 212-289-5514
McLean, Wilson Rep: The Newborn Group / 212-260-6700	Monteleone, John Rep: Mendola / 212-986-5680
→ McMacken, David / 707-996-5239 19481 Franquelin Pl., Sonoma, CA 95476 page 36	Montoliu, Raphael Rep: Ceci Bartels Assocs. / 314-781-7377
McNeel, Richard / 201-779-0802 140 Hepburn Rd., #14H, Clifton, NJ 07012	Moody, Donna / 203-438-6906 182 North St., Ridgefield, CT 06877
Meisel, Ann Rep: Mendola / 212-986-5680	Moore, Chris Rep: Bernstein & Andriulli / 212-682-1490
Mercie, Tina Rep: Les Mintz / 305-454-6566	Moore, Cyd Rep: Irmeli Holmberg / 212-545-9155
Mericle, Charise / 312-486-8719 1951 N. Wilmot, Chicago, IL 60647	Moore, Elizabeth / 213-667-2009
Meyer, Gary / 818-992-6974 21725 Ybarra Rd., Woodland Hills, CA 91364	Moores, Jeff Rep: Pamela Korn / 717-595-9298
Meyers, Steve / 518-399-0581	Mora, Francisco / 818-449-0356 45 N. Allen Ave., Pasadena, CA 91106
Milbourn, Patrick / 212-939-4594	Moran, Michael / 201-966-6229 39 Elmwood Rd., Florham Park, NJ 07932
Miller, Steve / 619-758-0804 2586 Majella Rd, Vista, CA 92084	Morawa, Amy / 212-938-5732 375 S. End Ave., #4K, NYC, NY 10280
Milnazik, Kimmerle / 215-259-1565 73-2 Drexelbrook Dr., Drexel Hill, PA 19026 Rep: Artworks / 212-627-1554 Rep: Terry Putscher / 215-569-8890	Morenko, Michael / 212-627-5920 255 W. Tenth St., #5FS, NYC, NY 10014
	Morin, Josee Rep: Marlena / 212-289-5514
→ Misconish, David / 404-231-9711 175D Peachtree Hills Ave. NE, Atlanta, GA 30305 page 7	Morris, Burton / 412-682-7963 400 Noble St., Pittsburgh, PA 15232 Rep: Cynthia Wacker / 412-928-8717 Rep: The Weber Group / 212-799-6532
	Morris, Frank Rep: Bill & Maurine Klimt / 212-799-2231

$$F = (a \times p)^4$$

Table (3.22). Illustration

Illustrators	Illustrators
Mortensen, Cristine Rep: Nadine Represents / 415-456-7711	Nelson, Hilber Rep: Kolea Baker / 206 764-1136
Mosberg, Hilary / 415-457-4088 Rep: Friend & Johnson / 214-855-0055	Nelson, Joelle Rep: Jane Jenni / 612-224-6763 page 25
Mullane, John Rep: Fran Seigel / 212-486-9644	Nelson, John / 602-829-8992 Rep: Ceci Bartels Assocs. / 314-781-7377 Rep: Irmeli Holmberg / 212-545-9155
Munck, Paula Rep: Jacqueline Dedell / 212-741-2539	Nelson, R. Kenton Rep: Friend & Johnson / 214-855-0055
Muns, Marjorie Rep: Joanne Hedge / 213-874-1661	Neski, Peter / 212-737-2521 315 E. 68th St., NYC, NY 10021
Murawski, Alex Rep: Gerald & Cullen Rapp / 212-889-3337	Nessim, Barbara / 212-219-1111 63 Greene St., NY, NY 10012 pages 40 - 41
Murray, John / 617-424-0024 page 39	Nible, Geri / 913-341-0724 / 816-767-2724 7800 Grant Lane, Overland Park, KS 66204
Murton, Simon Rep: Motion Artists / 213-851-7737	Nicodemus, Stephen / 213-876-4687 Rep: Linda de Moreta / 510-769-1421
Musso, Joseph Rep: Motion Artists / 213-851-7737	Niklewicz, Adam / 203-270-8424 44 Great Quarter Rd., Sandy Hook, CT 06482
Myers, Matt Rep: Lehmen Dabney / 206-325-8595	Nimoy, Nancy / 310-202-0773 10534 Clarkson Rd, LA, CA 90064
Mysakov, Leonid Rep: Irmeli Holmberg / 212-545-9155	Nitta, Kazushige Rep: David Goldman / 212-807-6627
Nacht, Merle Rep: Jacqueline Dedell / 212-741-2539	Nixon, Tony / 913-384-5444 7210 Robertson, Overland Park, KS 66204
Najaka, Marlies Rep: Gerald & Cullen Rapp / 212-889-3337	Nordell, Dale Rep: Jaz & Jaz / 206-282-8558
Nakamura, Joel Rep: Corey Graham / 415-956-4750	Northeast, Christian / 416-538-0400 48 Abell St., Toronto, Ontario, Canada M6J-3HZ
Nascimbene, Yan Rep: Lindgren & Smith / 212-929-5590	Notarile, Chris Rep: Mendola / 212-986-5680
Naugle, Diane / 805-374-1174 Rep: Linda de Moreta / 510-769-7421	O'Brien, Tim Rep: Peter & George Lott / 212-953-7088
Nelson, Bill / 212-683-1362 Rep: Richard Solomon / 212-683-1362	O'Connell, Mitch Rep: Daniele Collignon / 212-243-4209
Nelson, Craig / 818-363-4494 Rep: Bernstein & Andriulli / 212-682-1490 Rep: Christine Prapas / 503-246-9511	

Table (3.23). Illustration

Illustrators	Illustrators
O'Connor, Cathy Christy Rep: Mendola / 212-986-5680	Paraskevas, Michael Rep: Lindgen & Smith / 212-929-5590
O'Shea, Kevin Rep: Jaz & Jaz / 206-282-8558	Pardy, Cindy Rep: Daniele Collignon / 212-243-4209
Ochagavia, Carlos Rep: Jeff Lavaty & Assoc. / 212-355-0910	Parisi, Richard / 410-243-7217 3000 Chestnut Ave., #6, Baltimore, MD 21211 Rep: Vicki Morgan Assoc. / 212-475-0440
Okamura, Tim C. / 718-858-1980 57 Jay St., #1A, Brooklyn, NY 11201	Park, Chang / 718-651-3764 52-05 39th Rd., #2A, Woodside, NY 11377 page 51
Olbinski, Tomek Rep: Marlena / 212-289-5514	Parker, Edward Rep: Jacqueline Dedell / 212-741-2539
Olitsky, Eve / 203-561-5523 1476 Blvd., W. Hartford, CT 06119	Parker, Robert Andrew Rep: Riley Illustration / 212-989-8770
Oppenheimer, Jennie / 415-488-1047 PO Box 292, Lagunitas, CA 94938 Rep: Jan Collier / 415-383-9026	Parton, Steve Rep: S.I. International / 212-254-4996
Ortega, Jose / 212-772-3329 131 Ave. B, Charley Parker Pl., NYC, NY 10009	Pastrana, Robert M. / 818-548-6083 473 A Riverdale Dr., Glendale, CA 91204
Osborn, Jim / 615-385-4476 4801 Nevada Ave., Nashville, TN 37209	Patelis, Dimitrios Rep: Leslie Barany Communications / 212-627-8488 page 19
Osborne, Stephen Rep: Kathy Braun / 415-775-3366	Patti, Joyce Rep: Vicki Morgan Assoc. / 212-475-0440
Osiecki, Lori / 602-962-5233 123 W. Second St., Mesa, AZ 85201 Rep: Cliff Knecht / 412-761-5666	Paul Design, Art / 312-266-0621 175 East Delaware Place, Chicago, IL 60611
Ostrokolowicz, Debra / 508-943-8451 6 Malden Dr., Webster, MA 01570 page 30	Payne, C.F. Rep: Richard Solomon / 212-683-1362
Owen, Tania / 615-298-1444 2804 Brightwood Ave., Nashville, TN 37212	Peake, Kevin Rep: Tonal Values / 305-576-0142 page 43
Pace, Julie Rep: Lehmen Dabney / 206-325-8595 Rep: Mary Holland & Co. / 602-263-8990	Peale, Charles Rep: Asciutto Art Reps / 602-899-0600
Palen, Debbie Rep: Lisa Freeman / 317-920-0068	Peck, Everett Rep: Richard Salzman / 415-285-8267
Palmer, Gary / 704-376-4027 1735 Dilworth Rd. E., Charlotte, NC 28203 Rep: Kerry Reilly / 704-365-6111	Pelavin, Daniel / 212-941-7418 80 Varick St., Ste. 3B, NYC, NY 10013

$$F = (a \times p)^4$$

TABLE (3.24). ILLUSTRATION

Illustrators	Illustrators
Penca, Gary / 305-752-4699 8335 NW 20th St., Coral Springs, FL 33071	Polenghi, Evan / 718-499-3214 159 25th St., Brooklyn, NY 11232 Rep: Jean Conlon / 212-966-9897
Percivalle, Rosanne / 212-727-9158 132 W. 21st St. 12th Fl., NYC, NY 10011	Pope, Kevin / 812-824-6949 3735 Cleve Butcher Rd., Bloomington, IN 47401 Rep: Ceci Bartels Assocs. / 314-781-7377
Perez, Omaha / 718-636-6040 11 Lincoln Pl., #2R, Brooklyn, NY 11217	Porazinski, Rob / 312-745-9005 2218 N. Newland Ave., Chicago, IL 60635 Rep: Jim Hanson / 312-337-7770
Perkins, Ken Rep: Joanne Hedge / 213-874-1661	Porfirio, Guy Rep: Ceci Bartels Assocs. / 314-781-7377 Rep: Mary Holland & Co. / 602-263-8990
Peters, Bob Rep: Gerald & Cullen Rapp / 212-889-3337	Powell, Keith / 509-633-1737 P.O. Box 788, Grand Coulee, WA 99133
Pettit, David Rep: Motion Artists / 213-851-7737	Probert, Jean Rep: Ceci Bartels Assocs. / 314-781-7377
Phillips, Laura Rep: Bernstein & Andriulli / 212-682-1490 Rep: Joanne Hedge / 213-874-1661	Przewodek, Camille Rep: Gerald & Cullen Rapp / 212-889-3337
Picasso, Dan Rep: Joanie Bernstein / 612-374-3169	Punin, Nikolai / 212-727-7237 161 W. 16th St., #18E, NYC, NY 10011 Rep: Tonal Values / 305-576-0142 Rep: Harriet Kastaris / 314-773-2600
Pierazzi, Gary Rep: Kathy Braun / 415-775-3366	Pyle, Charles Rep: Lindgren & Smith / 212-929-5590 Rep: Melissa Brock / 510-521-2012
Pifko, Sigmund Rep: Gerald & Cullen Rapp / 212-889-3337	Racz, Michael / 718-956-0980
Pincus, Harry / 212-925-8071 160 Ave of the Americas, NYC, NY 10013	Ragland, Greg Rep: Kolea Baker / 206-784-1136
Pinkney, Jerry Rep: Gerald & Cullen Rapp / 212-889-3337	Raglin, Tim Rep: Lindgren & Smith / 212-929-5590
Pitts, Ted Rep: Scott Hull Associates / 513-433-8383	Ravanelli, Terry / 618-931-7459 2483 Waterman, Granite City, IL 62040 Rep: Harriet Kastaris / 314-773-2600
→ Piven, Hanoch / 212-691-5133 310 W. 22nd St., #4A, NY, NY 10011 page 48	Rediger, Deborah Rep: Ceci Bartels Assocs. / 314-781-7377
→ Plunkert, David / 410-235-7803 3647 Falls Rd., Baltimore, MD 21211 page 14	Reed, Mike Rep: Brooke & Company / 214-352-9192
Podevin, Jean-Francois / 310-945-9613 5812 Newlin Ave., Whittier, CA 90601	

TABLE (3.25). ILLUSTRATION

Illustrators	Illustrators
Reese, Ralph / 201-773-2481 81 Renaissance Dr., Clifton, NJ 07013	Rogers, Paul / 818-564-8728 12 S. Fair Oaks Ave. #202, Pasadena, CA 91105 Rep: Rita Marie / 213-934-3395
Rekosh, Jana Rep: Jaz & Jaz / 206-282-8558	Roman, Irena Rep: Daniele Collignon / 212-243-4209
→ Rendon, Maria / 909-889-8979 / 213-687-3664 6997 Perris Hill Rd., San Bernardino, CA 92404 page 50	Romeo, Richard / 305-472-0072 1066 NW 96th Ave., Fort Lauderdale, FL 33322
Richards, Kenn / 516-499-7575 3 Elwin Pl., E. Northport, NY 11731 Rep: Jerry Leff / 212-697-8525	Root, Kimberly Bulcken Rep: Jacqueline Dedell / 212-741-2539
Riedy, Mark Rep: Scott Hull Associates / 513-433-8383	Root, Lynn Green / 601-366-5780 4449 Wedgewood St., Jackson, MS 39211
Rieser, William / 415-389-0332 361 Megee Ave., Mill Valley, CA 94941 Rep: Rita Marie	Rosen, Jonathon / 718-499-3911 408 Second St., #3, Brooklyn, NY 11215
Rigie, Mitch Rep: David Goldman / 212-807-6627	Rosenberg, Ken Rep: Joanne Hedge / 213-874-1661 Rep: Hankins & Tegenborg / 212-967-9092
Risko, Robert / 212-255-2865 / 212-989-6987 155 W. 15th St., Ste. 4B, NYC, NY 10011	Rosenthal, Marc / 518-766-4191 #8 Route 66, Malden Bridge, NY 12115 Rep: Gerald & Cullen Rapp / 212-889-3337
→ Ritter, John / 415-922-8577 page 37	Rossi, Pam / 708-475-2533 908 Main St., #3, Evanston, IL 60202 Rep: Terry Squire / 919-772-1262
→ Roberts, Scott / 410-879-3362 6 N. Main St., Ste. 200, Bel Air, MD 21014 page 26	Roth, Robert G. / 816-444-7430 148 Lakebridge Dr., Kings Park, NY 11754 Rep: Jerry Leff / 212-697-8525
Robertson Typographic Ill. / 303-444-2787 1245 Pearl St., #200, Boulder, CO 80302	Roy, Joanna / 212-663-7876 549 W. 123rd St., NYC, NY 10027
Robertson, Terry / 213-221-5938 3654 Roseview Ave., LA, CA 90065	Rubess, Balvis / 416-927-7071 260 Brunswick Ave., Toronto, ON M5S 2M7
Robertson, Walter / 714-362-1848 Artesano 10 Tarmarac Pl., Alisa Viejo, CA 92656	Ruff, Donna / 203-866-8626 18 Crockett St., Rowayton, CT 06853
Robinette, John / 901-681-9668 5889 Ewing Dr., Memphis, TN 38119 Rep: The Williams Group / 404-873-2287	Ruiz, Art Rep: S.I. International / 212-254-4996
Rogers, Lilla Rep: Irmeli Holmberg / 212-545-9155	Russell, Bill / 415-474-4759 949 Filbert St., #5, SF, CA 94133 Rep: Reactor / 212-967-7699

$$F = (a \times p)^4$$

TABLE (3.26). ILLUSTRATION

Illustrators	Illustrators
Russo, Anthony / 401-624-9184 51 Fog Land Rd., Tiverton, RI 02878	Scholl, Oliver Rep: Motion Artists / 213-851-7737
Ryden, Mark / 818-355-5047 541 Ramona Ave., Sierra Madre, CA 91024	Schrier, Fred Rep: Lisa Freeman / 317-920-0068
Sabanosh, Michael / 212-947-8161 433 W. 34th St., #18B, NYC, NY 10001	Schudlich, Stephen Rep: Ceci Bartels Assocs. / 314-781-7377
Sadowski, Wiktor Rep: Marlena / 212-289-5514	Schulenburg, Paul / 508-385-8845 24 Captain Connolly Rd., Brewster, MA 02631
Saksa Art & Design / 609-259-7792 10 Hidden Hollow Dr., Hamilton Township, NJ 08620	Schuler, Mark E. / 913-384-0646 5410 W. 68th St., Prairie Village, KS 66208
Salerno, Steven Rep: Lindgren Smith / 212-397-7330	Schwab, Michael / 415-331-7621 80 Liberty Ship Way, #7, Sausalito, CA 94965 Rep: Madeline Renard / 212-490-2450
Sales, David Art / 212-505-7550 101 St. Marks Pl., Ste. 29, NYC, NY 10009	Schwartz, Daniel Rep: Richard Solomon / 212-683-1362
Salvati, Jim Rep: Joanne Hedge / 213-874-1661 Rep: Motion Artists / 213-848-7737	Schwarz, Joanie Rep: Vicki Morgan Assoc. / 212-475-0440
Sanjulian, Manuel Rep: S.I. International / 212-254-4996	Schweitzer, Dave Rep: Joanne Hedge / 213-874-1661
Sano, Kazuhiko / 415-381-6377 105 Stadium Ave., Mill Valley, CA 94941 Rep: Renard Represents / 212-490-2450	→ Sealock, Rick / 403-276-5428 112 C 17th Ave. N.W., Calgary, Alberta, Canada T2M OM6 page 4
Sasaki, Goro Rep: Bernstein & Andriulli / 212-682-1490	Seckler, Judy / 818-508-8778 11024 Acama St., #216, Studio City, CA 91602
Saunders, Robert / 617-566-4464 34 Station St., Brookline, MA 02146	Sekine, Hisashi Rep: Daniele Collignon / 212-243-4209
Sayles, John Rep: Jerry Leff / 212-697-8525	Sharp, Bruce Rep: Tania Kimche / 212-242-6367
Scanlan, David / 310-545-0773 1600 18th St., Manhattan Beach, CA 90266 Rep: Robin Stevens / 312-689-3442 / 312-670-0470	Shaw, Ned / 812-333-2181 2770 N. Smith Pike, Bloomington, IN 47404
Schneebalg, Martin / 718-599-6327 568 Driggs Ave., #1R, Brooklyn, NY 11211	Shaw, Stan Rep: Lehmen Dabney / 206-325-8595
Schofield, Mark / 206-623-9539 1201 First Ave. S., Seattle, WA 98134 Rep: Martha Prods. / 310-390-8663 Rep: Sharon Dodge / 206-622-7035	Shed, Greg Rep: Richard Salzman / 415-285-8267

TABLE (3.27). ILLUSTRATION

Illustrators	Illustrators
Shema, Bob / 214-402-0316 619 Rancho Circle, Irving, TX 75063 Rep: L. Jane Mills Co. / 214-946-6569	Soderlind, Kirsten Rep: Vicki Morgan Assoc. / 212-475-0440
Shigley, Neil / 619-451-1101 Rep: Carol Chislovsky / 212-677-9100	Soileau, Hodges / 203-852-0751 350 Flax Hill Rd., Norwalk, CT 06854
Short, Robbie / 404-565-7811 2903 Bentwood Dr., Marietta, GA 30062	Solomon, Debra / 212-473-0060 143 Greene St., #3, NYC, NY 10012
Simmons, Keith / 919-387-0042 107 Kilbreck Dr., Cary, NC 27511	Soloski, Tommy Rep: Les Mintz / 305-454-6566
Sipp, Geo / 404-876-0312 2720 Margaret Mitchell Dr., Atlanta, GA 30327	Sorren, Joe / 619-722-7777 Rep: Conrad Represents / 415-921-7140
Siudmak, Wojtek Rep: Marlena / 212-289-5514	South, Randy / 818-985-9306 360 Ritch St., Ste. 3201, SF, CA 94107 Rep: Betsy Hillman / 415-391-9181
Skutnik, Andrew / 718-768-6313 122 Prospect Park W., Brooklyn, NY 11215	Spalenka, Greg / 818-992-5828 / 212-741-9064 21303 San Miguel St., Woodland Hills, CA 91364
Smallish, Craig / 414-243-9711 Rep: Jim Hanson & Talent / 312-337-7770	Spector, Joel / 203-355-5942 3 Maplewood Dr., New Milford, CT 06776 Rep: Harvey Kahn / 201-467-0223 Rep: Jerry Leff / 212-697-8525
Smith, Douglas Rep: Richard Solomon / 212-683-1362	
Smith, Elwood H. / 914-876-2358 2 Locust Grove Rd, Rhinebeck, NY 12572 Rep: Maggie Pickard / 914-876-2358	Spencer Design, Joe / 818-760-0216 11201 Valley Spring Lane, N. Hollywood, CA 91602 Rep: Betsy Hillman / 415-391-1181 Rep: Fox Art / 213-653-6484
Smith, Jere Rep: Kolea Baker / 206-784-1136	Spino, Peter / 619-225-9476 3050 Kellogg St., San Diego, CA 92106 page 34
Smith, John C. / 206-742-4974 16217 22nd Dr. SE, Mill Creek, WA 98012 page 47	Spollen, Chris / 718-979-9695 362 Cromwell Ave., Ocean Breeze, NY 10305
Smith, Mark T. / 212-679-9485 / 310-281-5504 235 E. 22nd St., #13V, NYC, NY 10010 page 13	Sposato, John / 212-477-3909 43 E. 22nd St., NYC, NY 10010
Smith, Mary Ann / 212-691-3570 165 Perry St., #4D, NYC, NY 10014	Sprouls, Kevin / 609-965-4795 1 Schooner Ln., Sweetwater, NJ 08037
Smith, Rick Rep: Photo Comp / 212-720-2272	Stabin, Victor / 212-243-7688 84-21 Midland Parkway, Jamaica Estates, NY 11432
	Stahl, Nancy / 212-362-8779
Sneberger, Dan Rep: Fran Seigel / 212-486-9644	Stanislaw Fernandes / 212-533-2648 874 Broadway, #305, NYC, NY 10003

$$F = (a \times p)^4$$

Table (3.28). Illustration

Illustrators	Illustrators
Starrett, Terri Rep: Penny & Stermer Group / 212-505-9342	Stutzman, Mark / 301-334-4086 Eloqui 100 G Street, Mt. Lake Park, MD 21550
Steam, Inc. / 818-242-5688 103 W. California, Glendale, CA 91203 Rep: Vicki Morgan / 212-475-0440	Sullivan, James / 908-541-2926 26 Tulaski Ave., Carteret, NJ 07008
Stearney, Mark / 312-360-9033 621 S. Plymouth Ct., #202, Chicago, IL 60605	Suma, Doug Rep: Jae Wagoner / 310-392-4877
Steele, Robert Gantt / 415-923-0741 14 Wilmot St., SF, CA 94115 Rep: Lindgren & Smith / 212-929-5590 Rep: Jan Collier / 415-383-9026	Sumichrast, Jozef / 708-295-0255 465 Beverly Pl., Lake Forest, IL 60045 Rep: Renard Represents / 212-490-2450
Steirnagle, Michael Rep: Conrad Represents... / 415-921-7140 Rep: Photocom Inc. / 214-720-2272	Summers, Mark Rep: Richard Solomon / 212-683-1362
Stephen Gressak / 718-834-9198 59 Pineapple St., 5B, Brooklyn, NY 11201 Rep: Cathy Gouch / 415-285-9911	Sweeney, Glynis / 313-548-4381 346 W. Webster, Ferndale, MI 48220 Rep: Ceci Bartels Assoc. / 314-781-7377
Stermer, Dugald / 415-777-0110 600 The Embarcadero, SF, CA 94107 Rep: Jim Lilie / 415-441-4384	Swierzy, Waldemar Rep: Marlena / 212-289-5514
Sterrett, Jane / 212-929-2566 160 Fifth Ave., NYC, NY 10010	Syme, Hugh / 317-529-0978 / 818-508-7137 3868 South Spiceland Road, Newcastle, IN 47362 Rep: Randy Pate & Assoc. / 805-529-8111
Stevens, John / 516-579-5352 53 Clear Meadow, E. Meadow, NY 11554	Taback, Simms Rep: The Newborn Group / 212-260-6700
Stevenson, Dave Rep: Sylvia Franks / 310-276-5282	Tanhauser, Gary Rep: Richard Salzman / 415-285-8267
Stewart, J.W. Rep: Lindgren & Smith / 212-929-5590	Taylor, Dahl Rep: Vicki Morgan Assoc. / 212-475-0440
Stock, Jeff / 617-639-8384 Little Harbor, Marblehead, MA 01945	Taylor, David / 317-634-2728 Rep: Woody Coleman / 216-661-4222
Stribling-Sutherland, Kelly / 817-382-1253 1208 San Gabriel, Denton, TX 76205 Rep: Friend & Johnson / 214-559-0055	Taylor, Joseph / 708-328-2454 2117 Ewing Ave., Evanston, IL 60201 Rep: David Montagano / 708-527-3283 Rep: Mendola / 212-986-5680
Struzan, Drew / 818-578-7291 624 Eaton Dr., Pasadena, CA 91107 Rep: Gerald & Cullen Rapp / 212-889-3337	Teach, Buz Walker / 916-454-3556 2501 11th Ave., Sacramento, CA 95818
Stuart, Walter Rep: Richard Salzman / 415-285-8267	Teisher, Anne Rep: Sylvia Franks / 213-276-5282 Rep: Mary Holland / 602-263-8990

TABLE (3.29). ILLUSTRATION

Illustrators	Illustrators
Tenud, Tish / 916-455-0569 3427 Folsom Blvd, Sacramento, CA 95816	Tsuchiya, Julie Rep: Joanne Hedge / 213-874-1661
Terreson, Jeffrey / 914-764-4897 66 Hack Green Rd., Pound Ridge, NY 10576 Rep: Mendola / 212-986-5680	Tucker, Ezra Rep: Jim Lilie / 415-441-4384 Rep: France Aline Inc. / 213-933-2500
Tessler, John / 916-443-9080 1409 R St., Sacramento, CA 95814	Turgeon, Jim Rep: Penny & Stermer Group / 212-505-9342
Thewes, Thomas / 810-545-4053 1229 E. Lincoln, Royal Oak, MI 48067 pages 44 - 45	Turgeon, Pol / 514-273-8329 5187 Keanne-Mance #3, Montreal, Quebec, Canada H2V4K2 Rep: Lindgren & Smith / 212-929-5590
Thompson, Thierry Rep: Mendola / 212-986-5680	Turk, Stephen / 310-788-0682
Thorpe, Jim / 615-690-8655 1728 Blackwood Dr., Knoxville, TN 37923	Turner-Coleman, Stacy / 718-441-1114 92-11 91st. Ave., Apt. #1, Jamaica, NY 11421
Tiani, Alex Rep: Daniele Collignon / 212-243-4209	Uhl, David / 303-455-3535 1501 Boulder St., Denver, CO 80211
Tillinghast, Dave Rep: Corey Graham / 415-956-4750	Ulriksen, Mark Rep: Norman Maslon / 415-641-4376
Timmons, Bonnie / 610-380-0292 446 Springdell Rd., R.D.5, Coatesville, PA 19320 Rep: Joanne Palulian / 212-581-8338 / 203-866-3734	Unger, Judy Rep: Penny & Stermer Group / 212-505-9342
Tinkelman, Murray Rep: Jim Lilie / 415-441-4384	Unruh, Jack / 214-871-0187 2706 Fairmont, Dallas, TX 75201 Rep: Susan Wells / 404-255-1430 Rep: Ron Sweet / 415-433-1222
Toelke, Cathleen / 914-876-8776 P.O. Box 487, Rhinebeck, NY 12572	Uram, Lauren / 718-789-7717 838 Carroll St., Brooklyn, NY 11215
Tom, Jack / 203-452-0889 135 Lazy Brook Rd., Monroe, CT 06468	Vaccaro, Victor / 516-286-6266 6 Sunny Dr., Bellport, NY 11713
Tomasello, Sam / 718-728-4914 36-01 31st Ave., #4A, Astoria, NY 11106	Vanderbeek, Don Rep: Scott Hull Associates / 513-433-8383
Torp, Cynthia Rep: Jan Collier / 415-383-9026 Rep: Lindgren & Smith / 212-929-5590	Vargo, Kurt Rep: Pamela Korn / 717-595-9298
Torres, Carlos / 718-768-3296 1139 Prospect Ave., Ste. 1D, Brooklyn, NY 11218	Ventura, Andrea / 212-932-0412 2785 Broadway, #5I, NYC, NY 10025
Traulle, Abel / 714-775-7455 11605 Marigold Circle, Fountain Valley, CA 92708	Ventura, Marco Rep: Jacqueline Dedell / 212-741-2539
	Verkaaik, Ben Rep: Jeff Lavaty & Assoc. / 212-355-0910

$$F = (a \times p)^4$$

TABLE (3.30). ILLUSTRATION

Illustrators	Illustrators
Vitale, Stefano Rep: Lindgren & Smith / 212-929-5590	Weakley, Mark Rep: Susan Gomberg / 212-206-0066
Viviano, Sam / 212-242-1471	Weber, James / 614-777-0631 3637 Ridgewood Dr., Hilliard, OH 43026
Von Schmidt, Erich / 818-559-1490 859 N. Hollywood Way, #214, Burbank, CA 91505	Weinstein, Ellen / 212-675-4360 1 Union Square, #914, NYC, NY 10010
→ Von Ulrich, Mark / 212-989-9325 1 Union Sq. W., Studio 903, NYC, NY 10003 page 46	Welker, Gaylord / 213-965-9611 607 S. Detroit St., LA, CA 90036 Rep: Joan Kelly / 212-865-0692
Voo, Rhonda Rep: Repertoire / 214-369-6990	Weller, Don Rep: Daniele Collignon / 212-243-4209 Rep: Jae Wagoner / 310-392-4877
Wagner, Brett Rep: Sylvia Franks/The Crea / 310-276-5282	Wepplo, Mike Rep: Christine Prapas / 503-246-9511
Waller, Charles Rep: Martha Productions / 310-390-8663	Westerberg, Rob / 212-242-4319 424 W. 22nd St., #9, NYC, NY 10011
Walton, Brenda Rep: Conrad Represents... / 415-921-7140	Wexler, Ed / 818-888-3858 4701 Don Pio Dr., Woodland Hills, CA 91364
Ward, John / 516-546-2906 125 Maryland Ave., Freeport, NY 11520	→ White, Eric / 415-821-3839 1142 Castro St., SF, CA 94114 page 38
Warnick, Elsa Rep: Christine Prapas / 503-246-9511 Rep: Mary Holland & Co. / 602-263-8990	Whitehead, S.B. / 212-686-5250 200 E. 27th St. #5C, NYC, NY 10016
Warren, Jim / 310-423-0460 1260 E. 57th St., Long Beach, CA 90805 Rep: Alan Lynch / 908-813-8718	Wickart, Mark / 708-369-0164 6293 Surrey Ridge Rd., Lisle, IL 60532
Warshaw Blumenthal / 212-867-4225 104 E. 40th St., Ste. 504, NYC, NY 10016	Widener, Terry Rep: Michele Manasse / 215-862-2091
Watford, Wayne Rep: Ceci Bartels Assocs. / 314-781-7377 Rep: Martha Productions / 310-390-8663	Wiemann, Roy / 212-431-3793 P.O. Box 271, NYC, NY 10012 Rep: Jett & Associates / 502-635-1401
Watkinson, Brent Rep: Bernstein & Andruilli, / 212-682-1490 Rep: Joanne Hedge / 213-874-1661	Wiggins, Mick / 510-524-3076 Rep: Jacqueline Dedell / 212-741-2539
Watts, Stan / 818-889-9199 Rep: Mary Busacca / 415-776-4247 Rep: Ceci Bartels Assocs. / 314-781-7377	Wilcox, David Rep: The Newborn Group / 212-260-6700
Wawiorka, Matthew Rep: Lisa Freeman / 317-255-1197	Wiley, Paul / 800-627-8071 / 212-627-8071 410 W. 24th St., #12I, NYC, NY 10011
	Willardson & Assoc. Rep: Vicki Morgan Assoc. / 212-475-0440

$$F = (a \times p)^4$$

TABLE (3.31). ILLUSTRATION

Illustrators	Illustrators
Williams, Lorraine / 718-638-7203 36 Plaza St., 4B, Brooklyn, NY 11238	Yamashiro, Allen Rep: Lehmen Dabney / 206-325-8595
Wilton, Nicholas / 415-488-4710 PO Box 292, Lagunitas, CA 94938 Rep: Jan Collier / 415-383-9026	Yang, James Rep: David Goldman / 212-807-6627
Wimmer, Chuck / 216-526-2820 7760 Oakhurst Circle, Cleveland, OH 44141	Yankus, Marc / 212-242-6334 570 Hudson St., NYC, NY 10014
Winters, Greg / 818-798-7666 2139 Pinecrest Dr., Altadena, CA 91001	Yealdhall, Gary Rep: Tonal Values / 305-576-0142
Wisenbaugh, Jean Rep: Lindgren & Smith / 212-929-5590	Yelchin, Eugene Rep: Motion Artists / 213-851-7737
Witte, Michael Rep: Gerald & Cullen Rapp / 212-889-3337	Younger, Heidi Rep: Jacqueline Dedell / 212-741-2539
Wolf, Bruce Rep: Vicki Morgan Assoc. / 212-475-0440 Rep: Sweet Represents / 415-433-1222	Zeto, Toni / 310-393-5431 901 Tenth St., Ste. 301, Santa Monica, CA 90403
Wolf, Elizabeth / 202-686-0179 3717 Alton Pl. NW, Washington, DC 20016	Zick, Brian Rep: Ellen Knable & Assocs / 310-855-8855
Wolfe, Corey Rep: Nancy George / 213-655-0998	Zielinski, John Rep: Sal Barracca & Assoc. / 212-889-2400
Wolff, Punz / 201-385-6028 / 212-254-5705 457 Herkimer Ave., Haworth, NJ 07641	Ziemienski, Dennis Rep: Jim Lilie / 415-441-4384 Rep: Irmeli Holmberg / 212-545-9155
Wolynski, Voytek / 203-229-8533 56 Liberty St., New Britian, CT 06052	Ziering, Bob / 212-873-0034 151 W. 74th St., NYC, NY 10023 Rep: Gerald & Cullen Rapp / 212-889-3337
Woodman, Dave / 818-547-6019 750 Kings Rd., #224, LA, CA 90069 Rep: Elizabeth Poje / 310-556-1439	→ Zimmerman, Robert / 704-252-9689 RZimm@A0L.com page 21
Woodruff, Thomas / 212-924-4192 29 Cornelia St., #17, NYC, NY 10014	Zingarelli, Mark Rep: Pat Hackett / 206-447-1600
Woolley, Janet Rep: Alan Lynch / 908-813-8718	Zuber-Mallison, Carol Rep: Brooke & Company / 214-352-9192
Worthington, George / 214-255-6481 3118 Parker St., Irving, TX 75062	Zwingler, Randall Rep: Les Mintz / 305-454-6566
Wray, Wendy Rep: Vicki Morgan Associate / 212-475-0440	Zwolak, Paul Rep: Marlena / 212-289-5514
Yaccarino, Dan / 212-675-5335 Rep: Lindgren & Smith / 212-929-5590	

$$F = (a \times p)^4$$

Table (3.32). Illustration

Notes	Notes

the faster an object *moves*, the slower time *moves* .

(4.A)

the speed of light

is the

fountain of youth

$$\frac{\text{representatives}}{(\text{syndication} + \text{stock})} \times \text{photographers}$$

(4 . B)

RON BAXTER SMITH
NEW YORK 212 343 0132
REEL AVAILABLE UPON REQUEST

TORONTO
416 462 3040
REEL AVAILABLE UPON REQUEST

KURT COBAIN 1967-1994
SPIN
Rolling Stone
WOMEN IN ROCK
LIZ PHAIR
A Rocker is a Star is Born
George Bush's Heroin Connection
Robert Redford
R.E.M.'s 'Monster' New Album
BADLANDS: WHITE GANGS IN IOWA
SPIN
BECK
The Loser Takes All
By Mike Rubin
NINE INCH NAILS
This Little Piggie Went Agro
By Dorsey Steinke
The Unbearable Darkness of Being
JOHNNY CASH
By Barry Hannah
BEASTIE BOYS
MOST OF THESE
AGAIN SO DON
ANYTHING N
WERE THE DAY
OF MY CA
SO TO
KURT
ART + COMMERCE
2060737

PEOPLE, I WILL NEVER PHOTOGRAPH
THINK I AM SHOWING
THAN WHO
SAID
YOU
THEY
FRONT
THING
WORK
TH
FRANK w OCKENFELS 3

HAWKES

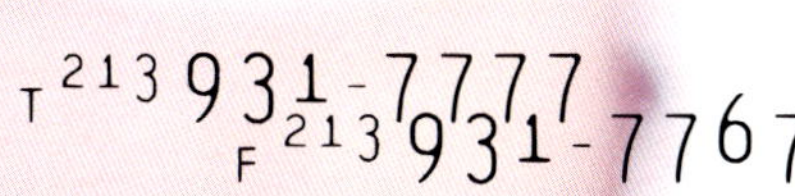

SCOGIN MAYO   REP|FRIEND & JOHNSON   DALLAS 214.559.0055   SAN FRANCISCO 415.927.4500   CHICAGO 312.943.7885   NEW YORK 212.808.0022

SCOGIN MAYO   REP|FRIEND & JOHNSON   DALLAS 214.559.0055   SAN FRANCISCO 415.927.4500   CHICAGO 312.943.7885   NEW YORK 212.808.0022

WARNING
PUBLIC NOTICE OF ATTACHMENT
bullets in
revolvers
ammuniti
19 4
POLICE
9mm LUGER
WT
LUGER
SHARPSHOOTER
Compton Blvd
105 EAST
Norwalk

CHROME DOME STUDIOS
Daniel Arsenault
Photographic Collage
Ruthless Records
Easy E
NY: 212 595 1125
LA: 310 641 8556
CH: 312 670 7737
SF: 415 325 9678
Studio 213 931 6441
Art Director: SEAN ALATORRE | MORBIDO BIZARRIO, L.A.

Michael Lavine Photography

represented by Rob Magnotta

at Edge 212.343.2260

represented by
AMY SOSINSKY at EDGE
photography
212 343
2260
jana leōn

GRAVITY · CHAOS ·
YTIVARG · A!TRENI ·
CHAOS

jana leōn

MICHAEL WONG

REPRESENTED BY

EDGE

NEW YORK CITY

212 343 2260

LOS ANGELES

213 954 9422

JOSEPH CULTICE

Studio 211 East 3rd Street #6R NYC, NY 10009 212 388 9003

Trent Reznor of Nine Inch Nails

GARY
HUSH

503 222 4786
PHOTO
GRAPHY

Thomas Heinser

415 495 0365

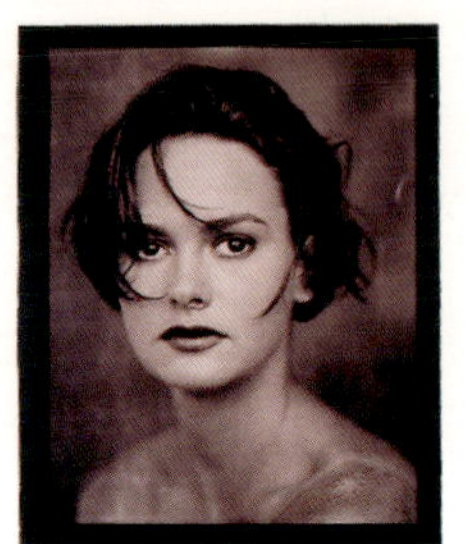

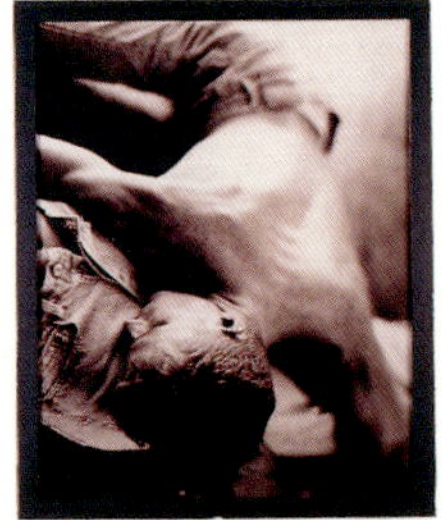

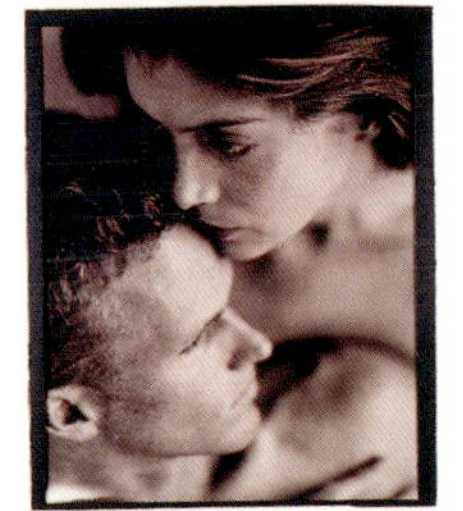

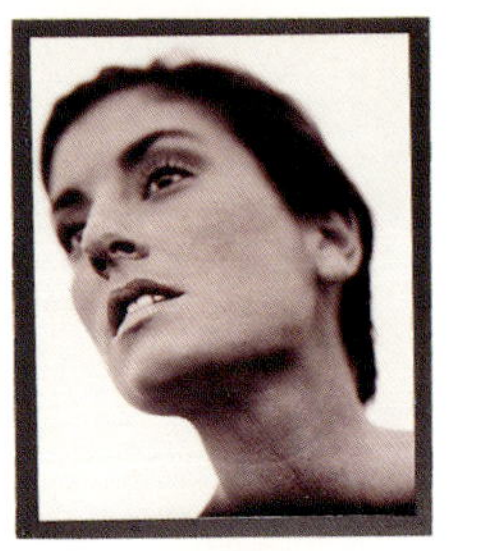

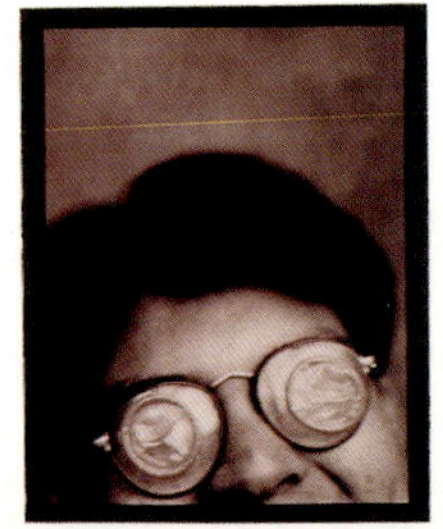

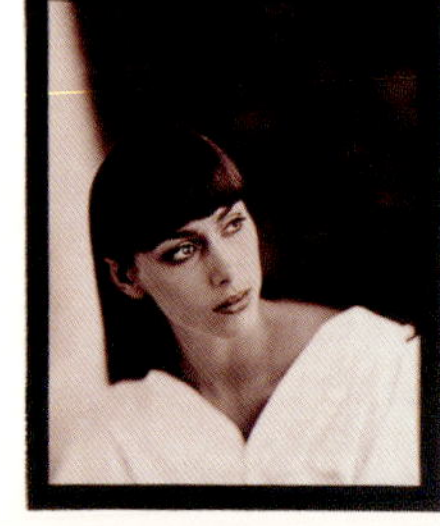

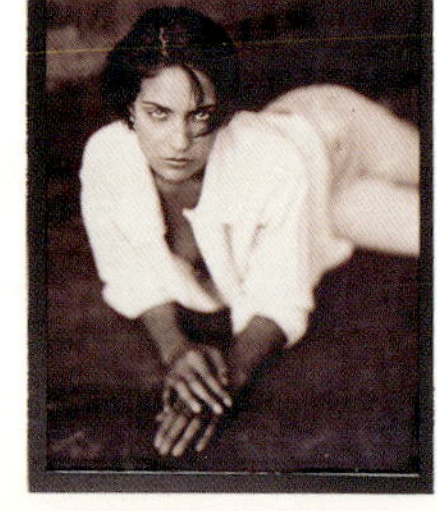

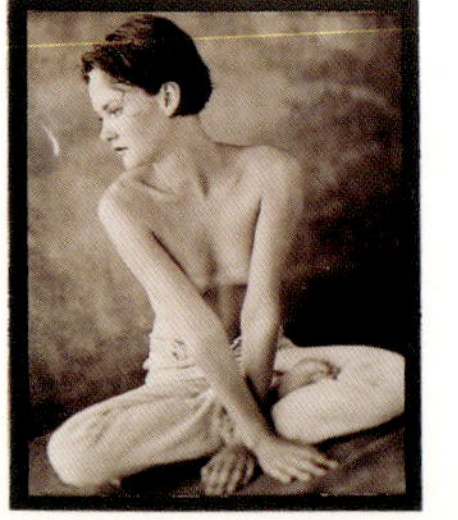

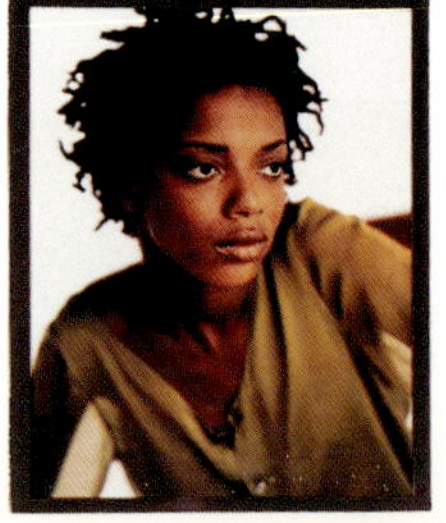

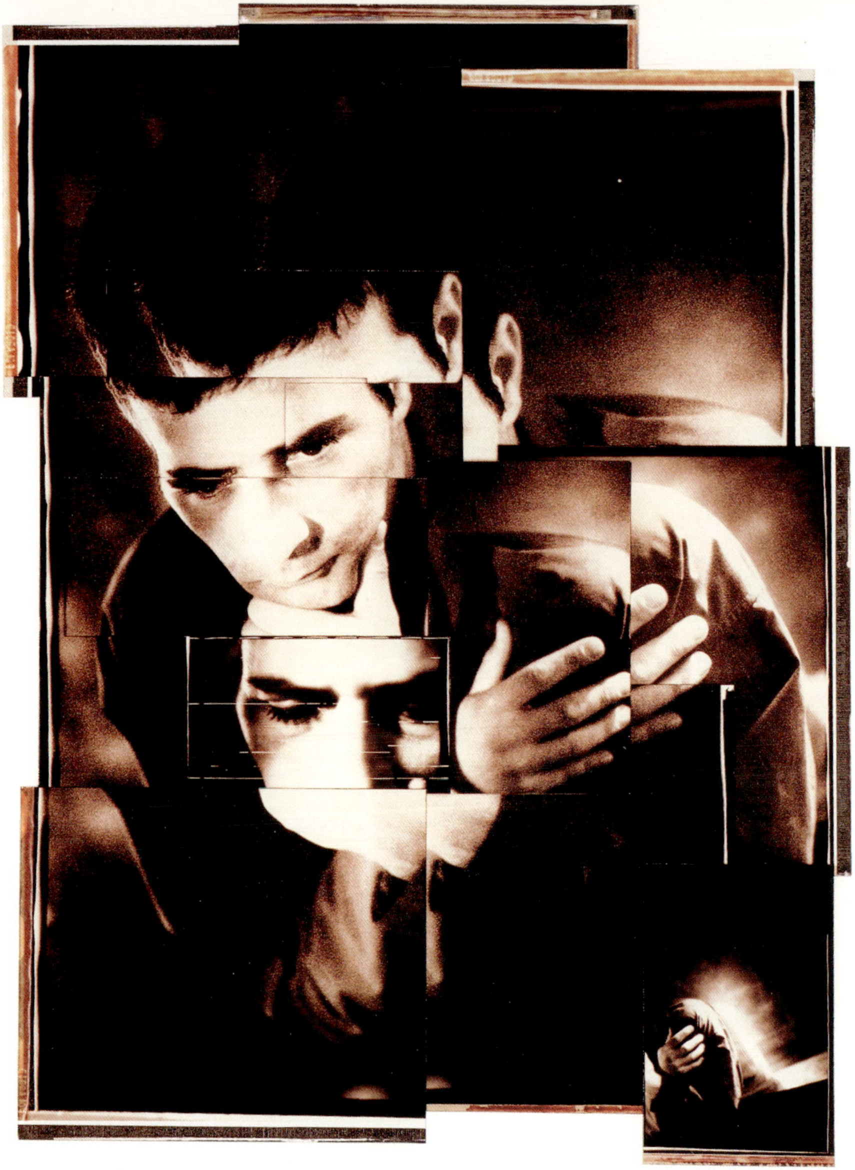

sanopinio
elatimago
verslumen

robertolding

Robert Olding Photography
3315 Sacramento Street, No.305, San Francisco, California 94118
Vox 415.905.5939 And Fax 415.931.2630

dennis galante new york city 212 529-5531

represented by samantha lewin 212 228-5530

5200 latona avenue northeast seattle wa 98105 206.633.3775
represented by lehmen dabney inc. 206.325.8595 fax 206.325.8594

BEV PARKER
212 645 0580

213.957.5780

Tracy
Lamonica

photography

Deborah Roundtree Photography
(213) 933-0297
Reps:

Los Angeles, David Zaitz (310) 207-4806…New York, Randy Cole (212) 679-5933

Dallas , Liz McCann (214) 526-2252…Chicago, Randi Fiat (312) 663-5300

BUTCH

BELAIR
BUTCH BELAIR IS REPRESENTED BY MICHAEL GINSBURG (212)679-8881

BUTCH
BELAIR

BUTCH BELAIR IS REPRESENTED BY MICHAEL GINSBURG (212)679-8881
BB

DARRYL ESTRINE
IS REPRESENTED
BY MICHAEL GINSBURG
(212)679-8881

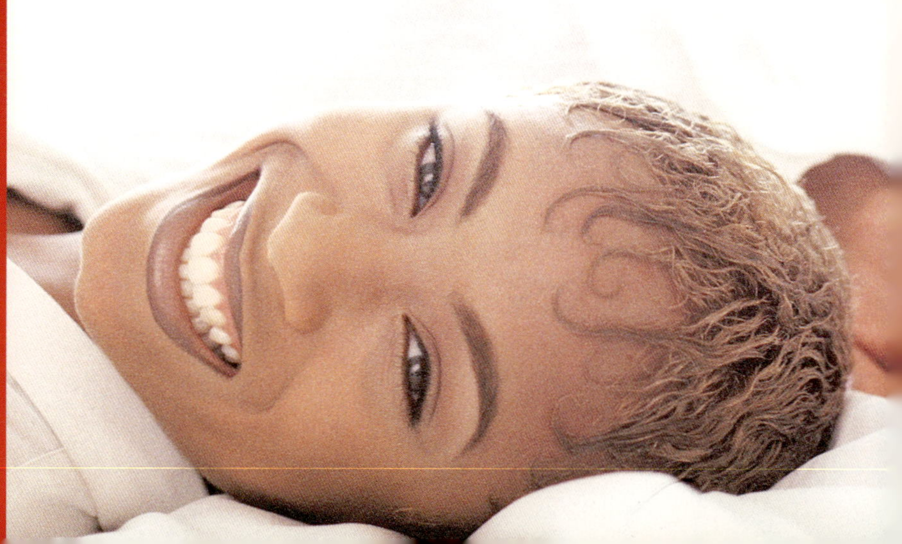

DARRYL ESTRINE

GLAMART
CHRIS SANDERS
SEVENTY THREE SPRING STREET
#502 | NEW YORK CITY 10012
212 343-0003 | FAX 343-0087
©1994 CHRIS SANDERS, INC.

CHRIS SANDERS IS REPRESENTED BY MICHAEL GINSBURG 212 679-8881
©1994 CHRIS SANDERS, INC.

JEFFREY WEISS
PHOTOGRAPHY
213 - 655 - 3519

Terminator II

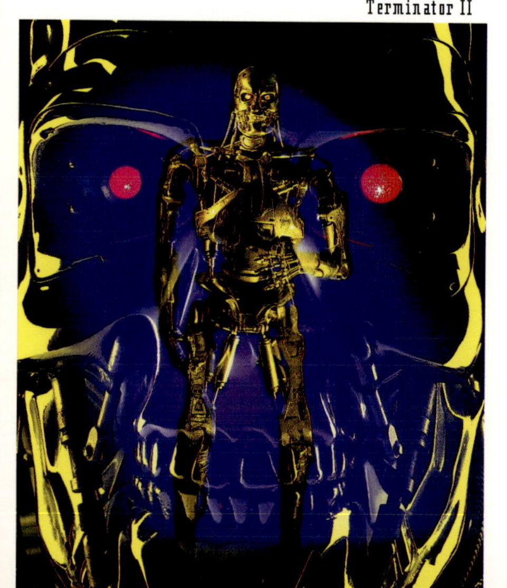

Jurassic Park

Edward Scissorhands

Valerie Gates

Photography&Film • 310.657.9700

ARTIST REPRESENTATIVE
TEL 415.863.4969
FAX 415.863.3937

S H I V E L Y

BLU R
VANS
MORROW SNOWBOARDS
BIKINI
BURTON SNOWBOARDS
RAY GUN
+
TREVOR . GRAVES
503.362.3102.
rid e
DESIGN
PHOTOGRAPHS

tyler **B** boley

photography

scattle 206 860 7166

WALDORF
415 5861170
rep. HENDRA

0 1 2 3 4 5 6 7 8 9

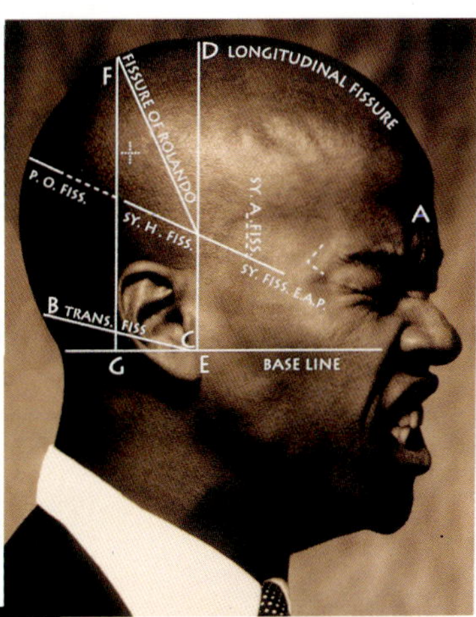
D LONGITUDINAL FISSURE
F FISSURE OF ROLANDO
P. O. FISS.
SY. H. FISS
SY. A. FISS.
SY. FISS. E.A.P.
A
B TRANS. FISS
G C E BASE LINE

iron pipe STUDIO 415 5435599

REUBEN NJAA

(nah)

VACHON

P H O T O G R A P H Y

185 Clara Street San Francisco California 94107   phone: 415.777.3273   fax: 415.957.1105
Represented by Bobbi Wendt phone: 415.487.2160 fax: 415.487.0129

P H O T O G R A P H Y

185 Clara Street San Francisco California 94107   phone: 415.777.3273   fax: 415.957.1105

Represented by Bobbi Wendt phone: 415.487.2160 fax: 415.487.0129

JOHN EDER • PHOTOGRAPHY • 213 661 9120

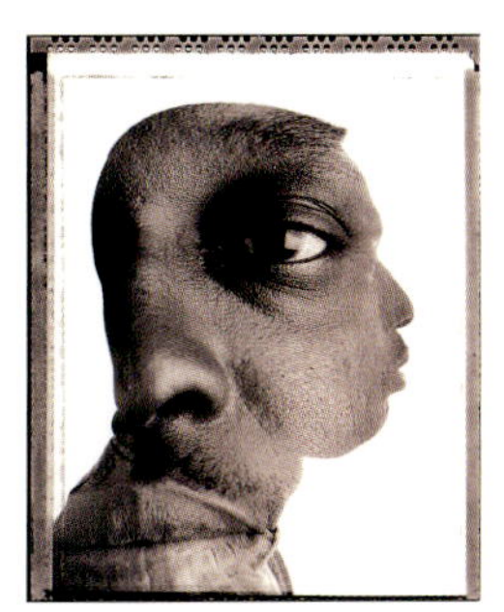

DAVE TEEL photography 213-658-6394

A b r a m s *Lacagnina*

alan abrams / francesca lacagnina / 206 624 7646

Neal Farris
294
829
5612

David Perry
415•487•1325

Michael Northrup
410•669•4705

Eric Van Den Brulle
212•721•2611

STOCK AVAILABLE THROUGH photonica

141 Fifth Avenue suite 8 south
NY, NY 10010 212•505•9000
Fax: 212•505•2200

ROBERT OLDING
415•905•5939

RIEDER & WALSH
412•621•1268

PAUL VOZDIC
212•388•8136

eric tucker

l.a.
310 452.1905

n.y.
212 228.7924
REPRESENTED BY: PATTI SILVERSTEIN

DESIGN: KEN LOH 805.263.9485

photography

PeterMichelena
213 465.5773 LA
212 645.7676 NY

PeterMicheleny
213 465.5773 LA
212 645.7676 NY

E.J. CARR

236 WEST 27TH STREET NY NY 10011

212 242 0818

E.J. CARR
236 WEST 27TH STREET NY NY 10001
212 242 0818

Greg Watermann shoots lots of famous celebrities in their best light

Randy Travis, Warner Bros Recording Artist

And sometimes he just shoots

GREG WATERMANN IS REPRESENTED BY BROOKE DAVIS 214-352-9192

Paul Elledge

P H O T O G R A P H Y

STUDIO TELEPHONE
312 733-8021

Paul Elledge

312 733-8021

D O R O T H Y   L O W
P H O T O G R A P H Y

213 957 0712

HUGH   KRETSCHMER

East Coast West Coast

SHARPE + ASSOCIATES

Los Angeles 310.641.8556

New York 212.595.1125

Studio 213.627.6554

Laura Wagner   213·465·5773 212·645·/676

[Bob LONDON]
[212] 966 4894
PHOTOGRAPHY

ANNALISA
2139391998
PHOTOGRAPHY

VISAGES
rps inc.

LEE STANFORD
PHOTOGRAPHY
420 5TH ST N. NO. 845
MPLS. MN. 55401
612.338.7901

m
3.
meredithparmelee
213.934.9969
rmelee
PHOTOGRAPHY
m

GARY
GOLDBERG
212
228 4820
agramonte-hynes design

ERNEST **WASHINGTON**
(4o4) 522+4488 photography

Sky Cries Mary/World Domination

Layne Staley/Rolling Stone

K a r e n   M o s k o w i t z

here: 206 860-1242   there: 213-627-3840

S. PETER LOPEZ

2 1 3 - 6 5 5 - 1 0 5 0

Karen Ollis

Photographic Illustration

Assignment•Fine Art•Stock

1847 Superior Avenue

Cleveland, Ohio 44114

216.781.8646

Fax 781.3040

ROBIN DAVIS　　✳　　404 876 6341

Scott Thomas imagery

CHUCK GOODENOUGH PHOTOGRAPHY

Voice: 213 881 9455   E-Mail: JHFG35A@prodigy.com   Fax: 213 881 9456

p h o t o
+
d i g i t a l

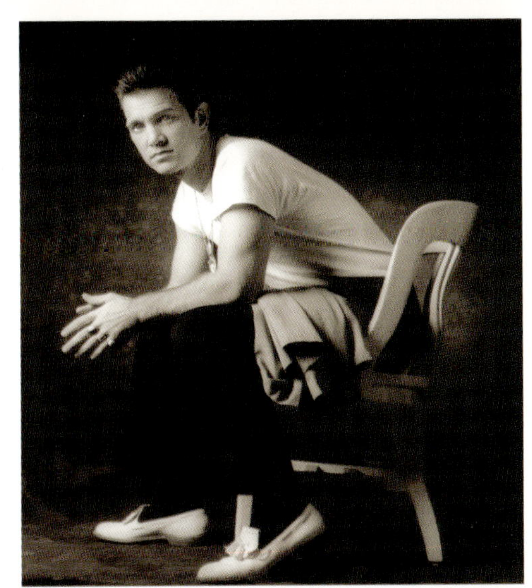

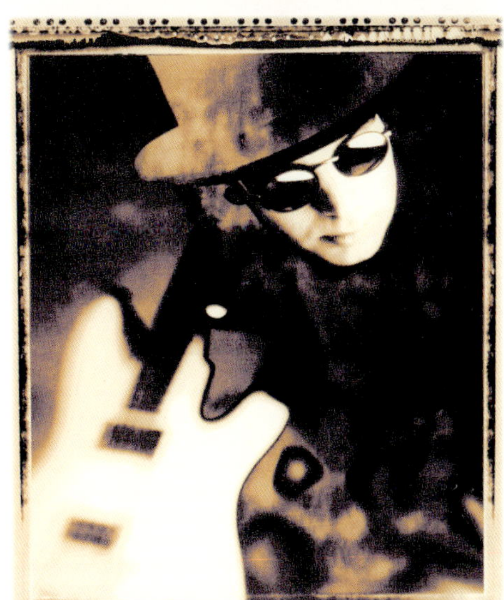

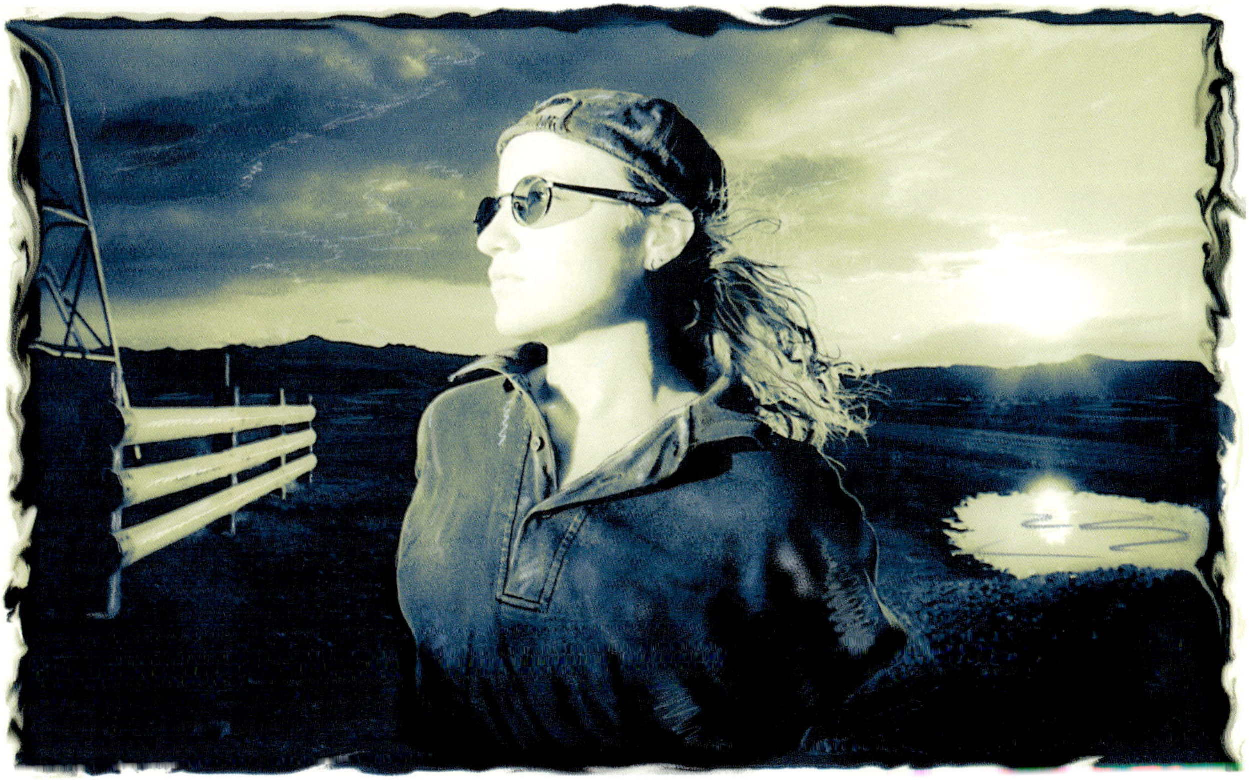

michael sexton

p h o t o + d i g i t a l

4 1 5 6 2 1 5 3 4 5

I might tend to play
my image,
Vito Acconci
almost automatically,
in front of a camera.
And maybe the camera
is about making
the image
or confirming
and establishing
and distributing
the image
as expected pose.
Mitchell Kearney   704-377-7662

WILLIAM S. BURROUGHS

ROBERT CARDIN STUDIO
SAN FRANCISCO, CALIFORNIA

ROBERT CARDIN STUDIO   142 TENTH STREET SAN FRANCISCO, CALIFORNIA 94103 FAX 415 255 1278 PHONE 415 255 4040

RJ MUNA
PHOTOGRAPHY

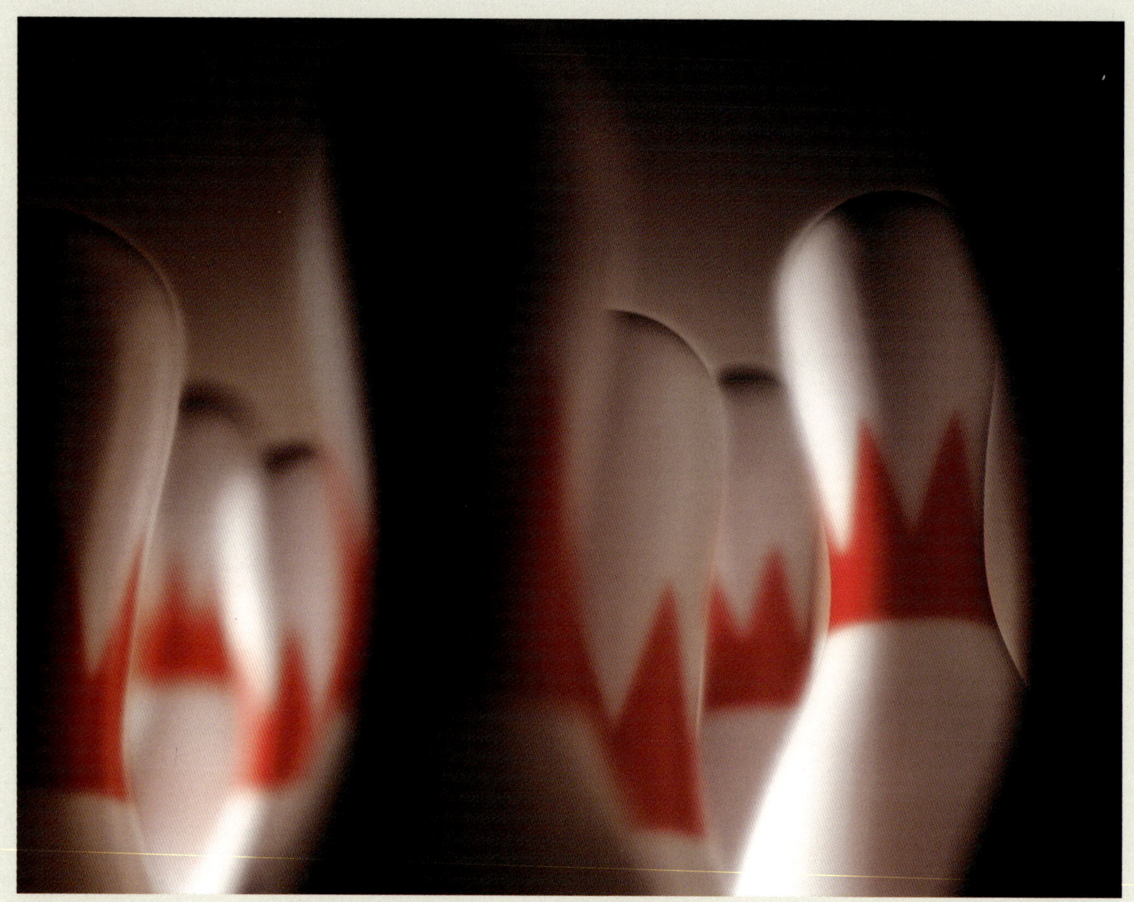

SAN FRANCISCO   415.468.8225

PARISH KOHANIM

TEL 404.892.0099
FAX 404.892.0156

P A R I S H   K O H A N I M

TEL 404.892.0099
FAX 404.892.0156

DAVID VANCE PHOTOGRAPHER 150 N.W. 164 STREET MIAMI, FL 33169 305 354 2083 305 354 2085 FAX 305 354 2085

DAVID VAN CE
DAVID VANCE
DAVID VANCE
DAVID VANCE

425 BROOME STREET 3R. NEW YORK, N.Y. 10013

212 925-0359

212 925-0359

425 BROOME STREET 3R. NEW YORK. N.Y. 10013

DEBORAH RAVEN

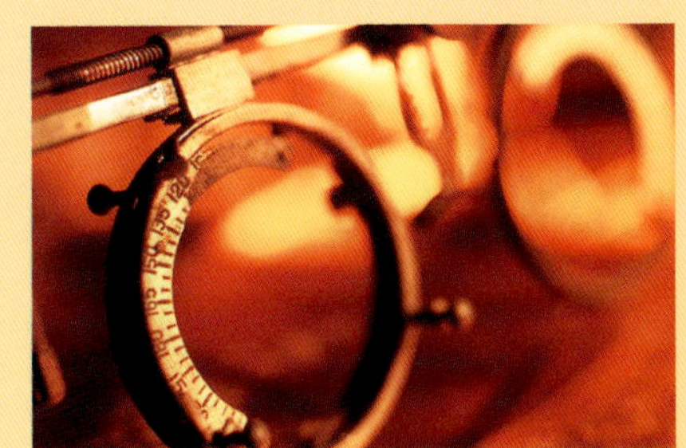

HARRINGTON
STUDIO

942 FOURTH AVENUE SOUTH, NASHVILLE, TN 37210

Trisha Yearwood / MCA Records

Indo G & Lil' Blunt / Luke Records

Tony Joe White / Remark Records

CAINES

BRUCE CAINES PHOTOGRAPHY   433 WEST 34TH STREET   NEW YORK CITY 10001

212 · 594 · 9443

scott
VAN
OSDOL

STUDIO 2
306 WEST 16TH STREET
AUSTIN, TEXAS 78701
512/ 469-9510

Cristo Rey de Las
Mechanistas

MICHAEL LLEWELLYN

TEL 213·223·1792

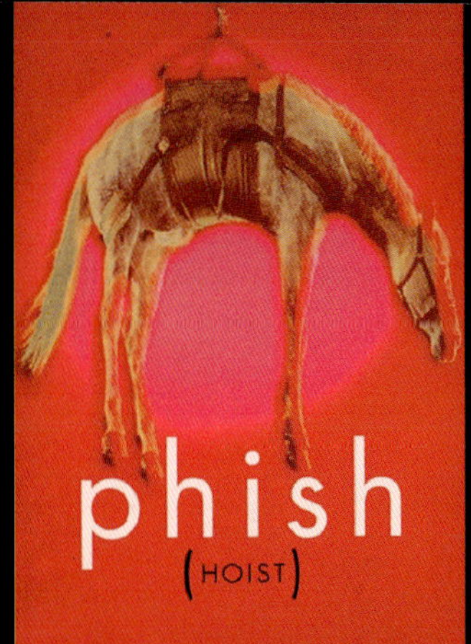

phish
(HOIST)

CHARLES MARAIA

New York City   212.206.8156

GARY SPECTOR

212 · 695 · 5140

ll me a gimp, call me paralyzed for me, but

TIME, OCTOBER 30, 1993   47

pretty much healed itself." says

ROBBIE McCLARAN 503-234-6588

st don't call me something that I'm not," he

within legal radioac-
tive limits—less
radioactive than
Denver."

s. "I'm not

THE NEW YORK TIMES MAGAZINE / JUNE 7, 1992

differently

led. I can't

walk. But I

also hate it

en people

MARCH 1993 • OUTSIDE

say 'wheel-

hair-bound.' People who can walk are not ar

DERRICK SCAMMELL IS A SPOKESPERSON FOR
THE DEPARTMENT OF ENERGY.

PHOTOGRAPHY BY ROBBIE McCLARAN

Thus t

boo s of heartbeat filled my
got ight, and my movements
simultaneously.

journey

I managed the drop and
bothering to aim, I fired. "Boo
and chaos swept the aisle
Damn, I missed!

I fired again and hit him in
bullet knocked him back, and
weapon discharged into the
three more times to create a
intensity, then turned and tw
my mother. I totally forgot I
my hand. I tucked it while jo
household appliance aisle.
there, I panicked and made
door. There among the other
shoppers, I found Mom. I
and ushered her away from t
Boy, was that you?" she a
it wasn't. "Kody, what happe
made no attempt to
attempt was a timely esca
silence, block after block.
looked at each other
ack across Western Ave
breathe better in reflection
Fuck him, he was gonna sh
my shooting as suspicion
very dangerous; we all knew

nightm
world.
ed by
perpet
unspea
crimes
survivi
of thei
locked
of deat
played
nation

MONSTER
23
TEXAS MONTHLY 87
"Part of me had been
expecting a Charles Manson
type. I wondered, could I
even speak to this man? And
then he came into the visit-
ing area. He had showered
and he had on a clean blue
shirt and his face was like
open field. He
to see me and
humann
loneliness
to. We were both human
beings."
Prejean would return to
Angola many times where
she would learn about
Sonnier, confront him about
the enormity of
he and his brother had com-
SAY-9-NOV/DEC 1993
AMNESTY INTERNATIONAL
ROBBIE McCLARAN 503-234-6588
"Monster" Kody Scott
Photography by Robbie McClaran
18   LOS ANGELES TIMES MAGAZINE, APRIL 4, 1993

greenbergphotography 212.594.5624 jill greenbergphotography 212.594.562

eenbergphotography212.594.5624 jill greenbergphotography212.594.5624 jil

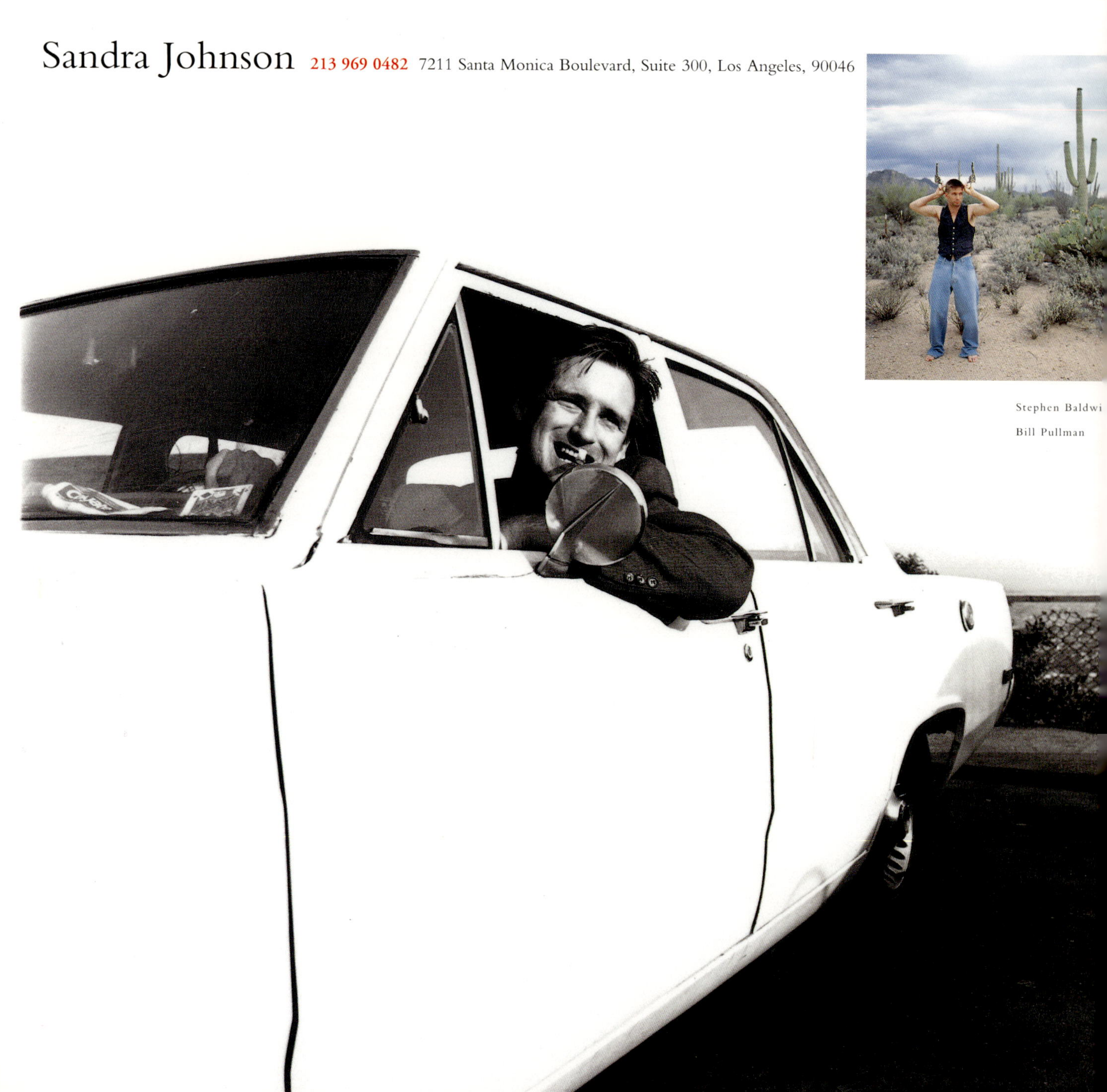

Sandra Johnson

213 969 0482   7211 Santa Monica Boulevard, Suite 300, Los Angeles, 90046

Henry Rollins
Michael Caton Jones
Sandra Bullock
Pauly Shore
Ice Cube

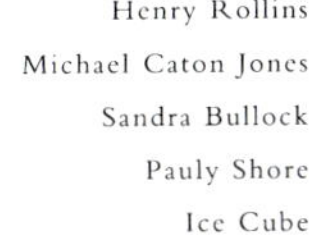

Sandra
Johnson
213 969 0482

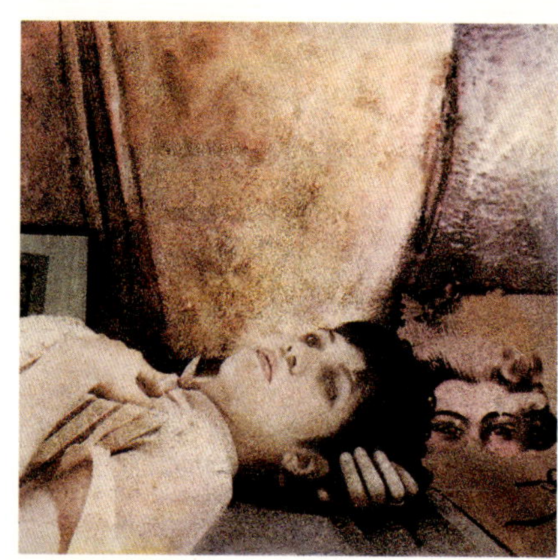

Leah Demchick photography tel/fax 212 873 5536

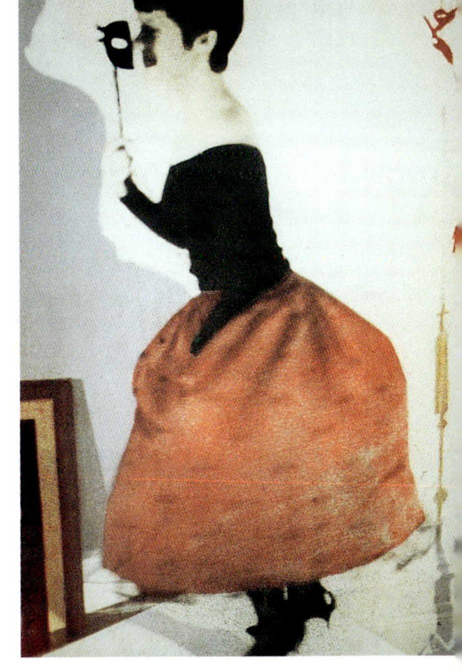

212·2·60·8858
Michael Mazzeo
MICHAEL MAZZEO
MICHAEL MAZZEO
DESIGN BY CAROLYN QUAN/STUDIO Q
MICHAEL

DIANE, LOS ANGELES, CALIFORNIA

JACK ROSENZWEIG, GLEN SUMMIT, PENNSYLVANIA

LL COOL J, LOS ANGELES, CALIFORNIA

michael grecco is represented by/in new york editorial + entertainment = sygma 212 675 7900
/advertising = susan miller 212 905 8400 / in los angeles/keswick hamilton/sygma 213 380 3933

RUSSELL SIMMONS, NEW YORK, NEW YORK

DIANE, LOS ANGELES, CALIFORNIA

ROBERT EVANS, LOS ANGELES, CALIFORNIA

/in new york editorial + entertainment = sygma 212 675 7900
ler 21... ...wick hamilton/sygma 213 380 3933

DEAD CAN DANCE, LOS ANGELES, CALIFORNIA

EL JOURGENSEN, AUSTIN, TEXAS

QUENTIN TARANTINO, LOS ANGELES, CALIFORNIA

marko lavrisha

4 15. 64 7. 95 50

marko
Lavrisha

4 15 . 64 7 . 95 50

MICHAEL MAZZEO
MICHAEL MAZZEO
MAZZEO
212.260.8858

michael grecco is represented by/in new york editorial + entertainment = sygma 212 675 7900
/advertising = susan miller 212 905 8400 / in los angeles/keswick hamilton/sygma 213 380 3933

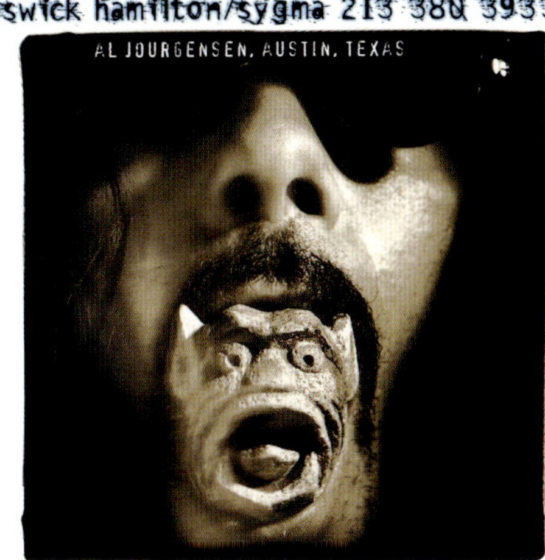

TINA AND THE B-SIDE MOVEMENT   "MONSTER"

CROUSER

MICHAEL CROUSER PHOTOGRAPHER 1624 HARMON PLACE SUITE 224 MINNEAPOLIS MN 55403

612 371 0551

MADRID

CROUSER

MICHAEL CROUSER PHOTOGRAPHER 1624 HARMON PLACE SUITE 224 MINNEAPOLIS MN 55403

612 371 0551

BUTLER
Photography

415 . 777 . 1656

DETROIT

LISA
SPINDLER
PHOTOGRAPHY

2900 EAST JEFFERSON • SUITE 3C • DETROIT, MI 48207 • 313.393.8538

SRGDESIGN
Anthony Artiaga
telephone: 818-505-0849 facsimile 818-760-7146
photography and music video

$$\frac{\text{representatives}}{(\text{syndication} + \text{stock})} \times \text{photographers} \, . \tag{4.1}$$

$$F = (a \times p)^4$$

TABLE (4.2). PHOTOGRAPHY

Photography Representatives	Photography Representatives
Achard, Philippe & Assoc. / 212-614-0962 611 Broadway, Ste. 841, NYC, NY 10012	Black Star / 212-679-3288 116 E. 27th St., 5th Fl., NYC, NY 10016
Aiges, Hillary / 212-247-2992	Black, Pamela / 212-979-2636 149 Fifth Ave., Ste. 800, NYC, NY 10010
Aline, France / 213-933-2500 1076 S. Ogden Dr., LA, CA 90019	Boghosian, Marty / 919-353-1813 201 E. 21st St., NYC, NY 10010
Anderson, Paula / 312-321-0848	Boho Studio / 212-334-8302 254 Elizabeth St., #5A, NYC, NY 10012
Archive Photo / 212-675-0115 / 800-688-5656 530 W. 25th St., NYC, NY 10001	Booth, Tom / 212-243-2750 425 W. 23rd St., #17A, NYC, NY 10011
→ Art + Commerce / 212-206-0737 755 Washington St., 2nd Fl., NYC, NY 10014 pages 4 - 5	Botaish Group, Janet / 310-314-1571 1503 Abbot Kinney Blvd., Venice, CA 90291
Ash, Michael / 212-807-6286 107 W. 25th St., NYC, NY 10001	Braun, Kathy / 415-775-3366 75 Water St., SF, CA 94133
Atols Hoffman / 312-222-0504 405 N. Wabash Ave., Ste 3002, Chicago, IL 60611	→ Brooke & Co. / 214-352-9192 4323 Bluffview Blvd., Dallas, TX 75209 pages 60 - 61
Austin, Yasuko / 213-467-1533 6922 Hollywood Blvd., #620, LA, CA 90028	Brown, Doug / 212-953-0088 60 E. 42nd ST., Ste.2028, NYC, NY 10165
Ayerst, Deborah / 415-567-3570 2546 Sutter St., SF, CA 94115	Burlingham, Tricia / 310-275-3495 10355 Ashton Ave., LA, CA 90024
Barany Communications, Leslie / 212-627-8488 121 W. 27th, Rm. 202, NYC, NY 10001	Bush, Nan / 212-226-0814 135 Watts St., NYC, NY 10013
Barba, Maria / 212-227-4110 65 Reade St, #3B, NYC, NY 10007	Byrnes Brady Barber / 212-875-0226 500 West End Ave., Suite 2A, NYC, NY 10024
Barboza, Ken / 212-505-8635 853 Broadway, #1603, NYC, NY 10003	C Pictures / 214-526-8004 3102 Oaklawn Ave., Dallas, TX 75219
Bartels Associates, Ceci / 314-781-7377 / 212-912-1877 3286 Ivanhoe, St. Louis, MO 63139	Cadenbach, Marilyn / 617-484-7437 149 Oakley Rd., Belmont, MA 02178
Beate Works / 213-653-5088 7916 Melrose, Suite #2, LA, CA 90046	Caputo, Elise / 212-725-0503
Beidler, Barbara / 212-979-6996 648 Broadway, #506, NYC, NY 10012	Carp, Stan / 212-362-4000 2166 Broadway, NYC, NY 10024
Bernstein & Andriulli / 212-682-1490 60 E. 42nd St., NYC, NY 10165	Cartel / 718-263-2010 135-11 Coolidge Ave., Kew Gardens, NY 11435
Bina Talent / 212-533-1734 108 E. 16th St., NYC, NY 10003	Casey, Judy / 212-255-3252 96 Fifth Ave., #1K, NYC, NY 10011

TABLE (4.3). PHOTOGRAPHY

Photography Representatives	Photography Representatives
Casey, Marge / 212-486-9575 245 E. 63rd St., NYC, NY 10021	→ Edge / 212-343-2260 596 Broadway, Ste. 1104, NYC, NY 10012 pages 12 - 15
Charles, Bill / 212-213-6810 220 E. 24th St., #6H, NYC, NY 10010	Epstein, Rhoni / 310-207-5937 11711 Gosen Ave., #5, LA, CA 90049
Clarke, Teri / 212-460-5022 57 East 11th Street, 6th Floor, NYC, NY 10003	Fandrich, Jeff / 214-324-3959 6102 E. Mockingbird, #192, Dallas, TX 75214
→ Cole, Randy / 212-679-5933 24 W. 30th St., 5th Fl, NYC, NY 10001 page 29	→ Fiat, Randi / 312-663-5300 1727 S. Indiana, Chicago, IL 60616 page 29
Comport, Allan / 813-579-4499 750 94th Ave. N, #203, St. Petersburg, FL 33702	Fox Art / 213-653-6484 8350 Melrose Ave., Ste. 201, LA, CA 90069
Conlon, Jean / 212-966-9897 461 Broome St., NYC, NY 10013	→ Friend & Johnson / 214-559-0055 3624 Oaklawn, Ste. 300, Dallas, TX 75219 pages 8 - 9
Connolly, Elyse / 212-598-4473 270 Park Ave. So., NYC, NY 10010	→ Friend & Johnson / 312-943-7885 676 St. Clair, #1550, Chicago, IL 60611 pages 8 - 9
Conrad, James / 415-921-7140 2149 Lyon St., #5, SF, CA 94115	→ Friend & Johnson / 415-927-4500 325 Wilson Way, Larkspur, CA 94939 pages 8 - 9
Cornelia Artists Rep. / 212-620-0544 145 Ave. of the Americas, Ste. 200, NYC, NY 10013	→ Friend & Johnson / 212-808-0022 325 E. 41st St., Ste. 604, NYC, NY 10017 pages 8 - 9
Cornell, Kathleen / 310-301-8059 737 Milwood Ave., Venice, CA 90291	Frith, Amy / 617-268-2506 131 G St., 3rd Fl., Boston, MA 02127
Creative Resource/Sylvia Franks, The / 310-276-5282 12056 Summit Circle, Beverly Hills, CA 90210	Gamma Liaison / 212-447-2505 11 E. 26th St., 17th Fl., NYC, NY 10010
Cuomo, Celeste / 214-443-9111 3311 Oaklawn Ave., #300, Dallas, TX 75219	Gamma Liaison / 213-469-2242 6606 Sunset Blvd., Ste. 201, LA, CA 90028
DLM / 212-297-0041 60 E. 42nd St., NYC, NY 10165	Gardner, Jean / 213-464-2492 444 N. Larchmont Blvd., Ste. 108, LA, CA 90004
Daley, Katie / 212-465-2420 245 W. 29th St., 16th Fl., NYC, NY 10001	George Reps / 310-399-1664 256 Horizon Ave., Venice, CA 90291
Day, Ursula / 212-979-8591 24 Fifth Ave., #531, NYC, NY 10011	→ Ginsburg, Michael / 212-679-8881 240 E. 27th St., #24E, NYC, NY 10016 pages 30 - 37
Dodge & Associates, Sharon / 206-622-7035 1201 First Ave. S., Ste. 202, Seattle, WA 98134	
→ Edge / 213-954-9422 5757 Wilshire Blvd., Pent. #20, LA, CA 90036 pages 12 - 15	

$$F = (a \times p)^4$$

TABLE (4.4). PHOTOGRAPHY

Photography Representatives	Photography Representatives
Green, Anita / 212-674-4788 718 Broadway, NYC, NY 10003	Keith, Kelly / 213-224-8288 618-D Moulton Ave., LA, CA 90031
Hackett, Pat / 206-447-1600 101 Yesler Way, #502, Seattle, WA 98104	⟶ Keswick Hamilton/Sygma / 213-380-3933 3519 W. Sixth St., LA, CA 90020 pages 118 - 119
Hall & Associates / 310-652-7322 1010 S. Robertson Blvd., #10, LA, CA 90035	Ketcham, Laurie / 212-481-9592 210 E. 36th St., #6C, NYC, NY 10016
Hanson & Talent, Jim / 312-337-7770 777 N. Michigan Ave., Chicago, IL 60611	Knable & Associates, Inc., Ellen / 310-855-8855 1233 S. La Cienega Blvd, LA, CA 90035
Harlib Associates, Inc., Joel / 312-573-1370 10 E. Ontario St., Ste.4708, Chicago, IL 60611	Kolea / 206-784-1136 2814 NW 72nd St., Seattle, WA 98117
Haynes, Dawn / 212-431-8631 185 Franklin, #3, NYC, NY	Korman, Alison / 212-727-1442 135 W. 24th St., PHA, NYC, NY 10011
⟶ Hedleston, Colleen / 212-595-1125 25 W. 68th St., #9A, NYC, NY 10023 pages 10 - 11, 66	Korn Associates, Elaine / 212-760-0057 372 Fifth Ave., #2E, NYC, NY 10018
Henry, John / 212-686-6883 237 E. 31st St., NYC, NY 10016	Kramer & Associates, Joan 310-446-1866 / 212-567-5545 10490 Wilshire Blvd., Ste. 1701, LA, CA 90024
Herron, Pat / 212-683-9039 80 Madison Ave., NYC, NY 10016	Kramer & Kramer / 212-645-8787 156 Fifth Ave., NYC, NY 10010
Image Bank / 212-529-6700	Kristo-Nagy, Elka / 212-255-7525
In Focus Associates / 212-779-3600 21 E. 40th St., Ste. 903, NYC, NY 10016	L.A. Rep / 213-656-1720 8149 Kirkwood Dr., LA, CA 90046
Jaz & Jaz / 206-282-8558 223 Prospect St., Seattle, WA 98109	LGI Photo Agency / 212-736-4602 241 W. 36th St., 7th Fl., NYC, NY 10018
Jenni, Jane / 612-224-6763 472 Portland Ave., St. Paul, MN 55102	⟶ LaCuesta, Karen / 415-863-4969 495 Carolina St., SF, CA 94107 page 39
Joyce, Tricia / 212-962-0728 80 Warren St., NYC, NY 10007	LaMoine Represents / 213-467-9730 6057 Melrose Ave., LA, CA 90038
Kamin & Assoc., Vincent / 312-787-8834 260 E. Chestnut, Ste. 3005, Chicago, IL 60611	⟶ Lehmen Dabney, Inc. / 206-325-8595 1431 35th Ave. So., Seattle, WA 98144 page 26
Karpe, Michele / 818-760-0491 11965 Woodbridge St., Studio City, CA 91604	Levin/Dorr / 212-627-9871 1123 Broadway, Ste 1015, NYC, NY 10010
Kasemeier, Ellen / 805-640-9262	⟶ Lewin, Samantha / 212-228-5530 page 24 - 25
Kauss, Jean Gabriel / 212-779-4440 147 E. 36th St., NYC, NY 10016	

$F = (a \times p)^4$

TABLE (4.5). PHOTOGRAPHY

Photography Representatives	Photography Representatives
Li, Liz / 212-889-7067 260 Fifth Ave., NYC, NY 10001	Moses, Janice / 212-779-7929 155 E. 31st St., NYC, NY 10016
London Features / 212-929-7007 405 W. 14th St., 4th Fl., NYC, NY 10014	Newman & Associates, Carole / 310-394-5031 1119 Colorado Ave., #23, Santa Monica, CA 90401
London, Valerie / 310-278-6633 9301 Alcott St., LA, CA 90035	→ Nonstock / 212-633-2388 91 Fifth Ave., Ste. 201, NYC, NY 10003 page 40
Ludlow, Catherine / 213-658-6920 750 N. Stanley Ave., LA, CA 90046	Onyx / 213-965-0899 7515 Beverly Blvd., LA, CA 90036
Lysohir, Chris / 212-741-3187 77 Seventh Ave., #12U, NYC, NY 10011	Outline / 213-954-9422 5757 Wilshire Blvd., Pent. #20, LA, CA 90036
Mann, Ken / 212-944-2853 20 W. 46th St., NYC, NY 10036	Outline / 212-226-8790 596 Broadway, Ste.1104, NYC, NY 10012
Marek & Associates / 212-924-6760 160 Fifth Ave., Ste. 914, NYC, NY 10010	Page, Jackie / 212-772-0346 219 E. 69th St., NYC, NY 10021
Martin, Deborah / 310-474-7277 / 212-490-2869 881 N. Beverly Glen, Bel Air, CA 90077	Paolantonio, Angela / 213-874-9880 6750 Mulholland Dr., LA, CA 90068
Marzena / 212-772-2522 229 E. 79th St., NYC, NY 10021	Parallax / 212-673-4335 125 E. 12th St., #1H, NYC, NY 10003
Maslov, Norman / 415-641-4376 879 Florida St., SF, CA 94110	Parvis, Frank / 212-473-5868 15 Washington Pl., NYC, NY 10003
→ McCann Co., The / 214-526-2252 4113 Rawlins St., Dallas, TX 75219 page 29	Pepper, Missy / 415-543-6881 35 Stillman, #206, SF, CA 94107
McKay, Colleen / 212-598-0469 229 E. Fifth St., #2, NYC, NY 10003	Photocom / 214-720-2272 3005 Maple Ave, #104, Dallas, TX 75201
Mead, Robert & Asooc. / 212-688-7474	→ Photonica / 212-505-9000 141 Fifth Ave. Suite 8 S, NYC, NY 10010 pages 52 - 53
Meo, Frank / 212-932-9236 54 Morningside Dr., #54, NYC, NY 10025	Pix Producers / 212-533-3800 380 Lafayette, 5th Fl., NYC, NY 10003
→ Miller, Susan / 212-905-8400 1641 Third Ave., #29A, NYC, NY 10128 pages 106 - 107, 118 - 119	Pizer, Alyssa / 310-440-3930 13121 Garden Land Rd., LA, CA 90049
Mills, Jane / 214-946-6569 600 N. Bishop, Dallas, TX 75208	Poje, Elizabeth / 310-550-1490 1001 S. Alfred St., LA, CA 90035
Monaco, David & Claudia / 212-647-0336 389 Bleeker St., NYC, NY 10014	Powell & Assocs., Alan Dean / 213-653-7041 655 N. Harper, LA, CA 90048

$$F = (a \times p)^4$$

Table (4.6). Photography

Photography Representatives	Photography Representatives
→ Prentice, Vicki & Associates / 310-826-1332 page 44	Schwartz, Deborah / 818-794-7371 1542 Whitefield Rd., Pasadena, CA 91104
Proof / 212-727-7445 7 W. 18th St.,, NYC, NY 10011	Scott, Freda / 415-398-9121 1015 Battery St., SF, CA 94111
Quinn, Lori / 415-546-9974	→ Sharpe + Assocs. / 310-641-8556 7536 Ogelsby Ave., LA, CA 90045 pages 10 - 11, 66
Ralph & Co. / 212-691-4277 24 W. 30th St., #5F, NYC, NY 10001	Shepherd, Judith / 212-242-6554 344 W. 23rd St., NYC, NY 10011
Rapp, Gerald & Cullen / 212-889-3337 108 E. 35th St., NYC, NY 10016	Shooting Star Int'l Photo Agency Inc / 212-447-0666 1178 Broadway, 4th. Fl., NYC, NY 10001
Rappaport, Jodi / 213-464-4481 6305 Yucca St., Ste.600 C, LA, CA 90028	Shooting Star Int'l Photo Agency, Inc. / 213-469-2020 1441 N. McCadden Pl., Hollywood, CA 90028
Retna Ltd. / 212-255-0622 18 E. 17th St., 3rd Fl., NYC, NY 10003	→ Silverstein, Patti / 212-228-7924 / 212-924-9710 205 Third Ave., #7F, NYC, NY 10003 pages 54 - 55
Rhyner, Renee / 214-922-7072 3100 Carlisle, Ste. 117, Dallas, TX 75204	Simitch, Leslie / 212-925-2668 270 Lafayette St., #1300, NYC, NY 10012
Richards, Julian / 212-219-1269 434 Greenwich St.,, NYC, NY 10013	Still Life Stock / 212-971-9178 / 800-982-9178 286 Fifth Ave., Suite 1206, NYC, NY 10001
Robinson, Gladys / 212-385-1861 49 Murray St., Grd Fl., NYC, NY 10007	Sullivan, Tom / 404-971-6782 3805 Maple Ct., Marietta, GA 30066
Robinson, Madeleine / 212-243-3138 31 W. 21st St., NYC, NY 10010	Swanstock / 602-622-7133 P.O. Box 2350, Tucson, AZ 85702
Rosenberg, Arlene / 212-675-7983 377 W. 11th St., NYC, NY 10014	Sweet Represents / 415-433-1222 716 Montgomery St., SF, CA 94111
Sacramone, Dario / 212-929-0487 302 W. 12th St., NYC, NY 10014	→ Sygma / 212-675-7900 322 Eighth Ave., 11th Fl, NYC, NY 10001 pages 118 - 119
Sampson, Corinna / 415-928-5070 1405 Gough St.,, SF, CA 94109	Those 3 Reps / 214-871-1316 2909 Cole, Ste. 118, Dallas, TX 75204
Samuels, Rosemary / 212-477-3567 14 Prince St., NYC, NY 10012	Toulon, Daryl / 212-867-2902 330 E. 39th St., #3E, NYC, NY 10016
Saunders Represents, Michele / 212-496-0268 84 Riverside Dr., NYC, NY 10024	Trela, Christopher / 212-956-2396 350 West 50th St., #27F, NYC, NY 10019
Savel, Carin / 718-768-3589	Turner/Collin / 212-243-6373 55 Bethune St., NYC, NY 10014
Scher, Dorothea / 212-689-7273 235 E. 22nd St., NYC, NY 10010	

Table (4.7). Photography

Photographers Representatives	Photographers
Umlas, Barbara / 516-329-0058 P.O. Box 1974, Amagansett, NY 11930	→ Zaitz, David / 310-207-4806 11830 Darlington, #10, LA, CA 90049 page 29
→ Visages Rps Inc. / 212-941-7550 560 Broadway, Ste. 407, NYC, NY 10012 page 70	Zari International / 212-388-8541 853 Broadway, Ste.1516, NYC, NY 10003
→ Visages Rps Inc. / 213-650-8880 7750 Sunset Blvd., LA, CA 90046 page 70	**Photographers**
Von Schreiber, Barbara / 212-460-5000 380 Lafayette, Ste. 300-C, NYC, NY 10003	Abbott, Waring / 212 925-6082 78 Franklin St., NYC, NY 10013
Watson & Kramer Associates / 212-431-4480 524 Broadway, NYC, NY 10012	→ Abrams Lacagnina / 206-624-7646 619 Western Avenue, Box 12, Seattle, WA 98104 page 50
Weiss, Caryn / 213-461-1084 6311 Romaine St., Ste. 7234, LA, CA 90038	Abranowicz, William C. / 201-948-4943 Rt.10 Box 10611, Newton, NJ 07860 Rep: Tricia Burlingham / 310-998-9176
Weiss, Debra / 213-656-5029 1123 1/2 N. Sweetzer Ave., LA, CA 90069	Accornero, Franco / 212-674-0068 620 Broadway, NYC, NY 10012
Weissberg, Elyse / 212-406-2566 299 Pearl St., NYC, NY 10038	Acevedo, Melanie / 212-964-4802 49 Warren St., #5`, NYC, NY 10007 Rep: Maria Barba / 212-227-4110
→ Wendt, Bobbi / 415-487-2160 152 Mississippi St., SF, CA 94107 pages 46 - 47	Adams, Butch / 801-532-5925 233 S. 600 West, Salt Lake City, UT 84101
Westheim, Lisa / 415-258-9908 160 Bungalo Ave., San Rafael, CA 94901	Adams, Eddie Rep: Eliane Laffont / 212-675-7900
White, Robert / 310-815-1923 / 818-244-4250 8741-A W. Washington, Culver City, CA 90232	Afanador, Ruven Rep: Giovanni Testino / 212-608-0888
Wiley, David / 415-986-8484 282 Second St., 2nd Fl., SF, CA 94105	Aguilera-Hellweg, Max Rep: Onyx / 213-965-0899
Wilson, Betty / 212-595-2124 9 W. 84th St., #2B, NYC, NY 10024	Akiyam, Ron / 201-943-3732 364 Palisade, #5A, Cliffside Park, NJ 07010
Winston West Ltd. / 310-275-2858 / 212-661-7279 195 S. Beverly Dr., Ste. 403, Beverly Hills, CA 90212	Allen, Greg / 213-461-9227 4616 Greenwood Pl., #4, Hollywood, CA 90027
Yellen/Lachapelle / 212-838-3170 420 E. 54th St., NYC, NY 10022	Allison, Ty / 310-396-1444 / 415-995-1772 912 Vernon Ave., Venice, CA 90291 Rep: Deborah Ayerst / 415-567-3570 Rep: Angela Paolantonio / 213-938-6071
Zaccaro, Jim / 212-744-4000 315 E. 68th St., NYC, NY 10021	

$$F = (a \times p)^4$$

TABLE (4.8). PHOTOGRAPHY

Photographers	Photographers

Anderson, Mark
Rep: LaMoine Represents / 213-467-9730

Anderson, Patrik
Rep: Art + Commerce / 212-206-0737

→ Annalisa / 213-939-3998
page 69

Arciero, Anthony / 312-772-7297
1643 N. milwaukee Ave., Ste. 2, Chicago, IL 60647

Aresu, Paul / 212-334-9494
Aresu/Goldring Studio
568 Broadway, #608, NYC, NY 10012

Armbruster, Paul / 212-691-8107
5 W. 21st St., NYC, NY 10010
Rep: Byrnes Brady Barber / 212-875-0226

Arnaud, Michel
Rep: Edge / 212-343-2260 / 213-954-9422

Arnold, Alice / 212-260-8872
28-30 Clinton St., #1A, NYC, NY 10002

Aroch, Guy
Rep: Bill Charles / 212-213-6810

→ Arsenault, Daniel / 213-931-6441
Rep: John Sharpe / 310-641-8556 / 212-595-1125
pages 10 - 11

→ Artiaga, Anthony / 818-505-0849
page 126

Astor, Josef / 212-307-5588
154 W. 57th St., Rm 845, NYC, NY 10019
Rep: Onyx / 213-965-0899
Rep: Barbara von Schrieber / 212-460-5000

Austin, Alan
Rep: Deborah Martin / 310-474-7277

Ava, Beth / 212-966-4407
480 Canal St., NYC, NY 10013

Avedon, Richard / 212-879-6325
407 E. 75th St., NYC, NY 10021

Avenaim, Jerry
Rep: Visages Rps., Inc. / 213-650-8880

Ayola, Brooks D. / 818-885-8402
21704 Devonshire St., #250, Chatsworth, CA 91311

Babini, Luca
Rep: Kramer & Kramer / 212-645-8787

Bachman, Bill
Rep: Joan Kramer & Assoc.
310-446-1866 / 212-567-5545

Badger, Rob / 415-927-3800
9 Ridge Way, Corte Madera, CA 94925-1337

Budowski, Cliff / 714-288-0889

Bak, Sunny / 213-933-6986
750 S. Spaulding Ave., #136, LA, CA 90036
Rep: Shooting Star / 213-469-2020

Baker, Jeff / 214-324-4162
7002 Santa Monica, Dallas, TX 75223

Baker, Nathan
Rep: Janet Botaish Group / 319-314-1571

Baker, Priscilla / 212-460-9747
93 First Ave.,#5D, NYC, NY 10003

Baker, Tony / 310-836-2407
8755 Washington Blvd., LA, CA 90232

Baldwin, Joel
Rep: Stockland Martel / 212-727-1400

Bali, Alain / 213-962-7933
7060 Hollywood Blvd, #503, LA, CA 90028

Banko, Phil / 206-621-7008
1201 First Ave. South, #332, Seattle, WA 98134
Rep: Jaz & Jaz / 206-282-8558

Baptiste, Beth / 212-691-5674

Barkentin-Blackburn, Pamela / 310-854-1941

Barker, Kent / 505-758-0970
Rep: Donna Baker / 214-526-8004

Barnes, Matt / 615-832-3297
P.O. Box 150904, Nashville, TN 37215

Barr, Christopher / 213-962-8602
Rep: Shooting Star / 213-469-2020

Table (4.9). Photography

Photographers	Photographers
Barry, David / 212-989-5273 15 Leroy, #5, NYC, NY 10014 Rep: Julian Richards / 212-219-1269	Berthiaume, Tom / 612-874-1999 2010 First Ave. S., Minneapolis, MN 55404 Rep: Anne Vande Creek
Bauer, Robert / 510-763-4819 / 213-270-4047 1057 Winsor Ave., Oakland, CA 94610	Bieber, Tim / 312-463-3590 3312 W. Belle Plaine, Chicago, IL 60618 Rep: Judy Wolff / 212-889-5353 Rep: Joel Harlib / 312-573-1370
Beals, Steven K. / 503-288-0550 807 Russel St., Portland, OR 97227	
Beckman, Janette / 212-477-3430 636 Broadway, Ste 1215, NYC, NY 10012	Binkley Knize / 312-477-1001 1920 N. Seminary, Chicago, IL 60614
Begleiter, Steven / 212-475-7498 303 Park Ave. South, #512, NYC, NY 10010	Biondo, Michael / 212-226-5299 464 Greenwich St., NYC, NY 10013
Bekker, Philip / 404-847-9777 5070 Trimble Road, Atlanta, GA 30342	Black, Steven / 415-459-3316 P.O. Box 550, San Anselmo, CA 94979
→ Belair, Butch Rep: Michael Ginsburg / 212-679-8881 pages 30 - 33	Blackman, Barry / 212-627-9777 40 W.25th St., NYC, NY 10010
Belcher, Dana / 212-645-8356 43 W. 24th St., #3A, NYC, NY 10010	Blais, John / 803-577-3132 77 Wentworth St., Ste. 5, Charleston, SC 29401
Bellissimo, John Rep: LGI / 212-736-4602	Blake, Rebecca / 212-439-8729 130 E. 62nd St., #1F, NYC, NY 10021 Rep: Jean Conlon / 212-966-9897
Bentham, John / 212-366-5686 / 416-588-2904	Blakeman, Robert / 213-624-6662 710 S. Santa Fe Ave., LA, CA 90021
Bentley, David / 312-829-2001 2059 W. Grand Ave., Chicago, IL 60612	Blakesberg, Jay / 415-621-2366 / 415-621-2366 P.O. Box 460054, SF, CA 94146 Rep: Keswick Hamilton/Sygma / 213-380-3933
Bercow, Larry / 212-941-5544 63 Crosby St., 3rd Fl., NYC, NY 10012	Bland, James / 214-467-0707 2430 Alco Ave., Dallas, TX 75211
Berg, Ron / 816-842-8480 415 Deleware, Kansas City, MO 64105	Bleyer Studio, Inc., Pete / 213-653-6567 807 N. Sierra Bonita Ave., LA, CA 90046
Berman, Howard / 212-925-2999 Bronstein/Berman & Associates 38 Greene St., NYC, NY 10013 Rep: Gary Hurewitz	Bloom, Teri / 212-475-2274
Bernier, Marc / 310-396-5064 600 Moulton Ave., Ste. 204, LA, CA 90031	Blosser, Robert Vance / 212-679-2802 34 E. 30th St., 2nd Fl, NYC, NY 10016
Bernstein, Bill / 212-334-3982 59 Thompson, #9, NYC, NY 10012	Bodi Productions / 212-947-7883 340 W. 39th St., NYC, NY 10018
Bernstein, Gary / 310-550-6891 8795 Washington Blvd, Culver City, CA 90230	Bogdanovich, Blake / 213-620-8776 500 Molino St., Ste. 103, LA, CA 90013

$$F = (a \times p)^4$$

TABLE (4.10). PHOTOGRAPHY

Photographers	Photographers
Bohm, Lesley / 213-625-8401 201 S. Santa Fe, #301, LA, CA 90012	Bray, Phil / 510-658-9740 3270 Ettie St., Oakland, CA 94608
Boley, Tyler / 206-860-7166 911 E. Pike, Ste. 333, Seattle, WA 98122 page 42	Brewer, Art / 714-661-8930 25262 Main Sail Dr., Dana Point, CA 92629
Bonge, Steve Rep: Leslie Barany Communic / 212-627-8488	Brewster, Debra / 818-956-3717 429-1/2 California Ave., Glendale, CA 91203
Bonner, Scott / 615-297-4029 / 615-385-9300 2700 Belmont Blvd., Nashville, TN 37212	Brill, James Rep: Marek & Assoc. / 212-924-6760
Bonnini, Steve / 503-239-5421 615 S.E. Alder, Ste. 300, Portland, OR 97214 Rep: Bob Mead / 914-835-0680 Rep: Nadine / 310-890-5999	Brody, Bob / 212-741-0013 5 W. 19th St., 2nd fl., NYC, NY 10011 Rep: Eunice Nathan / 212-772-1770
Bononi Vision Photography / 818-508-6542 6447 Bellaire Ave., N. Hollywood, CA 91606	Brosan, Roberto / 212-473-1471 873 Broadway, NYC, NY 10003 Rep: Jean Conlon / 212-966-9897
Boon, Sally / 212-673-8790 439 E. Ninth St., #6, NYC, NY 10009	Brown, George / 212-941-1786 39 Spring St., NYC, NY 10012
Borden, Frederik Rep: Renee Rhyner / 214-922-7072	Brown, Graham Rep: Jane Jenni / 612-224-6763
Bordnick, Barbara / 212-533-1180 39 E. 19th St., 3rd Fl, NYC, NY 10003 Rep: Zari Int. / 212-727-9145	Brown, Nancy / 212-924-9105 6 W. 20th St., NYC, NY 10011
Borges, Phil / 206-725-8322 4222 48th Ave. S., Seattle, WA 98118 Rep: Julee Geier / 206-725-8924	Brown, Robert E. / 818-409-0952 1104 Berkeley Dr., Glendale, CA 91205 Rep: Damien Steele / 213-747-4471
Borris, Dan / 212-989-6790 Rep: Edge / 212-343-2260 / 213-954-9422	Bryan-Brown, Marc / 212-594-1360 534 W. 35th st., NYC, NY 10001
Bourke, John-Francis / 212-889-4904 832 Sixth Ave., NYC, NY 10001	Buchsbaum, Jay David / 310-477-4289 / 818-222-2157 4706 Park Granada #188, Calabasas, CA 91302
Bracke, Victor / 213-625-1531 912 E. Third St., Ste. 106, LA, CA 90013	Buck, Chris / 212-343-9315 274 Mott Street, #5b, New York, NY 10012 Rep: Julian Richards / 212-219-1269
Bradley, Rodney Oman / 800-254-5071 / 319-365-5071 Rep: Paula Anderson / 312-321-0848	Buck, Monica / 212-645-1023 39 W. 14th. St., Ste. 406, NYC, NY 10011
Brakha, Moshe / 213-658-5799 P.O. Box 480399, LA, CA 90048 Rep: Michael Lohr / 213-658-5799	Buren, Jodi / 212-925-2316 116 Mercer St., NYC, NY 10012
Brandt, David Allen / 213-469-1399 1015 Cahuenga Blvd., Ste.14C, Hollywood, CA 90038	Burfield, Jason / 614-374-4428 P.O. Box 518, Reno, OH 45773

$$F = (a \times p)^4$$

Photographers	Photographers

Burns, Jerry / 404-522-9377
331 Elizabeth St., NE, Atlanta, GA 30307

Busacca, Larry / 212-633-8146
150 Fifth Ave., Ste. 220, NYC, NY 10010

Bush, Charles William / 213-466-6630
940 N. Highland Ave., #D, LA, CA 90038
Rep: Rhoni Epstein / 213-663-2388
Rep: Joan Jedell / 212-861-7861

→ Butler, Erik / 415-777-1656
577 Second St., #203, SF, CA 94107
pages 122 - 123

Butler, Robert
Rep: Elka Kristo-Nagy / 212-505-5607

Bybee / 415-863-6346
1811 Folsom St., SF, CA 94103

Byers, Bruce / 212-242-5846
220 W. 19th St., 10fl, NYC, NY 10011
Rep: Leffler/Badin / 212-877-2390

Cable, Wayne / 312-951-1799
401 W. Superior, 2nd Fl., Chicago, IL 60610
Rep: Nadine Ferrata / 312-663-9283

→ Caines, Bruce / 212-594-9443
433 W. 34th St., #7A, NYC, NY 10001
page 98

Calderero, James
Rep: Rick Wainman / 212-727-3091
Rep: Catherine Ludlow / 213-658-6920

Callahan, Kristin / 212-489-0521
535 W. 49th St., #5FW, NYC, NY 10019
Rep: London Features / 212-929-7007

Callis, Chris / 212-243-0231
91 Fifth Ave., 7th Fl., NYC, NY 10003
Rep: Marzena / 212-772-2522

Calocca-Provost, Norma / 909-592-3803
622 Arrow Hghwy, San Dimas, CA 91773

Cantrelli, Amy / 310-372-7744
1642 Wilcox, Hollywood, CA 90028

→ Cardin, Robert / 415-255-4546
142 Tenth St., SF, CA 94103
pages 86 - 87

Carney, Dennis / 615-889-5000
2804 Elmhill Pike, Nashville, TN 37214

Carney, Joann / 312-829-2332
401 N. Racine, Chicago, IL 60622
Rep: Tom Sasser / 312-856-9090

Carney, Lisa / 310-450-2931
418 Pier Ave., #213, Santa Monica, CA 90405

→ Carr, E.J. / 212-242-0818
236 W. 27th St., NYC, NY 10001
pages 58 - 59

Carroll, Chris / 212-334-1135
275 Church St., 4th Fl., NYC, NY 10013
Rep: Onyx / 213-965-0899

Casado, John / 213-666-5123
1858 Fanning St., LA, CA 90026

Castellanos, Mario / 818-280-6602
Rep: Caryn Weiss / 213-461-1084

Catanzaro/Mahdessian / 213-663-8810 / 310-456-1971

Cates, Gwendolen / 310-452-2724
825 Hampton Drive, Venice, CA 90291
Rep: Keswick Hamilton/Sygma / 213-380-3933

Ceppas, Cristiana / 415-543-3993
423 Tehama, 2nd fl., SF, CA 94103

Chalkin, Dennis / 212-929-1036
5 E. 16th St., NYC, NY 10003

Chang, Aaron / 619-231-0256

Chanteau, Pierre / 212-227-4931
80 Warren St., NYC, NY 10007
Rep: Vicki Spaeth / 212-349-4264

Chappell, Graham
Rep: Deborah Martin / 310-474-7277

Charles Watson, Lisa / 212-807-8600
119 W. 23rd St. #502, NYC, NY 10011

Chavez, Marina / 213-662-6515

$$F = (a \times p)^4$$

TABLE (4.12). PHOTOGRAPHY

Photographers	Photographers
Chesser, Mike / 213-934-5211 5290 W. Washington Blvd., LA, CA 90016	Colao, John Rep: L.A. Rep / 213-656-1720
Chevallier, Pascal Rep: Marek & Assoc. / 212-924-6760	Coll, Beatriz / 415-863-0699 2415 Third St., #265, SF, CA 94107
Chin, Ted / 212-674-1871 5 E. 19th St., NYC, NY 10003 Rep: Susan Miller / 212-905-8400	Collicott, Tom / 206-223-0038 619 Western Ave., Seattle, WA 98104 Rep: Kolea Baker / 206-784-1136
Chin, Walter Rep: Marek & Assoc. / 212-924-6760	Collin, Fran Rep: Turner/Collins / 212-243-6373
Chiossone, Carlos / 212-473-3616 7 E. 20th St., NYC, NY 10003	Collins, Chris / 212-633-1670 35 W. 20th St., NYC, NY 10011 Rep: DiBartolo/Lemkowitz / 212-297-0041
Chung, Ken Lei / 213-938-9117 5900 Venice Blvd, LA, CA 90019 Rep: Christine / 213-938-9117	Cook, Rod Rep: Bina / 212-533-1734
Churchill, Doug / 818-841-9615 3305 W. Alameda Ave., Burbank, CA 91505	→ Cooper, John F. / 212-545-0375 Rep: Susan Miller / 212-905-8400 pages 106 - 107
Cipolla, Karen / 212-619-6114 103 Reade St., NYC, NY 10013	Cooper, Sidney / 213-268-2627 1427 E. Fourth St., Ste. 2, LA, CA 90033
Claiborne, Barron Rep: Betty Wilson / 212-595-2124	Corbett, Jay / 212-366-1166 17 Little West 12th St., #205, NYC, NY 10014
Clark, Robert / 212-533-8814 220 Sullivan St., #4D, NYC, NY 10012	Corman, Richard / 212-799-2395 Rep: Stockland Martel / 212-727-1400
Clarke, Chandra / 415-957-9393 860 Second St., SF, CA 94107	Coupon, William / 212-941-5676 237 Lafayette, #10W, NYC, NY 10012
Claxton, William Rep: Visages / 212-941-7550	Covello, Linda / 201-568-0211
Clement, Michele / 415-695-0100 879 Florida Street, SF, CA 94110 Rep: Norman Maslov / 415-641-4376	Coxwell, Chris / 813-229-0323 Rep: Allan Comport / 813-579-4499
Clinch, Danny / 212-233-6170 65 Reade St., #3B, NYC, NY 10007 Rep: Maria Barba / 212-227-4110	Crocker, Will / 504-522-2651 Rep: Those 3 Reps / 214-871-1316
Clough, Terry / 212-255-3040 147 W. 25th St., NYC, NY 10001 Rep: Gail Gaynin / 212-580-3141	Cross, Dylan / 212-727-1977 136 W. 21st. St., 9th Fl., NYC, NY 10011
Cohl, Eddy Rep: Kramer & Kramer / 212-645-8787	Crosta, Laura / 310-376-2820 644 Tenth St., Hermosa Beach, CA 90254
	→ Crouser, Michael / 612-371-0551 1624 Harmon Pl., Ste. 224, Minneapolis, MN 55403 pages 120 - 121

TABLE (4.13). PHOTOGRAPHY

Photographers	Photographers

Crowley, Eliot / 213-851-5110 / 805-965-5458

Cruff, Kevin / 602-225-0273
2328 East Van Buren St., #103, Phoenix, AZ 85006
Rep: Kimberly Boege / 602-265-4389

Crum, Lee
Rep: Doug Brown / 212-953-0088

Cuff, Markus / 213-934-1721
456 S. Cochran Ave., LA, CA 90036
Rep: Shooting Star / 212-469-2020

Cuffaro, Chris
Rep: Edge / 213-954-9422 / 212-343-2260

→ Cultice, Joseph / 212-388-9003
211 E. 3rd St., #6R, NYC, NY 10009
pages 16 - 17

Curtis, Mel / 206-323-1230
2400 E. Lynn St., Seattle, WA 98112
Rep: Donna Jorgensen / 206-634-1880

Cutler, Craig / 212-473-2892
628-30 Broadway, Ste.403, NYC, NY 10012
Rep: Marzena / 212-772-2522

Cutting, Ann Elliott / 818-440-1974
163 W. Colorado Blvd., Pasadena, CA 91105
Rep: Valerie London / 310-278-6633

D'Orazio, Sante
Rep: Visages Rps., Inc. / 213-650-8880

Dakota, Michael / 305-325-8727
808 N.W. 8th St. Rd, Miami, FL 33136
Rep: Irene Dakota / 305-674-9975 / 212-221-3472

Dalla Chiesa, Carlo
Rep: Catherine Ludlow / 213-658-6920

Danelian, Stephen
Rep: Edge / 212-343-2260 / 212-954-9422

Daniels, Charles / 213-461-8659

Davenport, Neil
Rep: Outline / 213-954-9422 / 212-226-8790

Davies & Starr
Rep: Deborah Ayerst / 415-567-3570
Rep: Pix Producers / 212-533-3800

Davis, Dee / 615-832-9659
3630 Trousdale, Ste H, Nashville, TN 37204

→ Davis, Robin / 404-876-6341
665 Cooledge Ave. NE, Atlanta, GA 30306
page 80

Day, Lorraine
Rep: Beate Works / 213-653-5088

De Boismenu, Geoffroy
Rep: Betty Wilson / 212-595-2124

→ De Souza, Daniel / 415-777-3273
185 Clara St., #202, SF, CA 94107
Rep: Bobbi Wendt / 415-487-2160
pages 46 - 47

DeLeon, John / 818-571-8348
1304 Milam Pl., Monterey Park, CA 91755

DeMarchelier, Patrick
Rep: Bryan Bantry / 212-935-0200

DeVault, Jim / 615-269-4538
2400 Sunset Pl., Nashville, TN 37212

Delgado, Luis / 415-863-6504
499 Alabama, Ste. 101, SF, CA 94110

→ Demchick, Leah / 212-873-5536
pages 112 - 113

Dent, Fritz / 206-441-5072
103 Battery St., Seattle, WA 98121

Der, Rick / 415-824-8580
50 Mendell St., #10, SF, CA 94124

DiMarzio, Larry / 718-981-9286
1388 Richmond Terrace, Staten Island, NY 10310

DiSanto, AnnaMaria / 213-653-0345
Rep: Photo Features / 213-465-7957

DiScalfani, Robert / 212-966-8903
480 Broadway, Suite 403, NYC, NY 10013

Diadul, Robert
Rep: Kramer & Kramer / 212-645-8787

$$F = (a \times p)^4$$

TABLE (4.14). PHOTOGRAPHY

Photographers	Photographers
Dickson, Nigel / 416-366-4477 507 King St. East, Ste. 100, Toronto, Ontario, Canada M5A 1M3	Dutesco, Roberto Rep: Visages / 213-650-8880
Dill, Nicola / 310-573-1274	Dwass, Michael / 212-979-1893 111 E. 14th St., Ste. 214, NYC, NY 10003
Dixon, Philip Rep: Marek & Assoc. / 212-924-6760	Dyer, Alison / 213-665-7855 1356 Lucille Ave., LA, CA 90026 Rep: LaMoine Represents / 213-467-9730
Dockery, Alan / 213-662-8153 4679 Hollywood Blvd, LA, CA 90027	E, David Rep: Beate Works / 213-653-5088
Doje, Yuri / 416-366-8081 74 Bathurst St., Toronto, ON, Canada M5V 2P5	Eadon, Jack Rep: Sylvia Franks/Creative / 310-276-5282
Dokus, Peter / 213-462-5588 6112 Santa Monica Blvd, LA, CA 90038	Eccles, Andrew Rep: Edge / 212-343-2260 / 213-954-9422
Donahue, Patrick J. / 213-463-4165 1153 N. Highland Ave., LA, CA 90038	Edahl, Ed / 212-929-2002 236 W. 27th St., NYC, NY 10001
Douglas Brothers Rep: Onyx / 213-965-0899	→ Eder, John / 213-661-9120 page 48
Dreyfus, Joshua B. / 312-987-1892 727 South Dearborn, #511, Chicago, IL 60605	Edson, Steve / 617-924-2212 25 Otis St., Watertown, MA 02172
DuBose, George / 212-647-1873 142 W. 14th St., NYC, NY 10011	Edwards, Charles / 818-795-7114 163 Colorado Blvd., Pasadena, CA 91105
Dubler III, Douglas / 212-410-6300 162 E. 92nd St., NYC, NY 10128	Eisner, Sandra / 212-889-0338
Duke, Peter / 310-459-8630	Elgort Ltd., Arthur / 212-219-8775 136 Grand St., NYC, NY 10013 Rep: Marianne Houtenbos
Duke, William / 415-949-1344 90 Hillview Ave., Los Altos, CA 94022	Elias, Robert / 213-651-3222
Dunas, Jeff / 310-275-6111 / 212-242-1266 9021 Melrose Ave., Ste. 310, LA, CA 90069 Rep: Keswick Hamilton / Syg / 213-380-3933	→ Elledge, Paul / 312-733-8021 1808 West Grand Ave, Chicago, IL 60622 pages 62 - 63
Dunn, Larry / 603-641-6575 250 Commercial St., Manchester, NH 03101 Rep: Caron Shaffer	Ellman, Elaine / 212-925-7151 60 Gramercy Park, NYC, NY 10010
Dupuy, Gil Rep: Ceci Bartels / 314-781-7377	Emerson, Sam / 310-657-3630 348 S. Elm Dr., Beverly Hills, CA 90212
Durham, Michael / 615-262-2806 1169 Greenland Ave., Nashville, TN 37216	Emrich, Bill / 212-255-8704 115 W. 23rd St., #63, NYC, NY 10011

TABLE (4.15). PHOTOGRAPHY

Photographers	Photographers
Enfield, Jill / 212-777-3510 211 E. 18th St., NYC, NY 10003 Rep: Ralph Mennemeyer / 212-691-4277	Farber, Enid / 212-744-2845 425 E. 75th St., #3B, NYC, NY 10021
Engler, David / 612-680-4697 529 S. Seventh, #698, Minneapolis, MN 55415	Farber, Robert / 212-486-9090 207A E. 62nd St., NYC, NY 10021
English, Rick / 415-255-0751 1162 Bryant St., SF, CA 94103 Rep: Deborah English	⟶ Farris, Neal / 214-821-5612 500 Exposition, Suite104, Dallas, TX 75226 Rep: Ally Godfrey / 214-827-2559 page 51
Erickson, Jim / 919-833-9955 117 S. West St., Raleigh, NC 27603	Faye, Michael Rep: Janet Botaish Group / 310-314-1571
Erle, Steve / 213-965-8350 117 S. Gardner St., LA, CA 90036	Federici, Daniela Rep: Visages / 212-941-7550
Erler, Glen Rep: Jodi Rappaport / 213-934-8633	Fee, James Rep: David Maloney / 213-469-2020
Estrada & Rowley / 213-935-4364 4736 W. Washington Blvd., LA, CA 90016	Feingold, Deborah / 212-924-9710 133 W. 19th St., Ste. 5B, NYC, NY 10011 Rep: Patti Silverstein / 212-228-7924
⟶ Estrine, Darryl Rep: Michael Ginsburg / 212-679-8881 pages 34 - 35	Ferguson, Scott / 314-241-3811 710 N. Tucker #512, St. Louis, MO 63101 Rep: Teenuh Foster / 314-821-2278 Rep: Suzanne Craig / 918-749-9424
Etheredge, Sherry / 213-662-6021 1926 N. Alexandria, Ste. #2, LA, CA 90027	Ferrand, Olivier / 213-933-0952 155 S. Sycamore Ave., LA, CA 90036
Ewert, Steve / 312-733-5762 17 North Elizabeth, Chicago, IL 60607	Ferri, Fabrizio Rep: Art + Commerce / 212-206-0737
Exley, Jonathan / 213-661-4444 P.O. Box 46335, LA, CA 90046 Rep: Gamma Liaison / 212-447-2500	Ferri, Mark / 212-431-1356 463 Broome St., NYC, NY 10013 Rep: Kevin R. Schochat / 212-475-7068
Exum Rep: Bill Charles / 212-213-6810	Ferro, Jean / 213-462-0121 419 N. Larchmont Blvd, #64, LA, CA 90004 Rep: G.A. Management:Greg E / 310-285-9898
Factor, Davis Rep: Visages Rps., Inc. / 213-650-8880	Feurer, Hans Rep: Marek & Assoc. / 212-924-6760
Fagan, Dennis / 512-479-4103 610 Neuces St., Austin, TX 78701	Fewsmith, Phil / 213-644-1127 3913 Fountain Ave., LA, CA 90029
Fair, J. Henry / 212-674-6599 206 E. Ninth St., NYC, NY 10003	Fialaire, Regis Rep: Zari Int. / 212-388-8541
Fairchild, Paul / 415-321-7187 927 Hamilton Ave., Menlo Park, CA 94025	
Falls, John / 212-691-1933	

$$F = (a \times p)^4$$

TABLE (4.16). PHOTOGRAPHY

Photographers	Photographers
Fiere, Brad Rep: Joan Kramer & Assoc. 310-446-1866 / 212-567-5545	Freedman, Holly / 818-980-7568 Rep: Ellen Kasemeier / 805-640-9262
Finlay, Alastair / 212-334-8001 13-17 Laight St., 5th Fl, NYC, NY 10013	Freeman, Amanda / 213-662-7119 1401 Avon Park Terrace, LA, CA 90026 Rep: Catherine Ludlow / 213-658-6920
Fischer, Ken & Carl / 212-794-0400 121 E. 83rd St, NYC, NY 10028-0821	French, Andy / 212-678-2280
Fiscus, Jim / 214-821-4004 4101 Commerce, #4, Dallas, TX 75226 Rep: Byrnes Brady Barber / 212-875-0226	Fried, David / 201-743-6210 / 201-743-2602 314 Ridgewood Ave., Glen Ridge, NJ 07028
Flanagan, Lendon / 213-628-9627 929 E. 2nd St. Studio 107, LA, CA 90012	Friedman, Carol / 212-925-4951 60 Grand St., NYC, NY 10013
Ford, Carol Rep: Michele Karpe / 818-760-0491	Friedman, Glen / 212-353-8111 280 Park Ave. South, 14J, NYC, NY 10010
Forsman, John Reed Rep: Jean Gardner / 213-464-2492	Friedman, Steve / 212-864-2662 545 W. 111th St., #6K, NYC, NY 10025
Fortuna, Christopher / 212-274-9571 80 Varick, #2B, NYC, NY 10013	Frigo,Clare & Crnkovich, James Rep: Jane Jenni / 612-224-6763
Foulke, Douglas / 212-243-0822 140 W. 22nd St., NYC, NY 10011 Rep: Paula Krongard / 212-683-1020	Frohman, Jesse Rep: Marek & Assoc. / 212-924-6760
Frakes, Bill / 305-441-9048	Froomer, Brett / 212-533-3113 7 E. 20th St., NYC, NY 10003 Rep: Bernstein & Andriulli / 212-682-1490
Frame, Bob Rep: LaMoine Represents / 213-467-9730 Rep: Proof / 212-979-6440	Fuchs, Rafael / 212-529-0518 410 E. 13th St., #29, NYC, NY 10003
Franchina, Marco Rep: Winston West / 310-275-2858	Furman, Michael / 215-925-4233 115 Arch St., Philadelphia, PA 19106 Rep: Victoria Satterthwaite
Francis, Pam / 713-528-1672	Gadge / 212-586-1246
Frank, Dana / 212-340-4727	Gaget, Bruno / 212-219-1834 500 Broome St., NYC, NY 10013 Rep: OZ / 212-686-5277
Frank, Sandra / 415-365-8228 2636 Broadway, Redwood City, CA 94063	Gajdel, Edward / 416-535-4773 198 Crawford St., Toronto, Canada M6J 2V6 Rep: Djanka
Frantz, Ken / 312-951-1077 415 W. Huron St., Chicago, IL 60610	→ Galante, Dennis / 212-529-5531 29 E. 19th St., NYC, NY 10003 Rep: Samantha Lewin / 212-228-5530 pages 24 - 25
Frazier, Jeff / 615-320-7191 1305 Clinton St., Studio 200, Nashville, TN 37203	

TABLE (4.17). PHOTOGRAPHY

Photographers	Photographers
Galante, Jim / 212-529-4300 873 Broadway, Ste. 510, NYC, NY 10003	Gobits, Rolph Rep: Stockland Martel / 212-727-1400
Galella Ltd., Ron / 201-402-2366 12 Nelson Lane, Montville, NJ 07045	Goble, Brian / 212-219-0887 80 Varick St., NYC, NY 10013
Gamba, Mark / 212-387-0397 123 2nd Ave. #2, NYC, NY 10003	Goines, Susan / 213-665-5374 Rep: Kathleen Cornell & Co. / 310-301-8059
Gardlin, Martin / 212-534-1554	→ Goldberg, Gary / 212-228-4820 475 FDR Dr., L602, NYC, NY 10002 page 73
Garner, Kate Rep: Visages Rps., Inc. / 213-650-8880	Goldman, Michael / 212-966-4997 177 Hudson Street, NYC, NY 10013
Garrabrants, Doug / 213-622-5358 Rep: Julee Geier / 206-725-8924	Goldsmith, Jim / 212-460-5237 22 East 21 Street, #8f, New York, NY 10010
→ Gates, Valerie / 310-657-9700 Rep: Karen LaCuesta / 415-863-4969 page 39	Goldsmith, Lynn / 212-736-4602 241 W. 36th St., NYC, NY 10018
Getsug, Don / 312-939-1477 1255 S. Michigan, Chicago, IL 60605	Gonzales, Mando / 818-814-2876
Gillis, Greg / 312-733-2340 1117 West Lake, Chicago, IL 60607 Rep: Kelly Cleveland / 312-733-1908	Gonzalez, Danny / 212-734-5436 1045 Lexington Ave., #3B, NYC, NY 10021
Gipe, Jon / 602-230-8266 6747 N. 10th St., Phoenix, AZ 85014	→ Goodenough, Chuck / 213-881-9455 516 S. Anderson St., LA, CA 90033 JHF635A@prodigy.com page 82
Giraldo, Anita / 212-431-1193 480 Canal Street, 8th Fl., NYC, NY 10013	Gordon, Anthony Rep: Stockland Martel / 212-727-1400
Girardot, Guillaume Rep: Kramer & Kramer / 212-645-8787	Gorman, Greg Rep: Tricia Burlingham / 310-998-9176
Gissinger, Hans Rep: Monaco Reps / 212-647-0336	Gorton, D. / 601-352-1894 1232 Greymount Ave., Jackson, MS 39202 Rep: Onyx / 213-965-0899
Gittler, Ian / 212-633-9628 10 Sheridan Sq., NYC, NY 10013	Gould, Harrison / 212-929-9001 76 Ninth Ave., West PH, NYC, NY 10011
Glaviano, Marco Rep: Turner/Collins / 212-243-6373	Gould, Rick / 619-941-3223 993C So. Santa Fe Ave., Vista, CA 92083
Glembin, John / 212-929-6188 429 W. 14th St , NYC, NY 10014	Graham, Donald / 212-459-4767 / 213-656-7117 Rep: David Maloney / 212-675-7900
Glenn, Eileen / 312-666-7300 407 N. Elizabeth St., Chicago, IL 60622 Rep: Marlene Marino / 312-337-2976	Graham, Geoff / 410-675-5393 3233 O'Donnell St., Baltimore, MD 21244

$$F = (a \times p)^4$$

Table (4.18). Photography

Photographers	Photographers
Graham, Jim / 215-592-7272 720 Chestnut St., Philadelphia, PA 19106 Rep: LGI / 212-736-4602	Gruen, Bob / 212-691-0391 55 Bethune St., NYC, NY 10014 Rep: Starfile / 212-354-8327
Granata, Donna / 805-649-9366 / 310-452-4704 P.O. Box 2619, Ventura, CA 93002	Gruen, John Rep: Michael Ash / 212-807-6286
Graves, Trevor / 503-362-3102 8511 Macleay Rd. SE, Salem, OR 97301 page 41	Grumpy Bear Prods. / 603-654-6557 P.O. Box 125, Mt. Vernon, NH 03057
Gray, Katie / 212-722-6228 1160 5th Ave., Ste. 606, NYC, NY 10029	Gudnason, Torkil Rep: Judy Casey Inc. / 212-255-3252
Gray, Mike / 503-228-8203 938 NW Everett, Portland, OR 97209	Guice, Brad / 212-941-6096 232 W. Broadway, NYC, NY 10013 Rep: Janice Moses / 212-779-7929
Gray, Mitchel / 212-722-6228 1160 Fifth Avenue, Ste. 606, NYC, NY 10029	Guilburt, David / 310-457-8260
Gray, Todd / 818-763-6729 11201 Kling St., N. Hollywood, CA 91602	Guip, Amy / 212-674-8166 352 Bowery, #2, NYC, NY 10012
Grecco, Michael / 310-452-4461 Rep: Keswick Hamilton/Sygma / 213-380-3933 Rep: Susan Miller / 212-905-8400 Rep: Sygma / 212-675-7900 pages 118 - 119	Gunther, Matt / 310-273-4390 Guzman Rep: Jodi Rappaport / 213-464-4481 Rep: Frank Parvis / 212-473-5868
Green, Barbara / 213-661-0054	Gwinn, Beth / 615-385-0917 P.O. Box 22817, Nashville, TN 37202
Greenberg, Jill / 212-594-5624 322 Seventh Ave., Ste. 3F, NYC, NY 10001 pages 108 - 109	Gwynn, Cat / 213-660-5354 3765 Legion Lane, LA, CA 90039 Rep: Nadine / 310-829-5233
Greenfield, Lois / 212-925-1117 52 White St., NYC, NY 10013 Rep: John Henry / 212-686-6883	Gyssler, Glen / 312-843-2202 Rep: Jim Hanson / 312-337-7770
Greenfield-Sanders, Timothy Rep: Stockland Martel / 212-727-1400	Haber, Graham S. / 212-268-4148 348 W. 38th St., NYC, NY 10018
Gregoire, Peter / 212-967-4969 448 37th St., #12C, NYC, NY 10018 Rep: Laurie Ketcham / 212-481-9592	Haber, Michael Rep: Alyssa Pizer / 310-440-3930
Greyshock, Caroline / 213-658-1171 Rep: Caryn Weiss / 213-461-1084	Hagiwara, Brian / 212-674-6026 504 La Guardia Pl., NYC, NY 10012 Rep: Proof / 212-979-6440
Gross, Gary / 212-807-7141 235 West Fourth Street, NYC, NY 10014	Hagler, Skeeter / 214-526-5141 2919 Welborn, Suite 101, Dallas, TX 75219 Rep: Kathy Jane Hill / 214-559-0802

TABLE (4.19). PHOTOGRAPHY

Photographers	Photographers

Hagopian, Jim / 213-856-0018
915 N. Mansfield Ave., LA, CA 90038

Haiman, Todd / 212-391-0810
26 W. 38th St., NYC, NY 10018
Rep: Doug Brown / 212-953-0088

Halfin, Ross
Rep: Neil Zlozower / 213-653-6726

Hall, Glenn / 615-255-7971
315 Tenth Ave. N., Ste. 109, Nashville, TN 37203

Halper, Mark Robert / 213-687-7377
900 E. First St., #305, LA, CA 90012

Halpern, John / 212-439-4775
Rep: Fox Art., Inc. / 213-653-6484

Halsband, Michael / 212-889-2994
1200 Broadway, NYC, NY 10001

Hames, William / 310-287-1077
8743 W. Washington Blvd., Culver City, CA 90232

Hammond, Francis / 212-242-7519
526 W. 26th St., NYC, NY 10001

Hanauer, Mark / 213-462-2421
1153 N. Las Palmas, LA, CA 90038
Rep: Onyx / 213-965-0899

Hanson, Pamela
Rep: Leslie Simitch / 212-925-2668

Harbron, Patrick / 212-967-2111 / 213-856-2253
666 Greenwich St., Ste. 746, NYC, NY 10014

Harger, Eric / 415-626-0456
2325 Third St., #414, SF, CA 94107

Harmel, Mark / 213-936-4686
6135 Colgate Ave., LA, CA 90036
Rep: Lisa Zari / 212-727-9145

→ Harrington Studio / 615-248-6725
942 Fourth Ave. S., Nashville, TN 37210
pages 96 - 97

Harris, Mark / 213-939-3979

Harris, Neal / 212-734-1593
1571 York Ave., #5n, NYC, NY 10028

Hart, Tracy / 713-868-9606
The Heights Gallery
1438 Herkimer at 15th, Houston, TX 77008

Harvey, Philip / 415-861-2091
911 Minna St., SF, CA 94103

Harvey, Stephen / 213-934-5817
7801 W. Beverly Blvd, LA, CA 90036

Hashi
Rep: Stockland Martel / 212-727-1400

Hashimoto, Michael / 213-882-8599
7211 Sant Monica Blvd., Ste. 300, LA, CA 90046

Hastings, Daniel / 201-656-0255

Hastings, James / 212-929-2454
7 E. 14th st., NYC, NY 10003

Hastings, Ryan / 206-762-8691
309 S. Cloverdale, #C24, Seattle, WA 98108

Hathaway, Steve / 415-255-2100
400 Treat Ave., Ste. F, SF, CA 94110
Rep: Polly Smith / 415-989-6501

Hauser, Marc / 312-486-4381
1810 W. Cortland St., Chicago, IL 60622
Rep: Randi Fiat & Assoc. / 312-663-5300
Rep: The McCann Co. / 214-526-2252

→ Hawkes, William / 213-931-7777
5757 Venice Blvd., LA, CA 90019
pages 6 - 7

Hawkins, David / 615-256-8989

Heard, Gary Lee / 716-454-2796
72 Cascade Dr., Rochester, NY 14614

→ Heinser, Thomas / 415-495-0365
25 Zoe St., SF, CA 94107
pages 20 - 21

Heintz, Michael / 203-838-7599
15 N. Water St., S. Norwalk, CT 06854
Rep: Nan Wasson

Heisler, Gregory / 212-777-8100
568 Broadway, NYC, NY 10012

$$F = (a \times p)^4$$

Table (4.20). Photography

Photographers	Photographers
Henderson, Derek Rep: Visages Rps., Inc. / 213-650-8880	Holdorf, Thomas / 212-473-2602 534 E. Sixth St., #1, NYC, NY 10009
Henry, J. Greg / 213-850-5255	Hollywood, Barry Rep: Kramer & Kramer / 212-688-4364
Hershberger, Sally Rep: Janet Botaish Group / 310-314-1571	Holts, Ron / 301-589-7900 9153 Brookville Rd., Silver Spring, MD 20910
Hershko, Eli / 212-247-2992 Rep: Hillary Aiges	Holub, Ed / 212-206-0429 119 W. 23rd. St., #907, NYC, NY 10011
Herzhaft, Beth / 213-653-2364 431 N. Stanley Ave., LA, CA 90036	Holz, George / 212-229-0017 Rep: Onyx / 213-965-0899
Heuberger, William / 212-242-1532 140 W. 22nd St., NYC, NY 10011 Rep: Pamela Black / 212-979-2636	Holzemer, Buck / 612-824-3874 3448 Chicago Ave., Minneapolis, MN 55407
Heungman / 212-925-5965 16 Crosby St., NYC, NY 10013	Holzer, Richard / 214-393-4860 6036 Ridgecrest #213, Dallas, TX 75231
Heydt, Maggie / 708-501-4527 1250 Cherry St., Winnetka, IL 60093	Hood, Rusty / 714-846-6214 16281 Underhill Lane, Huntington Beach, CA 92647
Higashino, Mark / 212-979-2870 873 Broadway, #608, NYC, NY 10003	Hooper, Thomas / 212-691-0122 126 Fifth Ave., 5th Fl., NYC, NY 10011 Rep: Michael Schenker / 212-691-0122
Himmel, Lizzie / 212-683-5331 50 W. 29th St., #4W, NYC, NY 10001 Rep: Proof / 212-979-6440	Hope, Christina / 904-246-9689 2720 Third St S., Jackonville Beach, FL 32250 Rep: Lisa Zari / 212-727-9145
Hing/Norton / 212-683-4258 24 W. 30th. St., 8th. Fl., NYC, NY 10001 Rep: Randy Cole / 212-679-5933	Horvath, Peter Rep: Kolea Baker / 206-784-1136
Hinsdale, Greg Rep: Catherine Ludlow / 213-658-6920	House, Troy Rep: Jodi Rappaport / 213-464-4481 Rep: Achard & Assoc. / 212-614-0962
Hiro Studios, Inc. Rep: Nob Horde / 212-753-0462	Howrani, Ameen / 313-875-3123 2820 E. Grand Blvd, Detroit, MI 48211 Rep: Elizabeth Hollow / 313-875-3123
Hispard, Marc Rep: Jean Gabriel Kauss / 212-370-4300	Hummel, David / 612-322-4683 12763 Edgewater Path, Apple Valley, MN 55124
Hitz, Bradford Walker Evans / 310-392-9636 Rep: Caryn Weiss / 213-461-1084	Hunter, Rick / 210-223-3052 128 Main Plaza,, San Antonio, TX 78205
Hofmann, Ruedi Rep: Stockland Martel / 212-727-1400	Hunyady, Brooke Rep: Zari Int. / 212-388-8541
Holderer, Jon / 212-620-4260 37 W. 20th St., NYC, NY 10011	

F = (a × p)⁴

$$F = (a \times p)^4$$

Table (4.21). Photography

Photographers	Photographers

Hursey, Dana / 213-931-7577
4429 Bel Air Dr., La Canada, CA 91011

⟶ Hush, Gary / 503-222-4786
514 NW 11th St., #205, Portland, OR 97209
pages 18 - 19

Ionesco, Irina
Rep: Leslie Barany / 212-627-8488

Iooss, Walter
Rep: Stockland Martel / 212-727-1400

⟶ Irby, Kevin / 415-552-0671
1810 Harrison St., #10, SF, CA 94103
page 1

Israelson, Nels / 213-680-2414
311 Avery St., LA, CA 90013
Rep: Alyssa Pizer / 310-440-3930

Issermann, Dominique
Rep: JGK / 212-370-4300

Izu, Kenro
Rep: Jean Conlon / 212-966-9897

Izzo, Teresa / 800-370-5260 / 617-926-3966

Jacobson, Eric / 212-777-0070
45 E.20th St., 5th Fl., NYC, NY 10003

Jaffe, Ellen / 212-966-7206
248 Lafayette, NYC, NY 10012

Jasmin, Paul
Rep: Visages Rps., Inc, / 213-650-8880

Jefferies, Marc A. / 212-293-4208
1001 Woodycrest Ave, #7F, Bronx, NY 10452

Jeffers-Burghardt, Paige / 818-500-4852 / 818-500-4852
1051 Irving Ave., Glendale, CA 91201

Jennings, Steve / 415-883-0317
P.O. Box 9141, San Rafael, CA 94912
Rep: LGI / 212-736-4602

Jensen, David / 213-937-8926
Rep: Jodi Rappaport / 213-464-4481

Johnson, Jeff / 612-339-7929
529 S. Seventh St., Ste.698, Minneapolis, MN 55115

Johnson, Michael
Rep: Friend & Johnson / 415-927-4500 / 212-808-0022

⟶ Johnson, Sandra / 213-969-0482
7211 Santa Monica Blvd., Ste. 300, LA, CA 90046
pages 110 - 111

Jolly, Pat / 504-899-8994
1820 General Pershing St., New Orleans, LA 70115

Jones, Aaron / 505-466-1956
#3 Vaquero Rd., Santa Fe, NM 87505

Jones, Carolyn / 212-431-9696
167 Spring St., NYC, NY 10012
Rep: Barbara Von Schrieber / 212-460-5000

Jones, Lou / 617-426-6335
22 Randolph St., Boston, MA 02118
Rep: Lorie Savel

Jones, Sam / 213-658-5551
349 1/2 N. Hayworth Ave., LA, CA 90048

Jones, Spencer / 212-941-8165
23 Leonard St., NYC, NY 10013
Rep: Bill Charles / 212-941-8165

Jones, Will / 602-244-1971
1615 N. 36th St., Phoenix, AZ 85008

Jordano, Dave / 312-280-8212
1335 N. Wells, Chicago, IL 60610
Rep: Vincent Kamin & Assocs / 312-787-8834

Jurgens, Panja
Rep: Leslie Barany / 212-627-8488

Kahan, Eric / 212-243-9727
37 W. 20th St., NYC, NY 10011

Kaltman, Naomi
Rep: Caryn Weiss / 213-461-1084

Kam, Hendrik / 415-861-7093

Kander, Nadav
Rep: Stockland Martel / 212-727-1400

Kane, Gary / 212-677-4944
238 E. 14th St., #4D, NYC, NY 10003

$$F = (a \times p)^4$$

Photographers	Photographers
Karr, Dean / 213-625-8743 1201 E. Fifth St., Studio B, LA, CA 90013	Kenner, Fred / 215-238-9559 113 Arch St., Philadelphia, PA 19106
Kase, Ander / 310-204-1799 10829 Palms Blvd, Ste. 5, LA, CA 90034	Kenton, Basia Rep: Beate Works / 213-653-5088
Katvan, Moshe / 212-242-4895 40 W. 17th St., NYC, NY 10011 Rep: Ralph Mennemeyer / 212-691-4277	Kern, Geof Rep: Friend & Johnson / 214-855-0055 / 212-808-0022
Katz, Jeff / 213-463-0430 1038 N. Sycamore Ave., LA, CA 90038	Kessler, Joshua / 212-229-1540 9 E. 13th St., 4J, NYC, NY 10003
Katzenstein, David / 212-529-9460 23 E. Fourth St., 4th Floor, NYC, NY 10003	Key, Trevor Rep: Friend & Johnson / 212-808-0022 / 312-943-7885
Katzman, Mark / 314-241-3811 710 N. Tucker #512, St. Louis, MO 63101 Rep: Suzanne Craig / 918-749-9424 Rep: Teenuh Foster / 314-821-2278	Khornak, Lucille / 212-593-0933 425 E. 58th St., NYC, NY 10022
Kayne, Mark Rep: Winston West / 310-275-2858	Kim, Cherry / 212-727-3287 11 W. 17th St., 4th FL., NYC, NY 10011
Kazu Studio Ltd. / 312-348-5393 1211 W. Webster, Chicago, IL 60614	Kinney, Greg / 615-297-8084 238 Burlington Pl., Nashville, TN 37215
→ Kearney, Mitchell / 704-377-7662 301 E. 7th St., Charlotte, NC 28202 pages 84 - 85	Kirk, Neil Rep: Julia Kirk / 212-420-1794 Rep: Winston West, Ltd. / 310-275-2858
Keeley, Dennis / 310-833-1001 1001 Averill Ave., San Pedro, CA 90732 Rep: Caryn Weiss / 213-461-1084	Kirkland, Douglas / 213-656-8511 9060 Wonderland Park Ave., LA, CA 90046
Keith, Darren Rep: L.A. Rep / 213-656-1720	Kirkland, Gene / 818-509-2663 6363 Vicland Pl., N. Hollywood, CA 90606
Keith, Ron / 615-383-2225 1401 Acklen Ave., Nashville, TN 37212	Knight, Kevin / 212-532-9482 116 Lexington Ave., 3rd Fl., NYC, NY 10016
Kelly, Bill / 212-989-2794 Mesopotamia Productions 140 Seventh Ave., NYC, NY 10011 Rep: Elizabeth Veneskey / 212-989-2794	Knott, Grace Rep: Friend & Johnson / 214-855-0055
Kemmerling, Steve / 612-378-0571 153 26th Ave. SE, Ste. 101, Minneapolis, MN 55414	→ Kohanim, Parish / 404-892-0099 1130 W. Peachtree St., Atlanta, GA 30309 pages 90 - 91
Kennedy, David Michael / 505-473-2745 P.O. Box 254, Cerrillos, NM 87010	Kohlberg, Karin / 212-966-0485 34 White St., NYC, NY 10013
	Kolansky, Palma / 212-727-7300 55 Van Dam St., NYC, NY 10013
	Kopelow, Paul / 212-689-0685 135 Madison Ave., NYC, NY 10016

$F = (a \times p)^4$

Table (4.23). Photography

Photographers	Photographers

Koudis, Nick / 212-206-0606
30 W. 22nd St., 5th Floor, NYC, NY 10010

Kozyra, James / 212-229-1150
180 Varrick, 14th Floor, NYC, NY 10014
Rep: Elise Caputo / 212-725-0503

Krajcirovic, Maria
Rep: Jim Hanson & Talent / 312-337-7770

Kramer, David / 213-937-2121
5531 W. Washington Blvd., LA, CA 90016

Kratochivil, Antonin / 212-947-1589
448 W. 37th St., #69, NYC, NY 10013

→ Kretschmer, Hugh / 213-627-6554
1250 Long Beach Ave., Studio 117, LA, CA 90021
Rep: Sharpe & Assoc. / 310-641-8556 / 212-595-1125
page 66

Kroninger, Rick
Rep: Those 3 Reps / 214-871-1316

Kuehn, Karen / 212-477-1251
300 E. 4th St., #1D, NYC, NY 10009
Rep: Janice Moses / 212-779-7929

Kuhns, Pete / 212-675-2141
356 W. 20th St., #2A, NYC, NY 10011

Kwaku / 212-868-1597

La Monica, Michael / 305-573-6352

La Tona, Kevin / 206-285-5779
159 Western Ave. W., #454, Seattle, WA 98119

LaChapelle, David / 212-529-5385
Rep: Caryn Weiss / 213-461-1084

→ Lamonica, Tracy / 213-957-5780
page 28

Lane, Morris / 212-696-0498
212A E. 26th St., NYC, NY 10010

Lange, George / 310-396-1642
243 Hollister Ave., Santa Monica, CA 90405
Rep: Onyx / 213-965-0899

Lange, Paul
Rep: Kramer & Kramer / 212-645-8787

Lanker, Brian / 503-485-0070
1993 Kimberly Dr., Eugene, OR 97405

Lansel, Andre
Rep: Visages / 213-650-8880

Larrain, Gilles / 212-925-8494
95 Grand St., #1, NYC, NY 10013

Larsen, Kristine / 212-608-3813
12 John St., #9, NYC, NY 10038

Larson, Joel / 612-339-4924
917 North Fifth Street, Minneapolis, MN 55401

Lasky, Bob / 305-891-0550
1543 N.E. 123rd St., N.Miami, FL 33161

Laubmayer, Klaus
Rep: Elaine Korn Assoc. Ltd / 212-760-0057
Rep: Beate Works / 213-653-5088

Lauren, Joan / 213-651-4070

Laurita, Michele / 213-462-7937
6200 Banner Ave., #1, Hollywood, CA 90038

→ Lavine, Michael
Rep: Edge / 212-343-2260 / 213-954-9422
pages 12 - 13

→ Lavrisha, Marko / 415-647-9550
pages 116 - 117

Lawson, Phillip & Pamela / 213-656-3886
8809 Oakwilde Ln., Dept 1, LA, CA 90046

Leach, David / 212-288-1234
75 Spring St., NYC, NY 10012

Lee, Lewis / 214-819-3115
201 Regal Row, Dallas, TX 75247

Leeds, Liza / 718-934-3607
1714 Ave. V, Brooklyn, NY 11229

Lefkowitz, Jay Alan / 212-929-1036
5 E. 16th St., NYC, NY 10003
Rep: Chris Lysohir / 212-741-3187

Leialoha, Mark / 415-647-6588
3435 Army Street, SF, CA 94111
Rep: Jane Hoffman / 818-789-0624

Table (4.24). Photography

Photographers	Photographers
Leibovitz, Annie Rep: Art + Commerce / 212-206-0737	Lindfors, Tom / 312-489-3330 2136 W. Moffat, Chicago, IL 60647
→ Leon, Jana / 212-966-2050 Rep: Edge / 212-343-2260 page 14	Lindner, Frank / 718-768-5268 502 13th St., Brooklyn, NY 11215
Lepori, Dave / 408-279-0394 385 N. Third St., Ste. A3, San Jose, CA 95112	Lindsay & Milgate / 206-443-9527 1929 Third Ave, Seattle, WA 98101
Lesch, William / 602-622-6693 426 S. Otero Ave., Tucson, AZ 85701	Lindsay, Kurt / 206-443-9527 1929 Third Ave, Seattle, WA 98101
Levenson, Alan / 310-396-3456	Lipton, Joel / 213-934-8611 1039 S. Fairfax Ave, LA, CA 90019
Levere, Douglas / 212-274-1924 425 Broome St., 3M, NYC, NY 10013	Little, Blake Rep: Fox Art, Inc. / 213-653-6484
Levin, Roz / 201-944-6014 1 Wall St., Fort Lee, NJ 07024	Livzey, John / 213-469-2992 1510 N. Las Palmas, LA, CA 90028
Levine, Cynthia / 213-851-9982 Rep: Keswick Hamilton/Sygma / 213-380-3933	→ Llewellyn, Michael / 213-223-1792 2020 N. Main St., #011, LA, CA 90031 pages 100 - 101
Lewine, Rob / 213-654-0830 8929 Holly Pl., LA, CA 90046	Lombroso, Dorit / 310-450-0992 Rep: Rhoni Epstein / 310-207-5937
Lewis, Bonnie / 310-392-7700	→ London, Bob / 212-966-4894 565 Broadway #8W, NYC, NY 10012 page 68
Lewis, Robert / 212-475-6564 333 Park Ave So., 4th Fl., NYC, NY 10010	Long, Andrew / 512-441-0638 119 Academy Dr., Austin, TX 78704
Lewis, Steve / 617-723-8801 9 Center St., Exeter, NH 03833	Loper, John / 416-861-0287 93 Parliament St., #323, Toronto, Canada M5A 3Y7
Liberatore, Virginia / 212-645-3753 240 W. 15th St., #33, NYC, NY 10011	Lopez, Bret Rep: Anita Green / 212-674-4788
Lieberman, Ilona / 310-285-7838 8424 Santa Monica Blvd., West Hollywood, CA 90069	Lopez, Nola / 212-691-3521 415 W. 23rd St, #5C, NYC, NY 10011
Lieberman, Marcia Rep: Linda DeMoreta / 510-769-1421	→ Lopez, Peter / 213-655-1050 8306 Wilshire Blvd., #444, Beverly Hills, CA 90211 pages 76 - 77
Liepke, Peter / 212-247-7372 425 West 57th St., #1B, NYC, NY 10019	Lott, Kip / 214-826-8220
Lightner, Scott / 310-556-0221 270 N. Canon Dr., #1092, Beverly Hills, CA 90210	→ Low, Dorothy / 213-957-0712 6103 Melrose, LA, CA 90038 pages 64 - 65
Lindem, Holly / 213-656-6243	

Photographers	Photographers
Lowe, Edmund Rep: Jaz & Jaz / 206-282-8558	Malyszko, Mike / 617-426-9111 90 South St., Boston, MA 02111
Ludes, Wolfgang / 212-925-7584 Rep: Olive Head / 212-580-3323	Manangan, Paul / 212-366-9683 135 W. 26th St., 3rd Floor, NYC, NY 10001
Luna, Orlando / 305-662-7746 7009 SW 46th St., Miami, FL 33155	Manarchy, Dennis / 312-666-7400 656 W. Hubbard St., Chicago, IL 60610
Lupino, Stephan Rep: Leslie Barany / 212-627-8488	Mandel, Andrea / 312-829-4002 452 N. Morgan St., Chicago, IL 60622
Lyden, Paul / 508-745-5070 35 Congress St., Salem, MA 01970 Rep: LGI	Mann, Jean Paul Rep: Keswick Hamilton / 213-380-3933
Maas, Rita / 212-447-0410 40 W. 27th St., NYC, NY 10001 Rep: Anita Green / 212-674-4788	Marcus, Ken / 213-937-7214 6916 Melrose Ave., Hollywood, CA 90038
MacPherson, Andrew Rep: Jodi Rappaport / 213-464-4481	Maresca, Frank / 212-620-0955 236 W. 26th St., #903, NYC, NY 10001
MacWeeney, Alen / 212-473-2500 171 First Ave., NYC, NY 10003	Maraia, Charles / 212-206-8156 236 W. 27th St., #804, NYC, NY 10001 page 102
Maday, Tom / 312-235-1600 1643 N. Milwaukee, Chicago, IL 60647	Marill, Olivier / 818-985-4430 4206 Babcock Ave., Studio City, CA 91604 Rep: Allen Dean Powell / 213-653-7041
Mahdavian, Daniel / 212-465-2508 / 212-685-2331 275 Fifth Ave., NYC, NY 10016	Mark, Mary Ellen / 212-925-2770 / 212-925-1380 134 Spring St., #502, NYC, NY 10012 Rep: Art + Commerce / 212-206-0737
Maillard, Jean Claude / 212-439-6433 / 310-288-7911 Rep: Elaine Korn / 212-760-0057	Markus, Kurt / 406-756-9191 135 Lone Pine Rd., Kalispell, MT 59901 Rep: Maria Markus / 406-756-9191
Maisel, David / 415-380-8700 180 Sunset Way, Muir Beach, CA 94965 Rep: Norman Maslov / 415-641-4376 Rep: Bill Rabin & Assoc. / 312-944-6655	Martin, Christoph / 212-477-7336 20 Bond St., #7, NYC, NY 10012 Rep: Philippe Achard / 212-614-0962
Maisel, Jay / 212-431-5013 190 Bowery, NYC, NY 10012 Rep: Emily Vickers / 212-431-5013	Martin, Gene / 212-861-0811 157 E. 72nd St., #10A, NYC, NY 10021 Rep: Merry Erlich
Malabrigo, Mark / 212-420-8087	Martin, Mark / 615-331-4646 3630 Trousdale Dr., Ste. H&G, Nashville, TN 37204
Malignon, Jacques / 212-532-7727 34 W. 28th St., 6th Fl., NYC, NY 10001	Maser, Wayne Rep: Art + Commerce / 212-206-0737
Malluk, Eddie / 212-473-1127 205 Third Ave., Ste. 15M, NYC, NY 10003	Mason, Karen / 206-340-0644

$$F = (a \times p)^4$$

TABLE (4.26). PHOTOGRAPHY

Photographers	Photographers
Matura, Nedjeljko / 212-463-9692 119 W. 23rd St., #505, NYC, NY 10011 Rep: Trisha Buckley	McMullen, Patrick / 212-674-2153 12 Fifth Ave., 1R, NYC, NY 10011
Mauro, Aldo / 213-937-5967 5410 Wilshire Blvd., #405, LA, CA 90036	McRae, Michael / 801-328-3633 925 S.W. Temple, Salt Lake City, UT 84101
→ Mayo, Scogin / 214-941-0663 413 N. Bishop Ave., Dallas, TX 75208 Rep: Friend & Johnson / 214-559-0055 / 212-808-0022 pages 8 - 9	Means, Lisa / 214-826-4979 5915 Anita, Dallas, TX 75206 Rep: Jeff Fandrich / 214-324-3959
Mayor, Alan L. / 615-385-4706 3807 Murphy Rd., Nashville, TN 37209	Meeks, Raymond Rep: Marilyn Cadenbach / 617-484-7437
Mazur, Kevin / 516-957-1171 54 E. Sunrise Hwy, Lindenhurst, NY 11757	Mehr Licht Productions / 818-342-5505 18034 Ventura Blvd, #194, Encino, CA 91316
→ Mazzeo, Michael / 212-228-2004 417 Lafayette, NYC, NY 10003 Rep: Pomegranate Pictures / 212-260-8858 pages 114 - 115	→ Mei, Gallen / 305-453-9660 / 212-929-0540 1405 Gough St., SF, CA 94109 Rep: Corinna Sampson / 415-928-5070 Film / pages 4 - 5
→ McClaran, Robbie / 503-234-6588 pages 104 - 105	Meier, Raymond Rep: Michael Ash / 212-807-6286
McConagle, Russell / 312-225-5557 221 E. Cullerton, 6th fl, Chicago, IL 60616	Meisel, Steven Rep: Art + Commerce / 212-206-0737
McDaniel, Melody / 213-939-2312 Rep: Barbara Von Schreiber / 212-460-5000	Mendoza, Roberto / 717-686-1155 3013 Sunrise Lake, Milford, PA 18337
McDonald, Jock 46 Gilbert St., SF, CA 94103 Rep: Missy Pepper / 415-543-6881	Meola, Eric Rep: Stockland Martel / 212-727-1400
McEntee, Jamie / 305-527-4114 Creative Minds Photography 1038 NE 16th Ave., Ft. Lauderdale, FL 33304	Mercer, Lance / 206-528-1585 2540 N.E. 97th St., Seattle, WA 98115
McEntee, Kay / 517-631-7964 1308 Harwood Ct., Midland, MI 48640	Meredith, Diane / 713-862-8775 6203 Westcott, Houston, TX 77007
McGann, Catherine / 212-713-5548	Merlino, Ralph Rep: Joan Kramer & Assoc. 310-446-1866 / 212-567-5545
McGuire, Jim / 615-244-1947	Messer, Alan / 615-385-4706 Rep: Zari Int. / 212-727-9145
McLaughlin, Micheal Rep: Julian Richards / 212-219-1269	Metzner, Sheila / 212-865-1222 310 Riverside Dr., NYC, NY 10025
McLoughlin, James / 212-206-8207 980 Broadway, #306, Thornwood, NY 10594	Meyer, Kip / 212-683-9039 80 Madison Ave., NYC, NY 10016 Rep: Pat Herron

TABLE (4.27). PHOTOGRAPHY

Photographers	Photographers
Meyers, Barry / 301-585-8617 407 Thayer Ave., Silver Springs, MD 20910	Miller, Peter Darley / 310-836-8312 8800 Venice Blvd., LA, CA 90034
Meyerson, Arthur / 713-529-9697 2710 Bissonnet, Houston, TX 77005	Miller, Rex / 212-979-1802 250 Mercer St., A205, NYC, NY 10012
Micaud, Christopher / 212-473-7266 143 Avenue B, Phc, NYC, NY 10009 Rep: Judy Casey / 212-255-3252	Milne, Bill / 212-255-0710 140 W. 22nd St., NYC, NY 10011 Rep: Lisa Cichocki
Michaels, Jeffrey / 408-734-8814 Shades of Grey 1014 Morse Ave., #8, Sunnyvale, CA 94089	Mistretta, Martin / 212-675-1547 220 W. 19th St., NYC, NY 10011 Rep: Liz Li / 212-889-7067
Michelena, Peter / 213-465-5773 / 212-645-7676 pages 56 - 57	Mitchell, Ann / 818-842-6414 132 E. Providencia Ave., Burbank, CA 91502
Michelson, Randall / 213-465-3232 650 N. Bronson Ave., Ste. 142, LA, CA 90004	Modricker, Darren / 212-978-8877 / 215-732-8877 502 Park Ave., NYC, NY 10022
Michienzi, Shawn / 612-673-0594 1625 Hennepin Ave S., Minneapolis, MN 55403	Molenhouse, Craig / 818-901-9306 P.O. Box 7678, Van Nuys, CA 91409
Milazzo, Robert / 212-243-7191 126 W. 22nd St., 2nd Fl., NYC, NY 10011	Monk, Russell 443 King St., West, Toronto, Canada M5V 1K4
Miles, Bill / 617-426-6862 374 Congress St., Ste. 304, Boston, MA 02210	Moon, Sarah Rep: Barbara von Schreiber, / 212-580-7044
Miles, Jonnie / 212-865-7956 309 W. 99th St., NYC, NY 10025	Moran, Nancy / 212-505-9620 143 Greene St., NYC, NY 10012 Rep: Carol Cohn / 212-924-4450
Milford, Denise / 213-883-0836 2201 Maravilla Dr., LA, CA 90068	Morduchowicz, Daniel / 213-464-6114 6313 Yucca St., Hollywood, CA 90028
Millard, Robert / 818-247-4700 1435 Gardena Ave., #10, Glendale, CA 91204	Morello, Peter / 212-477-5101 Rep: Retna / 212-255-0622
Miller, Brad / 312-292-0875 1439 N. Milwaukee, Chicago, IL 60622	Morgan, Paul J. / 214-741-3908 / 212-330-8008 3408 Main St., Dallas, TX 75226
Miller, Don / 213-680-1896 447 S. Hewitt St., LA, CA 90013	Morgan, Scott / 310-392-1863 711 Hampton Dr., Venice, CA 90291 Rep: Deborah Ayerst / 415-567-3570
Miller, Frank / 612-935-8888	Morris, Bill / 212-274-1177 42 Greene St., NYC, NY 10013
Miller, Karen / 310-827-5921 312 Venice Way, Venice, CA 90291	
Miller, Michael Rep: LaMoine Represents / 213-467-9730	Morrison, John / 416-588-2746 / 416-535-1955 33 Jefferson Ave., Toronto, Canada M6K 1Y3

$$F = (a \times p)^4$$

TABLE (4.28). PHOTOGRAPHY

Photographers	Photographers
Morrison, Ted / 212-279-2838 286 Fifth Ave., NYC, NY 10001	Nash, Peter / 615-327-0400 1305 Clinton Street, Nashville, TN 37203
Moscati, Frank Rep: Joan Kramer & Assoc. 310-446-1866 / 212-567-5545	Nation, Bill Rep: Joan Kramer & Assoc. 310-446-1866 / 212-567-5545
→ Moskowitz, Karen / 206-860-1242 / 213-427-9340 1517 12th Ave., Seattle, WA 98122 page 75	Natkin, Paul / 312-871-7371 Photo Reserve 2924 N. Racine, Chicago, IL 60657
Moss, Gary / 213-255-2404	Neleman, Hans / 212-274-1000 77 Mercer St., NYC, NY 10012 Rep: Deborah Ayerst / 415-567-3570
Moss, Jean / 312-786-9110 1255 S. Michigan Ave., Chicago, IL 60605 Rep: Chris W. Glenn / 312-787-4459	Nelken, Dan / 212-532-7471 43 W. 27th St., NYC, NY 10001 Rep: Adele Q. Brown
Mougin, Claude Rep: Stockland Martel / 212-727-1400	Nelson, Geoffrey / 415-306-9563 2636 Broadway, Redwood City, CA 94063
Mueller, Eva Rep: Rania Abbasi / 212-334-8302	Newbury, Jeffery / 415-255-8470 333 Caledonia, Sausalito, CA 94965 Rep: Deborah Ayerst / 415-567-3570
Muller, Michael Rep: Edge / 212-343-2260 / 213-954-9422	Newton, Stanley D. / 310-392-9953 2532 Lincoln Blvd, Suite 56, Venice, CA 90291 Rep: Shooting Star / 213-469-2020
Mulligan, Joseph / 215-592-1359 239 Chestnut St., Philadelphia, PA 19106 Rep: Ralph Kerr / 215-592-1359	Nicks, Dewey Rep: Leslie Simitch / 212-925-2668
→ Muna, R.J. / 415-468-8225 225 Industrial St., SF, CA 94124 pages 88 - 89	Niero, John / 909-626-6223 2527 N. Mountain Ave., Claremont, CA 91711
Mundahl, Kurt / 212-334-8210 44 Lispenard St., #3, NYC, NY 10013	Nilsen, Frederik / 213-257-9566 5317 Abbot Pl., LA, CA 90042
Musilek, Stan / 415-621-5336 1224 Mariposa St., SF, CA 94109	Nilsson, Steven / 213-342-9458 2020 N. Main St., #230, LA, CA 90031
Myers, Jim / 214-698-0500 165 Cole St., Dallas, TX 75207 Rep: Those 3 Reps / 214-871-1316	Nissen, Melanie Rep: LaMoine Represents / 213-467-9730
Myron / 505-982-5055 5 Blue Jay Dr., Santa Fe, NM 87501	→ Njaa, Reuben / 210-271-0630 119 Blue Star, San Antonio, TX 78204 Rep: Vicki Prentice / 310-826-1332 page 44
Nahoum, Ken / 212-924-8880 55 Van Dam St., 16th Fl., NYC, NY 10013	
Nakamura, Tohru / 212-334-8011 112 Greene St., NYC, NY 10012	Noble, Richard / 213-655-4711 2866 Belden Dr., LA, CA 90046

TABLE (4.29). PHOTOGRAPHY

Photographers	Photographers

Nolton, Gary / 503-228-0844
107 NW Fifth Ave., Portland, OR 97209
Rep: Marianne Campbell / 415-433-0353
Rep: Ken Feldman / 312-337-0447

North Holtorf, & Co. / 404-350-8926
1895 Defoor Ave. NW, Atlanta, GA 30318

→ Northrup, Michael / 410-669-4705
2352 Eutaw Pl., Baltimore, MD 21217
page 52

Nozick & Nozick / 410-448-0278

O'Brien, Michael / 512-472-9205
500 San Marcos St., Suite 102, Austin, TX 78702

O'Connell, Bill / 617-437-7556
791 Tremont St., #116 W., Boston, MA 02118

O'Neill, Michael / 212-807-8777
459 West 18th St., NYC, NY 10011
Rep: Barbara Von Schreiber / 212-460-5000

→ Ockenfels 3, Frank W.
Rep: Art + Commerce / 212-206-0737
pages 4 - 5

Odle, Beth / 615-256-5512

→ Olding, Robert / 415-905-5939
3315 Sacramento St., #305, SF, CA 94118
pages 22 - 23, 53

Olivier, Rick / 504-522-7646
225 N. Peters, New Orleans, LA 70130

→ Ollis, Karen / 216-781-8646
1547 Superior Ave., Cleveland, OH 44114
pages 78 - 79

Olsen, Craig Cameron / 213-931-2916
1145 S. Spaulding, LA, CA 90019

→ Olson, Rosanne / 206-633-3775
5200 Latona Ave. NE, Seattle, WA 98105
Rep: Lehmen Dabney Inc. / 206-325-8595
page 26

Orlandi, Roberto
Rep: Jodi Rappaport / 213-934-8633

Orlik, Steve / 212-614-3243

Orn, Fridrik / 213-225-3599
2100 N. Main St., B-3, LA, CA 90031

Otte, Sylvia
Rep: Laurie Ketcham / 212-481-9592

Oudi / 212-777-0847
33 Bleecker Street, NYC, NY 10012
Rep: Sara Ravis

Ouellette, Chris
Rep: Gladys Robinson / 212-385-1861

Paczkowski, Joe / 612-673-0594
1625 Hennepin Ave S., Minneapolis, MN 55403

Page, Lee / 212-233-2227
68 Thomas, 5R, NYC, NY 10013

Pagliuso, Jean
Rep: Barbara von Schreiber, / 212-580-7044

Palmisano, Giorgio / 212-431-7719
309 Mott St., #4A, NYC, NY 10012

Panopoulos, Gerald / 212-242-3132
236 West 27th St., NYC, NY 10011

Papadopolous, Peter / 212-675-4459

Papas, BJ / 212-279-4817

Paras, Michael N. / 212-736-7835
350 Seventh Ave., Ste.2205, NYC, NY 10001

Pardines, B. Anthony / 213-663-0808
3181 1/2 Glendale Blvd., LA, CA 90039

Parian, Levon / 213-934-3685
5769 W. Venice Blvd., LA, CA 90019
Rep: Shooting Star / 212-469-2020

→ Parker, Bev / 212-645-0580
page 27

Parks, Greg / 213-665-1730
2126 Cove Ave., LA, CA 90039

→ Parmelee, Meredith / 213-934-9969
page 72

Pashley, Grove / 213-463-6363
1112 N. Beachwood Dr., LA, CA 90038

$$F = (a \times p)^4$$

Photographers	Photographers
Pasley, Richard Rep: LGI / 212-736-4602	Peterson, Richard / 303-893-3201 1415 Wewatta, #204, Denver, CO 80202
Peardon, Lisa Rep: L.A. Rep / 213-656-1720	Petoe, Denes / 212-213-3311 22 W. 27th St., NYC, NY 10001
Pearle, Eric / 214-943-1339 600 N. Bishop, Dallas, TX 75208 Rep: Jane Mills / 214-946-6569 Rep: Pix Producers, Inc. / 212-533-3800	Petrakes, George / 617-695-0556 242 E. Berkeley St., 5th Fl., Boston, MA 02118 Rep: Mary Jane
Pearson, John / 510-525-7553 1343 Sacramento St., Berkeley, CA 94702	Petrella, Howard / 206-935-1152
Pearson, Victoria / 213-225-0919 696 Moulton Ave, #E, LA, CA 90031 Rep: Michele Karpe / 818-760-0491	Pfriender, Stephanie Rep: Stockland Martel / 212-727-1400
Peden, John / 212-255-2674 155 W. 19th St., NYC, NY 10011 Rep: Monaco Reps / 212-647-0336	Phelps, Bill / 612-339-7731 1624 Harmon Place, Ste.225, Minneapolis, MN 55403
Pederson, Lane / 212-929-9001 76 Ninth Ave., #PH, NYC, NY 10011 Rep: Howard Fox / 212-794-1542	Philips, Steven John / 410-889-4622 3 Hardy Court, Blatimore, MD 21204
Peer, George Rep: Jane Jenni / 612-224-6763	Picayo, Jose / 212-989-8945 32 Morton St., NYC, NY 10014 Rep: Barbara Von Schreiber / 212-460-5000
Penn, Irving / 212-880-8811	Pierce, Richard Rep: Cornelia Artists Rep / 212-620-0544
Penny, Donald / 212-633-9650 10 W. 18th St., NYC, NY 10011	Pinderhughes, John / 212-463-9092 26 W. 17th St., Suite 703, NYC, NY 10011
Perlstein, Abram / 213-876-2862 Rep: Shooting Star / 213-469-2020	Pittman, Dustin / 212-242-3702 210 W. 16 St., NYC, NY 10011
Perno, Jack / 312-666-1495 1956 W. Grand, Chicago, IL 60622 Rep: Cindy Nelson / 312-666-1495 Rep: Randy Cole / 212-679-5933	Pizzarello, Charlie / 212-889-7022 18 W. 27th St., 9fl, NYC, NY 10001
Perry, David / 415-487-1325 610 22nd St., #309, SF, CA 94107 page 52	Pluchino, Joseph Rep: Bill Charles / 212-213-6810
Perry, Nigel Rep: LaMoine Represents / 213-467-9730	Polillio, Joe / 212-727-7450 6 W. 20th St., 2nd Fl., NYC, NY 10011
Pesota, Jack Rep: Bina / 212-533-1734	Porcas, Russell Rep: Colleen McKay / 212-598-0469
Peterson, David / 415-552-6954	Porcella, Philip Rep: Ella / 617-266-3858
	Porto, James / 212-966-4407 480 Canal St., NYC, NY 10013 Rep: DLM / 212-297-0041

TABLE (4.31). PHOTOGRAPHY

Photographers	Photographers
Posey, Carl / 212-248-5118 66 Pearl St., #203, NYC, NY 10004	Rankin-Smith, Pamela / 212-861-6836 150 E. 69th St., NYC, NY 10021
Powers, Lisa / 415-328-4633 Rep: Renee Hersey	Ransier, Richard / 213-258-2277
Predrag / 914-354-5555 Rep: Jim Zaccaro / 212-744-4000	Rapoport, Aaron / 213-883-0388 922 N. Formosa, Hollywood, CA 90046
Preston, Neal / 213-461-2788 P.O. Box 3473, Hollywood, CA 90078 Rep: Outline / 212-226-8790	Rasmussen, Tim / 212-647-1052 2 Horatio, #11D, NYC, NY 10014
Prezant, Steve / 203-256-8844 926 Reef Road, Fairfield, CT 06430	Rau, Andre Rep: Visages Reps / 212-941-7550
Prince, Len Rep: Levin/Dorr / 212-627-9871	Rausser, Stephanie / 510-654-9470 4053 Harlan, #203, Emeryville, CA 94608
Proctor, Daniel / 415-931-1515 3040 Clay St., SF, CA 94115	→ Raven, Deborah / 212-925-0359 425 Broome St., #3R, NYC, NY 10013 pages 94 - 95
Provost, David / 909-592-3803 622 Arrow Hghwy, San Dimas, CA 91773	Ravid, Joyce Rep: Onyx / 213-965-0899
Prozzo, Marco / 206-323-7900 1065 E. Prospect St., #103, Seattle, WA 98102	Reding/Cooper Rep: Zari Int. / 212-727-9145
Purvis, Charles Rep: Art + Commerce / 212-206-0737	Reed, Dudley Rep: Onyx / 213-965-0899
Putnam, Don / 800-438-6706 P.O.Box 24856, Nashville, TN 37202	Reens, Richard / 214-953-1855 2912 Maple Ave., Dallas, TX 75201
Quackenbush, Russell / 617-871-6977 604 Salem St., Rockland, MA 02370	Regnier, Michael / 816-472-8166
Quin, Clark / 617-451-2686 249 A Street, Boston, MA 02210	Reiher, Jim / 212-736-3131 31 W. 31st St., NYC, NY 10001
Raab, Michael / 212-533-0030 831 Broadway, NYC, NY 10003	Reisig & Taylor Rep: Edge / 213-954-9422 / 212-343-2260
Ragel, Jon / 213-654-4590 Rep: Onyx / 213-965-0899	Reitzel, Bill / 415-864-0510 580 19th St., SF, CA 94107
Randall, Robert / 312-226-9100 250 N Artesian, Chicago, IL 60612	Renard, Jean / 617-266-8673 142 Berkeley St., Boston, MA 02116
Rankin, Richard / 213-463-3755 4649 Beverly Blvd., #101, LA, CA 90004	Ressmeyer-Starlight, Inc. / 516-725-5100 179 North Side Dr., Sag Harbor, NY 11963
	Reznicki, Jack / 212-925-0771 568 Broadway, NYC, NY 10012 Rep: Elysse Weisberg / 212-406-2566

$$F = (a \times p)^4$$

TABLE (4.32). PHOTOGRAPHY

Photographers	Photographers
Rhea, Scott / 214-821-9387 4147 Commerce Studio 1, Dallas, TX 75226	Rolston, Matthew / 213-658-1151 8259 Melrose Ave., LA, CA 90046 Rep: Tressa Lucas / 213-658-6616
→ Rieder & Walsh / 412-621-1268 424 N. Craig St, Pittsburgh, PA 15213 page 53	Romy / 818-382-4749 859 Hollywood Way, #301, Burbank, CA 91505
Ripling, Earl / 212-727-2493 33 W. 17th St., NYC, NY 10011 Rep: Pamela Black / 212-979-2636	Rose, David / 212-226-7031 80 Varick, #2A, NYC, NY 10013
Ritts, Herb / 212-941-7550 560 Broadway, Ste. 407, NYC, NY 10012 Rep: Visages Rps. / 212-941-7550 / 213-650-8880	Rosenberg, Alan / 408-986-8484 1140 Walsh Ave., Santa Clara, CA 95050 Rep: David Wiley / 408-442-1821
Rizzo, John / 212-725-0650 163 Amsterdam, #189, NYC, NY 10023	Rosenberg, Howard / 213-484-0523 2520 Sunset Blvd., LA, CA 90026
Robbins, Bill / 310-314-7771 Rep: Susan Miller / 212-905-8400 Rep: Elizabeth Poje / 310-556-1439	Rosenberg, Merlyn / 213-660-1731 Rep: David Maloney / 212-675-7900
Robert, Francois / 312-787-0777 740 N. Wells, Chicago, IL 60610 Rep: Gary Hurewitz / 212-925-2999	Rosenthal, Barry / 212-645-0433 205 W. 19th St., NYC, NY 10011 Rep: Elyn Zelman
Roberts, Ebet / 212-316-3696 245 W. 107th St., #10C, NYC, NY 10025	Rosenthal, Mike / 212-929-5156 213 West 16th Street, #6, NYC, NY 10011
Robin, David / 415-863-8900 / 213-243-6475 818 Brannan, SF, CA 94103	Rosza, Johnny Rep: LaMoine Represents / 213-467-9730 Rep: Deborah Martin / 310-474-7277
Robledo, Maria / 212-406-3211 Rep: Friend & Johnson / 212-808-0022 / 415-927-4500	Rotem / 212-947-9455 259 W. 30th St., 16fl., NYC, NY 10001
Robledo, Maria I. / 212-406-3211 95 Reade St. #5S, NYC, NY 10013 Rep: Friend & Johnson / 214-855-0055	Roth, David / 213-664-9888
Rocco, Roberto Rep: LaMoine Represents / 213-467-9730	Rothfeld, Steven / 310-399-2460
Rock, Bob / 212-460-8258 873 Broadway, #302, NYC, NY 10003	→ Roundtree, Deborah / 213-933-0297 1662 S. Stanley Ave., LA, CA 90019 Rep: David Zaitz / 310-207-4806 Rep: Randy Cole / 212-679-5933 Rep: Liz McCann / 214-526-2252 Rep: Randi Fiat / 312-663-5300 page 29
Rock, Mick / 212-219-1650 5 White St., NYC, NY 10013	Rowe, Jeff / 512-478-1820 Lone Star Silver 304 Colorado St., Austin, TX 78701
Rodin, Christine / 212-242-3260 38 Morton St., 5A, NYC, NY 10014	Rubin, Bernard / 407-629-9484 786 Antonette Ave., Winter Park, FL 32789

TABLE (4.33). PHOTOGRAPHY

Photographers	Photographers

Rubin, Laurie / 312-348-2224
1113 Armitage, Chicago, IL 60614
Rep: Randi Fiat / 312-663-5300
Rep: The McCann Co. / 214-526-2252

Russell, John / 212-473-6562
144 Sullivan St., #23, NYC, NY 10012

Rutherford, Mike / 615-242-5953
623 Sixth Ave. So., Nashville, TN 37203
Rep: Debbie Rutherford

Ryan, Tom / 214-651-7085
2919 Canton St., Dallas, TX 75226
Rep: Friend & Johnson / 214-855-0055

Sabella, Jill / 206-285-4794

Sahihi, Ashkan
Rep: Julian Richards / 212-219-1269

Salisbury, John Patrick
Rep: Janet Botaish Group / 310-314-1571

Sallow, Jacki / 818-988-8810
Rep: LGI / 212-736-4602

Salvatori, Lou
Rep: Visages Rps. / 212-941-7550

Salzano, James / 212-242-4820
29 W. 15th St., NYC, NY 10011
Rep: Frank Meo / 212-353-0907

Sanchez, Albert
Rep: Caryn Weiss / 213-461-1084

→ Sanders, Chris / 212-343-0003
73 Spring St., #502, NYC, NY 10012
Rep: Michael Ginsburg / 212-679-8881
pages 36 - 37

Saragnese, Frank / 201-659-4655

Savio, Joanne / 212-941-7631
47 Walker St., NYC, NY 10013

Sax, Ken / 310-288-9634 / 310-785-0335
9188 W. Pico Blvd., #225, LA, CA 90035
Rep: L.A. Rep / 213-656-1720

Scales, Jeffrey / 212-316-0705
1945 Seventh Ave., NYC, NY 10026

Scarlett, Nora / 212-741-2620
37 W. 20th St., NYC, NY 10011
Rep: Gerald & Cullen Rapp, / 212-889-3337

Scavullo, Francesco
Rep: Tom Gallahger / 212-838-0930

Schafer, F. Scott / 818-440-9695
Rep: Valerie London / 310-278-6633

Schaffner, Sue / 212-741-2715
350 Bleeker, #6C, NYC, NY 10014

Schapiro, Steve / 310-276-0729
9536 Tullis Dr., Beverly Hills, CA 90210

Schatt, Roy
Rep: Leslie Barany / 212-627-8488

Schenck, Rocky / 213-465-1547
2420 Detour Dr., Hollywood, CA 90068

Schewe, Jeff / 312-951-6334
624 W. Willow, Chicago, IL 60614

Schiff, Nancy Rica / 212-679-9444 / 310-657-5436
24 W. 30th St., NYC, NY 10001

Schiffman, Bonnie / 213-937-8222
6455 Colgate Ave., LA, CA 90048
Rep: Onyx / 213-965-0899

Schles, Ken
Rep: Onyx / 213-965-0899

Schmid, Hannes
Rep: Jim Hanson / 312-337-7770

Schmid, Lothar
Rep: Visages Rps. / 212-941-7550

Schmidt, Eric / 818-574-1953
Rep: Elisabeth Poje

Schoenfeld, Michael / 801-532-2006
560 W. 200 So., Salt Lake City, UT 84101
Rep: Suzy

Schrack, Thea / 415-647-1174
Rep: Deborah Ayerst / 415-567-3570

Schraub, Paul / 408-426-4537
738 A Chestnut St., Santa Cruz, CA 95060

$$F = (a \times p)^4$$

TABLE (4.34). PHOTOGRAPHY

Photographers	Photographers
Schriddle, Daniel / 818-848-7723	Shoshana, Rose / 310-399-0467 / 310-399-4282 511 Hill St., Santa Monica, CA 90405
Schulman, Scott C. / 310-306-2191 4311 Lyceum Ave., LA, CA 90066	Shot in the Dark Photography / 206-441-5532 P.O. Box 61608, Seattle, WA 98121
Scott, Mark / 213-931-9319 Rep: Jean Gardner / 213-464-2492	Shotwell, Chuck Rep: Friend & Johnson / 214-855-0055 / 312-943-7885
Sebree, Robert / 213-225-3609 694 Moulton Ave., LA, CA 90031	Shrearer, Graham Rep: Visages Rps. / 212-941-7550
Sedlik, Jeff / 213-626-3323 940 E. Second St., #8, LA, CA 90012	Shung, Ken / 212-255-1332 / 518-537-5503 41 Union Square W., #735, NYC, NY 10003
Seeger, Jan / 213-626-2535 500 Molino, #216, LA, CA 90013	Sia, Joseph / 203-336-9221 955 Tunxis Hill Rd., Fairfield, CT 06430
Seidel, Mitchell / 201-798-2623 P.O. Box 1983, Hoboken, NJ 07030	Silbert, Layle / 212-677-0947 505 LaGuardia Pl., #16C, NYC, NY 10012
Seifert, Lisa / 212-645-2915 305 Spring St., #2B, NYC, NY 10013	Silfen, Alan / 310-587-4980 P.O.Box 17366, Beverly Hills, CA 90209
Seliger, Mark / 212-941-6548 96 Grand St., 3F, NYC, NY 10013 Rep: Proof / 212-979-6440	Silverman, Jay / 213-466-6030 920 N. Citrus Ave., Hollywood, CA 90038
Selkirk, Neil / 212-243-6778 515 W. 19th St., NYC, NY 10011	Silverstein, Joyce / 310-659-1831 P.O. Box 69A63, LA, CA 90069 Rep: Katz Pictures Ltd. / 071-814-9898
Sennet, Mark Rep: Onyx / 213-965-0899	Sim, Duncan Rep: Michael Ash / 212-807-6288
Serrao, Carlos / 213-954-1554 422 S. Detroit St., LA, CA 90036	Simhoni, George Rep: Robin Dictenberg / 212-620-0995
Sexton, Michael / 415-621-5345 page 83	Simmons, Erik Leigh / 617-268-4650 60 K Street, Boston, MA 02127
Shacter, Susan / 212-741-1476 7 E. 17th St., NYC, NY 10003 Rep: Elyse Connolly / 212-598-4473 Rep: Janet Botaish Group / 310-314-1571	Simon, Peter Angelo / 212-925-0890 520 Broadway, Ste. 702, NYC, NY 10012
Shaw, Kate / 312-664-5734 1827 Lincoln Park W., Chicago, IL 60614	Simons, Chip / 505-869-0344 1570 W. Bosque Loop, Bosque Farms, NM 87068
Sherif, Mohammed / 212-722-7439 400 E. 89th St., NYC, NY 10128	Sims, Jim Rep: Friend & Johnson / 214-855-0055 / 415-927-4500
Shively, Will / 614-464-0330 492 Armstrong St., Columbus, OH 43215 page 40	Sirota, Peggy Rep: Elyse Connolly / 212-598-4473 Rep: Tricia Burlingham / 310-998-9176

TABLE (4.35). PHOTOGRAPHY

Photographers	Photographers

Skid / 212-274-0525
558 Broome St., #4, NYC, NY 10013

Slavin, Neal
Rep: Barbara von Schreiber, / 212-580-7044

Smale, Brian / 212-684-1989
20 W. 27th St., 3rd Fl., NYC, NY 10001

Smith, Brian / 305-534-3130
4646 Pine Tree Dr., Miami Beach, FL 33140

Smith, Matthew Jordan
Rep: Deborah Martin / 310-474-7277

Smith, Michael P. / 504-866-8940 / 504-524-3296
1210 Short St., New Orleans, LA 70118

Smith, Michele A. H. / 213-469-6644
1933 N. Bronson Ave., #301, LA, CA 90068

Smith, Richard Hamilton
Rep: Atols & Hoffman / 312-222-0504

Smith, Rodney / 914-359-3814
Rep: Michael Ash / 212-807-6286

→ Smith, Ron Baxter / 212-343-0132 / 416-462-3040
pages 2 - 3

Smith, Sean / 212-366-5182
111 W. 11th St., 5RE, NYC, NY 10011

Smith, Seth / 214-428-4510
2401 S. Ervay, Suite 204, Dallas, TX 75215

Smith, Steve
Rep: Jean Gardner / 213-464-2492

Smothers, Bryan / 713-691-3242
834 W. 43rd, Houston, TX 77018

Snyder, Isabel
Rep: Jean Gabriel Kauss / 212-370-4300

Sokolik, Jim
Rep: Ceci Bartels / 314-781-7377

Solomon, Ike / 213-876-0604
3720 Barham Blvd., LA, CA 90068

Solomon, Paul / 212-760-1203
440 W. 34th St., NYC, NY 10001
Rep: Barbara Gordon / 212-686-3514

Soqui, Ted / 213-963-1261
2944 N. Santa Anita Ave., Altadena, CA 91001

Sord, Kristen / 212-663-3154
240 West 102nd St., #45, NYC, NY 10025

Spaeth, Dana / 212-475-4946
813 Broadway, #2, NYC, NY 10003

Spatz, Eugene / 212-777-6793
264 Sixth Ave., NYC, NY 10014

Spear, Geoff / 212-529-0778
152 Wooster, NYC, NY 10012

→ Spector, Gary / 212-695-5140
424 W. 33rd St., NYC, NY 10001
page 103

Spelman, Steve / 212-242-9381
88 Jane St., #5E, NYC, NY 10014

→ Spindler, Lisa / 313-393-8538
2900 E. Jefferson, #3C, Detroit, MI 48207
pages 124 - 125

Spinelli, Frank / 212-243-8318
22 W. 21st St., NYC, NY 10010
Rep: Dorothea Scher / 212-689-7273

Spiro / 212-947-7883
340 W. 39th St., NYC, NY 10018

Springsteen, Pamela / 213-874-9188
P.O. Box 93656, LA, CA 90093
Rep: Keswick Hamilton/Sygma / 213-380-3933

Sprinkle, Annie
Rep: Leslie Barany Communic / 212-627-8488

St. Nicholas, Randee
Rep: Caryn Weiss / 213-461-1084

Staedler, Lance
Rep: Jean Gabriel Kauss / 212-370-4300
Rep: LaMoine Represents / 213-467-9730

Stahman, Robert / 212-679-1484
1200 Broadway, NYC, NY 10001

$$F = (a \times p)^4$$

TABLE (4.36). PHOTOGRAPHY

Photographers	Photographers
Stambler, Wayne Rep: Keswick Hamilton Sygma / 213-380-3933	Studna, Carl / 310-475-6175
→ Stanford, Lee / 612-338-7901 420 Fifth St. N, Ste.845, Minneapolis, MN 55401 page 71	Sugarman, Lynn / 214-748-1019 1019 Dragon St., Dallas, TX 75207 Rep: Brooke & Co. / 214-352-9192
Stapleton, Kevin / 213-487-1609 712 Grandview St., LA, CA 90057	Sugerman, Debra / 512-469-9705 Rep: Barbara Wolf / 212-873-3579
Stasny, Horst Rep: Michele Karpe / 818-760-0491	Sullivan, Cleo Rep: Betty Wilson / 212-595-2124
Steiner, Christian / 212-724-1990 300 Central Park W., NYC, NY 10024	Sullivan, Lorinda / 212-629-4133 50 W. 34th St., #4C7, NYC, NY 10001
Sternbach, Scott / 201-433-0391	Summa, Ann / 213-680-1563 240 S. Broadway, #3F, LA, CA 90012 Rep: Onyx / 213-965-0899
Stevenson, Monica / 212-598-4201 88 E. 10th St., #3, NYC, NY 10003	Switzer, Maynard Rep: Bina / 212-533-1734
Stickler, Stephen / 213-259-0091 2100 Panamint Dr., LA, CA 90065 Rep: LaMoine Represents / 213-467-9730	Taflan, Jeff / 818-509-9747 12839 Moorpark St., #16, Studio City, CA 91604
Stiles, James / 212-627-1766 413-15 W. 14th St., NYC, NY 10014	Takei, Koji / 310-306-8086 4223 Glencoe Ave. Suite B119, Marina Del Rey, CA 90291 Rep: Kathy Braun / 415-775-3366
Stivers, Robert / 310-452-3737 / 505-982-0520 309 Montezuma #218, Santa Fe, NM 87501	Tamburo, Ted / 312-226-4884 400 N. Racine, Suite 105, Chicago, ILL 60622
Stoll, Lori / 213-626-6309 8016 W. 4th St., LA, CA 90048	Tangen, Peter / 818-985-1000
Stratton, Jimi / 404-351-7191 500 N. Bishop, D-1, Atlanta, GA 30318	Tanzer, Jessica / 415-861-1912 488 Castro, SF, CA 94114
Stringfellow, Kim / 415-864-6475 564 Mission, #657, SF, CA 94105	Tardio, Robert / 212-254-5413 9 East 19th St., NYC, NY 10003 Rep: Colleen McKay / 212-598-0469
Strongin, Jeanne / 212-473-3718 61 Irving Pl., NYC, NY 10003	Tcherevkoff, Michel / 212-229-1733 15 West 24th St., NYC, NY 10010 Rep: Madeleine Robinson / 212-243-3138
Stroppa, Jr., Anthony / 201-731-2430 65 Nicholas Ave., W. Orange, NJ 07052	
Stroube, Greg Rep: Ceci Bartels / 314-781-7377	
Studio B / 415-383-8658 1815 Shoreline Hwy., Muir Beach, CA 94965	→ Teel, David / 213-658-6394 page 49

TABLE (4.37). PHOTOGRAPHY

Photographers	Photographers

Tenneson, Joyce / 212-741-9371
114 W. 27th St., NYC, NY 10001
Rep: Michele Karpe / 818-760-0491

Terranova, Michael / 504-899-7328
4840 Camp St., New Orleans, LA 70115

Teuwen, Geert / 212-929-9001
76 Ninth Ave., #PH, NYC, NY 10011
Rep: Etienne Sibille

Thain, Alastair
Rep: Onyx / 213-965-0899

Thijsse, Leen
Rep: Stockland Martel / 212-727-1400

Thomas, Geoffrey Hargrave / 212-675-6451
470 W. 24th St., NYC, NY 10011

→ Thomas, Scott / 615-256-4406
630 Fogg St., Nashville, TN 37203
page 81

Thompson, Michael
Rep: Jed Root / 212-226-6600

Thurner, Jeffrey
Rep: Edge / 213-954-9422 / 212-343-2260

Tighe, Michael
Rep: Edge / 213-954-9422 / 212-343-2260

Tillinghast, Paul / 212-741-3764
20 W. 20th St., NYC, NY 10011

Tillman, Denny / 212-255-2977
222 W. 15th St. 10B, NYC, NY 10011

Tise, David / 415-777-0669
975 Folsom, SF, CA 94107
Rep: Brian King / 415-512-9535

Tisman, Jeff / 908-251-5810
11 Pawnee Rd., E. Brunswick, NJ 08816

Todd, Richard / 213-851-3698
1716 N. Vista St., LA, CA 90046

Tolot, Alberto
Rep: Catherine Ludlow / 213-658-6920

Toma, Kenji / 212-219-1113
560 Broadway, Ste.404, NYC, NY 10012
Rep: Michael Ash / 212-807-6286

Topleman, Lars / 503-224-4556
1314 NE Irving St., #214, Portland, OR 97209

Toy, Jo Ann / 212-969-0744
39 Spring Street, NYC, NY 10012

Trachtenberg, Robert / 213-938-4063
354 S. La Jolla, LA, CA 90048

Tran, Robert / 818-286-0907
Rep: Jim Hanson / 312-337-7770

Trent, Brad / 212-627-2147
666 Greenwich St., NYC, NY 10014
Rep: DLM / 212-297-0041

Tress, Arthur / 212-877-1305

Trindl, Gene / 818-785-1950
6337 Peach Ave., Van Nuys, CA 91411

→ Tucker, Eric / 310-452-1905
Rep: Patti Silverstein / 212-228-7924
pages 54 - 55

Tucker, Mark / 615-254-6802
508 Lea Ave., Nashville, TN 37203

Turbeville, Deborah
Rep: Marek & Assoc. / 212-924-6760

Turner, Danny / 214-826-1130
615 N. Good Latimer Exprswy, Dallas, TX 75204

Turner, Darren B. / 516-623-2844
854 Van Buren St., Baldwin, NY 11510

Turner, Pete / 212-765-1733
P.O. Box 203, Wainscott, NY 11975-0203
Rep: Elise Caputo / 212-725-0503

Twice Gibson / 213-549-9080
113 N. La Brea, LA, CA 90036

Tynan, Dana / 310-475-0212
1311 S. Beverly Glen Blvd., LA, CA 90024
Rep: Caryn Weiss / 213-461-1084

TABLE (4.38). PHOTOGRAPHY

Photographers	Photographers

Uchitel, Diego / 213-650-7348
8696 Cresent Dr., LA, CA 90046
Rep: Stockland Martel / 212-727-1400

Uhlmann, Gina / 312-871-1025
1872 N. Clybourn, #115, Chicago, IL 60614
Rep: Holly Kallick / 312-248-9310

Umans, Marty / 212-995-0100
29 E. 19th St., NYC, NY 10003
Rep: Dario Sacramone / 212-929-0487

Uzzle, Andy
Rep: Gamma Liaison / 212-447-2505

V Group, The / 212-666-8477
697 West End Ave., NYC, NY 10025

→ Vachon, Jean / 514-395-2227
95 Rue Prince, Montreal, Quebec, Canada H3C 2M7
page 45

Vadukul, Max
Rep: Art + Commerce / 212-206-0737

Vadukul, Nitin
Rep: Frank Parvis / 212-473-5868

Valeska, Shonna / 212-683-4448
140 E. 28th St., NYC, NY 10016

→ Van Den Brulle, Eric / 212-721-2611
page 52

→ Van Osdol, Scott / 512-469-9510
306 W. 16th St., #2, Austin, TX 78701
page 99

Van Overbeek
Rep: Brooke & Co. / 214-352-9192

Van Petten, Rob / 212-869-2190 / 617-426-8641
216 Seventh Ave. 4B, NYC, NY 10017

Van S, Mark / 206-624-6785
700 Virginia, Seattle, WA 98101

→ Vance, David / 305-354-2083
150 N.W. 164th St., Miami, FL 33169
pages 92 - 93

Vander Schuit, Carl / 619-539-7337
751 Turqoise St., San Diego, CA 92109

Varis, Photomedia / 213-874-0129
922 N. Formosa Ave., LA, CA 90046

Vaughan, Garth / 212-473-6543
10 Bleecker St., #1A, NYC, NY 10012

Vedros, Nick / 816-471-5488
215 W. 19th St., Kansas City, MO 64108
Rep: Kenney & Mead / 212-627-3400

Vega, Raul / 213-387-2058 / 212-633-0181
3511 W. Sixth St., LA, CA 90020

Ventola, Giorgio / 312-951-0880
368 W. Huron, Chicago, IL 60610
Rep: Bob Wolter

Vera, Cesar / 212-941-8594
Boho Studio
254 Elizabeth St., #5A, NYC, NY 10012
Rep: Rania Abbasi / 212-334-8302

Verglas, Antoine
Rep: Philippe Achard / 212-614-0962

Vieira, Mark A. / 510-537-8128
Rep: Keswick Hamilton/Sygma / 213-380-3933

Volkmann, Roy / 212-941-7730
Circle Studio
80 Varick St., #10B, NYC, NY 10013
Rep: Liz Li / 212-889-7067

Von Unwerth, Ellen
Rep: Art + Commerce / 212-206-0737

→ Vozdic, Paul / 212-388-8136
page 53

Vracin, Andrew / 214-688-1841
Rep: The McCann Co. / 214-526-2252

Wagenaar, David / 312-944-6330
1504 N. Fremont, Chicago, IL 60622
Rep: Beverly Long

TABLE (4.39). PHOTOGRAPHY

Photographers	Photographers
→ Wagner, Laura / 305-532-5405 / 213-876-8756 2421 Lake Pancoast Dr., #2F, Miami, FL 33140 page 67	Weinstein, Don / 213-461-0141 931 N. Citrus Ave., LA, CA 90038 Rep: LGI / 212-736-4602
Wahlberg, Chris / 415-821-6906 2660 Third St., SF, CA 94107	Weinstein, Michael / 212-925-2612 225 Lafayette St., Ste. 313, NYC, NY 10012
Wahlstrom, Richard Rep: Jim Hanson / 312-337-7770	Weisberg, Eugene / 212-219-3762 520 Broadway, #702, NYC, NY 10010
Wakagi, Shingo / 212-290-2419	→ Weiss, Jeffrey / 213-655-3519 page 38
→ Waldorf, David / 415-586-1170 / 415-543-5599 page 43	Weiss, Mark / 212-777-3034 628 Broadway, NYC, NY 10012 Rep: Michael Ginsberg / 212-679-8881
Wallace, Allen / 212-614-6635 220 E. 22nd St., 1G, NYC, NY 10010	Weiss, Mark / 908-291-2989 P.O. Box 398, Rumson, NJ 07760 Rep: Deena
Wallace, Randall / 212-242-2930 43 W. 13th St., Ste. 3F, NYC, NY 10011	Weissman/Photo/Graphics/Studio / 212-989-9694 463 West St., Suite B332, NYC, NY 10014
→ Washington, Ernest / 404-522-4488 488 Edgewood Ave., Atlanta, GA 30312 page 74	Welch, Nathaniel / 213-964-9675 543 N. Sycamore Ave., No 11, LA, CA 90036
→ Watermann, Greg Rep: Brooke Davis / 214-352-9192 pages 60 - 61	Werner, Susan / 213-850-6848 P.O. Box 480204, LA, CA 90048
Watson, Albert / 212-627-0077 777 Washington St., NYC, NY 10014 Rep: Elizabeth Watson	Westenberger, Theo / 212-732-5900 366 Broadway, NYC, NY 10013
Watson, Stuart / 213-663-0136 3712 Arbolada Rd., LA, CA 90027 Rep: Onyx / 213-965-0899	Westwood, Carol / 213-463-0829 501 N. Rossmore Ave., LA, CA 90004
Watson, Tres / 214-634-8737 1345 Chemical, Dallas, TX 75207	Wexler, Glen / 213-465-0268 736 N. Highland Ave., LA, CA 90038
Watts, Ben Rep: Kramer & Kramer / 212-645-8787	Whipple III, George Carroll / 212-949-0202
Watts, Cliff Rep: Jodi Rappaport / 213-934-8633	White, Dan / 816-421-2400 1000 Broadway, #301, Kansas City, MO 64105
Weber, Bruce Rep: Nan Bush / 212-226-0814	White, James / 212-563-4342 Rep: LaMoine Represents / 213-467-9730
Weingart, Ken / 212-979-8978	White, Timothy Rep: Stockland Martel / 212-727-1400 Rep: Onyx (L.A. only) / 213-965-0899

$$F = (a \times p)^4$$

TABLE (4.40). PHOTOGRAPHY

Photographers	Photographers
White/Packert / 617-423-0577 107 South St., 6 fl., Boston, MA 02111 Rep: Amy Frith / 617-268-2506	Witrogen, Ned / 305-672-5033 320 W. 25th St., Miami Beach, FL 33140
Whitlock, Neill / 214-948-3117 Rep: Friend & Johnson / 214-855-0055	Wohrman, Scott / 305-752-6297 P.O. Box 9728, Coral Springs, FL 33075
Whitman, Robert / 212-213-6611 1181 Broadway, 7th Fl., NYC, NY 10001	Wojcik, James / 212-431-0108 256 Mott St., #4, NYC, NY 10012
Whitsitt, Steven / 818-982-8160 6835 Laurel Canyon, #303, N. Hollywood, CA 91605	Wolfson, Ron / 818-990-9788 14355 Huston, #219, Sherman Oaks, CA 91423 Rep: London Features / 212-929-7007
Wilder, Brian / 603-431-2066 60 Market St., Portsmouth, NH 03801	→ Wong, Michael Rep: Edge / 212-343-2260 / 213-954-9422 page 15
Wilhelm, Dave Rep: Melissa Brock / 510-521-2012	Wood, James B. / 213-851-7722 7095 Hollywood Blvd., Hollywood, CA 90028 Rep: Hall & Assoc. / 310-652-7322 Rep: Sweet Represents / 415-433-1222
Wilkes, Stephen / 212-475-4010 48 E. 13th St., NYC, NY 10003 Rep: Doug Brown / 212-953-0088	Wu, Ron / 716-454-5600 / 212-321-9889 179 St. Paul St., Rochester, NY 14604
Williams, Everard / 818-683-3900 Rep: Sharpe & Assoc. / 310-641-8556	Yani, Hans Rep: Janet Botaish Group / 310-314-1571
Williams, Ron / 615-331-2500 105A Space Park, Nashville, TN 37211	Young, Russell / 818-952-5051 Rep: Keswick Hamilton Sygma / 213-380-3933
Williams, Steven Burr / 213-650-7906	Yurkovic, Gerhard / 212-674-2436 Rep: Ursula Day / 212-979-8591
Williardt, Kenneth 100 W. 23rd St, NYC, NY 10010 Rep: Marzena	Zagaris, Michael / 415-731-1517 803 Clayton, #3, SF, CA 94117
Wills, Bret / 212-925-2999 Bronstein/Berman & Assocs. 38 Greene St., NYC, NY 10013 Rep: Gary Hurewitz	Zahedi, Firooz Rep: Janet Botaish Group / 310-314-1571
Windham, Dale / 206-587-2332 900 First Ave S., Seattle, WA 98134 Rep: Jaz & Jaz / 206-282-8558	Zlozower, Neil / 213-653-6726 6341 Yucca, Hollywood, CA 90028
Winter, Nita / 415-927-4300 9 Ridge Way, Corte Madera, CA 94925-1337	Zoghlin, Ryan / 312-278-3504 1735 Paulina, Chicago, Il 60622
Winters, Dan / 213-957-5699 6383 Bryn Mawr Dr., LA, CA 90068 Rep: Kathryn Fouts	

particles *seeking* the next level of energy .
____

(5 . A)

the desperation
of radiation

$$(\text{tattoo artists} + \text{stylists} + \text{costumes} + \text{jewelry} + \text{hair} + \text{makeup}) + (\text{backdrops} + \text{props} + \text{model makers})$$

$$+ \ \text{magazines} \times \frac{\text{merchandising}}{\text{licensing}} \times (\text{movie studios} + \text{record labels})\,.$$

(5.B)

We're always out to lunch.

Breakfast, lunch or dinner for crew, talent and client,
The Mad Platter can do it all.
Whether it's wrap parties for a video shoot or any special event for
a photographer, we'll cater to your every whim.

310.657.1520

800.264.6805

JOHN WELLS

TELEVISIONS

UNIQUE TELEVISIONS FOR FILM / VIDEO / LOCATION AND STUDIO PHOTOGRAPHY
65 JAY STREET, BROOKLYN, NEW YORK 11201. TEL: 718. 624. 0650. REEL AVAILABLE

New York   Los Angeles   Yucca Valley

WALLER
CönCepT/ProDuKtion DeZine
213 484 1441

$$(\text{tattoo artists} + \text{stylists} + \text{costumes} + \text{jewelry} + \text{hair} + \text{makeup}) + (\text{backdrops} + \text{props} + \text{model makers})$$

$$+ \text{ magazines} \times \frac{\text{merchandising}}{\text{licensing}} \times (\text{movie studios} + \text{record labels}).$$

(5 . 1)

$$F = (a \times p)^4$$

TABLE (5.2). SUPPORT SERVICES

Tattoo Artists	Tattoo Artists
American Tattooing / 908-754-6390 43 Chatham St., N. Plansfield, NJ 07060	End of the Trail Tattoo / 209-524-9936 520 McHenry, Modesto, CA 95350
Avalon Tattoo Studio / 619-274-7635 1035 Garnet Ave., San Diego, CA 92109	Everett Tatto Emporium / 206-252-8315 2408 Broadway, Everett, WA 98203
Bill's Tattoo / 505-982-9421 711 Alarid, Santa Fe, NM 87501	Fine Line Studio / 203-526-2011 P.O. Box 332, Deep River, CT 06417
Black Wave Tattoo / 213-932-1900 118 S. La Brea, LA, CA 90036	Fun City Tattoo / 212-228-8851 / 212-534-4622 P.O. Box 20088, NY, NY 10009
Body Electric Studio / 213-954-1364 7274 1/2 Melrose Ave., LA, CA 90046	Goodtime Charlie's Tattooland / 714-827-2071 3246 W. Lincoln Ave., Anaheim, CA 92801
Body Marking Via Del Borgo Pi San Pietao 123/A, Bologna, Italy	Guilty & Innocent Productions / 312-404-6955 3105 N. Lincoln Ave., Chicago, Ill 60657
China Sea Tattoo / 808-533-1603 1033 Smith St., Honolulu, HI 96817	Horiyoshi III 3-123-ISE-CHO, Nishi-ku, Yokohama, Japan
Cynthesis Tattoo / 505-842-6511 1707 Five Points Rd. SW, Albuquerque, NM 87105	Ian of Reading 011-44-734598616, England
DeVita, Thom / 914-562-0622 23 Overlook Pl., Newburgh, NY 12550	King of Pain Tattoo 0.7 Voorburginal 141 1012 ES Amsterdam, The Netherlands
Don Ling's Removable Tattoos / 800-247-6817	Laguna Tattoo & Piercing / 714-497-3702 656 S. Pacific Coast Hwy, Laguna Beach, CA 92651
Dragon Moon Tattoo Studio / 410-768-6471 208 N. Crain Hwy., Glen Burnie, MD 21061	Lal Hardy / 081-444-8779 157 Sydney Rd., Muswell Hill, London, England N10 2NL
Dragon Tattoo / 408-286-8781 1520 W. San Carlos, San Jose, CA 95132	Lou's Tattoo Parlour / 305-532-7300 231 14th St., Miami Beach, FL 33139
Dragon Tattoo 13644 Grosvenor Rd., Surrey, B.C. V3R 5C9 Rep: Leslie Barany Communic / 212-627-8488	Midland Tattoo Centre Beecroft Road, Cannock, Staffs, England WS11 1JP
Dragon Tattoo / 808-622-5924 10 N. Kamehameha Hwy., Wahiawa, Hawaii 96786	New Moon Tattoos / 613-596-1790
East Side Tattoo / 212-388-0693	Permanent Mark 119 Loop Str., Cape Town, South Africa
Ed Hardy's Tattoo City / 415-433-9437 722 Columbus Ave., SF, CA 94133	Presitge Tattoo 12 Avenue Marbeau 94420 Le Plessis., Trivise, France
Electric Art Tattoo / 718-338-9546	
Enchanted Dragon, The / 602-323-2817 4243 E. Speedway Blvd., Tucson, AZ 85716	Red Dragon Tattoo / 804-230-7908 3910 Hull Street Rd., Richmond, VA 23224

TABLE (5.3). SUPPORT SERVICES

Tattoo Artists	Stylist Representatives
Schiffmacher, Henk Rep: Leslie Barany Communic / 212-627-8488	Celestine / 213-650-7181 8278 Sunset Blvd, LA, CA 90046
Seattle Tattoo Emporium / 206-622-6895 1106 Pike St., Seattle, WA 98101	Crystal Agency, The / 213-913-0700 / 212-978-4646 4237 Los Nietos Dr., LA, CA 90027
Shadow World Tattoo / 212-964-4727	→ Dawn 2 Dusk / 212-431-8631 185 Franklin St., Ste. 2, NYC, NY 10013 page 2
Shaw's Tattoo Studio / 512-758-1535 753 N. Commercial, Aransas Pass, TX 78336	→ Dawn 2 Dusk / 213-850-6783 8306 Wilshire Blvd., Ste. 412, Beverly Hills, CA 90211 page 2
Shotsie's / 201-633-1411 1275 Route 23 S., Wayne, NJ 07470	→ Dawn to Dusk / 305-532-5889 9181 W. Bay Harbor Dr., Ste. 14, Miami, FL 33154 page 2
Spider Webb Studio / 203-335-3992 1 Bostwick Ave., Bridgeport, CT 06605	Ennis, Inc. / 617-261-3970 451 D St., Boston, MA 02210
Spotlight Tattoo / 213-871-1084 5859 Melrose Blvd., LA, CA 90038	Jezebel / 212-673-5509 319 Ave. C, Apt. 8C, NYC, NY 10009
Sunset Strip Tattoo, Inc. / 213-650-6530 8418 W. Sunset Blvd., W. Hllywd, CA 90069	Joyce, Tricia / 212-962-0728 80 Warren St., NYC, NY 10007
Tattoo Art Museum / 415-775-4991 841 Columbus Ave., SF, CA 94133	Katie Daley/William J. Knight Agency / 212-465-2420 245 W. 29th St., 16th Fl., NYC, NY 10001
Tattoo Mania / 310-657-8282 8861 W. Sunset Blvd., Hollywood, CA 90069	Kauss, Jean Gabriel / 212-779-4440 147 E. 36th St., 3rd Rl., NYC, NY 10016
Tattoos by Johnny Junkfood / 045-224-930 Lysterstraat 21, Heerlen, Holand	L.A. Rep / 213-656-1720 8149 Kirkwood Dr., LA, CA 90046
Temptu / 212-675-4000 26 W. 17th St., NYC, NY 10011	Marek & Assocs., Inc. / 212-924-6760 170 Fifth Ave., NYC, NY 10010
Tux's Tattoo Studio / 410-761-7231	Network Representatives / 212-727-0044 454 W. 20th St., NYC, NY 10011
Wildcat Tattoo / 602-289-3904 719 E.3rd St., Winslow, AZ 86047	Perrella Management, Inc. / 212-247-4400 P.O. Box 1530, Radio City Station, NYC, NY 10101
Zeke's Tattoo / 910-346-9420 244 S. Wilmington Hwy., Jacksonville, NC 28540	→ Visages Rps Inc. / 212-941-7550 560 Broadway, #407, NYC, NY 10012 Photography / page 70
Stylist Representatives	→ Visages Rps Inc. / 213-650-8880 8748 Holloway Dr., W. Hllywd, CA 90069 Photography / page 70
Art + Commerce / 212-206-0737 755 Washington St., 2nd Fl, NYC, NY 10014	
Bina / 212-533-1734 108 E. 16th St., NYC, NY 10003	

$$F = (a \times p)^4$$

TABLE (5.4). SUPPORT SERVICES

Stylists Representatives	Stylists
Yellen/Lachapelle / 212-838-3170 420 E. 54th St., NYC, NY 10022	Bartlett, Victoria Rep: Marek & Associates / 212-924-6760
Z Agency, The / 212-529-3470 611 Broadway, #907, NYC, NY 10012	Behar, Robert Rep: Celestine / 213-650-7181
Zenobia Agency Inc. / 213-937-1010 130 S. Highland Ave., LA, CA 90036	Bernhard, Ivy / 212-925-1111 270 Lafayette, Ste. 401, NYC, NY 10012
Zoli Illusions & Style / 212-242-7050 3 W. 18th St., 5th Fl., NYC, NY 10011-4610	Bickson, Beth Rep: Celestine / 213-650-7181

Stylists

Stylists	Stylists
Aboitiz, Gemina Rep: Cloutier / 213-931-1323	Binder, Andrew Paul / 818-508-8621 12812 Landale St., Studio City, CA 91604
Aiken, Leslie Rep: HMS Bookings / 213-939-9100	Binder, Daryl Rep: LA Rep / 213-656-1720
Albright, Irene Rep: Tricia Joyce / 212-962-0728	Bizalion, Jean-Francois Rep: Ennis Inc. / 617-261-3970
Allyson, Dana Rep: Ivy Bernhard / 212-925-1111	Blanchard, Chris Rep: Team the Agency / 617-742-3444
Altuna, Charlie Rep: Celestine / 213-650-7181	Bloch, Philip Rep: Cloutier / 213-931-1323
Amelie Rep: Zoli Illusions / 212-242-7050	Blodwell, George Rep: Cloutier / 213-931-1323
Amzallag, Manuela Rep: Ennis Inc. / 617-261-3970 Rep: Katie Daley/William J. / 212-465-2420	Boucher, Suzanne Rep: Ennis Inc. / 617-261-3970
Anderson, Perrine Rep: Kramer + Kramer / 212-787-8787	Bowen, Kim Rep: Visages Rps Inc. / 213-650-8880
Ann & Co. / 615-297-7081 144 46th Ave. N., Nashville, TN 37209	Bradshaw, David Rep: Visages Rps Inc. / 212-841-7550
Apodaca, Marianne Rep: Cloutier / 213-931-1323	Breindel, Susan Rep: Susan Breindel / 212-841-7550
Ari Rep: Dion Peronneau / 213-299-4043	Brewster, Kithe Rep: Ivy Bernhard / 212-925-1111
Barish, Pamela Rep: LA Rep / 213-656-1720	Burnett, David Rep: Visages Rps Inc. / 212-841-7550
	Cabrera, Xavier Rep: Cloutier / 213-931-1323
	Calabro, Deborah Rep: Team the Agency / 617-742-3444

Table (5.5). Support Services

Stylists	Stylists
Campbell, Leslie Rep: HMS Bookings / 213-939-9100	Earabino, Stephen Rep: Visages Rps Inc. / 213-650-8880
Cannon / 212-366-6190 401 W. 24th St., Ste. #10, NY, NY 10011	Eisele, Eileen Rep: Ennis Inc. / 617-261-3970
Casey, Annie Rep: Ennis Inc. / 617-261-3970	Eisenhower, Michael Rep: Celestine / 213-650-7181
Cecca, Kim Rep: Network Reps / 212-727-0044	Ell, Erica Rep: Team the Agency / 617-742-3444
Cicolello, Veta / 212-316-2125 230 W. 108th St., #4B, NY, NY	Enrenfeld, Lauren Rep: Celestine / 213-650-7181
Collier, Rhett Rep: Celestine / 213-650-7181	Everard, Dean Rep: Ennis Inc. / 617-261-3970
Condit, Garth Rep: Visgaes Rps Inc. / 212-841-7550	Exaline / 615-399-1991
Cortina, George Rep: Ivy Bernhard / 212-925-1111	Farr, Kendall Rep: Kramer & Kramer / 212-757-8787
Cubert, Tova Rep: Zenobia Agency, Inc. / 206-340-0600	Feldmann, Sara Rep: Tricia Joyce / 212-962-0728
Cunniff, Jayne Rep: Katie Daley/William J. / 212-465-2420	Feuer, Eve Rep: Yellen/LaChapelle / 212-838-3170
Dallyn, Stacy Rep: Zenobia Agency, Inc. / 206-340-0600	Fitzgerald, Ann Rep: Team the Agency / 617-742-3444
Damonte, Pamela Rep: Ivy Bernhard / 212-925-1111	Flynn, Danny Rep: Visages Rps Inc. / 213-650-8880
DeMartino, Ricci Rep: Celestine / 213-650-7181 Rep: Zenobia Agency, Inc. / 415-621-7410	Fonteyne, Inge Rep: Visages Rps Inc. / 212-841-7550
Derrick, Gabrielle Rep: Team the Agency / 617-742-3444	France, Carine Rep: Zoli Illusions / 212-242-7050
Dickerson, Monika Rep: Celestine / 213-650-7181	Freeman, Meg Rep: Cloutier / 213-931-1323
Dominquez, Elaine Rep: Perrella Management / 212-247-4400	Fruitman, Sheva Rep: Kramer + Kramer / 212-787-8787
Dunn-Lee, Ionia Rep: Zoli Illusions & Style / 212-242-7050	Gambaccini, Sciascia Rep: Art + Commerce / 212-206-0737
	Gannon, Coleen Rep: Team the Agency / 617-742-3444

$$F = (a \times p)^4$$

TABLE (5.6). SUPPORT SERVICES

Stylists	Stylists
Gardner, Jeffrey Rep: Ivy Bernhard / 212-925-1111	Kale, Leslie Rep: Cloutier / 213-931-1323
Gardner, Leslie / 213-850-5453	Kerr, Ressa Rep: Visages Rps Inc. / 213-650-8880
Gill, Tanya Rep: Visages Rps Inc. / 213-650-8880	Khavkine, Solange Rep: Perrella Management / 212-247-4400
Godwin, Louise Rep: Perrella Managment / 212-247-4400	Kolbin, Jolie Rep: HMS Bookings / 213-939-9100
Goldman, Meg Rep: Ivy Bernhard / 212-925-1111	Krause Mora, Pamela / 213-650-1940 1400 N. Havenhurst Dr., LA, CA 90046
Goldstein, Lori Rep: Art + Commerce / 212-206-0737	Kutsugeras, Kelle Rep: Celestine / 213-650-7181
Goodman, Beth Rep: Cloutier / 213-931-1323	Labby, Karin Rep: Celestine / 213-650-7181
Gordon, Paris / 615-322-9368 Style Council 900 19th Ave. So., #1003, Nashville, TN 37212	Landig, Rhea Rep: Ivy Bernhard / 212-925-1111
Gore, Sarah Rep: Katie Daley/William J. / 212-465-2420	Lapsansky, Eileen Rep: Art + Commerce / 212-206-0737
Gravelle, Louisa Rep: Zenobia Agency, Inc. / 415-621-7410	Lawson, Dorothy Rep: HMS Bookings / 213-939-9100
HMS Bookings / 213-939-9100 1114 S. Ogden Dr., LA, CA 90019	LeClair, Debra Rep: Visages Rps Inc. / 213-650-8880
Harrison, Jane / 212-929-2993	Lee, Derek Rep: The Crystal Agency / 212-978-4646
Hartnett, Todd Rep: Ivy Bernhard / 212-925-1111	Leonard, Pauline Rep: Cloutier / 213-931-1323
Helfman, Lori Rep: Perrella Management / 212-247-4400	Lettieri, Caroline Rep: Celestine / 213-650-7181
Hengge, Helga Rep: Yellen/LaChapelle / 212-838-3170	Lewis, Iris Rep: Partos / 213-876-5500
Henry, Pat Rep: Katie Daley/William J. / 212-465-2420	Liguori, Debra Rep: Ivy Bernhard / 212-925-1111
Jenkins, Llewellyn Rep: Perrella Management / 212-247-4000	Little, Debrae Rep: The Crystal Agency / 213-913-0700
Jon Haugen, Calvin Rep: Celestine / 213-650-7181	Looker, Amy Rep: Team the Agency / 617-742-3444

TABLE (5.7). SUPPORT SERVICES

Stylists	Stylists
Magnum, Chaim Rep: Celestine / 213-650-7181	Moore, Lee Rep: Visages Rps Inc. / 213-650-8880
Make-up Creations / 213-463-8430 17815 Skypark Circle, #J, Irvine, CA 92714	Morris, Matthew Rep: Ivy Bernhard / 212-925-1111
Malakpour, Maryam Rep: Celestine / 213-650-7181	Morrison, Nikki Rep: Katie Daley/William J. / 212-465-2420
Marder, Gwen Rep: Katie Daley/William J. / 212-465-2420	Mottau, Christine Rep: Ennis Inc. / 617-261-3970
Marquez, Tracy Rep: Zenobia Agency, Inc. / 415-621-7410	Moultrie, Autumn Rep: Dion Peronneau / 213-299-4043
Martin, Chris Rep: Celestine / 213-650-7181	Newkirk, Scott Rep: Ivy Bernhard / 212-925-1111
Mason, Debi Rep: Art + Commerce / 212-206-0737	Palmer, Randy Rep: Cloutier / 213-931-1323
Mati, Veronique Rep: Tricia Joyce / 212-962-0728	Partos / 213-876-5500 3630 Barham Boulevard, Z 108, LA, CA 90068
Matula, Michael / 212-533-1160 Mud Honey 148 Sullivan St., NYC, NY 10012	Passanisi, Carmel Rep: Celestine / 213-650-7181
McQueen, Judith Rep: Dion Peronneau / 213-299-4043	Patner, Josh Rep: Ivy Bernhard / 212-925-1111
Mechem, Liz Rep: Ivy Bernhard / 212-925-1111 Rep: Zenobia Agency, Inc. / 213-937-1010	Paul, Donna Rep: Team the Agency / 617-742-3444
Medvene, Linda Rep: Cloutier / 213-931-1323	Paul, Kimberly Rep: Zenobia Agency, Inc. / 415-621-7410
Mel Grayson / 213-746-3593 746 E. 12th St., LA, CA 90021	Pelletier, Lysa Rep: Team the Agency / 617-742-3444
Michelle, Lisa Rep: The Crystal Agency / 213-913-0700	Phillips, Arianne Rep: Visages Rps Inc. / 213-650-8880
Michi Rep: Partos / 213-876-5500	Pretti, Kim / 818-776-8626 6036 Lindley Ave., Encino, CA 91316
Mills, Joey Rep: Perrella Management / 212-247-4400	Rede, Michele Rep: Visages Rps Inc. / 213-650-8880
Mingus, Keki Rep: Visages Rps Inc. / 212-841-7550	Repetti, Roseann Rep: Marek & Assocs. / 212-924-6760
	Robinson, Eric Rep: Zenobia Agency, Inc. / 206-340-0600

$$F = (a \times p)^4$$

TABLE (5.8). SUPPORT SERVICES

Stylists	Stylists
Rogiani, Elisabetta Rep: Kramer & Kramer / 212-757-8787	Stephenson, Dana Rep: Ennis Inc. / 617-261-3970
Ronk, Clara Rep: Network Reps / 212-727-0044	Style Architect / 212-749-0284 733 Amsterdam Ave., #24A, NYC, NY 10025
Ryder, Sylvia Rep: Celestine / 213-650-7181	Style Counsel / 615-320-0772 900 19th Ave. So., #1003, Nashville, TN 37212
Sanchez, Monique Rep: Zenobia Agency, Inc. / 206-340-0600	Styles, Stephanie Rep: Zari Int'l / 212-727-9145
Santiago / 212-315-1331 339 W. 48th St., NY, NY 10036	Swor, David Rep: Zenobia Agency, Inc. / 213-937-1010
Segal, Israel Rep: Ivy Bernhard / 212-925-1111	Tanabe, Gino Rep: Celestine / 213-650-7181
Serpa, Joseph Rep: Ennis Inc. / 617-261-3970	Tegtmeier, Christa Rep: Tricia Joyce / 212-962-0728
Silver, Pamela Rep: Yellen/LaChapelle / 212-838-3170	Telford, Jennifer Rep: Zenobia Agency, Inc. / 415-621-7410
Sinclaire, Paul Rep: Marek & Associates / 212-924-6760	Thielbar, Jan / 213-463-8430 17815 Skypark Circle, #J, Irvine, CA 92714
Smedley, Lisa Rep: Dion Peronneau / 213-299-4043	Thomas, Jeffrey Rep: Tricia Joyce / 212-962-0728
Smidley, Lisa Rep: Dion Peronneau / 213-299-4043	Trovati, Robertino Rep: Visages Rps Inc. / 213-650-8880
Smith, Randy Rep: Visages Rps Inc. / 212-841-7550	Trovati, Roberto Rep: Visages Rps Inc. / 212-841-7550
Sokolec, Jill Rep: Celestine / 213-650-7181	Turner, Vivian Rep: Cloutier / 213-931-1323
Solis, Denise Rep: Cloutier / 213-931-1323	Vernon-Lewis, Jane Rep: Zenobia Agency, Inc. / 213-937-1010
Stambuk, Rina Rep: Ennis inc. / 617-261-3970	Vidal, Raquel Rep: Ennis Inc. / 617-261-3970
Stark, Tui Rep: Ennis Inc. / 617-261-3970	Voss, Bonnie Orleans Rep: Yellen/Lachapelle / 212-838-3170
Steinberg, Ruth Rep: Zenobia Agency, Inc. / 213-937-1010	Waknin, Deborah Rep: Celestine / 213-650-7181
Steiner, Denise Rep: LA Rep / 213-656-1720	Warlow, Cindy Rep: Visages Rps Inc. / 213-650-8880

$F = (a \times p)^4$

TABLE (5.9). SUPPORT SERVICES

Stylists	Hair & Make-Up Representatives
Warren, Barbara Rep: The Crystal Agency / 213-913-0700	Bernhard, Ivy / 212-925-1111 270 Lafayette, Ste. 401, NYC, NY 10012
Whitacre, David Rep: Celestine / 213-650-7181	Bina / 212-533-1734 108 E. 16th St., NYC, NY 10003
White, Alexander Rep: Zoli Illusions / 212-242-7050	Bruno Le Salon / 212-581-9037 16 W. 57th St., NYC, NY 10019
Whitney, Nan Rep: Ennis Inc. / 617-261-3970	Celestine / 213-650-7181 8278 Sunset Blvd, LA, CA 90046
Willis, Ron Rep: Perrella Management / 212-247-4400	Cloutier Agency / 213-931-1323 7201 Melrose Ave., LA 90038
Wills, Laura / 212-677-6464 Screaming Mimi's 382 Lafayette St., NYC, NY 10003	→ Dawn 2 Dusk / 212-431-8631 185 Franklin St., Ste. 2, NYC, NY 10013 page 2
Wilson, Patti Rep: Marek & Associates / 212-924-6760	→ Dawn 2 Dusk / 213-850-6783 8306 Wilshire Blvd., Ste. 412, Beverly Hills, CA 90211 page 2
Witte, Paula Rep: Zenobia Agency, Inc. / 415-621-7410	→ Dawn to Dusk / 305-532-5889 9181 W. Bay Harbor Dr., Ste. 14, Miami, FL 33154 page 2
Wolf, Brana Rep: Art + Commerce / 212-206-0737	Creative Image / 213-655-9505 6363 Wilshire Blvd., Ste. 500, LA, CA 90048
Young, Lisa Rep: Zoli Illusions / 212-242-7050	Ennis, Inc. / 617-261-3970 451 D St., 9th Fl, Boston, MA 02210
Young, Mimi Rep: Art & Commerce / 212-206-0737	HMS Bookings / 213-939-9100 1114 S. Ogden Dr., LA, CA 90019
Zamorska, Basia Rep: Marek & Assocs. / 212-924-6760	Hallelujah! Artist Mgmt / 212-243-6608 81 Horatio St., #4-F, NYC, NY 10014
	Jezebel / 212-673-5509 319 Ave. C, Apt. 8C, NYC, NY 10009
Hair & Make-Up Representatives	Joyce, Tricia / 212-962-0728 80 Warren St., NYC, NY 10007
Achard & Associates, Inc.	Katie Daley/William J. Knight Agency / 212-465-2420 245 W. 29th St., 16th Fl., NYC, NY 10001
Art + Commerce / 212-206-0737 755 Washington St., NYC, NY 10014	Kauss, Jean Gabriel / 212-779-4440 147 E. 36th St., 3rd Rl., NYC, NY 10016
Atlantis Management / 212-924-1294 43 W. 16 St., #6H, NY, NY 10011	L.A. Rep / 213-656-1720 8149 Kirkwood Dr., LA, CA 90046
Bantry, Bryan / 212-935-0200 4 W. 58th St., PH, NYC, NY 10019	

$$F = (a \times p)^4$$

Table (5.10). Support Services

Hair & Make-Up Representatives	Hair & Make-Up
Marek & Assocs., Inc. / 212-924-6760 170 Fifth Ave., NYC, NY 10010	Allen, B'nard Rep: Dion Peronneau / 213-299-4043
Network Representatives / 212-727-0044 454 W. 20th St., NYC, NY 10011	Alvarez, Boushelle Rep: Tricia Joyce / 212-962-0728
Peronneau, Dion / 213-299-4043 4889 Linscott Pl., Ste. 4, LA, CA 90016	Andersson, Helene (Make-Up) Rep: Ivy Bernhard / 212-925-1111
Root Inc., Jed / 212-226-6600 225 Lafayette St., #909, NYC, NY 10012	Ando, Hiromi (Make-Up) Rep: Bryan Bantry / 212-925-0200
Team the Agency / 617-742-3444 63 Endicott St., #407, Boston, MA 02113	Andreoli, Rena Rep: Celestine / 213-650-7181
⟶ Visages Rps Inc. / 212-941-7550 560 Broadway, #407, NYC, NY 10012 Photography / page 70	Angell, Jeff Rep: HMS Bookings / 213-939-9100
⟶ Visages Rps Inc. / 213-650-8880 8748 Holloway Dr., W. Hllywd, CA 90069 Photography / page 70	Angileri, Enzo (Hair) Rep: Cloutier / 213-931-1323
Yellen/Lachapelle / 212-838-3170 420 E. 54th St., NYC, NY 10022	Antolin, Teddy (Hair) Rep: Visages Rps Inc. / 213-650-8880
Zenobia Agency Inc. / 213-937-1010 130 S. Highland Ave., LA, CA 90036	Apanasewicz, Terri Rep: Cloutier / 213-931-1323
Zoli Illusions & Style / 212-242-7050 3 W. 18th St., 5th Fl., NYC, NY 10011-4610	Aston, Chase Rep: Marek & Assocs. / 212-924-6760
	Aturo, Steven Rep: Team the Agency / 617-742-3444
Hair & Make-Up	Aucoin, Kevyn (Make-Up) Rep: Jed Root, Inc. / 212-226-6600
	Azuma (Hair) Rep: Hallelujah! / 212-243-6608
Ackenbarr, Gwen / 615-889-6840	Bacchini, Paola Rep: Zoli Illusions / 212-242-7050
Addabbo, Nello Rep: Zenobia Agency, Inc. / 206-340-0600	Bailey, Sarah Rep: HMS Bookings / 213-939-9100
Agostina (Make-Up) Rep: Celestine / 213-650-7181	Baker, Michael (Hair) Rep: Visages Rps Inc.
Agressott, Patricia (Hair) Rep: Visages Rps Inc. / 212-841-7550	Baldock, Lucy Rep: Celestine / 213-650-7181
Aleman, Michel (Hair) Rep: Bryan Bantry / 212-925-0200	Barnard, Eric Rep: Cloutier / 213-931-1323
Allasigga Rep: HMS Bookings / 213-939-9100	

$F = (a \times p)^4$

TABLE (5.11). SUPPORT SERVICES

Hair & Make-Up	Hair & Make-Up
Baroni, Giorgio Rep: Zenobia Agency, Inc. / 213-937-1010	Blanco, Daniel (Make-Up) Rep: Cloutier / 213-931-1323
Barr, Howard (Hair) Rep: Celestine / 213-650-7181	Boadi, Michael Rep: Atlantis Management / 212-924-1294
Barron, Lynn (Make-Up) Rep: Bryan Bantry / 212-935-0200	Boadi, Michael (Hair) Rep: Marek & Associates / 212-924-6760
Barry, Mitch (Hair) Rep: Bryan Bantry / 212-935-0200	Borgstrom, Katrina Rep: Celestine / 213-650-7181
Bech, Tina (Make-up) Rep: Bryan Bantry / 212-935-0200	Boursier, Kareen Rep: HMS Bookings / 213-939-9100
Beeman, Robert Rep: Team the Agency / 617-742-3444	Bowden, Patricia Rep: Katie Daley/William J. / 212-465-2420
Benevides, Rob / 212-228-9307 59 E. 3rd St., #3D, NY, NY 10003	Bowman, Brad / 213-466-8186
Benincasa, Lisa Rep: Perrella Management / 212-247-4400	Boyer, Ashley (Hair) Rep: Achard & Associates / 212-614-0962
Bensimon, Karen Rep: Yellen/LaChapelle / 212-838-3170	Breese, Jim (Make-Up) Rep: Atlantis Management / 212-924-1294
Bergomi, Emilio Rep: Zenobia Agency, Inc. / 213-937-1010	Breyer, Sherri Rep: Visages Rps Inc. / 213-650-8880
Berkowitz, Gary (Make-Up) Rep: Cloutier / 213-931-1323	Brown, Bobbi (Make-Up) Rep: Marek & Assocs. / 212-924-6760
Bernard, Tena Rep: Celestine / 213-650-7181	Brown, Peter / 212-684-7080 235 E. 22nd St., NYC, NY 10010
Bertellotti, Rae Rep: Team the Agency / 617-742-3444	Brunetti, Mary (Hair) Rep: Zoli Illusions / 212-242-7050
Bianco, Carmel Rep: Team the Agency / 617-742-3444	Calandra, Leonard (Hair) Rep: Kramer + Kramer, Inc. / 212-757-8787
Bieterman, Susan Rep: Zenobia Agency, Inc. / 206-340-0600	Calder, Martyn Foss (Hair) Rep: Visages Rps Inc. / 212-841-7550
Bilardi, Eric (Hair) Rep: Cloutier / 213-931-1323	Calo, Cheryl Rep: Zenobia Agency, Inc. / 213-937-1010 Rep: Zenobia Agency, Inc. / 415-621-7410
Birchall, John (Hair) Rep: Celestine / 213-650-7181	Calvo, Rudy (Make-Up) Rep: Dion Peronneau / 213-299-4043
Blancas, Paco (Make-Up) Rep: Atlantis Management / 212-924-1294	Campbell, Kenny (Make-Up) Rep: Kramer + Kramer / 212-797-8787

$$F = (a \times p)^4$$

Table (5.12). Support Services

Hair & Make-Up	Hair & Make-Up
Campo, Kim Rep: Ennis Inc. / 617-261-3970	Cooper, Fran (Make-Up) Rep: Kramer + Kramer, Inc. / 212-757-8787
Cantello, Linda (Make-Up) Rep: Atlantis Management / 212-924-1294	Cooper, Trina Rep: Achard & Associates / 212-614-0962
Carrillo, Kim (Make-Up) Rep: Celestine / 213-650-7181	Copeland, Christine Rep: HMS Bookings / 213-939-9100
Caruso, John (Hair) Rep: Bryan Bantry / 212-935-0200	Coppola, Monica Rep: Art + Commerce / 212-206-0737
Cate, Steven Rep: Zenobia Agency, Inc. / 213-937-1010	Cox, David (Hair) Rep: Celestine / 213-650-7181
Caydam, Alexis Rep: Kramer + Kramer / 212-757-8787	Creative Image / 213-655-9505 6500 Wilshire Blvd., LA, CA 90048
Cemal (Hair) Rep: Cloutier / 213-931-1323	Creighton, Colleen (Hair) Rep: Kramer + Kramer, Inc. / 212-575-8787
Char / 615-255-8346 20 Music Square W., #201, Nashville, TN 37203	Culp, James Rep: Zenobia Agency, Inc. / 206-340-0600
Chaston Betten Rep: Zenobia Agency, Inc. / 415-621-7410	D'Is, Yannick (Hair) Rep: Atlantis Management / 212-924-1294
Chilkes, Lesley (Make-Up) Rep: Art + Commerce / 212-206-0737	Daniele, Linda Rep: Jed Root, Inc. / 212-226-6600
Cicolello, Veta (Hair) / 212-316-2125 230 W. 108th St., #4B, NY, NY	Danon, Matt Rep: HMS Bookings / 213-939-9100
Cofano, Madeleine (Hair) Rep: Bryan Bantry / 212-935-0200	Davis, Kim (Make-Up) Rep: The Crystal Agency / 213-913-0700
Cohl (Hair) Rep: Bryan Bantry / 212-935-0200	De Fontbrune, Patrick (Make-Up) Rep: Celestine / 213-650-7181
Cole, Terri Forbes Rep: Zoli Illusions / 212-242-7050	De Rosa, Tom Rep: Zoli Illusions / 212-242-7050
Coleman, Christy (Make-Up) Rep: Jed Root, Inc. / 212-226-6600	Dellaria, Cal Rep: Ennis Inc. / 617-261-3970
Coleman, Ian Rep: Katie Daley/William J. / 212-465-2420	Demitt, Linda / 615-726-2222 1635 Broadway, Nashville, TN 37203
Combs, Cherie Rep: The Crystal Agency / 213-913-0700	Devine, Paul Rep: Ennis Inc. / 617-261-3970
Cooley, Richard Rep: Richard Cooley / 212-841-7550	Di Francesca, Betsy Rep: Zenobia Agency, Inc. / 213-937-1010

Hair & Make-Up	Hair & Make-Up
DiCecca, Rick Rep: Team the Agency / 617-742-3444 Rep: Zenobia Agency, Inc. / 415-621-7410	Fazio, Barbara (Hair) Rep: Yellen/LaChapelle / 212-838-3170
Diaz, Antonio Rep: Katie Daley/William J. / 212-465-2420	Fekkai, Frederic (Hair) Rep: Bryan Bantry / 212-935-0200
Dibase, Angelo Rep: LA Rep / 213-656-1720	Felker, Nadia / 206-285-8292 403 Roy St., Studio #27, Seattle, WA 98109
Diprima, Joanne Rep: Tricia Joyce / 212-962-0728	Ferrell, Eric Rep: Dion Peronneau / 213-299-4043
Dooley, Christine Rep: Ennis Inc. / 617-261-3970	Filippi, Paula Rep: Team the Agency / 617-742-3444
Dosunmu, Andrew Rep: Achard & Associates / 212-614-0962	Finnigan, Terence Rep: Visages Rps Inc. / 213-650-8880
Dubroff, Pati (Make-Up) Rep: Atlantis Management / 212-924-1294	Fiore, Franco Rep: Katie Daley/William J. / 212-465-2420
Dujic, Charles Rep: Celestine / 213-650-7181	Floyd, Roxanna (Make-Up) Rep: Zoli Illusions / 212-242-7050
Eason, Lynne Rep: LA Rep / 213-656-1720	Forster, Lisa Rep: Visages Rps Inc. / 212-841-7550 Rep: Zenobia Agency / 213-937-1010
Emmack, Lee Rep: Katie Daley/William J. / 212-465-2420	Foye, Frankie Rep: Celestine / 213-650-7181
Engelsman, Deborah Rep: Perrella Management / 212-247-4400	Francesca Tolot (Make-Up) Rep: Cloutier / 213-931-1323
Espegard, Gunn / 213-969-8354 2706 La Cuesta Dr., LA, CA 90046 Rep: Celestine / 213-650-7181	Franklin, Glenna (Make-Up) Rep: Yellen/LaChapelle / 212-838-3170
Eveyln, Vanessa Rep: Zoli Illusions & Style / 212-242-7050	Fredericke Rep: Celestine / 213-650-7181
Farman, Barbara Rep: Cloutier / 213-931-1323	Fugler, Howard (Hair) Rep: Bryan Bantry
Farolfi, Fulvia (Make-Up) Rep: Bryan Bantry / 212-935-0200	Gadson, Craig (Make-Up) Rep: Yellen/LaChapelle / 212-838-3170
Farrell, Melvone (Make-Up) Rep: Visages Rps Inc. / 213-650-8880	Gair, Joanne (Make-Up) Rep: Cloutier / 213-931-1323
Fass-Licata, Adele (Make-Up) Rep: Katie Daley/William J. / 212-465-2420	Gault, Sharon Rep: Cloutier / 213-931-1323

$$F = (a \times p)^4$$

TABLE (5.14). SUPPORT SERVICES

Hair & Make-Up	Hair & Make-Up
Geiger, Pam Rep: Bryan Bantry / 212-935-0200	Holston, Phoebe Rep: The Crystal Agency / 213-913-0700
Ghedri, Alice Rep: Hallelujah! / 212-243-6608	Hooke, Larry Rep: Zenobia Agency, Inc. / 415-621-7410 Rep: Zenobia Agency, Inc. / 206-340-0600
Giana (Make-Up) Rep: Kramer + Kramer, Inc. / 212-757-8787	Hopson, Maury (Hair) Rep: Bryan Bantry / 212-935-0200
Giannandrea (Hair) Rep: Celestine / 213-650-7181	Horgan, Debbie (Hair) Rep: Yellen/Lachapelle / 212-838-3170
Gilbert, Odile (Hair) Rep: Bryan Bantry / 212-935-0200	House, Jeffrey Rep: Zenobia Agency / 213-937-1010 Rep: Zenobia Agency / 415-621-7410
Gillespie, Pam Rep: Zenobia Agency, Inc. / 415-621-7410	Howe, Maryellen Rep: Zenobia Agency, Inc. / 213-937-1010
Gissler, Zanya Rep: Katie Daley/William J. / 212-465-2420	Howell, Daniel (Hair) Rep: Ivy Bernhard / 212-925-1111
Gorga, Kathleena Rep: Jezebel / 212-673-5509	Hutchings, Victor Rep: Zenobia Agency, Inc. / 415-621-7410
Gray, Tracey (Make-Up) Rep: Atlantis Management / 212-924-1294	Illusion / 615-352-4464 5115 Harding Rd., Nashville, TN 37205
Greco, Gary Rep: Team the Agecny / 617-742-3444	Ilnseher, Francois Rep: Bryan Bantry / 212-935-0200
Green, Gareth Rep: Zoli Illusions / 212-242-7050	Jadro, Laura (Make-Up) Rep: Celestine / 213-650-7181
Greenwell, Mary (Make-Up) Rep: Bryan Bantry / 212-935-0200	Jasper, Susie Rep: Cloutier / 213-931-1323
Greville-Morris, Jeanine (Make-Up) Rep: Cloutier / 213-931-1323	Jeffers, Helen Rep: Cloutier / 213-931-1323
Greville-Morris, Jeannie Rep: LA Rep / 213-656-1720	Jeffries, Ian (Make-Up) Rep: Jed Root / 212-226-6600
Habel, Nancy Rep: Zenobia Agency, Inc. / 206-340-0600	Jensen, Chuck Rep: Ivy Bernhard / 212-925-1111
Hajdukiewicz, James Rep: Cloutier / 213-931-1323	Jeung, Kathy (Make-Up) Rep: Visages Rps Inc. / 213-650-8880
Halperin, Lucy Rep: LA Rep / 213-656-1720	Johnson, Dale Rep: Visages Rps Inc. / 213-650-8880
Halterman, Troy (Hair) Rep: Art + Commerce / 212-206-0737	

TABLE (5.15). SUPPORT SERVICES

Hair & Make-Up	Hair & Make-Up
Johnson, Robert Rep: Zoli Illusions / 212-242-7050	King, Harry (Hair) Rep: Kramer + Kramer / 212-757-8787
Jones, Jeff Rep: HMS Bookings / 213-939-9100	King, Lindy (Hair) Rep: Kramer + Kramer / 212-757-8787
Joseph, Victor Rep: Cloutier / 213-931-1323	Kinion, Dina Rep: Zoli Illusions & Style / 212-242-7050 Rep: Ennis Inc. / 617-261-3970
Julien D'Ys (Hair) Rep: Atlantis Management / 212-924-1294	Kinks, Khamit (Hair) Rep: The Crystal Agency / 212-978-4646
Kahler, Mary L.Y.J. (Make-Up) / 917-451-9270	Knoll, Stephen (Hair) Rep: Kramer + Kramer / 212-757-8787
Kaliardos, James (Make-Up) Rep: Visages Rps Inc. / 212-841-7550	Kobari, Hiromi Rep: Perrella / 212-247-4400
Kang, Mina (Make-Up) / 213-384-1334 219 S. Ardmore Ave., LA, CA 90004	Krause Mora, Pamela / 213-650-1940 1400 N. Havenhurst Dr., LA, CA 90046
Karlo (Hair) Rep: Hallelujah! / 212-243-6608	Kraynak, Beki / 212-505-9844 134 E. 22nd St., #405, NYC, NY 10010
Karlyn, Bethany (Make-Up) Rep: Celestine / 213-650-7181	LaFontaine, Marie-Josee (Make-Up) Rep: Bryan Bantry / 212-935-0200
Kashuk, Sonia (Make-Up) Rep: Art & Commerce / 212-206-0737	Lamar (Make-Up) Rep: Marek & Associates / 212-924-6760
Katz, Beth Rep: Cloutier / 213-931-1323	Lana G. / 212-459-4008 511 Avenue of the Americas, Ste. 145, NYC, NY 10011
Kawahara, Karen (Make-Up) Rep: Cloutier / 213-931-1323	Lang, Wei (Make-Up) Rep: Tricia Joyce / 212-962-0728
Kelman, Jamie (Make-Up) / 212-529-3804 320 E. 22nd St., Apt. 6M, NY, NY 10010	Lara, Franklin (Hair) / 212-757-5360 Mitzu Salon 147 W. 57th St., NYC, NY 10019
Kendal, Diane (Make-Up) Rep: Art + Commerce / 212-206-0737	Lavett, Brent (Hair) Rep: Celestine / 213-650-7181
Keo, Richard (Hair) Rep: Cloutier / 213-931-1323 Rep: Art + Commerce / 212-206-0737	Lavoy, Johnny Rep: Team the Agency / 617-742-3444
Keoni (Hair) Rep: Cloutier / 213-931-1323 Rep: Yellen/LaChapelle / 212-838-3170	Le Duc, Josee Rep: Celestine / 213-650-7181
Kimura, Margaret (Hair) Rep: Cloutier / 213-931-1323	Leckie, Lorraine (Make-Up) Rep: Yellen/LaChapelle / 212-838-3170

$$F = (a \times p)^4$$

Hair & Make-Up	Hair & Make-Up
Lee, Kenn Rep: Zenobia Agency, Inc. / 206-340-0600	Makeup & Effects Lab, Inc. / 818-982-1483 7110 Laurel Canyon Blvd., E, N. Hollywood, CA 91605
Lemos, Francoise Rep: Team the Agency / 617-742-3444	Maldanado, Christopher (Make-Up) Rep: Dion Peronneau / 213-299-4043
Leonenko, Fedor Rep: Zenobia Agency, Inc. / 415-621-7410	Malige, Didier (Hair) Rep: Bryan Bantry / 212-935-0200
Levy, Sophie (Make-Up) Rep: Bryan Bantry / 212-935-0200	Maller, Bonnie (Make-Up) Rep: Bryan Bantry / 212-935-0200
Lewis, Laura Rep: Zenobia Agency, Inc. / 213-937-1010	Malouf, Kerry Rep: Visages Rps Inc. / 213-650-8880
Lilic, Sascha Rep: Tricia Joyce	Mancuso, Kevin (Hair) Rep: Jed Root, Inc. / 212-226-6600
Litt, Jani (Hair) / 212-262-8148 Garden in the Jungle 37 W. 56th St., NYC, NY 10019	Manders, Jasmine Rep: Celestine / 213-650-7181
Long Hair Rocks / 818-795-1272 2513 E. Colorado Blvd., Pasadena, CA 91107	Margin, Liz Rep: Team the Agency / 617-742-3444
Long, Lanier (Make-Up) / 212-772-8634 222 E. 84th St., #5A, NYC, NY 10028	Marin, Carlos Rep: Perrella / 212-247-4400
Longo, Vincent (Make-Up) Rep: Bryan Bantry / 212-935-0200	Markey, Denise (Make-Up) Rep: Kramer + Kramer, Inc. / 212-757-8787
Luca, Peggy Rep: Zenobia Agency, Inc. / 213-937-1010 Rep: Zenobia Agency, Inc. / 415-621-7410	Marks, Cheryl Rep: Celestine / 213-650-7181 Rep: Marek & Associates / 212-924-6760
Lucas, Patrick Rep: Zenobia / 213-937-1010	Marziali, Glenn (Make-Up) Rep: Bryan Bantry / 212-935-0200
Lucca, Jon Rep: Zenobia Agency, Inc. / 415-621-7410	Massarelli, Wayne Rep: HMS Bookings / 213-939-9100
Lucha, Tony (Hair) Rep: Jed Root, Inc. / 212-226-6600	Matsushima, Lori Rep: Cloutier / 213-931-1323
Lynch, Robyn Rep: Celestine / 213-650-7181	Matsuura, J.C. Rep: Visages Rps Inc. / 213-650-8880
Maderich, David Rep: Perrella Management / 212-247-4400	Mavestrand, Randi Rep: Zenobia Agency, Inc. / 213-937-1010
Make-up Creations / 213-463-8430 17815 Skypark Circle, Ste. J, Irvine, CA 92714	McBeth, Max Rep: Celestine / 213-650-7181

TABLE (5.17). SUPPORT SERVICES

Hair & Make-Up	Hair & Make-Up
McCarthy, Susan (Make-Up) Rep: Visages Rps Inc. / 212-841-7550	Neeko (Hair) Rep: The Crystal Agency / 213-913-0700
McGrath, Pat (Make-Up) Rep: Visages Rps Inc. / 213-650-8880	Nevio Rep: Jezebel / 212-673-5509
McKnight, Sam (Hair) Rep: Bryan Bantry / 212-935-0200 Rep: Visages Rps Inc. / 213-650-8880	Nichols, Edris E. (Hair) Rep: Atlantis Management
McRae, Donyale Rep: Jezebel / 212-673-5509	O'Connor, Judith Rep: Celestine / 213-650-7181
Melbourne, Jamie Rep: Atlantis Management / 212-924-1294	Occhipinti, Helena (Hair) Rep: Marek & Associates / 212-924-6760
Meranto, Jennifer Rep: Cloutier / 213-931-1323	Ohashi, Tomohiro Rep: Hallelujah! / 212-243-6608
Michaud, David Rep: Zenobia Agency, Inc. / 415-621-7410	Oribe / 212-319-3910 691 5th Ave., 10th Fl., NYC, NY 10022
Michaud, Julie Rep: Team the Agency / 617-742-3444	Orlando (Hair) Rep: Art + Commerce / 212-206-0737
Mirror, The / 615-329-0607 1102 16th Ave. So., Nashville, TN 37212	Osmundson, Wendy Rep: Cloutier / 213-931-1323
Monaci, Gina Rep: Visages Rps Inc. / 213-650-8880	Paige, Dick (Make-Up) Rep: Jed Root, Inc. / 212-226-6600
Mora, Luis (Hair) Rep: Atlantis Management / 212-924-1294	Palau, Guido (Hair) Rep: Jed Root, Inc. / 212-226-6600
Morelli, Roberto Rep: Perrella / 212-247-4400	Parfitt-Maister, Lisa (Hair & Makeup) Rep: Celestine / 213-650-7181
Morelock, Jody / 212-228-3097	Pecheux, Tom (Make-Up) Rep: Atlantis Management / 212-924-1294
Morgan, Anne Rep: Celestine / 213-650-7181	Pedis, Jan / 212-691-4260
Moyer, Tracy Rep: Celestine / 213-650-7181	Pierra (Hair) Rep: Atlantis Management / 212-924-1294
Mud Honey / 212-533-1160 148 Sullivan St., NYC, NY 10012	Pipino, Ric (Hair) Rep: Bryan Bantry / 212-935-0200
Mulholland, Moyra (Make-Up) Rep: Bryan Bantry / 212-935-0200	Procacci, Anna Marie (Make-Up) Rep: Hallelujah! / 212-243-6608
Nathanson, Kelly Rep: Jezebel / 212-673-5509	Radaelll, Serena (Hair) Rep: Cloutier / 213-931-1323

$$F = (a \times p)^4$$

TABLE (5.18). SUPPORT SERVICES

Hair & Make-Up	Hair & Make-Up
Rau, Mel (Make-Up) Rep: Atlantis Management / 212-924-1294	Salvarani, Monica (Make-Up) Rep: Celestine / 213-650-7181
Reiss-Andersen, Brigitte (Make-Up) Rep: Bryan Bantry / 212-935-0200	Sanguedolce, Sylvia / 718-224-2005
Renyer, Antonella (Make-Up) Rep: Cloutier / 213-931-1323	Santos, Eddie Rep: Perrella / 212-247-4400
Richards, Kendra (Make-up) Rep: Celestine / 213-650-7181	Sari Rep: Visages Rps Inc. / 213-650-8880
Riddle, Cheryl / 615-256-9937 20 Music Square W. #201, Nashville, TN 37203	Satoh (Hair) Rep: Hallelujah! / 212-243-6608
Rivette, Lia (Make-Up) Rep: Achard & Associates / 212-614-0962	Savic, Peter (Hair) Rep: Cloutier / 213-931-1323
Rodman, Letha (Make-Up) Rep: Ivy Bernhard / 212-925-1111	Scali, Vanessa (Make-Up) Rep: Atlantis Management / 212-924-1294 Rep: Team the Agency / 617-742-3444
Rooze, Robert de Rep: Perrella / 212-247-4400	Schiffman, Kathleen Rep: Team the Agency / 617-742-3444
Rose, Stephen (Hair) Rep: Art + Commerce / 212-206-0737	Sells, J.P. Rep: Zenobia Agency, Inc. / 415-621-7410 Rep: Zenobia Agency, Inc. / 206-340-0600
Rosen, Wendy Ann (Make-Up) Rep: Cloutier / 213-931-1323	Setaro, John (Hair) Rep: Celestine / 213-650-7181
Rougemont, Perrine (Hair) Rep: Kramer + Kramer, Inc. / 212-787-8787	Shaw, Makeup (Make-Up) Rep: Cloutier / 213-931-1323
Roy, Michele Rep: Team the Agency / 617-742-3444	Smith-Masters, Mariella (Make-Up) Rep: Bryan Bantry / 212-935-0200
Rumiko (Make-Up) Rep: Jed Root, Inc. / 212-226-6600	Smoot, Maria / 615-329-0607 The Mirror 1102 16th Ave. So., #205, Nashville, TN 37212
Rutledge, Derrick (Make-Up) / 202-269-3223 About Face 20203B N. Capitol St., NE, Washington, DC 20002 Rep: The Crystal Agency / 212-978-4646	Snow, Robert Rep: Visages Rps Inc. / 212-841-7550
Ryan, Kevin (Hair) Rep: Visages Rps Inc. / 213-650-8880	Snyder, Lydia (Make-Up) Rep: Kramer + Kramer, Inc. / 212-757-8787
Saba, Gabriel (Hair) Rep: Yellen/ LaChapelle	Sotomayor, Rudy Rep: HMS Bookings / 213-939-9100
Sachs, Melody / 310-915-1181	Spallas, Mitzi Rep: Cloutier / 213-931-1323

TABLE (5.19). SUPPORT SERVICES

Hair & Make-Up	Hair & Make-Up
Spearman, Eric Rep: Zoli Illusions & Style / 212-242-7050	Taricco, Nadia Rep: Cloutier / 213-931-1323
Spice (Hair) Rep: The Crystal Agency / 213-913-0700	Tonello, Michael Rep: Team the Agency
Sprague, Nancy Rep: Ivy Bernhard / 212-925-1111	Townsend, Jeanne Rep: Celestine / 213-650-7181
Springs, Carmon Rep: Kramer & Kramer / 212-757-8787	Tricomi, Edward (Hair) Rep: Atlantis Management / 212-924-1294
St. George, Edward Rep: Visages Rps Inc. / 213-650-8880	Twigg, Honey Rep: Achard & Associates / 212-614-0962
Stam, Ronnie (Hair) Rep: Yellen/LaChapelle / 212-838-3170	Uliana / 212-642-5021 783 Eighth Ave., #2C, NYC, NY 10036
Stave, Kian / 212-260-4377	Van Slee, Sandrine (Make-Up) Rep: Atlantis Management / 212-924-1294
Stockland, Jillayne (Make-Up) / 212-929-7151	Van Up, Tammy Rep: Zenobia Agency, Inc. / 415-621-7410
Storey, Lisa Jayne Rep: Visages Rps Inc. / 213-650-8880	Velasco, Danny Rep: Jezebel / 212-673-5509
Strettell, Jo (Make-Up) Rep: Visages Rps Inc. / 213-650-8880	Verel, Maria Rep: Art + Commerce / 212-206-0737
Strong, Collier Rep: Cloutier / 213-931-1323	Vetica, Robert Rep: Celestine / 213-650-7181
Stutzman, Jetty Rep: Cloutier / 213-931-1323	Vidal, Victor (Hair) Rep: Cloutier / 213-931-1323
Style Architect / 212-749-0284 733 Amsterdam Ave., #24A, NYC, NY 10025	Vigorelli, Gabriele (Hair) Rep: Bryan Bantry / 212-935-0200
Surprenant, Tom (Makeup EFX) Rep: Zenobia Agency, Inc. / 213-937-1010	Villanueva, Johnny (Hair) Rep: The Crystal Agency / 213-913-0700
Swan, Patrick Rep: Ivy Bernahrd / 212-925-1111	Vistica, Ina Rep: Katie Daley/William J. / 212-465-2420
Takahoshi, Mutsumi Rep: Yellen/Lachapelle / 212-838-3170	Von Wijnberge, Harie Rep: Zoli Illusions / 212-242-7050
Takako Rep: Perrella Management / 212-247-4400	Vrabl, Gui Rep: Perrella Management / 212-247-4400
Tamme, Bernhard (Hair) Rep: Celestine / 213-650-7181	Walker, Johnny (Hair) Rep: Visages Rps Inc. / 213-650-8880
Tang, Michelle Rep: Jezebel / 212-673-5509	

$$F = (a \times p)^4$$

Table (5.20). Support Services

Hair & Make-Up	Hair & Make-Up

<table>
<tr><td valign="top" width="50%">

Walter, Darin
Rep: Visages Rps Inc. / 213-650-8880

Ward (Hair)
Rep: Bryan Bantry / 212-935-0200

Ward, Ashley (Make-Up)
Rep: Bryan Bantry / 212-935-0200

Warn, Kerry
Rep: Kramer + Kramer / 212-797-8787

Warner Bros. (Makeup Dept.) / 818-954-2151
4000 Warner Blvd, Burbank, CA 91522

Weeks, Michael (Hair)
Rep: Dion Peronneau / 213-299-4269

Wells, Chris
Rep: Zenobia Agency, Inc. / 415-621-7410

Wells, Heidi
Rep: Ennis Inc. / 617-261-3970

Wells, Reggie (Make-Up)
Rep: Zoli Illusions / 212-242-7050

Westmoreland, Bill
Rep: Art + Commerce / 212-206-0737

Whelan, Nikki
Rep: Yellen/LaChapelle / 212-838-3170

Whitehead, Nicholas
Rep: The Crystal Agency / 213-913-0700

Wiedenmann, Diane (Hair)
Rep: Celestine / 213-650-7181

Wignes, Regina
Rep: Zenobia Agency, Inc. / 206-340-0600

Wilshire Wigs & Accessories (Hair)
213-875-2260 / 818-983-0874
13213 Saticoy St., N. Hollywood, CA 91605

Winters, Billy
Rep: Zenobia Agency, Inc. / 415-621-7410

Woodley, Jeffrey (Hair)
Rep: Zoli Illusions / 212-242-7050

</td><td valign="top" width="50%">

Zammit, Lucienne (Make-Up)
Rep: Cloutier / 213-931-1323

Costumes

American Costume Company / 818 764-2239
12980 Raymer St., N. Hollywood, CA 91605

Baron California Hats / 818-563-3025
1617 W. Burbank Blvd., Burbank, CA 91506

Becker, Susan / 213-851-6195

Bernini / 310-278-6287
362 N. Rodeo Dr., Beverly Hills, CA 90210

Bernini / 310-273-8786
335 N. Rodeo Dr., Beverly Hills, CA 90210

Bess, Jean / 615-832-2428

Bill Hargate Costume Inc. / 213-876-4432
1111 N. Formosa Ave., W. Hollywood, CA 90046

Breakstone, Bambi / 818-985-5665

Bruno, Richard / 818-781-6531 / 206-385-7149

Cash, Tara / 503-287-3857

Chrome Hearts / 213-874-3802
1027 N. Orange Dr., Hollywood, CA 90038

Cicolello, Veta / 212-316-2125
230 W. 108th St., #4B, NY, NY

Costume Collection / 818-503-0544
7318 Laurel Canyon Blvd, N. Hollywood, CA 91605

Costumes Rentals Corp. / 818-753-3700
11149 Van Owen St., N. Hollywood, CA 91605

Creative Costumes / 212-564-5552
330 W. 38th St., NYC, NY 10018

Dangerous Threads / 615-256-1033
105 Second Ave N., Nashville, TN 37203

Daniel, Betty Blair / 615-952-2200

</td></tr>
</table>

TABLE (5.21). SUPPORT SERVICES

Costumes	Costumes

Costumes (left column)

David's Outfitters / 212-691-7388
36 W. 20th St., NYC, NY 10011

Demonbreun, Wilma / 615-746-8531

EC2 Costumes / 213-934-1131
431 S. Fairfax Ave., 2nd Fl., LA, CA 90036

East Village Leather, Inc. / 212-533-8330
27 St. Mark's Pl., NYC, NY 10003

Elizabeth Lucas Collection, The / 310-451-4058
1021 Montana Ave., Santa Monica, CA 90403

Exaline / 615-399-1991

Geppetto Soft Sculpture, Inc. / 718-398-9792
107 Lexington Ave., Brooklyn, NY 11238

Gordon Novelty / 212-254-8616
933 Broadway, NYC, NY 10010

Hollywood Toys & Costumes
213-465-3119 / 213-622-0184
6562 Hollywood Blvd., Hollywood, CA 90028

Ian's / 212-838-3969
1151 Second Ave., NYC, NY 10021

Ian's / 212-420-1857
5 St. Mark's Pl., NYC, NY 10003

Island Electric / 212-346-9304
49 Market St., NYC, NY 10002

Junk for Joy / 818-569-4903
3314 W. Magnolia Blvd, Burbank, CA 91505

L.A. Gear / 310-822-1995
2850 Ocean Park Blvd., Santa Monica, CA 90405

Leathers & Treasures / 213-655-7541
7511 Melrose Ave., LA, CA 90046

Lily / 213-852-0667
8121 W. Third St., W. Hllywd, CA 90048

Manuel Exclusive Clothier / 615-321-5444
1922 Broadway, Nashville, TN 37203

Mel Grayson / 213-746-3593
746 E. 12th St., LA, CA 90021

Miller, Tammy S. / 615-321-5322 / 615-824-3952

Costumes (right column)

Motion Picture Costume Co. / 818-764-8191
6844 Lankershim Blvd, N. Hollywood, CA 91605

Paramount Costume Dept. / 213-956-5288
5555 Melrose Ave., Edith Head Bldg, Rm 200,
Hollywood, CA 90038-3197

Patricia Field / 212-254-1699
10 E. Eighth St., NYC, NY 10003

Performance Cosmetics/Costumes
615-256-0070 / 800-366-6701
1205 Church St., Nashville, TN 37203

Playmates / 213-464-7636
6438 Hollywood Blvd., LA, CA 90028

Pleasure & Cin / 213-937-6988
6125 Orange St., Ste. 104, L.A., CA 90048

Repeat Performance / 213-938-0609
318 N. LaBrea, LA, CA 90036

Retro Pieces Vintage Clothing / 615-329-3537
207 A Louise Ave., Nashville, TN 37203

Rockit Rags / 212-529-9070
33 St. Mark's Pl., NYC, NY 10003

Screaming Mimi's / 212-677-6464
382 Lafayette St., NYC, NY 10003

Soap Plant, The / 213-651-5587
7400 Melrose Ave., LA, CA 90046

Studio Cleaners / 310-838-1801
10800 Washington Blvd, Culver City, CA 90230

Style Council, The / 615-322-9368
900 19th Ave. S., #1003, Nashville, TN 37212

Suitably Yours / 818-957-8020 / 818-951-2160
3243 Foothill Blvd, La Crescenta, CA 91214

Trash & Vaudeville / 212-982-3590
4 St. Marks Pl., NYC, NY 10003

Universal City Studios / 818-777-3000 / 818-777-3438
100 Universal City Plaza, Universal City, CA 91608

Untitled / 212-505-9725
26 W. Eighth St., NYC, NY 10011

TABLE (5.22). SUPPORT SERVICES

Costumes

Warner Bros. Studio Facilities / 818-954-5692
3701 W. Oak, Burbank, CA 91522

Way We Wore, The / 415-822-1800
1094 Revere Ave., Ste. A29, SF, CA 94124

Western Costume Co. / 818-508-2119
11041 Vanouven St., N. Hollywood, CA 91605

Wheeler, Joni / 615-298-5664

World Domination Leather / 212-502-1162
440 W. 34th St., NYC, NY 10001
Rep: Victoria Watson / 212-575-8858

Jewelry

212 Jewelry / 212-243-5213
9 Christopher St., NYC, NY 10014

Axel / 212-777-7537
69 W. Ninth St., #4B, NYC, NY 10011

Chrome Hearts / 213-874-3802
943 N. Orange Dr., Hollywood, CA 90038

Dangerous Threads / 615-320-5890
2201 Elliston Pl., Nashville, TN 37203

Fletcher Jewelry, Philip / 212-219-1026
160 Prince St., NYC, NY 10012

Lassen, Andre
Rep: Leslie Barany / 212-627-8488

Necromance / 213-934-8684
7162 Melrose, LA, CA

Pleasure & Cin / 213-937-6988
6125 Orange St., Ste. 104, L.A., CA 90048

Rebellious Skull / 212-730-0269
55 W. 47th St., Rm. 200A, NYC, NY 10036

Scarbrough, Sparky / 602-924-4030
921 South Val Vista, #67, Mesa, AZ 85204

Streeter, Alex / 212-925-6496
152 Prince St., NYC, NY 10012

Jewelry

Studio Ze / 212-219-3304
598 Broadway, 2nd Fl., NY, NY 10012

Backdrops

Backdrop Solution, The / 312-993-0494
311 N. Des Plaines St., #603, Chicago, IL 60661

Davis Backdrops, Betsy / 212-645-4197
397 W. 12th St., NYC, NY 10014

Eastern Scenic Backdrops, Inc. / 212-244-2700
560 W. 34th St., NYC, NY 10001

Get Set / 214-748-4170
3406 Main, Dallas, TX 75226

Green Enterprises / 615-242-9632
607 Bass, Nashville, TN 37203

Modeworks Inc. / 212-226-4079
54 Leonard St., NYC, NY 10013

Neovision Design Inc. / 615-242-3164
2214 Metro Ctr.Blvd., Ste.105, Nashville, TN 37228

Oliphant Backdrops / 212-741-1233
20 W. 20th St., 6th Fl., NYC, NY 10011

Photo Backgrounds / 213-849-3255
1919 Empire Ave., Burbank, CA 91504

Quik Drop Box / 201-342-2893

Tamara Inc. Backdrops / 312-226-9066
1130 W. Monroe St., Chicago, IL 60607

Props

20th Century Props / 818-759-1192
11651 Hart St., N. Hllywd, CA 91605

Ace Banner / 212-620-9111
107 W. 27th St., NYC, NY 10001

Ang, Stephen
Rep: Zoli Illusions & Style / 212-727-0044

$$F = (a \times p)^4$$

TABLE (5.23). SUPPORT SERVICES

Props	Props
Aoki, H. / 212-564-4285 424 W. 33rd St., 10th Fl., NYC, NY 10001	Dean, Milton Rep: Perrella / 212-247-4400
Art Deco L.A.'s Prop House / 818-765-5653 7100 Case Ave., N. Hollywood, CA 91605	Drulu / 818-508-8621 12812 Landale St., Studio City, CA 91604
Art Wear / 212-431-9405 409 W. B'way, NYC, NY 10012	Eagle, Caryl Rep: Zenobia Agency, Inc. / 415-621-7410
Bandit Lites / 615-781-2777 219 Space Park S., Nashville, TN 37211	Eames, Tim / 310-455-3266 1104 Canyon Trail, Topanga, CA 90290
Bender, Thomas Roy / 213-462-6565 / 213-307-0773 1227 N. Genesee Ave., #4, W. Hllywd, CA 90046	Eclectic/Encore Properties / 212-645-8880 620 W. 26th St., NYC, NY 10001
Brooklyn Model Works / 718-834-1944 60 Washington Ave., Brooklyn, NY 11205	Ellis Mercantile Inc. / 213-933-7334 169 N. La Brea Ave., LA, CA 90036
Brusca Ice & Wood / 212-744-6986 2148 Second Ave., NYC, NY 10029	Falcaro, Millie / 212-727-0044 Rep: Network Reps / 212-727-0044
Build The Set Builder / 212-633-0348 59 Ninth Ave., Ste. 202, NYC, NY 10011	Filmtrix, Inc. / 818-980-3700 P.O. Box 715, N. Hollywood, CA 91603
Canter, Denise Rep: Visages Rps Inc / 212-841-7550	Gargoyles Ltd. / 212-255-0135 138 W. 25th St., NYC, NY 10001
Carpenter, Brent / 714-363-0825 19 Cala Moreya St., Laguna Niguel, CA 92677	Geppetto Soft Sculpture, Inc. / 718-398-9792 107 Lexington Ave., Brooklyn, NY 11238
Carroll Musical Instrument Rentals / 212-868-4120 351 W. 41st St., NYC, NY 10036	Gerry, Catherine / 212-769-4355 309 W. 90th St., NYC, NY 10024
Central Props / 212-265-7767 514 W. 49th St., NYC, NY 10019	Global Effects Inc. / 818-503-9273 7119 Laurel Canyon Blvd., N. Hollywood, CA 91605
Chandler, Mark Rep: Ivy Bernhard / 212-925-1111	Graphics For Industry / 212-889-6202 8 W. 30th St., 7th Fl., NYC, NY 10001
Character Shop, The / 818-718-0094 9033 Owen's Mouth Ave., Canoga Park, CA 91304	Green Enterprises / 615-242-9632 607 Bass St., Nashville, TN 37203
Churchman, Calvin Rep: Network Reps / 212-727-0044	Green, Hilary Rep: Celestine / 213-650-7181 Rep: Hilary Green / 213-937-1010
Cicolello, Veta / 212-316-2125 230 W. 108th St., #4B, NY, NY	Gregory, Steven Rep: Celestine / 213-650-7181
Cultural Design Ltd. / 212-594-8690 517 W. 46th St., NYC, NY 10036	Hahn, Mindy Rep: Celestine / 213-658-4181
Davis, Diane Rep: Zenobia Agency, Inc. / 415-621-7410	

$$F = (a \times p)^4$$

Table (5.24). Support Services

Props	Props
Hollywood Toys & Costumes 213-465-3119 / 213-622-0184 6562 Hollywood Blvd., Hollywood, CA 90028	Paramount Pictures / 212-373-7000 15 Columbus Circle, NYC, NY 10023
Interstate Theatrical Lighting / 615-329-2700 1416 Church St., Nashville, TN 37203	Prop Masters, Inc. / 818-846-3915 / 818-846-3957 912 W. Isabel St., Burbank, CA 91506
Keynote Piano Rentals / 212-777-1388 77 Bleecker St., NYC, NY 10012	Prop Services West, Inc. / 213-461-3371 915 N. Citrus Ave., LA, CA 90038
Lievre, Veronique Rep: Zenobia Agency, Inc. / 213-937-1010	Props For Today / 212-206-0330 121 W. 19th St., NYC, NY 10011
Magic Models, Inc. / 602-899-8830 14027 E. Williams Field Rd., Gilbert, AZ 85296	Props or Decor / 615-255-6767 114 13th Ave. N, Nashville, TN 72036
Make-up Creations / 213-463-8430 17815 Skypark Circle, Irvine, CA 92714	Rankin, Gardner Rep: Network Reps / 212-727-0044
Makeup & Effects Lab, Inc. / 818-982-1483 7110 Laurel Canyon Blvd. Bldg. E, N. Hollywood, CA 91605	Rock'n'Roll Construction / 201-216-9070 123 First St., Jersey City, NJ 07302
Marvin, Lennie / 818-841-5882 3110 Winona Ave., Burbank, CA 91504	Samardge, Sandy Rep: Network Reps / 212-727-0044
Metcalf Models / 214-748-2723 3309 Elm St., Dallas, TX 75226	Shaker, Suzanne Rep: Art + Commerce / 212-206-0737
Meyer, Richard / 718-885-3268 21 Schofield St., City Island, NY 10464	Studio Instrument Rentals / 212-627-7079 520 W. 25th St., NYC, NY 10001
Modern Artificial Flowers & Displays / 212-265-0414 517 W. 46th St., NYC, NY 10036	Tennessee Prod. Center, Inc. 615-577-5597 / 800-537-5972 10840 Chapman Hwy, Seymour, TN 37865
National Flag & Display / 212-675-5230 42 E. 20th St., 3rd Fl., NYC, NY 10003	Toy Specialists, The / 212-333-2206 333 W. 52nd St., 7th Fl., NYC, NY 10019
Neovision Design Inc. / 615-242-3164 2214 Metro Ctr. Blvd., Ste.105, Nashville, TN 37228	Universal City Studios / 818-777-3000 100 Universal City Plaza, Universal City, CA 91608
New York Prop Gallery / 212-399-0944 451 W. 54th St., NYC, NY 10019	Walt Disney Company, The / 818-560-1000 500 S. Buena Vista St., Burbank, Ca 91521
Niccolini / 212-243-2010 19 W. 21st St., NYC, NY 10010	Warner Bros. Studios / 818-954-6000 / 818-954-2171 4000 Warner Blvd., Burbank, CA 91522
Nights of Neon, Inc. / 818-982-3592 7442 Varna Ave., N. Hollywood, CA 91605	⟶ Wells Televisions, John / 718-624-0650 Brooklyn Factory 65 Jay St., Brooklyn, NY 11201 page 3
Paramount Pictures / 213-956-5000 5555 Melrose Ave., LA, CA 90038	Wheeler, Joni / 615-298-5664

$$F = (a \times p)^4$$

Props	Magazines
Woody, Freida Rep: Zenobia Agency, Inc. / 213-937-1010	Bikini / 310-452-6222 2110 Main, Ste. 100, Santa Monica, CA 90405
Magazines	Billboard Publications, Inc. / 212-764-7300 1515 Broadway, NYC, NY 10036
Advertising Age / 213-651-3710 / 800-992-9970 6500 Wilshire Blvd., Suite 2300, LA, CA 90048	Bomb Magazine / 212-431-3943 594 Broadway, 10th Fl, NYC, NY 10012
Advertising Age / 212-210-0170 220 E. 42nd St., NYC, NY 10017	Boston Globe, The / 617-929-2000 P.O. Box 2378, Boston, MA 02107
Adweek / 212-764-7300 1515 Broadway, NYC, NY 10036	Business Week Magazine / 212-512-2511 1221 Sixth Ave., 39th Fl., NYC, NY 10020
Adweek / 404-841-3333 6 Piedmont Center, Ste. 300, Atlanta, GA 30305	Buzz Magazine / 310-473-2721 11835 W. Olympic Blvd., Suite 450, LA, CA 90064
Allure Magazine / 212-880-8800 350 Madison Ave., NYC, NY 10017	CMJ New Music Monthly / 516-466-6000 11 Middle Neck Rd., Ste. 400, Great Neck, NY 11021
American Cinematographer 800-448-0145 / 213-969-4333 1782 N. Orange Dr., Hollywood, CA 90078	Cable Guide Magazine / 212-683-6116 475 Fifth Ave., Ste. 1207, NYC, NY 10017
American Photo / 212-767-6000 1633 Broadway, 43rd Fl., NYC, NY 10019	Cash Box Magazine / 212-245-4224 345 W. 58th St., Ste. 15W, NYC, NY 10019
Art & Design News / 317-849-6110 5783 Park Plaza Court, Indianapolis, IN 46220	Chicago Tribune, The / 312-222-3232 435 N. Michigan Ave., Chicago, IL 60611
Art Direction Magazine / 212-889-6500 10 E. 39th St., 6th Fl., NYC, NY 10016	Circus Magazine / 212-242-4902 6 W. 18th St., NYC, NY 10011
Associated Press, The / 212-621-1500 50 Rockefeller Plaza, NYC, NY 10020	Communication Arts Magazine / 415-326-6040 410 Sherman Ave., Palo Alto, CA 94306
Atlanta Magazine / 404-872-3100 Two Midtown Plaza 1360 Peachtree St., Ste. 1800, Atlanta, GA 30309	Conde Nast Traveler Magazine / 212-880-8800 360 Madison Ave., NYC, NY 10017
Atlantic Monthly, The / 617-536-9500 745 Boylston St., Boston, MA 02116	Cosmopolitan Magazine / 212-649-2000 224 W. 57th St., 8th Fl., NYC, NY 10019
BAM Magazine / 213-851-8600 6767 Forest Lawn Dr., Ste. 110, LA, CA 90068	Country Song Round Up / 201-843-4004 210 Route 4 E., Ste. 401, Paramus, NJ 07652
Baltimore Sun / 410-332-6000 501 N. Calvert, Baltimore, MD 21278	Creativity / 212-210-0170 220 E. 42nd St., 9th Fl., NYC, NY 10017
Bike Magazine P.O. Box 1028, Dana Point, CA 92629	Details Magazine / 212-420-0689 632 Broadway, 12th Fl., NYC, NY 10012
	Discover Magazine / 818-973-4150 500 South Buena Vista Street, Burbank, CA 91521

$$F = (a \times p)^4$$

TABLE (5.26). SUPPORT SERVICES

Magazines	Magazines
Elle Decor / 212-767-5800 1633 Broadway, 45th Fl, NYC, NY 10019	Health / 415-512-9100 301 Howard Street, 18th Fl., SF, CA 94105
Elle Magazine / 212-767-5800 1633 Broadway, 44th Fl., NYC, NY 10019	Hit Parader / 201-843-4004 210 Route 4 E., Paramus, NJ 02652
Emigre / 916-451-4344 4475 D St., Sacramento, CA 95819	Hollywood Reporter / 213-525-2000 5055 Wilshire Blvd., Ste. 600, LA, CA 90036
Entertainment Today / 818-566-4030 801 S. Main St., Burbank, CA 91506	How Magazine / 513-531-2222 F & W Publications 1507 Dana Ave., Cincinnati, OH 45207
Esquire / 212-649-4020 250 W. 55th St., NYC, NY 10019	Huh / 310-452-6222 2110 Main St., #100, Santa Monica, CA 90405
Film & Video / 213-653-8053 8455 Beverly Blvd., Suite 508, LA, CA 90048	In Fashion / 212-768-8450 29 W. 38th St., 15 Fl., NYC, NY 10018
Fitness Magazine / 212-463-1000 110 5th Ave., NYC, NY 10011	Indianapolis Star, The / 317-633-9279 307 N. Pennsylvania St., Indianapolis, IN 46206-0145
Forbes Magazine / 212-620-2200 60 Fifth Ave., NYC, NY 10011	Interview / 212-941-2900 575 Broadway, 5th Fl., NYC, NY 10012
Foundations / 212-645-1360 1133 Broadway, Suite 1220, NYC, NY 10010	Jazz Times / 301-588-4114 7961 Eastern Ave., Ste. 303, Silver Springs, MD 20910
Gavin / 415-495-1990 140 Second St., 2nd Fl., SF, CA 94105	Jazziz / 904-375-3705 3620 N.W. 43rd St., Ste. D, Gainsville, FL 32606
Gazette Newspapers / 310-433-2000 5225 E. 2nd St., Long Beach, CA 90803	L.A. Weekly / 213-465-9909 6715 Sunset Blvd., LA, CA 90028
Gentlemen's Quarterly / 212-880-8548 350 Madison Ave., 6th Fl., NYC, NY 10017	Life Magazine / 212-522-1212 Time-Life Building, 4th Fl Rockefeller Center, NYC, NY 10020
Glamour Magazine / 212-880-8062 350 Madison Ave., 11th Fl, NYC, NY 10017	Location Update / 213-483-9889 2301 Bellevue Ave., 5th Fl., LA, CA 90026
Graphic Design: USA / 212-534-5500 1556 Third Ave., #405, NYC, NY 10128	Los Angeles Times / 213-237-5000 Times Mirror Square, LA, CA 90053
Graphis / 212-532-9387 141 Lexington Ave., NYC, NY 10016	MacWorld / 415-243-0505 501 Second Street, San Francisco, CA 94107
Guitar Player / 415-358-9500 411 Borel Ave., #100, San Mateo, CA 94402	Mademoiselle Magazine / 212-880-8800 350 Madison Ave., NYC, NY 10017
Guitar World / 212-807-7100 1115 Broadway, 8th Fl., NYC, NY 10010	Men's Journal / 212-484-1616 1290 Sixth Ave., 2nd Fl., NYC, NY 10104
Harper's Bazaar / 310-392-1181 3000 Ocean Park Blvd., Santa Monica, CA 90405	

TABLE (5.27). SUPPORT SERVICES

Magazines	Magazines
Metal Edge / 212-780-3512 233 Park Ave. S, NYC, NY 10003	New York Post / 212-815-8000 210 South St., NYC, NY 10002
Metropolis / 212-722-5050 177 E. 87th St., NYC, NY 10128	New York Times / 212-556-1234 229 W. 43rd St., NYC, NY 10036
Millimeter / 212-477-4700 826 Broadway, 4th Fl, NYC, NY 10003	New Yorker, The / 212-536-5400 20 W. 43rd St., NYC, NY 10036
Mirabella / 212-447-4600 200 Madison Ave., 8th Fl., NYC, NY 10019	Newsweek Magazine / 212-445-4000 251 W. 57th St., NYC, NY 10019-1894
Money Magazine / 212-522-1212 1271 Ave. of the Americas, NYC, NY 10020	Omni / 212-496-6100 1965 Broadway, NYC, NY 10023
Mother Jones / 415-665-6637 731 Market St., Ste. 600, San Francisco, CA 94103	Option / 310-474-2600 1522 Cloverfield Blvd, Ste. B, Santa Monica, CA 90404
Movieline / 310-282-0711 1141 S. Beverly Dr., LA, CA 90035	Outside Magazine / 505-989-7100 400 Market St.St., Santa Fe, NM 87501
Ms. Magazine / 212-551-9595 230 Park Ave., 7th Fl., NYC, NY 10169	PC World / 415-978-3333 501 Second St., SF, CA 94107
Music City News / 615-329-2200 50 Music Sq. W., #601, Nashville, TN 37203	Paper Magazine / 212-226-4405 529 Broadway, NYC, NY 10012
Music Connection / 213-462-5772 6640 Sunset Blvd., LA, CA 90028	Parade Magazine / 212-450-7000 711 Third Ave., NYC, NY 10017
Musician Magazine / 212-536-5208 1515 Broadway, 11th Fl., NYC, NY 10036	Penthouse / 212-496-6100 1965 Broadway, NYC, NY 10023
NYPress / 212-941-1130 295 Lafayette St., NYC, NY 10012	People Magazine / 310-268-7200 10880 Wilshire Blvd., LA, CA 90024
Nashville Scene / 615-244-7989 209 Tenth Ave. S Ste. 222, Nashville, TN 37203	Philadelphia Inquirer / 215-854-2000 P.O. 8263ad St., Philadelphia, PA 19101
National Geographic / 202-857-7000 1145 17th St., N.W., Washington, DC 20036	Photo District News / 212-536-5222 1515 Broadway, NYC, NY 10036
New York Daily News / 212-210-2100 220 E. 42nd St., NYC, NY 10017	Playboy Magazine / 800-621-4105 680 N. Lakeshore Dr., Chicago, IL 606011
New York Magazine / 212-880-0700 755 Second Ave., 3rd Floor, NYC, NY 10017	Powder/Snowboarder Magazine / 714-496-5922 P.O. Box 1028, Dana Point, CA 92629
New York Newsday / 212-251-6800 2 Park Ave., NYC, NY 10016	Premiere / 212-725-3437 2 Park Ave., 4th Fl., NYC, NY 10016
	Print Magazine / 212-463-0600 104 Fifth Ave., NYC, NY 10011

$$F = (a \times p)^4$$

Table (5.28). Support Services

Magazines	Magazines
Pulse / 916-373-2450 2500 Dell Monte St., W. Sacramento, CA 95691	Town & Country Magazine / 212-903-5000 1700 Broadway, 30th Fl., NYC, NY 10019
Ray Gun / 310-452-6222 2110 Main St., #100, Santa Monica, CA 90405	Travel & Leisure / 212-382-5600 1120 Ave. of the Americas, NYC, NY 10036
Rip Magazine / 310-858-7100 9100 Wilshire Blvd., Beverly Hills, CA 90210	Travel Holiday / 212-366-8700 28 W. 23rd St., NYC, NY 10010
Rolling Stone / 212-484-1616 1290 Ave. of Americas, 2nd Fl, NYC, NY 10104	U.S. News & World Report / 202-955-2000 2400 N Street, NW, Washington, D.C. 20037-1196
San Antonio Express News / 210-225-7411 P.O. Box 2171, San Antonio, TX 78297-2171	US Magazine / 212-484-1616 1290 Sixth Ave., 2nd Fl., NYC, NY 10104
Select / 212-929-9473 153 W. 18th St., #1, NYC, NY 10011	USA Today / 703-276-3400 1000 Wilson Blvd., Arlington, VA 22209
Self Magazine / 212-880-8800 350 Madison Ave., NYC, NY 10017	Vanity Fair / 212-880-8800 350 Madison Ave., 4th Fl., NYC, NY 10017
Shoot / 213-525-2267 5055 Wilshire Blvd., LA, CA 90036	Variety / 213-857-6600 5700 Wilshire Blvd., Ste. 120, LA, CA 90036
Shoot / 212-764-7300 1515 Broadway, 14th Fl., NYC, NY 10036	Vibe / 212-522-7092 205 Lexington Ave., 3rd Fl, NYC, NY 10016
Sierra Magazine / 415-776-2211 730 Polk St., SF, CA 94109	Village Voice / 212-475-3300 36 Cooper Sq., NYC, NY 10003
Spin Magazine / 212-633-8200 6 W. 18th St., 11th Fl., NYC, NY 10011_4608	Vogue Magazine / 212-880-8800 350 Madison Ave., 13th Fl., NYC, NY 10017
Step by Step Graphics / 309-688-2300 6000 N. Forest Park Dr., E. Peoria, IL 61614	W Magazine / 212-630-3520 7 W. 34th St., 7 W. 34th St., NYC, NY 10001
Sucess Magazine / 212-551-9500 230 Park Ave., NYC, NY 10169	Wall Street Journal / 212-416-2000 200 Liberty St., 9th Fl, NYC, NY 10281
TV Guide / 212-819-3700 P.O. Box 201, NYC, NY 10013	Washington Post Magazine / 202-334-7585 1150 15th Street NW, Washington, DC 20071
Texas Monthly / 512-320-6900 P.O. Box 1569, Austin, TX 78767_1569	Whittle Communications / 615-595-5000 333 Main Ave., Knoxville, TN 37902
Time Magazine / 212-522-1212 Time Life Bldg. Rockefeller Center, NYC, NY 10020	Wired / 415-222-6200 520 Third St., 4th Fl., SF, CA 94107
Time Magazine / 310-268-7213 11766 Wilshire Blvd., Ste. 1800, LA, CA 90025	Working Mother / 212-551-9500 230 Park Ave., 7th Fl., NYC, NY 10169
	Worth Magazine / 212-223-3100 575 Lexington Ave., NYC, NY 10022

TABLE (5.29). SUPPORT SERVICES

Magazines	Merchandising

Magazines

YM Magazine / 212-878-8700
685 Third Ave., 28th Fl., NYC, NY 10017

Merchandising

20th Century Fox Licensing & Merchandising
310-203-2863
2121 Ave. of the Stars, Ste. 500, LA, CA 90067

AJM Marketing Enterprises / 708-240-1100
1515 Woodfield Road, Schaumburg, IL 60173

Aim / 412-683-2900
3812 Penn Ave., Pittsburgh, PA 15201

Alaska Momma, Inc. / 212-679-4404
303 Fifth Ave., 20th Fl, NYC, NY 10016

Ami! Art Makers International, Inc. / 813-360-9700
P.O. Box 67185, St. Pete Beach, FL. 33736-7185

Anheuser-Busch, Inc. / 314-577-4773
2700 S. Broadway, St. Louis, MO 63118

Animagic Entertainment Group, Inc. / 212-734-5909
444 E. 82nd St., Ste. 28C, NYC, NY 10028

Applause, Inc. / 818-992-6000
P.O. Box 4183, Woodland Hills, CA 91365-4183

Arts Uniq / 615-526-3491
P.O. Box 3085, Cookeville, TN 38502

Aspen Leaf / 800-525-0264
6700 Smith Road, Denver, CO 80207

Backstage Pass / 416-665-8890
740 Supertest Rd., Downsview, Ontario,
Canada M3J 2M5

Balzout, Inc. / 800-926-0169
1605 Fourth Ave., Charlston, WV 25312

Bang! Promotions / 212-260-5741

Bay Area Display S.F., Inc. / 415-864-8440
75 Barney Pl., SF, CA 94107

Benton, Jim / 810-644-5875
3170 Middlebury Rd., Bloomfield Township, MI 48301

Merchandising (continued)

Best Emblem & Insignia / 718-392-7171
37-11 35th Ave., Astoria, NY 11101

Bigfoot 4X4, Inc. / 314-731-8112
6311 N. Lindbergh Blvd., Hazelwood, MO 63042

Blue Grape Merchandising / 212-274-9552
536 Broadway, 4th Fl., NYC, NY 10012

Body & Soul / 212-595-0800
1926 Broadway, 5th Fl., NYC, NY 10023

Bradford Licensing Associates / 201-509-0200
209 Cooper Ave., Upper MontClair, NJ 07043

Brockum / 416-777-1811
111 George St., 3rd Fl., Toronto, Ont. M5A 2N4

Brockum Distribution Services / 818-884-4298
23800 Archwood St., West Hills, CA 91307

Brockum Int'l / 071-487-4782 / 071-487-3253
78 Harley House, Marylebane Rd.,
London, England NWI 5HW

Brown & Bigelow, Inc. / 612-293-7046
345 Plato Blvd. E., St. Paul, MN 55107

Browntowne Creations / 312-943-5751
300 W. Hill St., Unit 310, Chicago, IL 60610

Bubba Brands / 803-849-0601
139 Market St., Charleston, SC 29401

Cal Pacific / 310-822-5835
20201 Sherman Way, Canoga Park, CA 91306

Carolco Licensing / 310-289-7138
8800 Sunset Blvd., LA, CA 90069

Cheryl Ann Johnson, Inc. / 212-737-4344
514 E. 89th St., NYC, NY 10128

Chocolate Rock Records / 800-228-4442 / 212-532-0371
PO Box 360, Murray Hill Station, NYC, NY 10016

Cine Group / 514-524-7567
1151 Alexandre-DeSeve, Montreal,
Quebec, Canada H2L 2T7

Concept Licensing / 818-222-2956
5000 N.Pkwy. Calabasas, Calabasas, CA 91302

$$F = (a \times p)^4$$

Merchandising	Merchandising
Creatif Licensing Corp. / 914-241-6211 31 Old Town Crossing, Mt. Kisco, NY 10549	Giant / 310-289-5560 8900 Wilshire Blvd., Beverly Hills, CA 90211
Creative Glassics, Inc. / 908-901-6400 60 Park Ave., Lakewood, NJ 08701	Giordano Art, Ltd. / 718-631-9660 45-22 Zion St., Little Neck, NY 11362
Creative Licensing Corp. / 310-479-6777 2551 S. Bundy Dr., LA, CA 90064	Good Swag Dude, The / 212-772-0283 / 800-833-7565 525 E. 71st St., NYC, NY 10021
Crystal Enterprises / 818-884-4298 23800 Archwood St., W. Hills, CA 91307	Great Entertainment Merchandise / 212-603-7984 825 8th Ave., 27th Fl., NY, NY 10019
Curtis Archives / 317-633-2070 1000 Waterway Blvd., Indianapolis, IN 46202	Guisewite Studio / 213-871-8283 c/o Hollywood Ctr. Studios 1040 N. Las Palmas Ave., Bldg 25, LA, CA 90038
Curtis Management Group / 317-633-2050 1000 Waterway Blvd., Indianapolis, IN 46202	Hakan & Associates, Inc., Brian P. / 913-492-7900 8245 Nieman Rd., #126, Lenexa, KS 66214
Data East / 708-345-7700 990 Janice Ave., Melrose Park, IL 60160	Hamilton Projects, Inc. / 212-684-4388 215 Lexington Ave., 11th FL., NYC, NY 10016
Dic Animations, Inc. / 818-955-5636 303 N. Glenoaks Blvd., Burbank, CA 91502	Harley-Davidson, Inc. / 414-342-4680 3700 W. Juneau Ave., Milwaukee, WI 53208
Direct Merchandising / 818-982-3375 7440 Fulton Ave., N. Hollywood, CA 91605	Harmon Pictures Corporation, Larry / 213-463-2331 7080 Hollywood Blvd., #202, Hollywood, CA 90028
Direxion Entertainment / 212-274-9800 63 Greene St., #402, NYC, NY 10012	Hummel Licensing/McIntyre Associates / 201-633-7090 1211 Hamburg Turnpike, Wayne, NJ 07470
EMCI / 203-327-6545 24 Richmond Hill Ave., 8th Fl, Stamford, CT 06901	Image Marketing / 800-769-1260 4635 N.Olcott Ave., Harwood Heights, IL 60656
Earnshaw Publications / 212-563-2742 225 W. 34th St., Rm 1212, NYC, NY 10122	Ingle Co. / 310-820-8841 11661 San Vicente Blvd., LA, CA 90049
Famous Fido's, Inc. / 312-761-6029 1533 W. Devon, Chicago, IL 60660	Insignis Corporation / 615-321-3377 1915 Charlotte Ave., Ste. 200, Nashville, TN 37203
Farris Color Visions, Inc. / 404-897-1597 165 Sixth St., N.E., Ste. 101, Atlanta, GA 30308	International Management Group / 212-541-5640 420 W. 45th St., NYC, NY 10036
Fashion Victim / 800-522-7247 954 W. Washington St., Chicago, IL 60607	J&K Distributors / 714-842-2637 17555 Cameron St., Huntington Beach, CA 92647
Federal Duck Stamp Program / 202-208-4354 Dept. of Interiors 1849 C St. N.W., Ste. 2058, Washington, DC 20240	King Features / 212-455-4480 235 E. 46th St., 4th Fl, NYC, NY 10017
Fine Line Cinema / 212-649-4943 888 Seventh Ave., 19th Fl., NYC, NY 10106	Landmark Entertainment Group / 818-753-6700 5200 Lankersheim Blvd., N. Hollywood, CA 91601
First In Fashion USA / 310-855-1218 1074 S. La Cienega Blvd, LA, CA 90035	Larry Tucker, Inc. / 201-307-8888 188 Broadway, Woodcliff Lake, NJ 07675

TABLE (5.31). SUPPORT SERVICES

Merchandising	Merchandising
Lee Arnold Promotions / 414-351-9088 6944 N. Port Washington Rd., Milwaukee, WI 53217	Pacific Sportswear & Emblem Co. 800-872-8778 / 800-266-8778 6160 Fairmont Ave., Ste. F, San Diego, CA 92120
Lindberg Licensing & Promotion, Inc. / 914-961-5614 69 Tanglewylde Ave., Bronxville, NY 10708	Paramount Communications / 213-956-5000 5555 Melrose Ave., Hollywood, CA 90038-3197
LucasArts Entertainment Corporation / 415-662-1788 P.O. Box 2009, San Rafael, CA 94912	Ready For Duty / 212-465-9755 560 W. 43rd St., Ste. 10M, NYC, NY 10036
Lucy & Me / 206-775-8826 13710 41st N.E., Seattle, WA 98125	Red Sail Merchandising / 415-981-5900 909 Montgomery St., STe. 104, SF, CA 94133
MDI Grafx Inc. (Decals) / 800-274-3225 1407 Barclay Blvd., Buffalo Grove, IL 60089	Richards & Southern / 615-859-4121 P.O. Box 37, Goodlettsville, TN 37070
MGM Licensing & Merchandising / 212-708-0300 1350 Ave. of the Americas, NYC, NY 10019	Rock Embassy, Inc. / 212-307-1185 1776 Broadway, 19th Fl., NYC, NY 10019
Mack Trucks, Inc. / 215-439-2601 400 Mack Blvd., Allentown, PA 18105	Roth, Jay A. & Associates / 310-398-0300 2210 Wilshire Blvd., Santa Monica, CA 90403-5787
Master Card International / 212-649-4600 888 Seventh Ave., NYC, NY 10106	Sandana / 909-677-1737 40895 Vista Murrieta, Murrieta, CA 92562
Master Graphics / 205-887-8744 175 S. Gay St., Auburn, AL 36830	Scholastic, Inc. / 212-529-6300 740 Broadway, 8th Fl, NYC, NY 10003
Milton Bradley / 413-525-6411 443 Shaker Rd., East Longmeadow, MA 01028	Secret Identitee Merchandising 213-857-5520 / 818-506-3350 8075 W. Third St., #306, LA, CA 90048
Moda International Corp. / 212-687-7640 230 Park Ave., Ste. 924, NYC, NY 10169	Sherman Specialties / 516-546-7400 / 800-645-6513 114 Church St., Merrick, NY 11520
Motion Promotions / 212-219-3460 44 Walker St., NYC, NY 10013	Sid Tech / 310-274-4662 9033 Wilshire Blvd., Beverly Hills, CA 90211
Mr. K. Sportswear, Inc. / 212-213-4830 19 W. 26th St., NYC, NY 10010	Sony Pictures / 310-280-8595 10202 W. Washington Blvd, Culver City, CA 90232
National Sporting Goods Association / 708-439-4000 1699 Wall St., Ste. 700, Mt. Prospect, IL 60056	Sony Signature / 415-247-7400 2 Bryant St., 3rd Fl., SF, CA 94105
Neil Enterprises, Inc. / 708-913-8866 / 800-621-5584 940 Forest Edge Dr., Vernon Hills, IL 60061	Sony Signatures / 310-280-7788 10202 W. Washington Blvd., Culver City, CA 90232
Nice Man Merchandising / 612-493-2200 8752 Montecello Lane, Ste.100, Maple Grove, MN 55369	Storm, Inc. / 212-685-0404 41 Madison Ave., 5th Fl., NYC, NY 10010
Nice Man Merchandising / 212-941-6650 72 Spring St., Ste.1100, NYC, NY 10012	TTC Animation Licensing, Inc. / 718-459-8151 10A 63rd St., Regal Park, NY 11374
Not Fade Away Graphics Co. / 914-339-1087 P.O. Box 2092, Kingston, NY 12401	

$$F = (a \times p)^4$$

TABLE (5.32). SUPPORT SERVICES

Merchandising	Record Labels
Ten Ninety Nine Promotions / 301-949-8517 P.O. Box 21422, Washington, D.C. 20009-0922	Atlantic Records / 212-275-2000 75 Rockefeller Center, NYC, NY 10019
Tucker Group, The Walt / 818-547-1955 5225 San Fernando Rd. W., LA, CA 90039	Atlantic Records / 310-205-7450 9229 Sunset Blvd., LA, CA 90069
Turner Home Entertainment / 212-852-6819 420 Fifth Ave., NYC, NY 10018	Atlantic Records / 615-327-9394 1812 Broadway, Nashville, TN 37203
Universal Licensing Corp. / 816-932-6680 4900 Main St., Kansas City, MO 64112	BMG Music / 212-930-4000 1540 Broadway, NYC, NY 10036
Upgroup / 615-367-9653 1100 Kermit Dr., Ste. 100, Nashville, TN 37217	BMG/RCA / 213-468-4000 6363 Sunset Blvd., Hollywood, CA 90028
VPI / 212-581-0400 225 W. 57th St., NYC, NY 10019	BMG/RCA / 615-664-1200 1 Music Circle N., Nashville, TN 37203
Viacom Enterprises / 212-258-6000 1515 Broadway, 29th Fl., NYC, NY 10036	BNA Entertainment / 615-780-4400 1 Music Circle N., Nashville, TN 37203
Warjo Promotions, Inc. / 212-627-2800 236 W. 27th St., NYC, NY 10001	Blue Note Records / 212-492-5300 1290 Ave. of Americas, NYC, NY 10104
Warner Bros. Consumer Products / 818-954-7980 4000 Warner Blvd., Tower, Burbank, CA 91522	Capitol Records / 212-492-5300 1290 Ave. of the Americas, NYC, NY 10104
Western Publishing / 414-633-2431 1220 Mound Ave., Racine, WI 53404	Capitol Records / 213-462-6252 1750 N. Vine St., Hollywood, CA 90028
Wild Oats / 800-527-6287 502 S. Main St., Cape May Ct. House, NJ 08210	Capricorn Records / 615-320-8470 120 30th Ave. North, Nashville, TN 37203
Winterland / 415-597-9700 100 Harrison St., SF, CA 94105	Charisma / 212-603-8700 1790 Broadway, NYC, NY 10019

Record Labels

Record Labels	Record Labels
A&M Records / 213-469-2411 1416 N. La Brea Ave., Hollywood, CA 90028	Columbia Records / 310-449-2100 2100 Colorado Ave., Santa Monica, CA 90404
A&M Records / 212-333-1328 825 Eighth Ave., NYC, NY 10019	Columbia Records / 212-833-8000 550 Madison Ave., NY, NY 10022
Arista Records / 212-489-7400 6 W. 57th St., NYC, NY 10019	Curb Records / 818-843-2872 3907 W Alemeda Ave., 2nd Fl., Burbank, CA 91505
Arista Records / 213-655-9222 8370 Wilshire Blvd., 3rd Fl., Beverly Hills, CA 90211	Curb Records / 615-321-5080 47 Music Square East, Nashville, TN 37203
Arista Records / 615-780-9100 7 Music Circle N., Nashville, TN 37203	David Geffen Co. / 310-278-9010 9130 Sunset Blvd., Los Angeles, CA 90069
	Def Jam / 212-229-5200 160 Varick St., NYC, NY 10013

TABLE (5.33). SUPPORT SERVICES

Record Labels	Record Labels
EMI Music Publishing / 615-256-6610 35 Music Square E., Nashville, TN 37203	Interscope Records / 310-208-6547 10900 Wilshire Blvd., Ste. 1230, LA, CA 90024
EMI Records Group / 310-659-1700 8730 Sunset Blvd. 5th Fl., LA, CA 90069	Island Records / 310-276-4500 8920 Sunset Blvd., 2nd Fl., LA, CA 90069
EMI Records Group / 212-492-1200 1290 Ave. of Americas, 38th Fl., New York, NY 10104	Island Records / 212-477-8000 400 Lafayette St., NYC, NY 10003
East West Records America / 310-205-7420 9229 Sunset Blvd., 8th Fl., LA, CA 90069	JVC Jazz / 213-878-0101 3800 Barham Blvd., Ste. 305, LA, CA 90068
East West Records America / 212-275-2500 75 Rockefeller Plaza, NYC, NY 10019	Jive Records Chicago / 312-942-9700 700 N. Green, Ste. 200, Chicago, IL 60622
Epic Records / 212-833-8000 550 Madison Ave., NYC, NY 10022	Legacy-Division of Sony Music / 212-445-4321 550 Madison Ave., 31 Fl., NYC, NY 10022
Epic Records / 310-449-2100 2100 Colorado Ave., Santa Monica, CA 90404	Liberty Records / 615-269-2000 3322 West End Ave., 11th Fl., Nashville, TN 37203
GRP Records / 212-424-1000 555 W. 57th St., 10th Fl., NYC, NY 10019	MCA Records / 212-841-8000 1755 Broadway, 8th Fl., NYC, NY 10019
Geffen Records / 310-278-9010 9130 Sunset Blvd., LA, CA 90069	MCA Records / 818-777-4500 70 University City Plaza, Universal City, CA 91608
Geffen Records / 212-841-8600 1755 Broadway, NYC, NY 10019	MCA/Decca Records / 615-244-8944 60 Music Sq. E., Nashville, TN 37203
Giant / 310-289-5500 8900 Wilshire Blvd., Ste. 200, Beverly Hills, CA 90211	Maverick / 213-852-1177 8000 Beverly Blvd., LA, CA 90048
Giant / 615-256-3110 1514 S St., Nashville, TN 37212	Mercury Records / 212-333-8000 825 Eighth Ave., NYC, NY 10019
Giant Records / 212-275-4673 1290 Ave. of Americas, Ste. 410, NYC, NY 10019	Mercury Records / 310-996-7200 11150 Santa Monica Blvd., Ste. 1100, LA, CA 90025
Hollywood Records / 818-560-5670 500 S. Buena Vista St., Burbank, CA 91521	Mercury Records / 615-320-0110 66 Music Square W., Nashville, TN 37203
IRS / 310-841-4100 3520 Hayden Ave., Culver City, CA 90232	Modern Records / 213-658-7600 6535 Wilshire Blvd., Ste. 101, LA, CA 90048
IRS Records / 212-334-2170 594 Broadway, #901, NYC, NY 10012	Morgan Creek Records / 818-954-4800 4000 Warner Blvd., Bldg 76, Burbank, CA 91522
Imago Records / 310-289-7799 822 N. La Cienega Blvd., LA, CA 90069	Motown / 212-424-2000 1350 Sixth Ave., 20th Fl., NYC, NY 10019
Imago Records / 212-246-6644 152 W. 57th St., 44th Fl., NYC, NY 10019	Motown / 213-468-3500 6255 W. Sunset Blvd., 17th Fl., LA, CA 90028

$$F = (a \times p)^4$$

TABLE (5.34). SUPPORT SERVICES

Record Labels	Record Labels
Polydor Records / 615-329-4434 1222 16th Ave. S., 3rd Fl., Nashville, TN 37212	Sony Music / 212-833-8000 550 Madison Ave., NYC, NY 10022
Polygram / 212-333-8000 825 Eighth Ave., 24th Fl, NYC, NY 10019	Sony Music / 310-449-2100 2100 Colorado Ave., Santa Monica, CA 90404
Polygram / 310-996-7200 11150 Santa Monica Blvd., 10th Fl., LA, CA 90025	Sony Tree / 615-726-8300 8 Music Sq. W., Nashville, TN 37203
Priority Records / 213-467-0151 6430 Sunset Blvd., Ste. 900, Hollywood, CA 90028	Sparrow Records / 615-371-6800 Box 5010, Brentwood, TN 37024-5010
Priority Records / 212-527-8000 32 W. 18th St., NY, NY 10011	Stash Records / 212-243-4321 140 W. 22nd St., 12th Fl., NY, NY 10011
Private Music / 310-859-9200 9014 Melrose Ave., LA, CA 90064	SubPop / 206-441-8441 1932 First Ave., Ste. 1103, Seattle, WA 98101
RCA Records / 212-930-4000 1540 Broadway, NYC, NY 10036	Tommy Boy Records / 212-388-8300 902 Broadway, NYC, NY 10010
Relativity / 212-337-5300 79 Fifth Ave., 16th Fl., Hollis, NY 10003	Touche Records Co. / 510-524-4937 P.O. Box 96, El Cerrito, CA 94530
Relativity / 310-212-0801 20525 Manhattan Place, Torrance, CA 90501	Virgin Records / 212-586-7700 1790 Broadway, NYC, NY 10019
Reprise / 615-320-7525 1815 Division St., Nashville, TN 37203	Virgin Records in America / 310-278-1181 338 N. Foothill Rd., Beverly Hills, CA 90210
Reprise / 212-275-4500 75 Rockefeller Plaza, 20th Fl, NYC, NY 10019	Warner Bros. Records / 818-846-9090 3300 Warner Blvd., Burbank, CA 91505
Reprise / 818-953-3750 3300 Warner Blvd., Burbank, CA 91505	Warner Bros. Records / 615-748-8000 24 Music Square E., Nashville, TN 37203
Reunion Records / 615-320-9200 2910 Poston Ave., Nashville, TN 37203	Warner Bros. Records / 212-275-4500 75 Rockefeller Plaza, NYC, NY 10019
Road Runner Records / 212-219-0077 225 Lafayette St., Ste. 407, NYC, NY 10012	Windham Hill Records / 415-329-0647 P.O. Box 9388, Stanford, CA 94309
SBK Records / 212-492-1200 1290 Sixth Ave., NYC, NY 10104	Word Records / 615-385-9673 3319 West End Ave., Ste. 200, Nashville, TN 37203
SBK Records / 310-659-1700 8730 Sunset Blvd., 5th Fl., LA, CA 90069	Zoo Entertainment / 213-468-4200 6363 Sunset Blvd., Hollywood, CA 90028
Sire Records / 818-846-9090 3300 Warner Blvd., Burbank, CA 91505	Zoo Entertainment / 212-930-4935 1540 Broadway, 34th Fl., NYC, NY 10036
Sony Music / 615-742-4321 34 Music Square East, Nashville, TN 37203	Zoo/Praxis / 615-320-1200 1700 Hayes St., Ste. 302, Nashville, TN 37203

Table (5.35). Support Services

Notes	Notes

$$F = (a \times p)^4$$

Table (5.36). Support Services

Notes	Notes

$$F = (a \times p)^4$$

Notes	Notes

α-particle
2He⁴
(fig. 32)
(c)
glass
(fig. 49)
(fig. 28)
B   F
b   f
(fig. 10)
v₀
t
v
A   S   B
(fig. 34)
F   G
(fig. 24)
(fig. 25)
(fig. 26)
M
P
895
1000
50
446
θ
26.5°   100
W
Earth
w
P
W
(fig. 6)
(fig. 9)
(fig. 5)
v   m
(fig. 38)
L
F
W
P
(fig. 1)
(fig. 15)
F
S
(fig. 30)
N S
(a)
compass
magnet
r. 14)
h
W
(fig. 40)